# Computer Games: Interface, Design and Applications

# Computer Games: Interface, Design and Applications

Edited by
Oscar Moore

www.willfordpress.com

Published by Willford Press,
118-35 Queens Blvd., Suite 400,
Forest Hills, NY 11375, USA

ISBN: 978-1-68285-764-9

**Cataloging-in-Publication Data**

Computer games : interface, design and applications / edited by Oscar Moore.
    p. cm.
Includes bibliographical references and index.
ISBN 978-1-68285-764-9
1. Computer games. 2. Computer games--Design. 3. Computer interfaces.
4. Application software. I. Moore, Oscar.
GV1469.15 .C66 2020
794.8--dc23

For information on all Willford Press publications
visit our website at www.willfordpress.com

# Contents

# Preface

The purpose of the book is to provide a glimpse into the dynamics and to present opinions and studies of some of the scientists engaged in the development of new ideas in the field from very different standpoints. This book will prove useful to students and researchers owing to its high content quality.

A computer game is a video game. It is played on a personal computer rather than a dedicated arcade machine or video game console. Its defining characteristics include greater capacity in processing, video output and input; and more diverse and user-determined gaming software and hardware. The high-end computer gaming systems usually have more processing resources at its disposal. This can be utilized to improve the visual fidelity of the game relative to other programs. Unlike other gaming platforms, computer games are not owned and administered by a single group. The Steam distribution service and the Microsoft Windows operating system are the two dominating software for a computer gaming system. The ever-growing need of advanced technology is the reason that has fueled the development in the field of computer games in recent times. This book is a complete source of knowledge on the present status of this important field of technology. With state-of-the-art inputs by acclaimed experts of this field, it targets students and professionals.

At the end, I would like to appreciate all the efforts made by the authors in completing their chapters professionally. I express my deepest gratitude to all of them for contributing to this book by sharing their valuable works. A special thanks to my family and friends for their constant support in this journey.

Editor

# Dead Reckoning using Play Patterns in a Simple 2D Multiplayer Online Game

## Wei Shi,[1] Jean-Pierre Corriveau,[2] and Jacob Agar[2]

[1] *Faculty of Business and I.T., University of Ontario Institute of Technology, Oshawa, ON, Canada L1H 7K4*
[2] *School of Computer Science, Carleton University, Ottawa, ON, Canada K1S 5B6*

Correspondence should be addressed to Wei Shi; wei.shi@uoit.ca

Academic Editor: Abdennour El Rhalibi

In today's gaming world, a player expects the same play experience whether playing on a local network or online with many geographically distant players on congested networks. Because of delay and loss, there may be discrepancies in the simulated environment from player to player, likely resulting in incorrect perception of events. It is desirable to develop methods that minimize this problem. Dead reckoning is one such method. Traditional dead reckoning schemes typically predict a player's position linearly by assuming players move with constant force or velocity. In this paper, we consider team-based 2D online action games. In such games, player movement is rarely linear. Consequently, we implemented such a game to act as a test harness we used to collect a large amount of data from playing sessions involving a large number of experienced players. From analyzing this data, we identified play patterns, which we used to create three dead reckoning algorithms. We then used an extensive set of simulations to compare our algorithms with the IEEE standard dead reckoning algorithm and with the recent "Interest Scheme" algorithm. Our results are promising especially with respect to the average export error and the number of hits.

## 1. Introduction

Consumers have spent 20.77 billion US dollars on video games in the United States alone in 2012 [1]. 36% of gamers play games on their smart phones and 25% of gamers play on their wireless device. 62% of gamers play games with others, either in-person or online [2]. Multiplayer online games (MOGs) make up a huge portion of one of the largest entertainment industries on the planet. Consequently, maximizing a player's play experience while playing a MOG is key for the success of such games.

MOGs are a kind of distributed interactive simulation (DIS), which is defined by the IEEE standard 1278.1 as an infrastructure that links simulations of various types at multiple locations to create realistic, complex, and virtual worlds for the simulation of highly interactive activities. DISs are intended to support a mixture of virtual entities with computer controlled behaviour (computer generated forces), virtual entities with live operators (human in-the-loop simulators), live entities (operational platforms and test

and evaluation systems), and constructive entities (war games and other automated simulations) [3]. Data messages, known as protocol data units (PDUs), are exchanged on a network between simulation applications. Delay and loss of PDUs are the two major issues facing DISs. *Delay* (or equivalently, network latency) refers to the time it takes for packets of PDUs to travel from sender to receiver. This delay is usually taken to be caused by the time it takes for a signal to propagate through a given medium, plus the time it takes to route the signal through routers. *Jitter* is a term used as a measure of the variability over time of delay across the network [4]. *Loss* (often higher when delay is higher) refers to lost network packets as a result of signal degradation over a network medium, as well as rejected packets and congestion at a given network node. Delay and loss cause a DIS to suffer from a lack of consistency between remote participants, jittery movement of various entities, and a general loss of accuracy in the simulation. Consequently, MOGs are inherently more difficult to design and produce than a traditional locally played video game: the distributed nature of the former entails finding solutions to many architectural problems irrelevant for the latter. In particular, players playing in geographical locations thousands of kilometers away from each other need to have their actions appear to be executed in the same virtual space.

Thus, the main objective when designing the architecture of a networked video game is to maximize the user's playing experience by minimizing the appearance of the adverse effects of the network during play. When a network message (packet) is sent, there is a time delay called *lag* between the sending of the packet and the reception of the packet. Late or lost packet transmission has the effect of objects in a scene being rendered at out-of-date or incorrect locations. If objects are simply rendered at their latest known position, their movement is, as a result, jittery and sporadic. This is because they are being drawn at a location where they actually are not, and this looks unnatural.

Dead reckoning algorithms predict where an object should be based on past information. They can be used to estimate a rendering position more accurate to the true path of the object. This ensures that once the player receives the true position of the object, the positional jump to the correct location is either nonexistent or much smaller, creating the illusion that this object is behaving normally.

Lag compensation techniques are not restricted to MOGs but in fact apply to any distributed interactive simulation (DIS) application. DISs are used by military, space exploration, and medical organizations amongst others. In such contexts, improving the "user experience" ultimately entails improving the quality of such applications.

The key idea behind dead reckoning is that predicting the position of an object makes it unnecessary to receive an update for that object's motion every time it moves. Such updates are required only when there is a change in the motion. This allows for a greater degree of network lag and loss and lowers the number of update messages that are required to be sent over the network.

Traditional prediction schemes predict player position by assuming that each player moves with a constant force or velocity. Because player movement is rarely linear in nature, using linear prediction cannot maintain an accurate result. However, few of the dead reckoning methods that have been proposed focus on improving prediction accuracy by introducing new methods of predicting the path of a player. The "Interest Scheme" presented in [5] is one such innovative approach. It specifically focuses on improving prediction accuracy in a 2D tank game. The key contribution of the "Interest Scheme" is that it does so by assuming that a player's surrounding objects will have some anticipative effect on the player's path. An important restriction however is that a tank cannot "strafe" to the left and right of the forward vector but has to rotate to change direction. In this paper, we instead consider traditional team-based 2D action games (e.g., first-person, third-person, or top-down shooters) wherein players can move freely in all directions, making a player's movement highly unpredictable, and thus highly prone to inaccuracies. We propose a prediction scheme that takes *user play patterns* into account. In order to determine such patterns, we first implemented a 2D top-down multiplayer online game titled

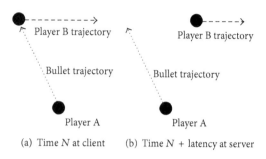

(a) Time $N$ at client    (b) Time $N$ + latency at server

FIGURE 1: Inconsistency without time warping.

"Ethereal," which serves as our test environment. Ethereal is a 2D multiplayer competitive game of 2 opposing teams in which players have freedom to move in all directions without gravity. A key facet of Ethereal is that it records not only all keyboard and mouse input of all players, but also all game world variables (such as game object and item positioning, world geometry information, and game events). We then conducted multiple play testing sessions, each involving numerous experienced players. From observing these players playing Ethereal and from subsequently analyzing half of the collected large dataset, we identified a set of typical player behaviours (i.e., play patterns). We used these patterns to create a new dead reckoning algorithm (and its associated parameters) called *EKB* (for *Experience knows best*). Another key facet of Ethereal is its ability to play back the recorded input data while simulating different network conditions. This allowed us to use the other half of our dataset to compare, under different network conditions, different versions of our path prediction algorithm with two well-known dead reckoning algorithms.

In the rest of this paper, we first discuss existing work on path prediction in the next section. Then, we introduce in Section 3 our initial EKB algorithm. In Section 4, we discuss two enhancements to this algorithm. Then, in Section 5, we present our experimental framework and compare our three versions of the EKB algorithm. Our experiments comparing the different versions of EKB with two well-known dead reckoning algorithms are summarized in Section 6. Finally, the generalization of our results, as well as other future work, is briefly discussed in the last section of the paper.

## 2. Related Work

*2.1. Effects of Delay, Jitter, and Loss on Users.* In [6], qualitative studies were conducted to determine the effects of adverse network states on the player. Participants were asked to comment on the quality of play at different levels of lag and jitter. Figures 1 and 2 of that paper show the mean opinion score (MOS) versus the amount of lag (ping) and jitter, respectively. Their findings clearly show that higher quantities of lag and jitter are correlated with a lower player experience.

In [7], the mean scores of players (the players' performance based on kills made and deaths suffered) were studied in *Unreal Tournament 2003* (a typical first person shooter video game). Through a series of 20 different scenarios of lag,

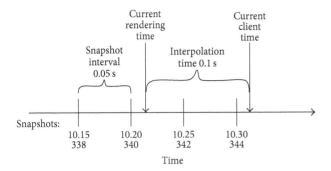

FIGURE 2: Object interpolation [17, 18].

with different players experiencing different amounts of lag, it was shown that high lag has a substantial negative effect on player performance. These findings are outlined in Figure 1 of that paper: it shows the scores of players unimpaired by bad network conditions versus those players experiencing bad network conditions.

A player's score in a shooting based game is a common metric used when measuring the effects of unfavourable network conditions on the player experience. Findings have been consistent that a higher degree of network loss, delay, and/or jitter results in fewer successful shots or kills made and a lower player score [6, 7, 9, 10]. For example, Aggarwal et al. [9] ran tests in a fast-paced tank shooting game called *BZFlag*, Wattimena et al. [6] gathered data from the popular shooting game *Quake IV*, and Ishibashi et al. [11] developed a distributed version of *Quake III* to test in. The performance of a player in these types of video games is based highly on reflexes and instant user input, and as a result, even fraction of second delays in the network can affect player performance. But these metrics should only be considered for a select genre or type of game. For example, in [12], running tests in the popular real-time strategy (RTS) PC Game *Warcraft III*, it was found that latency of up to 3 seconds has only marginal effects on the performances of players. This is a result of the strategic nature of the RTS genre, wherein strategic planning (as opposed to split second decision making) is more important to good performance. However, under high network lag or loss scenarios, a player's *perception* of the quality of the game can be hindered. As shown in [6], the adverse effects of the network will yield a perception of poor gaming quality. This is a result of either sporadic or jumpy positioning of game objects, or of a delay between the issuing a command for an action and the execution of that action.

*2.2. Consistency.* Action games use a client-server architecture to keep client-side computation to a minimum and allow for a scalable amount of players within the game world. This architecture also minimizes cheating by maintaining the game server as the single authority on all game events. In a client-server model action game, the server is the authority on game events and sends the clients game events, including the actions of other players. Client machines take input from the user and send this information to the server.

A MOG must achieve the illusion that players are playing in the same game world, when in reality they are geographically in different locations. In fact, in a MOG, players do not technically play in the same game space and are all only receiving a best-guess approximation of the game world. Given that the server is the authority on all game events, the clients must perform some form of time synchronization with the server. There are many ways to do this, each method with their own strengths and weaknesses. A discussion of these methods lies outside the focus of this paper. In summary, these distributed time synchronization techniques involve time-stamps and/or estimating lag times between machines. The time synchronization method used in our simulations is similar to the method described by Simpson in [13]: to ensure time is still synchronized, a client periodically sends a packet to the server time-stamped with the current time of the client. The server, on reception of this, immediately time-stamps the packet with its own current time and sends it back to the client. The client, from this, can determine how long it took the packet to get to the server and back again (round trip time or RTT) because of the time stamp. The client can also determine the exact time of the server, assuming it takes the same amount of time to get to and from the server (RTT/2). From here, the client will adjust its time delta between simulation ticks until its time matches the server. The client adjusts its time over several updates of the simulation because a large time jump all at once would cause objects in the scene to jump as well. If the time discrepancy is smoothed out over several frames, then there is no time-jump and the movements of the player are perceived as normal. Furthermore, because out-of-date packets and events are not important and we only need to know about the latest information regarding any given object, it is possible to employ proactive queue management techniques to drop old obsolete events in the face of arriving fresher event packets [14].

Local lag as proposed in [10, 15] refers to a network lag hiding technique wherein a delay is introduced between when an input is given and when its execution takes place. This hides lag and improves simulation accuracy because it effectively allows some time for the input packet to reach the server and subsequently to reach the other clients. Local lag allows all parties involved to receive a given event before its execution. Without local lag, in order to stay perfectly time-synchronized, a client or server would have to simulate the object or event forward to the current time, as it will have been received after its execution was supposed to take place. While this method is very effective at ensuring the time-synchronization of distributed events, it introduces a delay between when a player issues a command and when it is executed. This can be a problem, depending on what type of input the player gives. A player is more likely to notice delay regarding player movement or mouse movement input than delay regarding firing or shooting. The common method in most popular action games, for this reason, is to introduce a delay when dealing with firing or shooting, but to have no delay in regard to player movement or mouse movement input. For this reason, in our research simulation, we decided to employ no local lag for player movement but to introduce a small amount of delay for weapons firing. This allows us to benefit from local lag, without causing the annoyance of having player movement delay.

In [10], Liang and Boustead go on to propose a method to further reduce the negative effects of lag. Since a packet, due to jitter and different lag between players, can arrive at odd intervals, and even out of order, events need to be sorted in such a way to maintain temporal accuracy. To account for this, the common method used in the video game industry is a technique called time warp. Time warp refers to the "rewinding" of the simulation to execute events at the appropriate time. This ensures that events happen the way they are supposed to, as well ensuring consistency between different parties geographically. In [16], a variation of a time-warp system is proposed that features a trailing state synchronization method wherein instead of rewinding to time stamps when detecting a change, whole game states are simulated that are slightly behind the current time as to allow more time for late information to arrive. When an inconsistency is detected, the leading state need only roll back to a previous state.

As illustrated in Figure 1, assume player A has a network delay of 150 ms to the server and player A shoots a bullet at player B. According to player A's view (left side of Figure 1, Figure 1(a)), it looks like the bullet hit player B. But since the network message took 150 ms to reach the server, according to the lag of player B, the hit is not registered because player B has moved out of the way in the time it took for the message to arrive at the server (right side of Figure 1, Figure 1(b)). Time warp ensures this does not occur, by rewinding player A to its position 150 ms ago when the bullet was fired to check for the collision (that is, to make the server side looks like the left side of this figure Figure 1(a)). The simulation testbed used for our research includes this time warping technique, to help secure against the ill effects of lag.

### 2.3. Object Interpolation.

A common solution to reduce the jittery movement of rendered objects, as outlined by the popular video game development community *Valve*, is to draw game objects in the past, allowing the receiver to smoothly interpolate positional data between two recently received packets [17, 18]. The method works because time is rewound for that object, allowing current or past information about an object to represent the future information of that object. Then to draw the object, a position is interpolated from information ahead of and behind the new current position (which is actually in the past), as shown in Figure 2. Without information ahead of when rendering occurs, we can at best draw it at its current known position, which, as mentioned before, yields jittery rendering. As long as the rewind time (or interpolation time) is greater than lag, it should be possible to interpolate the position of the object. Interpolation times are traditionally a constant value or equal to the amount of lag to the server at any given time. The method used in our work is a constant interpolation value of 100 ms, as is used in the popular action game *Half-Life 2* [17, 18]. It is a value sufficient enough to cover a large percentage of the lag or loss that will occur.

### 2.4. Dead Reckoning.

As previously mentioned, the main goal of network compensation methods is to minimize the perceived influence of adverse network conditions on the player. Dead reckoning is a widely used method to achieve this goal. Dead reckoning is defined as any process to deduce the approximate current position of an object based on past information. In a MOG, this is done so that during high lag and loss conditions in the network, the client can approximate an object's position more accurately. That is, when data is lost or lost beyond what interpolation can solve, the current position of an object needs to be predicted. Without prediction, an object would only be rendered at the latest known position, causing discrepancies in simulation state and great jitter in object motion. When relying on dead reckoning, an assumption is made about the nature of game objects, such as adherence to certain forces or likelihoods. With small amounts of lag and loss, dead reckoning does a great job concealing the fact that there was missing information about an object.

The most common and traditional method of dead reckoning involves doing a linear projection of information received from the server about this object. An IEEE standard dead reckoning formula [3] is given by

$$P = P_0 + V_0 \Delta t + \frac{1}{2} A_0 \Delta t^2, \qquad (1)$$

where $P$, $\Delta t$, $P_0$, $V_0$, and $A_0$ represent the newly predicted position, elapsed time, original position, original velocity, and original acceleration, respectively. This equation works well to accurately predict an object, assuming that the object does not change direction. This method of prediction can become inaccurate after a time, especially for a player object, whose movement is very unpredictable.

When the receiver finally receives the actual current position from the server, after having predicted its position up until now, there will be some deviation between the predicted position and the actual position. This error difference is known as the *export error* [5, 8, 9]. Minimizing the *export error* has the effect of lowering the appearance of lag in the simulation.

In [9], the difference between a time-stamped and a nontime-stamped dead reckoning packet is explored. Without time-stamping a dead-reckoning packet, the receiver cannot be entirely sure when the packet was generated, and as a result, discrepancies between the sender and receiver's view of the world will exist. Time synchronization between players and time-stamping dead reckoning packets means that the receiving user can execute a received packet in proper order and in the exact same conditions as they were when generated. It is widely acknowledged that time synchronization, while adding network traffic, greatly improves simulation accuracy and reduces the export error [9, 10, 19–22].

As previously mentioned, traditional prediction schemes forecast a player's position by assuming each player moves using constant force or velocity. However, because player movement is rarely linear in nature, using linear prediction fails to maintain an accurate result. Furthermore, Wolf and Pantel explore and discuss the suitability of different prediction methods within the context of different types of video games [23]. They conclude that some prediction schemes are better suited to some types of games than to others. More specifically, they look at five traditional prediction schemes: constant velocity, constant acceleration, constant input position, constant input velocity, and constant input acceleration. Each prediction scheme is compared to the others in the context of a sports game, a racing game, and an action game. As a result of the evaluation of these different prediction methods in each game, these authors demonstrate that different prediction schemes are better suited to different types of games. For example, it is shown that predicting with a constant input velocity is best suited to sports games; a constant input acceleration is best for action games; predicting with constant acceleration is best suited to racing games, and for action games, constant velocity and constant input position predictions also offer a relatively low prediction error.

Among existing dead reckoning methods, few focus on improving prediction accuracy via genuinely new (i.e., nontraditional) methods for predicting the path of a player. We discuss below some of these innovative approaches.

Traditionally, dead reckoning algorithms dictate that the server should send a positional update to clients when an object strays from its predicted path by some threshold. Thus, a dead reckoning algorithm that successfully improves path prediction does not only minimize the appearance of lag but also minimizes network traffic as well. Duncan and Gracanin [24] propose a method, called the Pre-Reckoning scheme, that sends an update just before it is anticipated that an object will exceed some threshold. To anticipate a threshold change, the angle between the current movement and the last movement is analyzed. If this angle is large enough, it is assumed that the threshold will be crossed very soon, and a dead reckoning packet is sent. The Pre-Reckoning algorithm yields better results when variability in player movement is low.

Cai et al. [25] present an autoadaptive dead reckoning algorithm that uses a dynamic threshold to control the extrapolation errors in order to reduce the number of update packets. The results suggest a considerable reduction in (the number of) update packets without sacrificing accuracy in extrapolation. While having a dynamic threshold for predicting objects does result in less data needing to be sent over the network, it does not eliminate the requirement for increasingly accurate prediction schemes. A dynamic threshold allows farther away objects to not require a high a degree of accuracy, but regardless, closer objects still need to be predicted accurately. Furthermore, the method outlined in [25] assumes a perspective view on the world, such that farther away objects are smaller and less visible. However, in a 2D video game, in which an orthographic view is utilized, all objects in view are of normal size, and therefore almost all of the objects are of interest to the user.

Work has also been done in using neural networks to enhance the accuracy of dead reckoning [26, 27]. In [26], McCoy et al. propose an approach that requires each controlling host to rely on a bank of neural network predictors trained to predict future changes in an object's velocity. Conversely, the approach proposed by Hakiri et al. in [27]

is based on a fuzzy inference system trained by a learning algorithm derived from neural networks. This method does reduce network loads. While these methods have been shown to improve performance of dead reckoning, they impose extra computation on each host prior to the launching of a game and, more importantly, ultimately depend on extensive training. That is, the statistical nature of such predictors entails they must learn from very large datasets. Our proposed solution rests on the notion of *play patterns*. Machine learning could have been used to learn such play patterns from the large datasets we have gathered, but we have relied on our ability to initially recognize such patterns manually. Thus, we will not discuss further, in the context of this paper, techniques that require statistical learning.

Delaney et al. [28] describe a hybrid predictive technique that chooses either the deterministic dead reckoning model or a statistically based model. The claim of these authors is that their approach results in a more accurate representation of the movement of an entity and a consequent reduction in the number of packets that must be communicated to track that movement remotely. The statistical model rests on repeatedly observing players race to a same goal location in order to determine the most common path used. In turn, this path is used to predict the path of a player towards the same goal location. The difficulty with such an approach is that it rests on the notion of shared goal locations, which is not readily applicable to most genres of games. However, the idea of a hybrid approach to path prediction is an interesting one to which we will return later.

Finally, Li et al. propose a method called the "Interest Scheme" [5, 8] for predicting the location of a player-controlled object. That approach shows an increased accuracy of path prediction beyond traditional dead reckoning models specifically in a 2D tank game, with levels of lag up to 3000 ms. The strength of the Interest Scheme lies in the way it uses the surrounding entities of a given player-controlled entity to better predict what actions the user will take. The method works on the assumption that a player's directional input is affected by its surroundings, such as items and enemy players. Due to the introduction of an extra computational burden, especially when network conditions are adequate for play, a hybrid method is introduced into the "Interest Scheme." This method involves using traditional dead reckoning algorithms up until a fixed threshold of prediction time. However, "Interest Scheme" is designed for one very specific type of game. Thus, as previously mentioned, the success of the "Interest Scheme" is not reproducible in a traditional team-based action game.

While all the prediction methods referred to above are capable of predicting player movement relatively accurate, more elaborate methods should be considered to handle high amounts of lag. This is required by the non-deterministic manner in which players typically move in any given video game. Once there is a high amount of network delay, traditional methods of dead reckoning become too inaccurate, and the *export error* starts to become too large. Ultimately players start to notice a loss of consistency [6, 7, 18, 23, 29]. Some work, in particular the Interest Scheme outlined by Li et al. [5, 8], has been done from this standpoint. The algorithms that we will now introduce are in the same vein. Methodologically, our proposed solutions will be compared with the IEEE standard dead reckoning algorithm [3] (hereafter referred to as TDM for "traditional dead reckoning method") and the "Interest Scheme" (hereafter IS) algorithm [5, 8].

## 3. The EKB Algorithm

In this section, we introduce our proposed method of prediction algorithm: *experience knows best* (EKB). We start by describing our movement prediction algorithm, which rests on the combined use of different velocities. Next, each of these velocities is discussed. We then describe some enhancements to our algorithm, followed by a discussion of its parameter space. In order to clarify the algorithm description, hereafter we use *TPlayer* to refer to the target player for prediction. The *last known position* is the latest position data that was received over the network. The *last known position time (LKPT)* refers to the time stamp associated with the *last known position*. The *last known velocity* is the velocity associated with the LKPT.

*3.1. Combination of Velocities.* Our approach involves predicting a player's position by predicting the potential behaviours that a player may adopt. To do so, using half of the data collected during the play sessions of Ethereal, we identified behaviours that are assumed to affect the player's next movement. These behaviours each take the form of a velocity that is exerted on the players, affecting where they will be located next. These behaviour velocities are applied at different strength levels depending on what is occurring in the game from the point of view of the player at hand. These velocities are based on the positions and states of other objects in the scene. Velocities are applied as either an attraction or repulsion towards or away from a given position in space. The magnitude of these velocities depends on several factors such as the distance to the object and the strength or weakness of the player.

The following velocities are employed in our work: the follow velocity, the bravery velocity, and the alignment velocity. They will be explained at length in the next subsection. Here we first describe how they are combined to act on a player.

Each velocity takes into account other players in the game world in order to determine direction and magnitude. They do so only if a given player is within a specified static distance threshold. In our current experiments, we set this distance to the size of the screen. Any player outside of such a region of interest is not considered in the computing of a behaviour velocity.

In order to simplify how the velocities interact with each other, we separate player behaviour into two categories: *in battle* behaviours and *out of battle* behaviours. When the player is *in battle*, the player's position is calculated by combining the follow and the align velocities. When *out of battle*, the player's position is calculated by combining the follow and the align velocities. Let us elaborate.

Whether the *TPlayer* is *in battle* or not is chosen as a simple distance check to the closest enemy, as outlined in

| (1) **if** the player is in battle **then** |
|---|
| (2)  $\vec{V}_r = \left(\vec{V}_{\text{follow}} \times q\right) + \left(\vec{V}_{\text{bravery}} \times (1 - q)\right)$ |
| (3) **else** |
| (4)  $\vec{V}_r = \left(\vec{V}_{\text{follow}} \times r\right) + \left(\vec{V}_{\text{align}} \times (1 - r)\right)$ |
| (5) **end if** |

ALGORITHM 1: Apply velocities.

(4). If there exists an enemy within the battle threshold $W$, then the player is said to be *in battle*. Equation (2) calculates the distance from the current player position ($\vec{C}$) to a given enemy player ($\vec{P}_e$). For our results, we used a threshold of $W = 800$ as this seemed to accurately represent when a player was engaged in combat or not in the context of our game. Consider

$$D_{e_i} = \left|\vec{P}_{e_i} - \vec{C}\right| \tag{2}$$

$$closestEnemyDist = \min\left\{D_{e_1}, D_{e_2}, \ldots, D_{e_n}\right\} \tag{3}$$

$$InBattle = \begin{cases} \text{true} & \text{if } closestEnemyDist \leq W \\ \text{false} & \text{otherwise.} \end{cases} \tag{4}$$

Algorithm 1 shows how the velocities are handled. $\vec{V}_r$ is the final resultant velocity that is used to predict a player's position. Coefficients $q$ and $r$ are static values that are less than 1 and greater than 0 (the values of $q$ and $r$ will be explained shortly). They dictate how much of each velocity is used.

In summary, we first separate a player's behaviour into two states: *in battle* and *out of battle*. We then exert different velocities based on a player's current state. Finally, these velocities are combined into a resultant velocity $\vec{V}_r$ as outlined in Algorithm 1 to calculate the player's predicted position $\vec{C}_{\text{pred}}$ at the next simulation tick from this player's current position $\vec{C}$ (as shown in (5)). Consider

$$\vec{C}_{\text{pred}} = \vec{C} + \vec{V}_r. \tag{5}$$

We use $q = 0.5$ and $r = 0.6$. This is the result of trial and error tests to see what works best.

Finally, for convenience, we now give in Table 1 an explanation of each parameter that is used in the descriptions of our algorithms. The Nomenclature section lists lists these parameters, as well as all variables used in our algorithms.

*3.2. Main Theoretical Component: Velocities.* We now elaborate on each of the proposed velocities.

*3.2.1. Follow.* The follow velocity arises from our observation that the player moves towards friendly players and the player groups with these friendly players (e.g., other teammates). It is computed by taking the average position of all friendly players within a specified radius and having the player move towards that location. Furthermore, the speed of differentiation of this velocity does not depend on the distance of other

TABLE 1: Parameter space.

| Parameter | Value | Description |
|---|---|---|
| $W$ | 800 | Static distance threshold to differentiate between a player *in battle* or *out of battle* |
| $k$ | 0.4 | Coefficient used in (14) to determine how much smaller we scale the strength of the friendly team |
| $u$ | 200 | Maximum distance a player will aim to run towards or away from the friend epicenter depending on how strong each team is |
| $l$ | 0.1 | Coefficient used to modify $m$ (introduced below and defined in Nomenclature) so that it is in the correct range |
| $R$ | 60 | Upper bound on $m$ that ensures that there is always some transition that occurs from the old velocity $\vec{V}_0$ to the new velocity |
| $q$ | 0.5 | Sets how much of each follow and bravery velocity is used to create the resultant movement velocity if in battle |
| $r$ | 0.6 | Sets how much of each follow and alignment velocity is used to create the resultant movement velocity if out of battle |
| $h$ | 40 | Threshold angle used to determine the angle above which the change in velocity needs to be before a change in direction is registered |
| $x$ | 350 | Minimum threshold of lag below which the EKB method is always used |

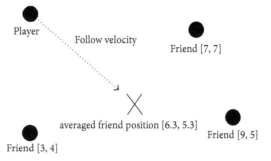

FIGURE 3: Follow velocity.

players, but it is instead always set to the maximum speed of the *TPlayer*. From our observations, the follow velocity is the most important behaviour velocity to exert on a player. This is because, in multiplayer online games, a player's actions generally proceed from a team-based strategy:

$$\vec{E}_f = \frac{\sum_{i=1}^{i=n_f} \vec{P}_{f,i}}{n_f} \qquad (6)$$

$$\vec{V}_{\text{follow}} = \frac{\vec{E}_f - \vec{C}}{\left|\vec{E}_f - \vec{C}\right|} \times S. \qquad (7)$$

Equation (6) calculates the averaged position of all friendly ($f$) players within a given threshold, where $\vec{P}_f$ is the position of a friend and $n_f$ is the number of players of that type within the predefined region of interest (ROI). Equation (7) represents the velocity from the *TPlayer* current position $\vec{C}$ to the average position of all friendly players. $S$ is the maximum speed of the *TPlayer*. The follow velocity is illustrated in Figure 3.

To gather friendly and enemy player data, we impose a maximum distance that a player can be before it is not considered in any calculations. The game window is 1280 pixels wide and 960 pixels tall, and so the maximum distance for considering players is 1280 pixels in the $x$-axis and 960 in the $y$-axis.

*3.2.2. Align.* The alignment velocity arises from a player's tendency to travel in a group with friendly players. The alignment velocity takes into account all friendly players' velocities within a specified radius. The closer a friendly player is, the more weight it carries in affecting the direction of the alignment velocity. The alignment velocity's magnitude is a function of how many friendly players are within the specified radius and how close they are. Consider

$$D_f = \begin{cases} D_{f\text{MAX}} & \text{if } D_f \geq D_{f\text{MAX}} \\ D_{f\text{MIN}} & \text{if } D_f \leq D_{f\text{MIN}} \end{cases} \qquad (8)$$

$$\vec{D}_{\text{align}} = \sum_{i=1}^{i=n_f} \left( \vec{V}_{f,i} \times \left(1 - \frac{D_{f,i} - D_{f,i_{\text{MIN}}}}{D_{f,i_{\text{MAX}}} - D_{f,i_{\text{MIN}}}}\right) \right) \qquad (9)$$

$$\vec{V}_{\text{align}} = \begin{cases} \vec{D}_{\text{align}} & \text{if } \left|\vec{D}_{\text{align}}\right| \leq S \\ \dfrac{\vec{D}_{\text{align}}}{\left|\vec{D}_{\text{align}}\right|} \times S & \text{otherwise.} \end{cases} \qquad (10)$$

Equations (9) and (10) outline the alignment velocity. $D_f, \vec{V}_f, D_{f\text{MIN}}$ and $D_{f\text{MAX}}$ represent the distance to the friendly player, the velocity of the friendly player, the minimum distance to consider for friendly players, and the maximum distance to consider for friendly players, respectively. If the result of (9) is greater than the player's speed $S$, then $\vec{V}_{\text{align}}$ is set to $S$. $D_{f\text{MIN}}$ and $D_{f\text{MAX}}$ are each a predefined threshold. $D_{f\text{MIN}} = 60$ pixels because a player's diameter is approximately this amount, and a player within this distance is likely not be distinguished by the *TPlayer*. $D_{f\text{MAX}} = 1000$ pixels because the friendly player in question is certainly visible at this distance. Though a player may be visible up to 1600 pixels (the diagonal distance of the screen space), an object outside of 1000 pixels is unlikely to affect the alignment of the *TPlayer*.

*3.2.3. Bravery.* The bravery velocity arises from the observed behaviour of a player's tendency to fall back when outnumbered by the enemy and the tendency to advance on the enemy while winning. To obtain the bravery velocity, the total strength of all nearby friends and the total strength of all nearby enemies are calculated. The strength of each team is calculated by adding up the health and ammo values of each player. The relative strength of the friendly army versus the enemy army determines the direction of the resulting velocity. If the friendly army is stronger, the bravery velocity is positive, namely, towards the enemy. Otherwise, it is negative, consequently, away from the enemy forces. The higher the magnitude of the velocity is, the farther the *TPlayer* will move away or towards the enemy:

$$\vec{E}_e = \frac{\sum_{i=1}^{i=n_e} \vec{P}_{e,i}}{n_e} \qquad \vec{E}_f = \frac{\sum_{i=1}^{i=n_f} \vec{P}_{f,i}}{n_f} \qquad (11)$$

$$I_p = \frac{H_p}{\mathrm{MH}_p} + \frac{A_p}{\mathrm{MA}_p} \qquad (12)$$

$$Z_f = \sum_{i=1}^{i=n_f} I_{f,i} \qquad Z_e = \sum_{i=1}^{i=n_e} I_{e,i} \qquad (13)$$

$$\vec{D}_{\mathrm{bravery}} = \left( \vec{E}_f + \left( \frac{\left(\vec{E}_e - \vec{E}_f\right)}{\left|\left(\vec{E}_e - \vec{E}_f\right)\right|} \right) \right.$$
$$\left. \times \left( u \times \frac{\left(kZ_f + I_c\right) - Z_e}{\max\left(\left(kZ_f + I_c\right), Z_e\right)} \right) \right) - \vec{C} \qquad (14)$$

$$\vec{V}_{\mathrm{bravery}} = \frac{\vec{D}_{\mathrm{bravery}}}{\left|\vec{D}_{\mathrm{bravery}}\right|} \times S. \qquad (15)$$

In (12), $I_p$ is the influence of given player (whether a friendly player, enemy player, or the current player) in terms of its strength. $H$, MH, $A$, and MA are the health, maximum health, ammo value, and maximum ammo of the player, respectively. This influence value is then combined into either the enemy or friendly team influence value, depending on which team the *TPlayer* is, represented by $Z_f$ or $Z_e$ in (13). $Z_f$ and $Z_e$ are each made up of all the players on the given team that are within a predefined threshold. $\vec{D}_{\mathrm{bravery}}$ in (14) is the direction vector used for the bravery velocity. $u$ is a coefficient, that is, the maximum distance that a player will run away or towards the enemy and $k$ is a coefficient that modifies the strength of the friendly influence. This is to model the fact that a player will consider his/her own strength over his/her allies' strength in a combat situation. The *TPlayer* is either moving towards or away from the enemy, in relation to the averaged friend position. This is illustrated in Figure 4. Equation (15) is the actual velocity used for bravery.

$k$ is a coefficient used in (14) to determine how much smaller we scale the strength of the friendly team. This is done for two reasons. First, a player will tend to consider his own strength when in combat and will not adjust her behaviour if their friends are strong or weak. Second, since enemy players are more often far away than friendly players, they often fall outside the maximum distance for considering players. Thus, many enemy players that the player may be aware of are not considered in the strength calculations because they are simply too far away. This is easily adjusted by using $k$. In our simulations, we set $k = 0.4$. We found through trial and error that this yielded the best results and behaviour that best reflected reality. $u$ is the maximum distance a player will aim to run towards or away from the friend epicenter depending on how strong each team is. We set $u$ to 200 pixels,

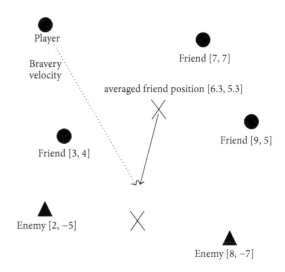

FIGURE 4: Bravery velocity when friendly team is stronger.

as, through trial and error, this is the value that resulted in the best prediction accuracy.

## 4. Algorithm Enhancements

*4.1. Smooth Transition.* In Algorithm 1, $\vec{V}_r$ is the final resultant velocity that is used to predict the player's position. After extensive experiments, we notice the following: if the player's velocity is immediately set to $\vec{V}_r$, the result is most often an inaccurate account of the player's movement. This is due to ignoring the player's *last known velocity*. The *last known velocity* is the last velocity information received in the last received position packet. (We use "position packet" synonymously with "dead reckoning packet," which refers to the information received from the server describing player information.) To alleviate this, we perform a smooth transition of the player from the *last known velocity* to the one determined by the combined velocities (see (16)). $\vec{V}_j$ is the velocity that should be used as the velocity of the player and $j$ is the number of updates that have occurred since the last known velocity $\vec{V}_0$. The more updates that have passed since the last known velocity was received (i.e., the larger the value of $j$), the larger the value of $\vec{V}_r$ is and the smaller the value $\vec{V}_0$ is. Once $j$ reaches the size of $m$ (discussed below), then we exclusively use $\vec{V}_r$ to determine $\vec{V}_j$ as follows:

$$\vec{V}_j = \begin{cases} \frac{m-j}{m}\vec{V}_0 + \frac{j}{m}\left(\vec{V}_r\right) & \text{if } j \leq m \\ \vec{V}_r & \text{otherwise} \end{cases} \qquad (16)$$

$$m = \begin{cases} l \min \{closestEnemyDist, \\ \qquad closestFriendDist\} & \text{if } m \leq R \\ R & \text{otherwise.} \end{cases} \qquad (17)$$

The calculations for $m$ are shown in (17). $m$ is proportional to the distance between the player and the closer of the closest friendly or enemy player. This is due to the following

(1) **if** the desired $A^*$ end destination location has changed since the last update **then**
(2)     recalculate an $A^*$ path to the desired location for $\vec{V}_{\text{follow}}$ and $\vec{V}_{\text{bravery}}$.
(3) **end if**
(4) **if** the next $A^*$ node in the path is reached **then**
(5)     increment the desired node location to the next node in the $A^*$ path.
(6) **end if**
(7) Use the next desired node location to calculate the vectors for $\vec{V}_{\text{follow}}$ and $\vec{V}_{\text{bravery}}$.
(8) **if** the player is in battle **then**
(9)     $\vec{V}_r = \left(\vec{V}_{\text{follow}} \times q\right) + \left(\vec{V}_{\text{bravery}} \times (1-q)\right)$
(10) **else**
(11)     $\vec{V}_r = \left(\vec{V}_{\text{follow}} \times r\right) + \left(\vec{V}_{\text{align}} \times (1-r)\right)$
(12) **end if**

ALGORITHM 2: $A^*$.

(1) **if** the amount of time since the last position packet was received ($Q$) is less than or equal to $x$ ms **then**
(2)     predict the player's position using the EKB
(3) **else if** the player has not changed direction since $LKPT - Q$ time **then**
(4)     predict the player's position using the TDM
(5) **else**
(6)     predict the player's position using the EKB
(7) **end if**

ALGORITHM 3: Hybrid approach.

observation: a player is more likely to react to a player that is close to it and is less likely to continue at the current velocity. $l$ is a coefficient used to modify $m$ so that it is in the right scale (we found that $l = 0.1$ works best). $R$ is the upper bounds on $m$.

We used $l = 0.1$ because it allows for the best transition from the old velocity $\vec{V}_0$ to the new velocity calculated by EKB. We used $R = 60$. This value represents a maximum allowable time to still consider the old velocity $\vec{V}_0$ in the calculations. An $R$ of 60 corresponds to 1 second.

### 4.2. Incorporation of $A^*$.

We employ the $A^*$ path finding algorithm [30] to further improve the accuracy of our initial algorithm. The use of the $A^*$ algorithm proceeds from observing a player's tendency to avoid walls and find an efficient path through space to a desired location. This ensures that the *TPlayer's* predicted path avoids wall objects and looks more realistic. The implementation of the $A^*$ path finding algorithm in our scheme involves modification to the follow and bravery velocities, whereas the alignment velocity remains the same. $\vec{V}_{\text{follow}}$ and $\vec{V}_{\text{bravery}}$ now point towards a desired position that is along the $A^*$ path, rather than pointing towards only the final destination. For $\vec{V}_{\text{follow}}$, this desired location is the average position of all nearby friendly players. For $\vec{V}_{\text{bravery}}$, this desired location is $\vec{D}_{\text{bravery}} + \vec{C}$. A shortest path to this desired location avoiding all obstacles is then calculated. Algorithm 2 outlines how $A^*$ is incorporated into our prediction scheme.

### 4.3. Hybrid Approach.

In order to further improve the prediction accuracy and reduce the number of packets transmitted across the network, we develop a hybrid scheme as follows.

(i) Below $x$ ms of lag, EKB is always used. This is because according to our experiment results EKB performs best under this lag range.

(ii) If a player has been moving in the same direction for less than or equal to the same amount of time as the network delay, then we assume the player will continue to move in this direction and thus we use TDM for the prediction.

(iii) Otherwise, EKB is used.

The hybrid method is detailed in Algorithm 3. We use $x = 350$, because below this threshold the EKB method performs significantly better than TDM and IS (as will be discussed later). The amount of time between the *current time* and the *LKPT* is how long we have not received a position packet from the server, that is, how long we have not known the true position of the *TPlayer*. We call this $Q$ time. Equation (18) describes its calculation:

$$Q = currentTime - LKPT. \qquad (18)$$

*LKPT* is the time stamp of the last received positional information received with regard to the *TPlayer*. We use $Q$ as the amount of time before the *LKPT* to check to see if the player has changed direction. If the *TPlayer* has not changed direction since $LKPT - Q$, then it is assumed that the player will continue in this direction, and the TDM is used.

```
(1) initialize count to one
(2) initialize directionChange to false
(3) while count is less than Q do
(4)     if the angle between the velocity at t = last received and
            the velocity at t = last received minus count's is above
            a threshold angle h. then
(5)         set directionChange to true.
(6)     end if
(7)         increment count by dt.
(8) end while
```

ALGORITHM 4: Check player direction change.

To determine whether a player has changed direction, we use the method outlined in Algorithm 4.

$h$ is a threshold angle used to determine the angle above which the change in velocity needs to be before a change in direction is registered. We use $h = 40$ degrees, so that if a player changes direction by 45 degrees, it is detected as a change in direction. $x$ is the minimum threshold of lag below which the EKB method is always used.

## 5. Experimental Parameters and Results

*5.1. Overhead Introduced by Our EKB Algorithm.* Our algorithm computes a player's desired position based on several calculations. The constituents of this algorithm that add complexity include the A* algorithm, as well as the calculation of (a) the follow vector, (b) the align vector, and (c) the bravery vector. Computing each of these vectors requires looping through nearby players, and therefore the time complexity is $O(n)$, where $n$ is the number of players. The time complexity of the A* calculation depends on heuristics. It is essentially a guided breadth-first search on the tiles (or grid) of the game world. In our implementation, the complexity is $O(D^2)$, where $D$ is the depth of the solution path. Each of these calculations is computed at most once per prediction, and there are at most $n$ players that require prediction. So the total time complexity of algorithm EKB is $O(nD^2 + n^2)$.

*5.2. Experiment Conditions.* In order to collect players' input, replay the collected data (for data analysis and pattern extraction), and conduct empirical and comparative evaluations, we implemented an interactive distributed test environment. This test environment takes the form of a multiplayer online game named Ethereal. We designed the test environment so that player activities would be similar to those that would be seen in any traditional action game. Players, each on a separate computer, can make a connection to the server machine to join the distributed interactive system, wherein players can interact with each other in real-time. Once a connection is made to the server, each player chooses a team to join and can then start playing the game. In Ethereal, players assume the role of a single entity that can move in all directions on a 2D plane freely. Also, they can use the mouse to aim and shoot. Gameplay is such that there are two

FIGURE 5: A snapshot from Ethereal.

teams, both pitted against each other in competition. Points are awarded to a team when a player from that team kills a player from the opposing team. A team wins when it reaches a certain amount of points before the other team does. A screenshot from the game can be seen in Figure 5.

To ensure adequate observations and depth of analysis, we implemented a replay system to record all events and inputs from play sessions and to conduct analysis based on this replay data. This allows us to do multiple predictions per update (i.e., tick) of the simulation on all players in the game without worrying about the analysis and collection of our results slowing down the simulation for the players during a play test. The replay system is a server-side implementation that is designed to accurately playback all game actions and events exactly as they were recorded. The replay system records all relevant information from a play session as it happens. It records player input, births time (i.e., player spawn time), death time, and state snapshots. Player input records consist of a time stamp, directional information, and mouse input at every update of the simulation. A "player snapshot" is taken every 5 seconds to ensure nothing becomes desynchronized. A player snapshot consists of all state information that is important to gameplay, namely: player position, velocity, health, and ammo. An example of such "replay raw data" can be found after the References section. The complete dataset is available at http://www.jakeagar.com/sessionInputsAndMapsAndConfigs.zip.

After recording all necessary data, the system can then play it back. This is done by spawning a given player at its

TABLE 2: Session parameters for algorithm evaluation.

|  | Number of players | Run time |
| --- | --- | --- |
| Session 1 | 10 | 15 minutes |
| Session 2 | 14 | 35 minutes |
| Session 3 | 15 | 28 minutes |

recorded birth time. Then, as the simulation progresses, the time stamp of the input record that is next to execute is checked. If it is time to execute this input, it gets executed. The same is done for the snapshot records. Once the death time of the player is reached, the player is killed. In this way, all recorded data is played back, such that an entire game play session can be observed after it has been recorded. Our test environment also has the capability to run and evaluate dead reckoning schemes and to measure and record metrics associated with each such scheme. At each update of the playback simulation, the replay system can check any number of criteria in order to decide if a simulated dead reckoning prediction should be made. To do so, the replay system must know the positional history of all objects. It achieves this by recording player positional data at each update of the simulation. When a dead reckoning prediction is called upon, the replay system "looks back in time" to the relevant simulated last known position. From the latter, it can predict a position at the current time, as well as measure how accurate the prediction is (by comparing it to the current position). That is, since the replay system makes only simulated dead reckoning predictions, we can easily compare such predictions against the actual player data. In particular, we can compute how far away the predicted position is from the actual position and measure the number of packets that would be sent by the current dead reckoning scheme (as will be explained shortly).

For the training and evaluation of our algorithm, we ran in total 3 play sessions of our 2D networked multiplayer game Ethereal. Table 2 outlines the number of players in and duration (i.e., "run time") of each session used for our algorithm evaluation. All participants were avid for professional video game players, male, between the ages of 17 and 30, and they were either undergraduate students, graduate students, or graduates. We used sessions 1 and 3 (25 participants) for our evaluations. We chose this many players as they constitute a representative set of set of the actual players that would be seen in an online game playing community. Furthermore, this size of sample follows suit with the sample sizes of similar studies. Finally, teams within a game were organized with respect to the configuration of the room so that players sitting close to each other were on the same team, allowing them to discuss strategy.

The play sessions were conducted in a local-area network (LAN) scenario, and thus while playing, players experienced near perfect network conditions. That is, lag was in the order of 5–50 ms at any given time. We then simulated lag on the players' input data from the replay files.

*5.3. Performance Testing and Metrics.* We experimented with different prediction methods, analyzing them with our replay

system. We can setup any amount of delay into the simulation and test the predicted position against the actual position of any player. At the time of making a prediction, we can then measure different metrics. We measured the average export error (AEE), the number of hits, and the number of packets sent. We use these metrics to evaluate our EKB method, as well as the two other dead reckoning schemes we selected: the TDM [3] and the IS [5, 8]. We believe that these metrics accurately test and contrast the accuracy of these dead reckoning schemes. Let us elaborate.

AEE is the average distance from the predicted position and the actual position of the player for all predictions made. To calculate it, we take the median of all export errors at fixed intervals of time (e.g., 300 ms, 600 ms, etc.) to determine the general accuracy of an algorithm. The calculation of AEE is shown in (19). $\vec{P}_t$ and $\vec{E}_t$ are, respectively, the actual position of the player and the predicted position of the player at time $t$. Here, $n$ is the total number of predictions made throughout the lifetime of all replay data. The AEE is a measurement of how similar the estimated behaviour of a player is related to the true and actual movement of a player. The AEE is the best metric in determining the accuracy of any given prediction method:

$$\text{AEE} = \frac{\sum_{i=0}^{i=n} \left| \vec{P}_{t,i} - \vec{E}_{t,i} \right|}{n}. \qquad (19)$$

The next metric we take is hits. A *hit* is defined as when the predicted location is within a specific threshold (measured in pixels) of the actual position. It is taken at specific points in time. This metric measures how many times the prediction scheme has predicted a position correctly. Whenever the position of the player is accurately predicted as a hit, this means that the play experience is improved for the player because it means that the estimated player position will not have to be corrected to the actual player position.

We also measure the number of packets that need to be transmitted over the network during each session of play. This is done by assuming that a packet only needs to be sent when the predicted position of the player is more than a certain static threshold $g$ distance away from the actual position of the player. We use a threshold of $g = 45$ because it is less than the width of a player. Measuring the number of packets sent is done in order to evaluate network traffic (which, ideally, should be as low as possible). Network bandwidth is often a performance bottleneck for distributed interactive simulations. When there are less packets that need to be sent per object, the game can replicate more objects over the network. We present packets sent as a single integer, representing the total number of packets that have been sent throughout all play sessions that were conducted.

To ensure we test our prediction scheme against other prediction schemes in identical situations of play, we make a prediction and measure its accuracy as often as possible. Instead of simulating realistic lag onto the players at the moment of play, we test our prediction scheme at every update of the simulation during replay playback (of the recorded replay data). Furthermore, at each tick of the simulation, we test lag at varying degrees of network delay.

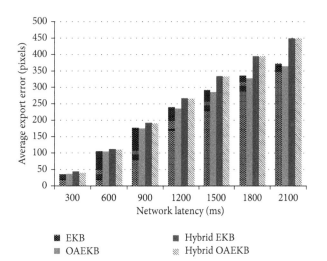

FIGURE 6: AEE of EKB and its variations.

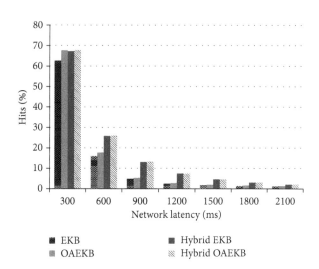

FIGURE 7: Hit percentages, EKB at threshold $g = 45$.

TABLE 3: AEE of EKB and its variations.

|          | EKB   | OAEKB | Hybrid EKB | Hybrid OAEKB |
|----------|-------|-------|------------|--------------|
| 300 ms   | 37.8  | 36.9  | 44.1       | 42.3         |
| 600 ms   | 106.9 | 104.8 | 112.6      | 112.5        |
| 900 ms   | 178.9 | 175.2 | 192.2      | 192.2        |
| 1200 ms  | 241.6 | 235.8 | 267.1      | 266.9        |
| 1500 ms  | 293.6 | 285.7 | 334.7      | 334.0        |
| 1800 ms  | 337.3 | 327.8 | 395.2      | 394.1        |
| 2100 ms  | 374.9 | 364.5 | 449.4      | 448.5        |

TABLE 4: Hit percentages and EKB at threshold $g = 45$.

|          | EKB   | OAEKB | Hybrid EKB | Hybrid OAEKB |
|----------|-------|-------|------------|--------------|
| 300 ms   | 62.6% | 67.7% | 67.2%      | 67.7%        |
| 600 ms   | 15.9% | 17.7% | 25.8%      | 26.0%        |
| 900 ms   | 4.8%  | 5.3%  | 13.1%      | 13.3%        |
| 1200 ms  | 2.5%  | 2.8%  | 7.5%       | 7.4%         |
| 1500 ms  | 1.7%  | 2.0%  | 4.6%       | 4.5%         |
| 1800 ms  | 1.4%  | 1.7%  | 3.0%       | 3.0%         |
| 2100 ms  | 1.2%  | 1.4%  | 2.1%       | 2.1%         |

At each tick, we simulate lag at 7 different levels, 300 ms apart. We test prediction at 300 ms of delay, 600 ms of delay, and so on up to 2100 ms of delay. We do 7 predictions per update of the simulation for each and every player in the game. We use nonrandom, deterministic lag intervals to ensure that analysis and comparison are done absolutely fair, such that nothing is left to chance. We test against lag up to approximately 2 seconds because lag scenarios above 2 seconds of network lag are not likely in today's online video games. Combining testing prediction at every update of the simulation with an all-encompassing approach to lag simulation allows the testing of every possible game scenario at every level of lag with each dead reckoning scheme. Finally, we remark that jitter is not addressed in this work.

*5.4. Experimental Results and Their Analysis.* In this subsection, the results of our experiments with our different versions of EKB are described. The discussion is organized with respect to each metric we consider: AEE, then number of hits, and finally packets sent.

*5.4.1. Average Export Error.* The average export error (AEE) is the discrepancy between the actual location of the player and the predicted location of the player (in pixels). Figure 6 and Table 3 compare the EKB method against the obstacle avoiding EKB (OAEKB) method that uses A$^*$, the hybrid EKB, and the hybrid OAEKB method. These figures show the

effect of introducing the A$^*$ algorithm on the AEE. While the introduction of the path finding algorithm A$^*$ does not improve prediction accuracy drastically, it does result in more realistic predicted motion of the player, as a player controlled by a human user will tend to avoid obstacles to achieve their objectives. AEE increases as prediction time increases. This is because as the prediction time increases, so does the time since the last player's true position was known. This suggests that the EKB performs better under higher latency conditions.

From Figure 6, we can compare the OAEKB and hybrid OAEKB Recall that movement in the hybrid method can use TDM or EKB, depending on how linear a player's past behaviour is. We introduced the hybrid method to increase the number of hits and decrease the number of packets sent. While it does this effectively, it also has the effect of lowering the accuracy of the AEE.

*5.4.2. Number of Hits.* Figure 7 shows the number of hits at different levels of network latency for EKB, OAEKB, hybrid EKB, and hybrid OAEKB. Table 4 shows the same data. The number of hits without using the hybrid method was much lower than with, and this is why we introduced the hybrid method. The fact that the hybrid method has the effect of improving the number of total hits while at the same time lowering AEE accuracy demonstrates that although the position of the player is often accurately predicted, it does

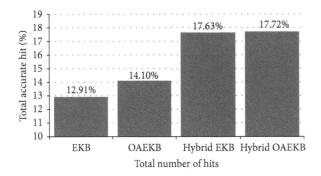

FIGURE 8: Total hit percentages, EKB at threshold $g = 45$.

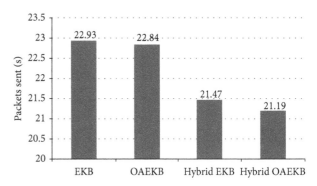

FIGURE 9: Packets per second, EKB at threshold $g = 45$.

not mean that the position of the player is overall better approximated. The hybrid method improves the number of hits because it allows for frequent predictions of the player moving in a straight line, during which time it is exactly accurate in predicting the player (as long as the player is moving linearly). Without the hybrid scheme, the EKB does approximate the player relatively accurate but does not produce as many exact predictions of player position.

As can be seen in Figure 8, the hybrid OAEKB method improves on the number of hits made by EKB. It can also be seen that while introducing A* into EKB did not provide relevant improvements to AEE, it increased the total number of accurate predictions made (as shown in Figure 8). This further provides evidence that A* allows our algorithm to more accurately predict the movement of the player.

*5.4.3. Number of Packets Sent.* We also measure the number of dead reckoning packets (or position packets) that need to be sent through the network. The "packets sent" metric is produced not by using fixed intervals of lag like for the AEE and hit metrics. Instead, as explained earlier, we work under the assumption that a packet is sent only when the predicted position is a certain threshold $h$ distance away from the actual position of the player. To calculate packets sent per second, we add up all the packets that would be sent in this way for each dead reckoning algorithm and then divide it by total time (of the play session) such that we obtain a measure of packets sent per second.

Figure 9 shows the number of packets required to be sent by the different versions of EKB. We observe that the hybrid method reduces the number of packets that need to be sent.

In summary, our experiments show that the OAEKB is best suited to produce the lowest AEE, and the hybrid OAEKB method is best suited for increasing the number of hits and reducing network traffic. In the next section, we will compare the different versions of EKB with TDM [3] and IS [5, 8].

## 6. Comparative Evaluation

*6.1. Average Export Error.* Figure 10 and Table 5 show the AEE introduced by the TDM, IS, EKB, OAEKB, hybrid EKB, and hybrid OAEKB algorithms. From this figure we can see that the OAEKB considerably lowers the overall prediction

TABLE 5: AEE comparison with high latency.

|  | TDM [3] | IS [5, 8] | EKB |
|---|---|---|---|
| 300 ms | 35.6 | 38.2 | 37.8 |
| 600 ms | 109.1 | 110.0 | 106.9 |
| 900 ms | 198.7 | 191.7 | 178.9 |
| 1200 ms | 293.3 | 271.8 | 241.6 |
| 1500 ms | 388.8 | 345.7 | 293.6 |
| 1800 ms | 484.2 | 413.8 | 337.3 |
| 2100 ms | 579.5 | 477.7 | 374.9 |
|  | OAEKB | Hybrid EKB | Hybrid OAEKB |
| 300 ms | 36.9 | 44.1 | 42.3 |
| 600 ms | 104.8 | 112.6 | 112.5 |
| 900 ms | 175.2 | 192.2 | 192.2 |
| 1200 ms | 235.8 | 267.1 | 266.9 |
| 1500 ms | 285.7 | 334.7 | 334.0 |
| 1800 ms | 327.8 | 395.2 | 394.1 |
| 2100 ms | 364.5 | 449.4 | 448.5 |

error when predicting at large amounts of network delay. This is a consequence of the OAEKB's strong ability to approximate the position of the player. It considers various factors that would affect the player in the context of the game and uses these to predict the path of the player. The OAEKB performance at high lag is demonstrated by the slope of OAEKB's AEE-prediction time relationship decreasing as high levels of prediction time are reached, while the TDM and IS seem to take a relatively linear increase in AEE as prediction time is increased.

From Figure 10, it can be seen that while the hybrid OAEKB yields significantly worse AEE overall compared to the OAEKB results, it still outperforms the TDM and IS.

*6.2. Hits Percentages.* We then measure the number of times each algorithm makes an accurate *hit*. Figure 11 lays out the number of hits that were recorded at each given time interval. Table 6 shows the same data as Figure 11. Hybrid EKB and Hybrid OAEKB performed relatively well, especially at very low amounts of lag (300 ms). The TDM is a close second in terms of number of hits to the hybrid OAEKB. The strength of the TDM is its ability to predict an object moving in a linear direction. So while hybrid OAEKB can better predict

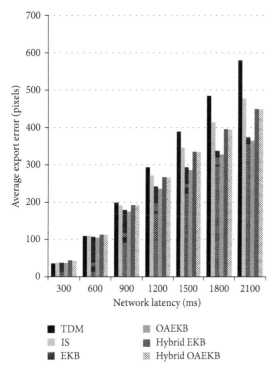

FIGURE 10: Average export error comparison.

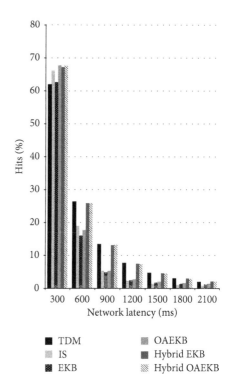

FIGURE 11: Hit percentages at threshold $g$ = 45.

TABLE 6: Hit percentages at threshold $g$ = 45.

|          | TDM [3]   | IS [5, 8]  | EKB         |
|----------|-----------|------------|-------------|
| 300 ms   | 61.9%     | 66.1%      | 62.6%       |
| 600 ms   | 26.3%     | 19.0%      | 15.9%       |
| 900 ms   | 13.4%     | 5.3%       | 4.8%        |
| 1200 ms  | 7.6%      | 2.3%       | 2.5%        |
| 1500 ms  | 4.6%      | 1.4%       | 1.7%        |
| 1800 ms  | 2.9%      | 1.1%       | 1.4%        |
| 2100 ms  | 1.9%      | 0.8%       | 1.2%        |
|          | OAEKB     | Hybrid EKB | Hybrid OAEKB|
| 300 ms   | 67.7%     | 67.2%      | 67.7%       |
| 600 ms   | 17.7%     | 25.8%      | 26.0%       |
| 900 ms   | 5.3%      | 13.1%      | 13.3%       |
| 1200 ms  | 2.8%      | 7.5%       | 7.4%        |
| 1500 ms  | 2.0%      | 4.6%       | 4.5%        |
| 1800 ms  | 1.7%      | 3.0%       | 3.0%        |
| 2100 ms  | 1.4%      | 2.1%       | 2.1%        |

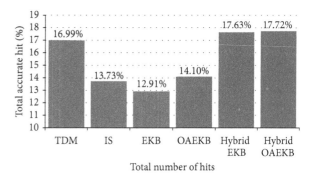

FIGURE 12: Total number of accurate hits at threshold $g$ = 45.

period of time. The IS assumes that the player will maintain the original velocity $\vec{V}_0$ for only a relatively short amount of time.

### 6.3. Number of Packets Sent.

We also measure the number of packets that need to be transmitted over the network during each time interval we monitor. Figure 13 shows hybrid OAEKB improves prediction accuracy over TDM and IS while sending as few packets as TDM. The difference in packets sent between TDM and hybrid OAEKB is negligible, whereas IS needs to send a significantly higher number of packets.

It is worth noting that, compared to TDM, EKB significantly reduces AEE but yields relatively poor improvements/results with respect to the number of hits and the number of packets sent. This is because the AEE is a measure of overall accuracy, while hits and packets sent are concerned

a player's overall behaviour, the TDM can better predict a player's behaviour when moving in the same direction (which players will often do).

The total number of hits as shown in Figure 12 is calculated by taking a mean calculation of all the previous hit percentage results. Hybrid OAEKB and Hybrid EKB performed best, followed very closely by the TDM. This is because the TDM predicts very accurately when a player moves in a single direction, which is often the case. The IS performed poorly because it failed to account for the case when a player would move in a straight line for an extended

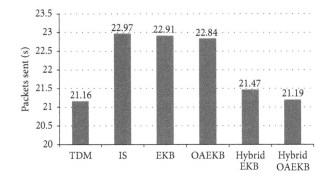

FIGURE 13: Comparison of packets sent per second.

with making a binary observation of whether the prediction was within a small threshold $h$ or not. The strength of the TDM is in its ability to perfectly predict the player, as long as this player is moving in a constant direction. The strength of hybrid OAEKB is that it selectively chooses to predict the player moving in a constant direction or to a defined behaviour. In this way, AEE can be improved without adversely affecting the number of hits made or the number of packets sent.

Finally, contrary to IS, hybrid OAEKB improves the prediction accuracy without increasing the network traffic. And while the number of packets sent is not improved over TDM, hybrid OAEKB does result in more realistic player movement on account of the significant improvements made to the AEE.

## 7. Conclusion

In light of the limitations observed in existing work on dead reckoning, we have proposed here a new prediction scheme that relies on user play patterns. Our research takes place in the context of a 2D top-down multiplayer online game we have developed. In such typical team-based action game, a player's movement is highly unpredictable and is therefore highly prone to prediction inaccuracies, thus emphasizing the need for a better prediction method. We have evaluated our three proposed algorithms against the IEEE standard dead reckoning algorithm [3] and the recent "Interest Scheme" algorithm [5, 8]. In particular, we have shown that while our hybrid OAEKB is best suited to improve hits and packets sent, its use also reduces the improvement to AEE we get from EKB and OAEKB, while still outperforming the other two dead reckoning algorithms we considered.

We emphasize that both the proposed play patterns and algorithms proceed from the data collected for a specific 2D multiplayer competitive game opposing two teams and in which players have freedom to move in all directions without gravity. We observe that traditional 3D first-person shooter games, such as *Unreal Tournament*, *Quake III*, and *Counter-Strike*, employ mostly 2-dimensional player motion (aside from jumping). Thus, our algorithms could be well-suited for these kinds of games as well. However, our algorithms specifically assume there are teams of players. Thus, the generalization of our results to other types of games still constitutes future work. Furthermore, we remark that we still adopt a simple approach to prediction. More complex schemes that (in the spirit of swarm artificial intelligence) would enable a player to simultaneously use multiple strategies (taking into account many possible scenarios) are beyond the scope of our current research.

Additionally, we would like to explore the potential for our method to take into account past decisions and play styles of the player to increase prediction accuracy. Our method assumes all players are interested at the same rate in following teammates and reacting to enemy players. In reality, many players possess differing play styles and skill levels and will react differently in any given situation. Utilizing machine learning or data analytics with this in mind could provide greatly improved results. Just by playing, a user could see automatically personalized improvements in prediction.

We would also like to experiment with taking into account the play styles associated with different weapons or character classes in order to increase prediction accuracy. Many games have different ways to interact in the world such as different weapons and characters to use that can greatly change how a player interacts with teammates and enemies. Building a framework that would allow knowledge of such factors could increase prediction accuracy even further.

We would like to improve upon how the desired position is calculated for the player. While A* made improvements to the method, these improvements were quite minimal. This may be caused by the fact that the position that is currently being used to predict where the player would like to be is fundamentally incorrect. More work should be done in finding exactly where the player would like to be at any given time.

Another difficult question we hope to eventually address pertains to the possibility that users could possibly adapt their input based on the network latency they are currently experiencing.

Finally, work needs to be done in order to reduce the number of packets that are sent over the network. Though each of the 3 versions of the EKB results in improved AEE and hits over the two other dead reckoning methods we considered, it does so with no improvement to network traffic.

## Appendix

Box 1 is an example of the raw gameplay data recorded from a play session. Map, Us, U, UI, N, P, Pos, Sy, Alignment, Si, Is, I, T and B, X, and Y represent the current map, the list of all users, information for a single user, the user's identification number, the user's name, starting information of a user's player, starting position, character type, team, spawn time of the player, list of input data, individual input entry, time of input, character representing directional and mouse input, the X position of the mouse cursor, and the Y position of the mouse cursor respectively, respectively.

```
<Map>ProvingGrounds.xml</Map>
<Us>
<U>
<Ui>0</Ui>
<N>Unnamed</N>
<P>
<Pos>
<X> −2560</X>
<Y>1024</Y>
</Pos>
<N>Unnamed</N>
<Sy>4</Sy>
<Alignment>0</Alignment>
<Si>3621</Si>
</P>
<Is>
<I>
<T>3723</T>
<B>0</B>
</I>
<I>
<T>3740</T>
<B>0</B>
</I>
<I>
<T>3757</T>
<B>0</B>
</I>
<I>
<T>3774</T>
<B>8</B>
<X> −1827.08</X>
<Y>1147.52</Y>
</I>
<I>
<T>3791</T>
<B>8</B>
</I>
<I>
<T>3808</T>
<B>8</B>
</I>
```

Box 1

## Nomenclature

$W$ : Static distance threshold to differentiate between a player *in battle* or *out of battle*

$k$: Coefficient used in (14) to determine how much smaller we scale the strength of the friendly team

$u$: Maximum distance a player will aim to run towards or away from the friend epicenter depending on how strong each team is

$l$: Coefficient used to modify $m$ (explained below) so that it is in the correct range

$R$: Upper bound on $m$ that ensures that there is always some transition that occurs from the old velocity $\vec{V}_0$ to the new velocity

$q$: Sets how much of each velocity (follow and bravery) is used to create the resultant movement velocity if *in battle*

$r$: Sets how much of each velocity (follow and align) is used to create the resultant movement velocity if out of battle

$h$: Threshold angle used to determine the angle above which the change in velocity needs to be before a change in direction is registered

$x$: Minimum threshold of lag below which the EKB method is always used

*TPlayer*: The player whose position is being predicted (target player)

$\vec{C}$: The current position of the *TPlayer*

$S$: The top movement speed of the *TPlayer*

$\vec{E}_f, \vec{E}_e$: Vector representing the epicenter of either friend or enemy players

$\vec{V}_{\text{follow}}$: Movement vector used to predict movement towards an epicenter of players

$\vec{D}_f, \vec{D}_e$: Distance from the *TPlayer* to a given friendly (or enemy) player

$\vec{P}$: Position of a given player

$\vec{D}_{\text{align}}$: Initial movement vector used to predict align behaviour before setting the magnitude limit $S$

$\vec{V}_{\text{align}}$: Movement vector used to predict movement aligning to friendly players' movement

$H, A, \text{MH}, \text{MA}$: Current health, current ammo, max health, and max ammo of a given player

$\vec{I}_p$: Influence of a given player

$\vec{Z}_f, \vec{Z}_e$: Sum of player influences (either friend or enemy)

$\vec{D}_{\text{bravery}}$: Initial movement vector used to predict bravery behaviour before setting magnitude to $S$

$\vec{V}_{\text{bravery}}$: Movement vector used to predict bravery behaviour

*closestEnemyDist*: Distance to closest enemy player

*InBattle*: True or false value based on in the player is said to be *in battle*

$\vec{V}_r$: Combination of other movement vectors used to predict the new position of the *TPlayer*

$\vec{V}_j$: Prediction movement vector used to smooth the *last known velocity* into $\vec{V}_r$

$j$: Number of updates since the *last known velocity*

$m$: Number of updates since the *last known velocity* to fully transition from $\vec{V}_j$ to $\vec{V}_r$

$Q$: Amount of time that has passed the *last known velocity*.

## Acknowledgment

The authors gratefully acknowledge financial support from the Natural Sciences and Engineering Research Council of Canada (NSERC) under Grant no. 371977-2009 RGPIN.

## References

[1] Entertainment Software Association, *Essential Facts about the Computer and Video Game Industry*, 2013.

[2] Entertainment Software Association, *Essential Facts about the Computer and Video Game Industry*, 2011.

[3] "IEEE standard for distributed interactive simulation application protocols," IEEE Standards Board, 1995.

[4] D. E. Comer, *Computer Networks and Internets*, Prentice Hall, 2008.

[5] S. Li, C. Chen, and L. Li, "A new method for path prediction in network games," *Computers in Entertainment*, vol. 5, no. 4, article 8, 12 pages, 2008.

[6] A. F. Wattimena, R. E. Kooij, J. M. van Vugt, and O. K. Ahmed, "Predicting the perceived quality of a first person shooter: the Quake IV G-model," in *Proceedings of the 5th ACM SIGCOMM Workshop on Network and System Support for Games (NetGames '06)*, Singapore, October 2006.

[7] P. Quax, P. Monsieurs, W. Lamotte, D. de Vleeschauwer, and N. Degrande, "Objective and subjective evaluation of the influence of small amounts of delay and jitter on a recent first person shooter game," in *Proceedings of the 3rd ACM SIGCOMM Workshop on Network and System Support for Games (NetGames '04)*, pp. 152–156, Portland, Ore, USA, September 2004.

[8] C. Chen and S. Li, "Interest scheme: a new method for path prediction," in *Proceedings of the 5th ACM SIGCOMM Workshop on Network and System Support for Games (NetGames '06)*, Singapore, October 2006.

[9] S. Aggarwal, H. Banavar, A. Khandelwal, S. Mukherjee, and S. Rangarajan, "Accuracy in dead-reckoning based distributed multi-player games," in *Proceedings of the 3rd ACM SIGCOMM Workshop on Network and System Support for Games (NetGames '04)*, pp. 161–165, Portland, Ore, USA, September 2004.

[10] D. Liang and P. Boustead, "Using local lag and timewarp to improve performance for real life multi-player online games," in *Proceedings of the 5th ACM SIGCOMM Workshop on Network and System Support for Games (NetGames '06)*, Singapore, October 2006.

[11] Y. Ishibashi, Y. Hashimoto, T. Ikedo, and S. Sugawara, "Adaptive Δ-causality control with adaptive dead-reckoning in networked games," in *Proceedings of the 6th ACM SIGCOMM Workshop on Network and System Support for Games (NetGames '07)*, pp. 75–80, Melbourne, Australia, September 2007.

[12] M. Claypool, "The effect of latency on user performance in real-time strategy games," in *Proceedings of the 2rd Workshop on Network and System Support for Games (NetGames '03)*, pp. 3–14, Redwood City, Calif, USA, May 2003.

[13] Z. B. Simpson, "A stream-based time synchronization technique for networked computer games," 2010, http://www.minecontrl.com/zack/timesync/timesync.html.

[14] C. E. Palazzi, S. Ferretti, S. Cacciaguerra, and M. Roccetti, "Interactivity-loss avoidance in event delivery synchronization for mirrored game architectures," *IEEE Transactions on Multimedia*, vol. 8, no. 4, pp. 874–879, 2006.

[15] M. Mauve, J. Vogel, V. Hilt, and W. Effelsberg, "Local-lag and timewarp: providing consistency for replicated continuous applications," *IEEE Transactions on Multimedia*, vol. 6, no. 1, pp. 47–57, 2004.

[16] E. Cronin, B. Filstrup, A. R. Kurc, and S. Jamin, "An efficient synchronization mechanism for mirrored game architectures," in *Proceedings of the 1st Workshop on Network and System Support for Games (NetGames '02)*, pp. 67–73, 2002.

[17] Valve, "Source Multiplayer Networking.," Valve Developer Community, 2011, https://developer.valvesoftware.com/wiki/Source_Multiplayer_Networking.

[18] Y. W. Bernier, "Latency Compensating Methods in Client/Server In-game Protocol Design and Optimization," Valve Developer Community, 2009, https://developer.valvesoftware.com/wiki/Latency_Compensating_Methods_in_Client/Server_In-game_Protocol_Design_and_Optimization#Footnotes.

[19] Y.-J. Lin, K. Guo, and S. Paul, "Sync-MS: synchronized messaging service for real-time multi-player," in *Proceedings of the 10th IEEE International Conference on Network Protocol (ICNP '02)*, pp. 1092–1648, 2002.

[20] Y. Zhang, L. Chen, and G. Chen, "Globally synchronized dead-reckoning with local lag for continuous distributed multiplayer games," in *Proceedings of the 5th ACM SIGCOMM Workshop on Network and System Support for Games (NetGames '06)*, Singapore, October 2006.

[21] F. W. B. Li, L. W. F. Li, and R. W. H. Lau, "Supporting continuous consistency in multiplayer online games," in *Proceedings of the 12th Annual ACM International Conference on Multimedia (MULTIMEDIA '04)*, pp. 388–391, New York, NY, USA, October 2004.

[22] S. Ferretti, "Interactivity maintenance for event synchronization in massive multiplayer online games," Technical Report UBLCS, Bologna, Italy, 2005.

[23] L. C. Wolf and L. Pantel, "On the suitability of dead reckoning schemes for games," in *Proceedings of the 1st Workshop on Network and System Support for Games (NetGames '02)*, pp. 79–84, 2002.

[24] T. P. Duncan and D. Gracanin, "Pre-reckoning algorithm for distributed virtual environments," in *Proceedings of the Winter Simulation Conference*, vol. 2, pp. 1086–1093, December 2003.

[25] W. Cai, F. B. S. Lee, and L. Chen, "An auto-adaptive dead reckoning algorithm for distributed interactive simulation," in *Proceedings of the 13th Workshop on Parallel and Distriuted Simulation (PADS '99)*, pp. 82–89, May 1999.

[26] A. McCoy, T. Ward, S. McLoone, and D. Delaney, "Multistep-ahead neural-network predictors for network traffic reduction in distributed interactive applications," *ACM Transactions on Modeling and Computer Simulation*, vol. 17, no. 4, article 16, Article ID 1276929, 2007.

[27] A. Hakiri, P. Berthou, and T. Gayraud, "QoS-enabled ANFIS Dead Reckoning algorithm for distributed interactive simulation," in *Proceedings of the 14th IEEE/ACM International Symposium on Distributed Simulation and Real-Time Applications (DS-RT '10)*, pp. 33–42, Fairfax, Va, USA, October 2010.

[28] D. Delaney, T. Ward, and S. McLoone, "On reducing entity state update packets in distributed interactive simulations using a hybrid model," in *Proceedings of the 21st IASTED International*

*Multi-Conference on Applied Informatics*, pp. 833–838, February 2003.

[29] W. Palant, C. Griwodz, and P. Halvorsen, "Evaluating dead reckoning variations with a multi-player game simulator," in *Proceedings of the 16th Annual International Workshop on Network and Operating Systems Support for Digital Audio and Video (NOSSDAV '06)*, pp. 4:1–4:6, Newport, RI, USA, May 2006.

[30] S. Russell and P. Norvig, *Artificial Intelligence: A Modern Approach*, Prentice Hall, 1995.

**2**

# 30 : 2: A Game Designed to Promote the Cardiopulmonary Resuscitation Protocol

**Imma Boada,**[1] **Antonio Rodriguez-Benitez,**[1] **Juan Manuel Garcia-Gonzalez,**[1] **Santiago Thió-Henestrosa,**[2] **and Mateu Sbert**[1,3]

[1]*Graphics and Imaging Laboratory, University of Girona, 17071 Girona, Spain*
[2]*Departament Informatica, Matemàtica Aplicada i Estadística, University of Girona, 17071 Girona, Spain*
[3]*School of Computer Science and Technology, Tianjin University, Tianjin 300072, China*

Correspondence should be addressed to Imma Boada; imma.boada@udg.edu

Academic Editor: Michela Mortara

Cardiopulmonary resuscitation (CPR) is a first-aid key survival technique used to stimulate breathing and keep blood flowing to the heart. Its effective administration can significantly increase the survival chances of cardiac arrest victims. We propose 30 : 2, a videogame designed to introduce the main steps of the CPR protocol. It is not intended for certification and training purpose. Driven by the 2010 European Resuscitation Council guidelines we have designed a game composed of eight mini games corresponding to the main steps of the protocol. The player acts as a helper and has to solve a different challenge. We present a detailed description of the game creation process presenting the requirements, the design decisions, and the implementation details. In addition, we present some first impressions of our testing users (25 children, five of each age from 8 to 12 years old and 12 males and 13 females). We evaluated clarity of instructions and three settings of the game: the aesthetics of scenarios, the playability, and the enjoyability of each mini game. All games were well punctuated, and there are no significantly differences between their sex. The proposed game can be a suitable tool to disseminate and promote CPR knowledge.

## 1. Introduction

In the last years, computer-based learning has emerged as an effective tool to promote learning and develop cognitive skills [1]. This approach combines serious learning with interactive entertainment providing many benefits in terms of learning and motivation [2–5]. According to Kebritchi and Hirumi [6], there are five main reasons for the effectiveness of computer-based learning: first, it uses action instead of explanation; second, it creates personal motivation and satisfaction; third, it accommodates multiple learning styles and skills; fourth, it reinforces mastery of skills; and fifth, it provides an interactive and decision-making context. In addition, computer games provide other benefits such as complex and diverse approaches to learning processes and outcomes, interactivity, ability to address cognitive as well as affective learning issues, and motivation for learning [7].

If we consider all these benefits and also that there is an extended use of portable gaming platforms among young people, we can conclude that computer-based games are a perfect channel to promote learning contents [8, 9]. In this context, we propose 30 : 2, a computer game designed to promote the cardiopulmonary resuscitation protocol among citizens and especially among children. The game is not intended for certification and training purpose but to increase awareness and improve knowledge about cardiopulmonary resuscitation.

Cardiopulmonary resuscitation (CPR) is an emergency lifesaving procedure that is done when someone's breathing or heartbeat has stopped. The procedure combines rescue breathing, to provide oxygen to the lungs, and chest compressions to keep oxygen-rich blood flowing until the heartbeat and breathing can be restored. Permanent brain damage or death can occur within minutes if blood flow stops. However, immediate CPR can double or triple survival rates and, CPR plus defibrillation within 3 to 5 minutes of collapse, can produce survival rates as high as 49 to 75% [10–14].

Since 1960, when Kouwenhoven et al. [15] published an article stating that anyone, anywhere, could perform CPR, providing CPR has become an essential competency not only for expert but also for lay people. Different organizations, such as the European Resuscitation Council (ERC) [14], the Red Cross, and the American Heart Association [16], have defined guidelines that describe how resuscitation should be undertaken both safely and effectively. In addition, many countries have initiated CPR programmes to train lay rescuers in CPR and several strategies have been used to teach it including mass training [17], or video self-instruction [18], among others. Unfortunately, the rate of bystander CPR at cardiac arrest is still very low, less than 20% [19]. There is a lack of awareness of the availability of CPR training for the public and lack of interest [20]. Therefore, any proposal that enhance CPR dissemination and promotion will be welcome. With this idea in mind, we created 30:2 a computer game designed to introduce, in an enjoyable way, the main steps of the CPR protocol to children and lay people. The game is composed of eight mini games corresponding to the main steps of the CPR protocol proposed by the ERC 2010 [14]. Each mini game presents a different challenge and different levels of difficulty to maintain the attention of the player. The game name, 30:2, comes from the key step of the CPR protocol that performs 30 compressions and 2 ventilations.

## 2. Related Work

In this section, we briefly describe the CPR protocol which is the basis of our game. Then, we review different applications that have been proposed to learn this protocol and some of the studies that have been carried out to promote it among nonexpert audience.

*2.1. The Basic Life Support Protocol.* The basic life support protocol defines the procedures that have to be carried out when a victim of a cardiac arrest is found. We will follow the protocol defined by the ERC 2010 [14] and represented in Figure 1. According to this protocol we have to proceed as follows. (1) Check the perimeter to make sure the situation is safe. (2) Check the victim for a response by gently shaking his shoulders and asking loudly if he is all right. (3a) If the victim responds, leave him in the position in which you found him ensuring there is no further danger; try to find out what is wrong with him/her and get help if needed. (3b) If he victim does not respond, shout for help, turn the victim onto his back, and then, open the airway placing your hand on his forehead and gently tilt his head back with your fingertips under the point of the victim's chin; lift the chin to open the airway. (4) Keeping the airway open, look, listen, and feel for breathing. (5a) If he is breathing normally, turn him into the recovery position. Send or go for help (call 112 or local emergency number for an ambulance) and continue to assess that breathing remains normal. (5b) If the breathing is not normal or absent, send someone for help and to

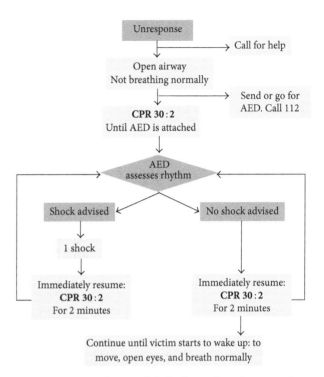

FIGURE 1: Automated external defibrillator algorithm according to 2010 ERC guidelines.

find and bring an automatic external defibrillator (AED) if available; or if you are on your own, use your mobile phone to alert the ambulance service. Leave the victim only when there is no other option. (6) Start chest compression and rescue breaths in a ratio of 30:2. To perform compressions, you must place your hands vertically above the victim's chest and press down on the sternum. Pressure depth has to be between 5 and 6 cm and at a rate of at least 100 compressions per minute, but not exceeding 120. After 30 compressions open the airway again and perform two rescue breaths, blowing steadily into the mouth while watching for the chest to rise, taking about 1 second as in normal breathing. Continue with chest compressions and rescue breathes, in a ratio of 30:2, and stop to recheck the victim only if he starts to wake up: to move, open eyes, and breathe normally. Otherwise, do not interrupt resuscitation. (7) If the victim recovers, put him in the lateral security position.

*2.2. State of the Art on CPR Applications.* Different methods have been proposed to teach CPR. Below we describe some of them (see Table 1 for a summary).

On the one hand, there are video training applications such as Save-a-Life simulator [21], an interactive online video simulation that tests the player knowledge of helping someone suffering from sudden cardiac arrest, and CPR-and-Choking [22], an application that provides instant information on how to perform CPR and how to aid a choking victim. On the other hand, there are handheld device applications such as CPR Game [23], a cardiac arrest simulator on iOS platform focused on advanced CPR training; iResus [24], an application for smart phone, designed to improve

TABLE 1: Some of the proposed applications to introduce CPR or some of the steps of the protocol.

| Application type | |
|---|---|
| Video training | Save-a-Life simulator [21], CPR-and-Choking [22] |
| Handheld device | CPR Game [23], iResus [24], iCPR [25, 26], M-AID [27], CPR simulator [21], and LifeSaver [28] |
| PC platform | Mini-VREM [29], AED Challenge [30] |
| Serious games | JUST [31], MicroSim [32], Staying Alive [33], LISSA [34], Relive [35], Viva!Game [36], and HeartRun [37] |

the performance of an advanced life support provider in a simulated emergency situation; iCPR [25, 26], an iPhone application designed for both lay persons and healthcare professionals able to detect the rate of chest compressions performance by using the built-in accelerometer; M-AID [27], a first-aid application for mobile phones that uses yes or no questions to judge an ongoing situation giving to the user detailed instructions of how to proceed; CPR simulator [21], a set of CPR exercises including adult, child, and infant CPR simulator that runs through the CPR sequence; and LifeSaver [28] a simulator proposed by the UK Resuscitation Council that fuses interactivity with live-action film. In addition, some applications for PC platforms are Mini-Virtual Reality Enhanced Mannequin (Mini-VREM) [29] which is a CPR feedback device with motion detection technology including Kinect, sensor and software specifically designed to analyse chest compression performance and provide real-time feedback in a simulation training setting; and AED Challenge [30], an application that provides online automated external defibrillation and CPR skill practice and testing with realistic scenarios. Finally, in the serious games context, some games for CPR training are JUST [31], an immersive virtual reality situation training system for nonprofessional health emergency operators; MicroSim Prehospital [32] designed for prehospital training on emergency medical services; and Staying Alive [33], an online 3D simulator which provides a learning experience of saving a virtual patient from cardiac arrest in four minutes. LISSA [34] is a serious game with actions turning around an emergency situation represented in a 3D virtual environment with the victim, the helper, and all the auxiliary tools that may require the emergency. The player has to save the victim applying the CPR actions that are evaluated and used to update the game score. When game is over LISSA returns a performance report. This game is used to complement CPR teaching. Other serious games are Relive [35], a first person 3D adventure where the player faces different rescue situations and can test the quality of his CPR directly; Viva!Game [36], a Web-based serious game designed to create awareness on cardiac arrest and cardiopulmonary resuscitation; and HeartRun [37], a mobile simulation game to train resuscitation and targeted at giving school children an understanding of CPR and getting them to take action.

Focusing on the audience, different experiences have been carried out to introduce CPR among children. Uray et al. evaluated the feasibility of life supporting first-aid training as a mandatory subject for 6-7-year-old children of primary schools [38]. They stated that resuscitation skills should be learnt at school, since children are easily motivated, learn quickly, and retain skills [39]. Jones et al. indicated that children of 9 years should be taught to perform CPR, including chest compressions [40]. In addition, the good results obtained in different experiences that have been carried out all over the world have motivated associations such as the ERC, the American Heart Association, and the American Academy of Pediatrics to recommend teaching resuscitation to school children [41–43].

From previous experiences, it makes sense to consider the development of a new game to introduce the CPR protocol to children. In addition, considering the current state of the art, we have seen that most of reported methods are based on multimedia approaches where video, text, and audio are combined to reproduce in a practical case the CPR protocol. In some cases, users can also interact by answering questions that drive them to the correct sequence of the protocol. A similar approach is followed in the case of serious games where instead of real actors they use avatars. Finally other applications just focus on the CPR maneuver. In our case, we propose a different approach to engage children attention on CPR. The axis of our game is also the CPR protocol but we consider the protocol steps independently. For each step, we create a mini game with a challenge that helps the user to retain the key procedure of the step, with enough variety of challenges to maintain the attention of the player and avoid boring him doing the same action for a long time.

## 3. Game Description

To describe the 30 : 2 videogame, we are going to follow the educational game development approach (EGDA) proposed by Torrente et al. [44]. This approach covers all tasks from game design to implementation and evaluation. It is built around four basic principles. The first is a procedure-centric approach that gives importance to capturing the procedural knowledge of the domain. In our case, this knowledge is provided by the ERC protocol that determines the steps that have to be carried out in case of sudden heart attack (see Section 2.1). The second is the collaboration between experts. In our case, the development team works in close collaboration with physicians specialized in cardiopulmonary resuscitation. The third is the agile development with agile tools. In our case, we apply an iterative process that includes analysis, game design, implementation, and quality assurance. The fourth is the low-cost game model. In our case, due to budget restriction our proposal considers 2D animations instead of 3D realistic models that require a much bigger budget. Below, we give a more detailed description of the main steps of the development process.

*3.1. Analysis.* The analysis phase was done in collaboration with experts on CPR that are in charge of CPR instruction

FIGURE 2: The steps of the basic life support protocol that have been selected to define the proposed game. We will create one mini game per selected step.

at our university and also at middle schools. For the school courses, they present the ERC guidelines to children, using the material provided by the ERC, and they also use a mannequin to practice. The purpose of the courses is to make children familiar with CPR concepts. The 30 : 2 game was conceived as a complement to these classes and as a way to preserve the acquired CPR knowledge. With this idea in mind, to delineate the objectives of our game, we considered the ERC guidelines presented in Section 2.1 and, assessed by the experts, we identified the steps and the key procedures of the protocol to be considered. The selected steps are represented in Figure 2 and correspond to the main case of the protocol in which the victim requires the CPR maneuver. We do not take into account the situations described in step (3a) or (5a).

The pedagogical approach used to design the game is based on the experiential learning theory, where educators aim engaging learners in direct experience to increase their knowledge, skills, and values [45]. Experience occurs as a result of interaction between human beings and an environment in forms of thinking, seeing, feeling, handling, and doing [45]. In our case, this experience is going to take place in an artificial environment where a victim has to be recovered from a heart attack by applying the CPR protocol. There are five instructional strategies rooted in the concept of learning through experiences. These are learning by doing, experiential, guided experiential, case-method teaching, and combination of experiential and inquiry-based learning [6]. In our case, we considered the learning by doing strategy. Schank et al. [46] posited seven instructional events to

facilitate this experience. In the analysis phase, we defined these instructional events as follows:

(1) Goals definition: our objective is to introduce the main steps of the CPR protocol to the children. With this purpose we decided to create eight mini games, one for each CPR step.

(2) Mission: the mission is to save a heart attack victim by correctly applying the CPR steps. This mission is decomposed in eight submissions one for each CPR step.

(3) Cover story: there is a heart attack victim in a park and the player has to save him. We decided to create a common scenario for all the mini games and we adapted it to each mini game's requirements.

(4) Roles: the player who acts as a rescuer.

(5) Operation scenarios: all mini games take place in a park; we will provide different views of the park depending on the actions to be carried out.

(6) Provided resources: each mini game has a different challenge. Provided resources will be adapted to it. Game instructions will be given using the keywords of the protocol steps.

(7) Provided feedback: when the challenge is achieved a well done message will appear as well as the keywords of the protocol step.

In addition, we will support different levels of difficulty to keep a high level of engagement. We will support two playing modes. In the first mode, the player will play mini games individually, one by one to reach the maximum level of each mini game. In the second mode, the player will follow the complete sequence of mini games at the same level to see the whole protocol each time. For the CPR courses, we consider that the second mode is the most suitable. To increase the chance to perform the whole CPR process, we give five lives to the player, represented as hearts. In this way if the player fails in one step he has the chance to repeat it. Having several lives, we consider that players engagement in the game will increase as well as, in turn, their intrinsic motivation [47, 48]. In addition, we also use written positive feedback to increase feelings of competence and autonomy, which in turn lead to increased motivation [49].

*3.2. Game Design.* To design the game, we considered that the player acquires the role of a helper who has to save the victim of a cardiac arrest by applying the main steps of the CPR protocol. To guide the player between mini games at the beginning of each one we present the instructions of the step protocol as highlighted keywords, with the goal that the player could retain them easily. In addition, at the end of the mini game, we show the obtained score and the achieved steps. The player has five lives represented as five hearts. To solve the mini game challenge we have a predefined time that is defined according to the level of difficulty. Below we describe the different mini games. For each mini game, we will describe its pedagogical objective which is related with some procedure of the protocol, the scenario, the challenge, the interaction required to achieve the challenge, how we create the different levels of difficulty, and the messages with keywords.

*3.2.1. Mini Game 1 (Isolate Victim).* This mini game is related with step (1) of the protocol. Its pedagogical objective is to transmit to the player that when there is a victim the helper has to check the perimeter to make sure the situation is safe. We designed a game where the main scene is a park with a lot of people. People are represented as hearts of different colours and the victim as a broken heart. All hearts are on movement and the player has to press on the broken heart. Then, it will appear a security perimeter represented as a circle around the victim. The player has to move hearts out from the perimeter to isolate the victim. In this case, the player interacts by pressing on the broken heart and dragging and dropping on the hearts inside the security position. To create the different levels of difficulty we increase the number of hearts and also the used colours. At the beginning, all hearts have the same colour and then, as level of difficulty increases, new colours are added. In addition, time will be adapted to the level, allotted time decreases when difficulty level increases.

The text that appears in the game corresponds to keywords of the represented step. Before starting the game, a screen appears with the current score, the level of difficulty, and the game instructions. In this case, the text is *find and isolate the victim.* Once the game starts, the message *find*

*the victim* and *isolate it* appears. At the end, the message *victim is in a secure position* appears.

*3.2.2. Mini Game 2 (Check Conscious).* This mini game is related with step (2) of the protocol. Its pedagogical objective is to transmit that to check the victim conscious; the helper has to shake his shoulder and ask if he is all right. We designed a game where the scene is a frontal view of the victim with the helper hand on the victim shoulder. In addition, there are glyphs with a question mark on the screen. These are of different colours and shapes; some icons add points and others subtract. Each time we click on a correct glyph, the hand will move victim shoulder to simulate the shaking procedure. The player has to achieve as much points as possible by pressing the correct glyphs. In this case, the player interacts by pressing on the correct icons. The levels of difficulty are related with the number of glyphs that appear and also their speed; the greater the difficulty, the greater the number of glyphs and speed. In addition, playing time will be adapted to the level; allotted time decreases when difficulty level increases.

As in the previous mini game the text that appears in the game corresponds to keywords of the represented step. Before starting the game, a screen appears with the current score, the level of difficulty, and the game instructions which are *check victim's response.* Once the game starts the message *press blue and yellow glyphs* appears. In the middle of the game the message *are you all right* appears and at the end, the message *victim is unconscious* appears.

*3.2.3. Mini Game 3 (Ask for Help).* This mini game is related with the first part of step (3b) of the protocol. Its pedagogical objective is to transmit that if the victim is not conscious, the helper has to shout for help. We designed a game where the scene represents a helper beside the victim. The helper has a speech balloon that has to be completed with the word *help.* Glyphs with letters fall down from the top of the screen and the player has to select the letters to write help. If letters are not selected in the correct order, he has to start again. The player has to complete the *help* word in the available time. In this case, the player interacts by pressing on the glyphs with the correct letters. The levels of difficulty are related with the falling speed of icon letters. In addition, time will be adapted to the level; allotted time decreases when difficulty level increases.

Again the text that appears in the game corresponds to keywords of the represented step. Before starting the game, a screen appears with the current score, the level of difficulty, and the game instructions which are *Ask for Help.* When the game starts the text *press the correct letters* appears as well as, at the end, *well done! Help is on the way!*

*3.2.4. Mini Game 4 (Check Breath).* This mini game is related with the first part of step (3b) and step (4) of the protocol. Its pedagogical objective is to transmit that if the victim is not conscious, in order to check breath the helper has to perform the tilt and chin lift by correctly placing hands on the head and move the victim's head back to open air way. Then, look at the thorax to see if it is moving and, finally, listen if the victim is breathing. We designed a game with the victim lying on the floor. We have a lateral view of his body and different glyphs representing right and left hands, ears, and eyes that will appear on the screen. The player has to select the hands and drop them to the correct head position to perform the tilt and chin lift. Then, place an eye glyph on the thorax and the ear near the victim's face. In this case, the player interacts by pressing on the glyph and dragging it to the correct position. The levels of difficulty are related with the number of glyphs and their speed. In addition, time will be adapted to the level; allotted time decreases when difficulty level increases.

The message that appears before starting the game is *check breath by performing tilt-chin maneuver; look at the thorax and listen respiration*. Once the game starts the messages *drag hands to correct positions* and *place eye on the thorax and ear on the face* appear. The final message is *victim is not breathing*.

*3.2.5. Mini Game 5 (Call Emergency).* This mini game is related with step (5b) of the protocol. Its pedagogical objective is to transmit that if the victim is not breathing, the helper has to call emergency number and ask for a defibrillator. We designed a game where the scene represents the front face of a mobile showing the numbers and the screen to see the dialed numbers. The player has to dial the correct emergency number in the available time. In this case, the player interacts by pressing on the phone numbers. To obtain different levels of difficulty the phone numbers change their position. In addition, time will be adapted to the level; allotted time decreases when difficulty level increases.

The message that appears before starting the game is *call emergency and ask for a defibrillator*. Once the game starts the message *call emergency* appears as well as, at the end, *well done! Emergency is on the way*.

*3.2.6. Mini Game 6 (Remove Clothes).* This mini game is related with step (6) of the protocol. Its pedagogical objective is to transmit that we need to uncover the thorax of the victim to perform the CPR maneuver. We designed a game where the scene represents a front plane of the victim with different layers of clothes (a scarf, a jacket, a shirt, etc.). The player has to remove, in the available time, all the clothes until thorax is uncovered. In this case, the player interacts by pressing on the screen following the shape of the scarf and the zip or pressing on the buttons. The levels of difficulty are related with the layers of clothes, which increase with the level of difficulty. In addition, allotted time will be adapted to the level; allotted time decreases when difficulty level increases.

The message that appears at the beginning is *remove clothes to uncover thorax*. Once the game starts, the message *remove clothes appropriately* appears as well as, at the end, *well done! Thorax uncovered*.

*3.2.7. Mini Game 7 (Perform CPR).* This mini game is related with step (6) of the protocol. Its pedagogical objective is to show the key maneuver of the CPR protocol. The player should learn how to place hands position and where, the rhythm, and the number of compressions that has to be

done. In addition, he has to learn that after compressions he has to perform two rescue breaths in a ratio of 30 : 2. Moreover, he has to learn that compressions are at least of 5 cm. We designed a game with a set of icons to select correct hand positions and placement. In addition, there is a central menu with two icons one for compressions and the other for ventilations, an indicator to show compression depth and another to indicate ventilation degree. This menu has a central board to indicate if maneuver is correct or not. The four considered degrees of correctness are critic, bad, good, and perfect. The player has to perform compressions and ventilations correctly. The player interacts pressing on the correct icons. In this case, the levels of difficulty are related with the accuracy at which CPR maneuver is performed.

The message that appears at the beginning is *perform CPR maneuver*. Once the game starts, the messages that appear are *select correct hands position, perform 30 : 2*, and *put defibrillator patches*. At the end, the final message is *well done! The victim has recovered*.

*3.2.8. Mini Game 8 (Security Position).* This mini game is related with the last step of the CPR protocol. Its pedagogical objective is to show the movements that have to be done to place the victim in the lateral security position. In this position, the mouth is downward so that fluid can drain from the patient's airway; the chin is well up to keep the epiglottis opened. Arms and legs are locked to stabilize the position of the patient. We designed a game where the scene represents a lateral view of the victim. The player has to press on the correct parts of the body and perform the correct movements to place the victim in the security position. The player interacts by pressing on the correct part of the victim's body and dragging it to the correct position. In this case, the levels of difficult are related with the available time which decreases when difficulty level increases.

The message that appears at the beginning is *place the victim in the lateral security position*. Once the game starts the message that appears is *press on the body parts and move* and at the end *well done! Victim is in lateral security position*.

*3.3. Implementation.* To implement the game we used Unity3D, a cross-platform game engine, that can support Mac OSX and WindowsXP/Vista/7/8. It supports three scripting languages: JavaScript, C#, and a dialect of Python called Boo. All three are equally fast and interoperate, and can use the underlying. NET libraries support databases, regular expressions, XML, file access, and networking. Although scripting is frequently considered as limited and slow, in Unity3D scripts are compiled to native code and run nearly as fast as C++. In the project, all the game scripts have been programmed in C#.

The proposed game has been programmed as a finite state machine, where each state can contain different state machines. We used a generic home-implemented state machine library to implement the game flow. This library allows the definition of each state machine, the states that compose it, the actions each state will perform, and its transitions, in a very detailed way. The library only needs

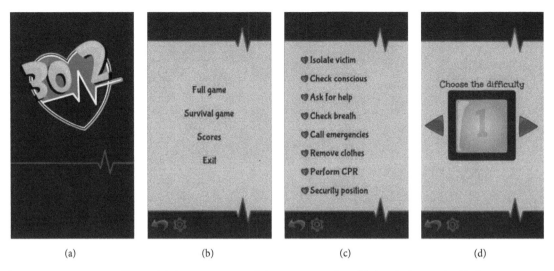

FIGURE 3: Game screens corresponding to (a) the main page and the menus to select (b) the playing mode, (c) the mini game, and (d) the difficulty level.

the user to define what a particular element requires: (i) for each state machine, we have to define the first state to be executed; (ii) for each action, we define the actual action that it will perform; (iii) for each transition, we define the condition for the transition and the next state to which it will move if condition is true (this allows the reutilization of transitions if the condition and destination match); and (iv) in each state, we define the list of actions that it will perform, the substate machines it contains (if any), the transitions it has, and if it is a final state. All the implementation references are generic and are checked during compilation. In this way, we ensure that all references are correct and avoid the continuous errors search. In addition, since elements are not instantiated until they are needed, performance increases considerably. The library also contains a static class that is used as a log. This class allows the subscription of delegates to the class, so that subscribed functions receive the log messages. We have also implemented a library to control scores. This library stores the score independently for each level, allowing us to personalize each level and how it calculates its score and stores them in a manager that allows us to determine what to do with the obtained scores. An important feature of the proposed implementation is that it can be easily upgradable to new CPR guidelines.

When the user starts the game, the general state machine will be initialized and this will initialize player information such as the score. The first state of this machine is the first mini game, Isolate Victim. When the Isolate Victim mini game starts, the difficulty level information and the submachine of the selected level are initialized. In the first state of this submachine, the user has to press on the broken heart. The action that allows pressing on all the hearts will be activated. When the player presses a heart it checks if it is the broken one or not. If it is an unbroken one, it will remain in the same state; otherwise, it will activate the transition to go to the next state. In the new state, the action to remove unbroken hearts from the perimeter of the broken one will be activated.

In this state, we continuously control that no hearts are into the perimeter. If there are, it remains in the same state. Once no more hearts are into the perimeter no more transitions are possible. Since this state is the last one, the submachine will finish and will inform its father state that it has finished. The father state will notify the score of the completed level to be stored in the score manager. Then, according to the game mode and the level, it will go to the next mini game or to the next level of the same mini game.

*3.4. Quality Assurance.* To ensure the game was stable and free of programming errors we continuously perform tests at different levels. We also used as testers members of our laboratory not related with the project but familiar with video games. Once all mini games were approved by our team, we performed tests with nonexperimented users with special attention to children. During tests we analysed playful experience to ensure that mini games were enjoyable enough. During these tests different proposals were done by the users and these led to different modifications on the mini games. To test the educational value after a testing session, we asked users to write the eight steps of the protocol to evaluate if they were able to reproduce them. In all the tests, they were able to do it.

## 4. Results

To present the results we will show different screens of the game grouped by mini games. For a complete demo of the game you can visit http://gilabparc.udg.edu/jocs/30_2/trailer .mov.

First images corresponding to some of the menus are presented in Figure 3. From (a) to (d), we can see the main screen with the game logo (see Figure 3(a)); the menu to select the playing modes (*Full* to play all the steps of the protocol, *Survival* to achieve the upper level of one mini game before

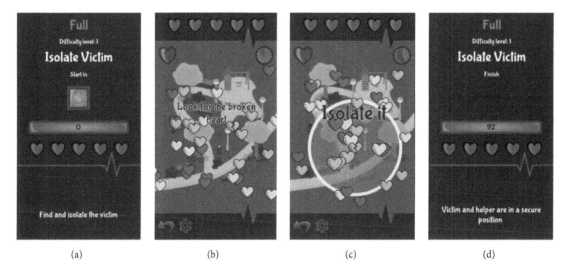

FIGURE 4: Screens of the Isolate Victim mini game. (a) Init screen with game instructions. (b) Before detecting the broken heart. (c) After detection of victim with the security perimeter from which hearts have to be removed. (d) Final screen where we can see the game score and the message that victim and helper are in a secure position.

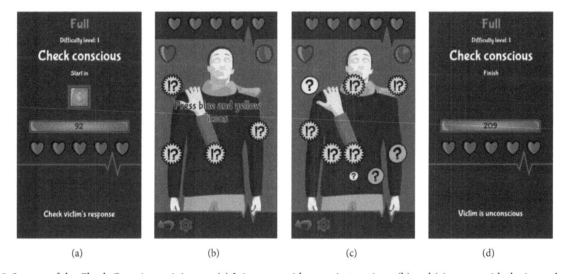

FIGURE 5: Screens of the Check Conscious mini game. (a) Init screen with game instructions. (b) and (c) scenes with the icons that have to be pressed to shake shoulder, only blue and yellow icons add points. (d) Final screen with the game score and the message that the victim is unconscious.

playing the next mini game, *Scores* to check the score, and *Exit* to exit the game); the menu to select the mini game we want to play (see Figure 3(c)); and the selector of the difficulty level once the game has been selected (see Figure 3(d)).

Figure 4 corresponds to the Isolate Victim mini game. From (a) to (d), we can see the init screen with game instructions and a timer that indicates when the game will start. We can also see the number of lives that the player has, in this case five hearts (see Figure 4(a)). This screen configuration is the same for all the mini games. The second image indicates what we have to do to isolate the victim. Note that we have hearts of different colours (see Figure 4(b)). Once we have pressed on the broken heart, the security perimeter appears and we have to isolate the victim as the message indicates (see Figure 4(c)). The last screen is the one

that appears when the game is over. It indicates that the victim and the helper are in a secure position (see Figure 4(d)).

Figure 5 corresponds to the Check Conscious mini game. From (a) to (d), we can see the init screen with game instructions (see Figure 5(a)). The second image indicates what we have to do to check consciousness: press blue and yellow icons (see Figure 5(b)). Once we have pressed on the correct icons we will see how the hand moves the victim's shoulder (see Figure 5(c)). The last screen indicates that victim is unconscious (see Figure 5(d)).

Figure 6 corresponds to the Ask for Help mini game. From (a) to (d), we can see the init screen with game instructions (see Figure 6(a)). The second image indicates what we have to do to ask for help and also the icons with letters falling in the screen (see Figure 6(b)). Once correct

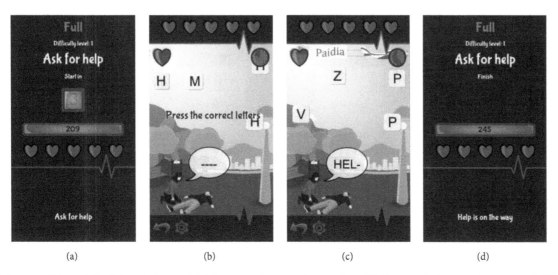

FIGURE 6: Screens of the Ask for Help mini game. (a) Init screen with game instructions. (b) Scene with the empty balloon and falling letters. (c) Scene with some of the help letters completed. (d) Final screen with the game score and the message that help is on the way.

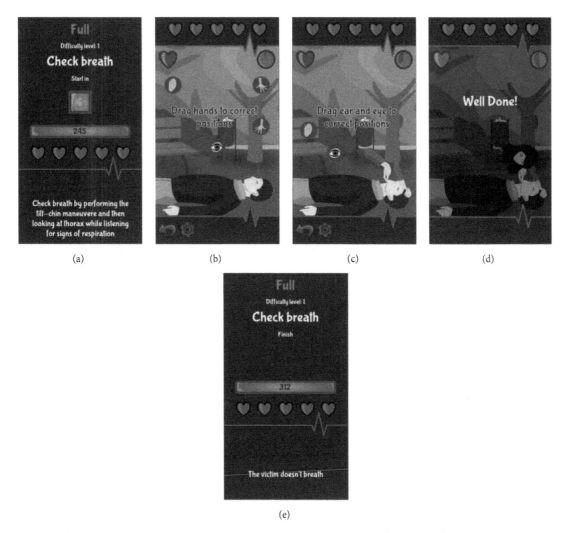

FIGURE 7: Screens of the Check Breath mini game. (a) Init screen with game instructions. (b) Scene with the icons that have to be placed in the correct positions. (c) Tilt-chin maneuver once hands have been correctly placed. (d) Look and listen for breath once eye and ear icons have been correctly placed. (e) Final screen with the score and the message that the victim is not breathing.

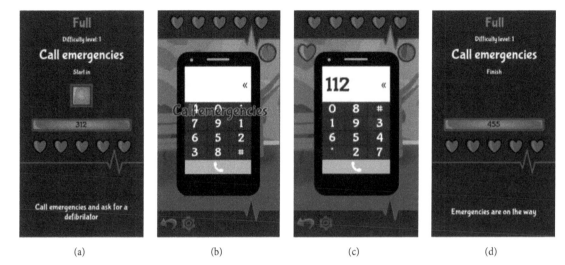

(a)                                    (b)                                    (c)                                    (d)

FIGURE 8: Game screens corresponding to the Ask for Help. (a) Init screen with game instructions. (b) Main screen with phone numbers and (c) once the player has dialed the correct number. (d) Final screen with the obtained score and the message that help and defibrillator are on the way.

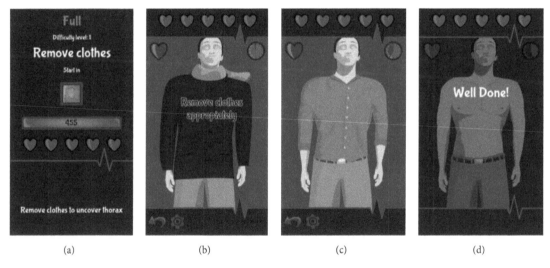

(a)                                    (b)                                    (c)                                    (d)

FIGURE 9: Game screens corresponding to the Remove Clothes mini game. (a) Init screen with game instructions. (b) Main scene with the victim wearing all the clothes. (c) After removing the scarf and the jacket. (d) Victim with the uncovered thorax.

letters are selected they appear in the speech balloon (see Figure 6(c)). The last screen indicates that help is on the way (see Figure 6(d)).

Figure 7 corresponds to the Check Breath mini game. From (a) to (e), we can see the init screen with game instructions indicating that we have to perform the tilt-chin maneuver and look and listen for breath (see Figure 7(a)). The second image shows the different icons of the game. As you can see, there are left and right hands to perform the tilt-chin maneuver and eyes and ears to look and listen. The icons have to be placed in the correct parts of the body victim (see Figure 7(b)). Once hands are correctly placed, the helper hands appear to show the correct hands placement on the victim (see Figure 7(c)). The next screen shows the helper head position which appears once eye and ear icons

are correctly placed (see Figure 7(d)). The last screen indicates that the victim is not breathing (see Figure 7(e)).

Figure 8 corresponds to the Call Emergencies mini game. From (a) to (d), we can see the init screen with game instructions (see Figure 8(a)). The second image shows the phone with all the numbers (see Figure 8(b)). During the game, the numbers change their positions (see Figure 8(c)). The last screen indicates that emergencies are on the way (see Figure 8(d)).

Figure 9 corresponds to the Remove Clothes mini game. From (a) to (d), we can see the init screen with game instructions that indicate we have to uncover the victim thorax (see Figure 9(a)). The second image shows the victim with all the clothes (see Figure 9(b)). The next one shows the victim once the scarf and the jacket have been removed

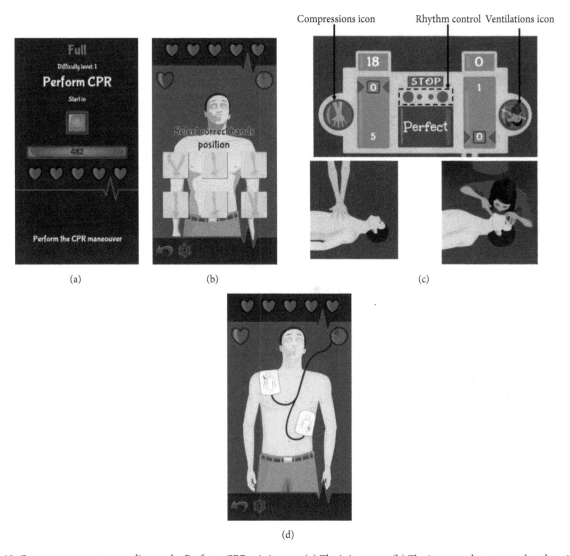

FIGURE 10: Game screens corresponding to the Perform CPR mini game. (a) The init screen. (b) The icon to select correct hand positions. (c) The menu to perform compressions and ventilations. (d) Defibrillator patches after performing CPR maneuver.

(see Figure 9(c)). The last one shows the victim with the uncovered thorax (see Figure 9(d)).

Figure 10 corresponds to the Perform CPR mini game which represents the key point of the protocol. From (a) to (d), we can see the init screen with game instructions (see Figure 10(a)). To start the game, the player has to select the correct hand positions. There will appear icons with different hands positions and the player has to select the correct one (see Figure 10(b)). Figure 10(c) represents the menu designed to control compressions and ventilations performance. In the middle of this board we can see if the performed action has been correct or not. Note that in the board we can also see the number of compressions and ventilations that have been performed and also indicators of the compression depth and ventilation degree. Once the maneuver has finished the defibrillator arrives and the player has to place the patches in the correct place (see Figure 10(d)).

Figure 11 corresponds to the Security Position mini game. From (a) to (e), we can see the init screen with game instructions (see Figure 11(a)). To start the game, the player has to move the victim by pressing on arms or legs of his body (see Figure 11(b)). Once the correct part is pressed, an icon appears as the one showed at the bottom of Figure 11(c). In next figure, we can see the victim after moving his arm (see Figure 11(d)). The last image represents the victim in the lateral security position (see Figure 11(e)).

*4.1. First Users' Impressions.* To test the game we selected 25 children, five of each age from 8 to 12 years old, and 12 males and 13 females. They played the game as many times as they wanted and then, we asked for clarity of instructions and three settings of the game: the aesthetics of scenarios, the playability, and the enjoyability of each mini game. For all four questions users should answer their impression in a scale

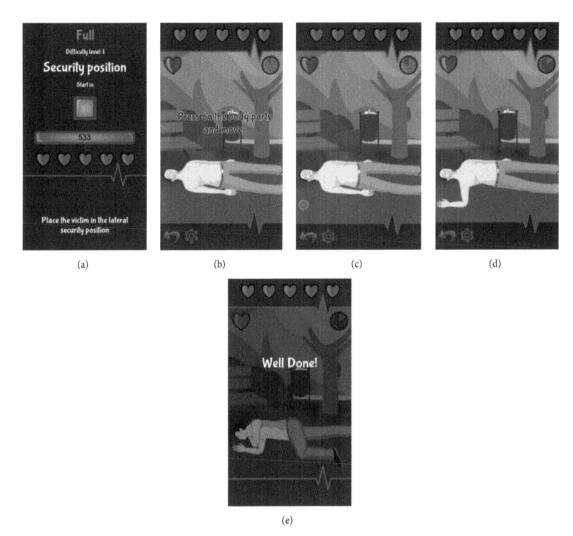

FIGURE 11: Game screens corresponding to the Security Position mini game. (a) The main scene. (b) The icon that appears to move the arm. (c) After moving the arm. (d) The victim in the lateral security position.

from 1 to 5 where 1 recalls to *I do not like at all* and 5 to *I like a lot*. In order to summarize the results, a mean of all three settings was calculated. Table 1 shows mean and standard deviation of answers. Regarding the clarity of instructions, all 8 mini games have values higher than 3 and 6 of them (1, 2, 3, 5, 6, and 7) even higher than 4. On the other hand, the settings mean presents the same results except in Game 8 with a mean of only 2,43. The last column of Table 2 shows there is no significant difference between sexes on the answer, according the $p$ values obtained by a Mann-Whitney $U$ test. Due to the low size of our sample we plan to repeat the experiment with a larger one.

## 5. Conclusions and Future Work

The correct application of cardiopulmonary resuscitation protocol can increase the chances of survival for victims of cardiac arrest. Due to the importance of this procedure, many initiatives have been proposed to disseminate it. However, it is still unknown for a large number of people, and new strategies to promote it are needed. In this paper, we have proposed a game with this purpose and specially targeted to children. Following the cardiopulmonary resuscitation guidelines proposed by the European Resuscitation Council 2010 and assessed by experts, we have converted the main procedures of these guidelines into eight different mini games. Each mini game represents one of the key processes of the protocol and is presented to the player as a challenge. Playing with them makes the player learn the protocol. Our first experiments show us the suitability of the game as a channel to disseminate the protocol, mainly among children. As an immediate work we will update the game to adapt it to the ERC guidelines proposed in 2015 and we will create/improve the scenarios and challenges to preserve the player interest. For instance, in mini game five, we will include the dispatcher assisted CPR instruction. Moreover, we will carry out a further evaluation with a larger sample. In addition, we will evaluate the efficacy of the game to improve the willingness and quality of basic life support in a clinical setting.

TABLE 2: Mean and standard deviation of 25 testers' answers related to clarity of instructions and three settings of the game: the aesthetics of scenarios, the playability, and the enjoyability of each mini game.

| | | Mean | Standard deviation | Mann-Whitney $U$ $p$ value |
|---|---|---|---|---|
| Game 1 | Clarity | 4,28 | 0,61 | 1,00 |
| Isolate Victim | Settings mean | 4,16 | 0,43 | 0,17 |
| Game 2 | Clarity | 4,36 | 0,57 | 0,53 |
| Check Conscious | Settings mean | 4,12 | 0,41 | 0,96 |
| Game 3 | Clarity | 4,56 | 0,51 | 0,08 |
| Ask for Help | Settings mean | 4,24 | 0,35 | 0,59 |
| Game 4 | Clarity | 3,68 | 0,75 | 0,81 |
| Check Breath | Settings mean | 3,52 | 0,42 | 0,40 |
| Game 5 | Clarity | 4,56 | 0,51 | 0,85 |
| Call Emergencies | Settings mean | 4,45 | 0,29 | 0,61 |
| Game 6 | Clarity | 4,46 | 0,51 | 0,85 |
| Remove Clothes | Settings mean | 4,19 | 0,36 | 0,41 |
| Game 7 | Clarity | 4,16 | 0,55 | 0,51 |
| Perform CPR | Settings mean | 4,16 | 0,59 | 0,27 |
| Game 8 | Clarity | 3,4 | 0,58 | 1,00 |
| Security Position | Settings mean | 2,43 | 0,46 | 0,91 |

## Competing Interests

There are no competing interests.

## Acknowledgments

This work has been funded in part by grants from the Spanish Government (no. TIN2013-47276-C6-1-R) and from the Catalan Government (no. 2014-SGR-1232).

## References

[1] M. Prensky, *Digital Game-Based Learning*, McGraw Hill, New York, NY, USA, 2001.

[2] T. M. Connolly, E. A. Boyle, E. MacArthur, T. Hainey, and J. M. Boyle, "A systematic literature review of empirical evidence on computer games and serious games," *Computers and Education*, vol. 59, no. 2, pp. 661–686, 2012.

[3] J. P. Gee, "Learning by design: good video games as learning machines," *E-Learning*, vol. 2, no. 1, pp. 5–16, 2005.

[4] D. W. Shaffer, *How Computer Games Help Children Learn*, Palgrave Macmillan, New York, NY, USA, 2006.

[5] F. Ke, "A case study of computer gaming for math: engaged learning from gameplay?" *Computers and Education*, vol. 51, no. 4, pp. 1609–1620, 2008.

[6] M. Kebritchi and A. Hirumi, "Examining the pedagogical foundations of modern educational computer games," *Computers and Education*, vol. 51, no. 4, pp. 1729–1743, 2008.

[7] H. F. O'Neil, R. Wainess, and E. L. Baker, "Classification of learning outcomes: evidence from the computer games literature," *Curriculum Journal*, vol. 16, no. 4, pp. 455–474, 2005.

[8] M. Virvou and E. Alepis, "Mobile educational features in authoring tools for personalised tutoring," *Computers and Education*, vol. 44, no. 1, pp. 53–68, 2005.

[9] P. Lavín-Mera, P. Moreno-Ger, and B. Fernández-Manjón, "Development of educational videogames in m-learning contexts," in *Proceedings of the 2nd IEEE International Conference on Digital Game and Intelligent Toy Enhanced Learning (DIGI-TEL '08)*, pp. 44–51, Banff, Canada, November 2008.

[10] T. Kitamura, T. Iwami, T. Kawamura et al., "Nationwide improvements in survival from out-of-hospital cardiac arrest in Japan," *Circulation*, vol. 126, no. 24, pp. 2834–2843, 2012.

[11] T. Nishi, T. Maeda, K. Takase, T. Kamikura, Y. Tanaka, and H. Inaba, "Does the number of rescuers affect the survival rate from out-of-hospital cardiac arrests? Two or more rescuers are not always better than one," *Resuscitation*, vol. 84, no. 2, pp. 154–161, 2013.

[12] Y. Tanaka, J. Taniguchi, Y. Wato, Y. Yoshida, and H. Inaba, "The continuous quality improvement project for telephone-assisted instruction of cardiopulmonary resuscitation increased the incidence of bystander CPR and improved the outcomes of out-of-hospital cardiac arrests," *Resuscitation*, vol. 83, no. 10, pp. 1235–1241, 2012.

[13] J. Herlitz, J. Engdahl, L. Svensson, M. Young, K.-A. Ängquist, and S. Holmberg, "Characteristics and outcome among children suffering from out of hospital cardiac arrest in Sweden," *Resuscitation*, vol. 64, no. 1, pp. 37–40, 2005.

[14] G. Abbas, A. Alfonzo, H. R. Arntz et al., "European Resuscitation Council Guidelines for Resuscitation 2010 Section 1. Executive summary," *Resuscitation*, vol. 81, no. 10, pp. 1219–1276, 2010.

[15] W. B. Kouwenhoven, J. R. Jude, and G. Knickerbocker, "Closed-chest cardiac massage," *Journal of the American Medical Association*, vol. 173, no. 10, pp. 1064–1067, 1960.

[16] American Heart Association, "Emergency Cardiovascular Care online education," http://www.onlineaha.org.

[17] Y. T. Fong, V. Anantharaman, S. H. Lim, K. F. Leong, and G. Pokkan, "Mass cardiopulmonary resuscitation 99—Survey results of a multi-organisational effort in public education in

cardiopulmonary resuscitation," *Resuscitation*, vol. 49, no. 2, pp. 201–205, 2001.

[18] E. L. Einspruch, B. Lynch, T. P. Aufderheide, G. Nichol, and L. Becker, "Retention of CPR skills learned in a traditional AHA Heartsaver course versus 30-min video self-training: a controlled randomized study," *Resuscitation*, vol. 74, no. 3, pp. 476–486, 2007.

[19] C. Vaillancourt, J. Grimshaw, J. C. Brehaut et al., "A survey of attitudes and factors associated with successful cardiopulmonary resuscitation (CPR) knowledge transfer in an older population most likely to witness cardiac arrest: design and methodology," *BMC Emergency Medicine*, vol. 8, article 13, 2008.

[20] A.-B. Thoren, A. Axelsson, and J. Herlitz, "The attitude of cardiac care patients towards CPR and CPR education," *Resuscitation*, vol. 61, no. 2, pp. 163–171, 2004.

[21] Medtronic Foundation, CPR Simulator, 2012, http://www.cpr-sim.com/.

[22] CPR Choking, 2011, http://www.stonemeadowdevelopment.com/StoneMeadowDevelopment/CPR&Choking.html.

[23] EM Gladiators LLC, CPR Game, 2011, http://www.freenew.net/iphone/cpr-game-20/466678.htm.

[24] D. Low, N. Clark, J. Soar et al., "Does use of iResus© application on a smart phone improve the performance of an advanced life support provider in a simulated emergency?" *Resuscitation*, vol. 81, no. 2, supplement, p. S10, 2010.

[25] A. Alessandri, *iCPR—iPhone App for CPR Training*, 2009, http://www.icpr.it/.

[26] F. Semeraro, F. Taggi, G. Tammaro, G. Imbriaco, L. Marchetti, and E. L. Cerchiari, "ICPR: a new application of high-quality cardiopulmonary resuscitation training," *Resuscitation*, vol. 82, no. 4, pp. 436–441, 2011.

[27] R. Zanner, D. Wilhelm, H. Feussner, and G. Schneider, "Evaluation of M-AID, a first aid application for mobile phones," *Resuscitation*, vol. 74, no. 3, pp. 487–494, 2007.

[28] LifeSaver, 2012, https://life-saver.org.uk/.

[29] Indiegogo Inc. Mini-VREM, 2012, http://www.mini-vrem.it/.

[30] Insight Instructional Media, *AED Challenge*, 2011, http://aed-challenge.com/.

[31] M. Ponder, B. Herbelin, T. Molet et al., "Interactive scenario immersion: health emergency decision training in just project," in *Proceedings of the International Workshop on Virtual Reality Rehabilitation*, pp. 87–101, 2002.

[32] Laerdal Medical, "MicroSim Prehospital," 2012, http://www.laerdal.com/gb/docid/12984879/MicroSimPrehospital.

[33] Ilumens, *Staying Alive 3D*, 2011, http://www.stayingalive.fr/index_uk.html.

[34] V. Wattanasoontorn, I. Boada, and M. Sbert Lissa, "A serious game to learn cardiopulmonary resuscitation," in *Proceedings of the 8th International Conference on Foundations of Digital Games, Games for Learning Workshop (FDG '13)*, 2013.

[35] F. Semeraro, A. Frisoli, G. Ristagno et al., "Relive: a serious game to learn how to save lives," *Resuscitation*, vol. 85, no. 7, pp. e109–e110, 2014.

[36] Viva! Game, http://www.viva2013.it/viva-game.

[37] B. Schmitz, R. Klemke, J. Walhout, and M. Specht, "Attuning a mobile simulation game for school children using a design-based research approach," *Computers and Education*, vol. 81, pp. 35–48, 2015.

[38] T. Uray, A. Lunzer, A. Ochsenhofer et al., "Feasibility of Life-supporting First-aid (LSFA) training as a mandatory subject in primary schools," *Resuscitation*, vol. 59, no. 2, pp. 211–220, 2003.

[39] M. S. Link, "CPR for kids: please try this at home," *Journal Watch Cardiology*, vol. 28, pp. 234–239, 2007.

[40] I. Jones, R. Whitfield, M. Colquhoun, D. Chamberlain, N. Vetter, and R. Newcombe, "At what age can schoolchildren provide effective chest compressions? An observational study from the Heartstart UK schools training programme," *British Medical Journal*, vol. 334, no. 7605, pp. 1201–1203, 2007.

[41] D. L. Isbye, L. S. Rasmussen, C. Ringsted, and F. K. Lippert, "Disseminating cardiopulmonary resuscitation training by distributing 35 000 personal manikins among school children," *Circulation*, vol. 116, no. 12, pp. 1380–1385, 2007.

[42] American Academy of Pediatrics Committee on Injury, Violence, and Poison Prevention, "Prevention of drowning in infants, children, and adolescents," *Pediatrics*, vol. 112, pp. 437–439, 2003.

[43] L. A. Pyles and J. Knapp, "Role of pediatricians in advocating life support training courses for parents and the public," *Pediatrics*, vol. 114, no. 6, pp. e761–e765, 2004.

[44] J. Torrente, B. Borro-Escribano, M. Freire et al., "Development of game-like simulations for procedural knowledge in health-care education," *IEEE Transactions on Learning Technologies*, vol. 7, no. 1, pp. 69–82, 2014.

[45] J. Dewey, *Experience and Education*, Simon and Schuster, New York, NY, USA, 1938.

[46] R. C. Schank, T. R. Berman, and K. A. Macpherson, "Instructional-design theories and models: a new paradigm of instructional theory," in *Learning by Doing*, C. M. Reigeluth and N. J. Mahwah, Eds., pp. 633–651, Lawrence Erlbaum Associates, Mahwah, NJ, USA, 1999.

[47] E. L. Deci and R. M. Ryan, *Intrinsic Motivation and Self-Determination in Human Behavior*, Plenum, New York, NY, USA, 1985.

[48] E. L. Deci and R. M. Ryan, "The "what" and "why" of goal pursuits: human needs and the self-determination of behavior," *Psychological Inquiry*, vol. 11, no. 4, pp. 227–268, 2000.

[49] C. Burgers, A. Eden, M. D. van Engelenburg, and S. Buningh, "How feedback boosts motivation and play in a brain-training game," *Computers in Human Behavior*, vol. 48, pp. 94–103, 2015.

# 3

# Development of a Gesture-Based Game Applying Participatory Design to Reflect Values of Manual Wheelchair Users

**Alexandre Greluk Szykman, André Luiz Brandão⑩, and João Paulo Gois**

*Federal University of ABC–UFABC, Avenida dos Estados 5001, Santo André, Brazil*

Correspondence should be addressed to André Luiz Brandão; brandao@daad-alumni.de

Academic Editor: Michael J. Katchabaw

Wheelchair users have been benefited from Natural User Interface (NUI) games because gesture-based applications can help motor disabled people. Previous work showed that considering values and the social context of these users improve game enjoyment. However, the literature lacks on studies that address games as a tool to approach personal values of people with physical disabilities. Participatory design encompasses techniques that allow absorbing and reflecting values of users into technologies. We developed a gesture-based game using participatory design addressing values of wheelchair users. To manage the development of our game, we permitted creativity and flexibility to the designers. Our design is aligned to the Game SCRUM and make use of concepts from the Creative Process. The products of each stage of the design that we applied are both a gesture-based game and its evaluation. We tested the *enjoyment* (immersion, difficult while playing, etc.) of users for the game that we developed thought game-based quantitative and qualitative analyses. Our results indicate that the game was able to provide a satisfactory entertaining experience to the users.

## 1. Introduction

Practicing exercises has been proven to develop physical, social, and cognitive capabilities of wheelchair users [1, 2]. Further, researchers showed that exercises lead wheelchair users to have a better life quality than able-bodied people who do not practice [3]. Nevertheless, in the current social context, wheelchair users have reduced opportunities to participate in group physical activities [1, 2]. Researchers have been tackling this issue with the development of exergames, where users perform physical exercises while interacting with the mechanics of digital games [1, 4]. User interaction with exergames often employs Natural User Interface (NUI) through motion capture [5]. There is evidence that people with disabilities, including wheelchair users, become motivated while practicing solo or group exercises through interaction with NUI-based games [6].

Szykman et al. [6] described the panorama of the research involving people with physical disabilities and NUI-based games developed until the year of 2015. The authors sought answers to the question "How are researchers conducting studies with NUI games and people with physical disabilities?". Szykman et al. [6] evidenced the importance of the development of NUI games for people with disabilities through two main observations: (1) 35% of the users who went through a treatment involving NUI games declared some form of improvement in life quality and (2) 95% of the researchers that measured the users' enjoyment for the developed games pointed out that the users had a positive experience.

Most of the gesture-based games have their main focus on the development of the rehabilitation of the users [6]. Examples for rehabilitation are games whose users' interface is structured upon the necessary movements for physiotherapy after a stroke or cerebral palsy. Szykman et al. also observed that there is a small number of games that focus on the inclusion of people with physical disabilities into society. An example of inclusion is a game that allows people with an amputated arm to play together with able-bodied people.

From the designing side, Gerling et al. [7] analyzed the importance of cooperation between experts and wheelchair users in the development of games with participatory design (PD). The authors concluded that expert designers who are not wheelchair users had more positive expectations about the representation of disabilities in a game content than wheelchair users. We understood that the process as a whole has benefited from the balance between insights of those two roles. They also mentioned that the manner in which the disability is represented in the games influences the positive experience of the game. In general, the enjoyment was higher when the act of overcoming the handicap was represented in a manner that empowered users [7]. That insight converges to the conclusions of Hutzler et al. [8] and Szykman et al. [6] about representing tools for overcoming disabilities as personal values of users in the game.

In 2016, Gerling et al. [9] represented the values of young powered wheelchair users in the design of gesture-based games through the application of PD techniques. The authors elicited the participants' values for self-perception, gaming preferences, and gesture-based play. The results, based on testimonials from the users, showed that the positive player experience of the game was substantially satisfying with the representation of their values in content [9].

We describe the design that we conducted to the creation of a gesture-based game with manual wheelchair users. We based the design aligning it to Game SCRUM and on concepts of participatory design. Besides, the design activities that occurred during our design also took into account aspects of Creative Process to aid the emerging of users' values. We measured the enjoyment, e.g., immersion and difficult while playing, of users towards the developed game with quantitative and qualitative analysis. The evaluation of the game indicates that the design that we applied lead to a productive game. The contribution of this paper is the description of the design of a gesture-based game that reflects values of wheelchair users employing participatory design. Specifically, this work aims to develop a game focused on entertainment that reflects the values of the wheelchair users with the purpose of entertainment.

We organize this paper as follows. In Section 2 we present value-guided approaches, from seminal studies to those closer to our approach. In Section 3 we present our design, detailing the set of sessions that composed it as well as aspects of the game we developed. After that, in Section 4 we evaluate the gesture-based game that we developed, in which wheelchair users and their relatives played together. In Section 5 we discuss how the concepts we employed influenced the design. We also compare our design sessions with those ones in previous studies and discuss the values emerged along the PD sessions. In Section 6 we detail limitations of our study. In Section 7 we conclude the present work.

## 2. Value-Guided Approaches to Design

The interest for and the distinct conceptualizations of human values have been continuously present in several areas, e.g., computer ethics, social informatics, and participatory design [11]. Nonetheless, a significant challenge when taking into account values in the design process arises. Precisely, values, which are naturally controversial or conflicting, not always are natural to be detected and incorporated into the technology. Such a challenge, as well as the different views of values, has led the HCI community and correlated

research areas to produce fruitful studies, reflections, and methodologies to elucidate values into the development of technologies. One common aspect of the main studies is that values must be dominant and central in the design process [12–15].

Friedman and colleagues presented seminal studies about the *value-sensitive design* (VSD) [11, 16, 17]. The starting point of VSD is the values that center the human well-being, dignity, rights, and justice and welfare. The VSD methodology relies on an iterative process that combines a tripod of studies: conceptual, empirical, and technical [11]. Such studies provide a rich set of questions, from philosophical to technical aspects, to be answered and refined along the design process.

Cockton [13] addressed the importance of redefining, focusing, and, consequently, recreating Human-Computer Interaction (HCI) as a design discipline. From a historical reflection of HCI, beginning at the System-Centered 70s to the Context-Centered 90s, Cockton converged to the Value-Centered HCI. For value-centered design, the author argues that the framework must be tailored around three processes [18]: opportunity identification, design, and evaluation and iteration.

These previous works provided comprehensive value-centered frameworks, as well as taxonomies and lists of general values. However, recently, authors have made significant questions about such studies [12, 14, 15, 19]. They are concerned about proposing more dynamical and flexible approaches for identifying and applying values in the design process. Iversen et al. [12] firstly paid attention to how PD has deviated from its original principles, i.e., from the Scandinavian traditions. The authors highlighted that the use of PD methods, e.g., the most common, having stakeholders during the design process, does not qualify a work as PD. They emphasize that PD is "about negotiating values". According to them, values are dynamic and emerge by a dialogical process, distinctly from previous studies [20]. The values interact recursively with the design process while permeating the whole process. In that sense, Iversen et al. approached techniques to mediate the emergence of values in the design process [21]. Halloran et al. [19] grasp values as a spontaneously emerging and dynamic resource for codesigners. They found that values are susceptible to changes; more specifically, the main question is not about identifying values, but a process for rethinking the values. They observed the need for a codesign approach that, as well as making use of preselected values, also integrates values that emerge during the process.

The theme of values has also permeated game design [22–25]. Flanagan et al. [23] emphasize the difficulty of designers in balancing their values with those from other sources. In their work, the authors proposed a framework, based on a working list of important values related to the project. Such values arise from designers, stakeholders, users, and previous work, project goals, and further hypotheses. Kultima and Sandovar [24] also proposed a set of categories of game design values, among them, the value of artistic expression, social impact, and commercial values.

For wheelchair users' games, Gerling et al. [9] presented the closest work to our approach. The authors employed

PD for developing a gesture-based game centered on players with mobility impairment. The authors focused on players' preferences and perspectives on the value of gesture-based play. It is worth mentioning that the studies from Gerling and colleagues [9, 10] are very expressive in addressing the development of gesture-based games for wheelchair users with participatory design. They observed that previous work [4, 26, 27] about wheelchair users with gesture-based games did not employ participatory design during their development. In counterpart, their resulting studies [7, 9, 28] led to relevant insights in including wheelchair users as designers in the game development as well as considering values in the design process.

Based on previous studies [6, 9], we noticed the importance of exploring the value of a gesture-based game for wheelchair users. As Iversen et al. [12], in our work, values emerged from a dialogical process, however, the tight schedule imposed by SCRUM leads to not having several sessions for refinement of the values. As observed by Friedman [16], the identification of codesigners is one of the most relevant steps while conducting a value-sensitive design. We also believe this observation is significantly relevant. In this sense, we seek codesigners that are both wheelchair users and sports practitioners. Particularly, they are tennis practitioners. We also considered as our codesigners the coaches of the wheelchair players.

## 3. Designing a Gesture-Based Game with Wheelchair Users

The design team consisted of eight members: the five codesigners (three wheelchair users and two able-bodied, who are their tennis coach and physiologist.), henceforth named *participants,* and three authors of this study, henceforth called *researchers.*

The coach and physiologist have a degree in physical education and are the oldest participants. Among the wheelchair users, people are from elementary school to undergraduate in health sciences. All of them are tennis practitioners. Also, the wheelchair users enjoy playing digital games. Notably, the men like to play fighting and soccer games while the girl enjoys dancing games.

The researchers not only acted as facilitators and developers but also have participated in design activities. We invited the codesigners among members of the tennis organization *CR Tennis Academy,* in the city of São Caetano do Sul, Brazil. We identified the participants by labels, summarized in Table 1. Fiorilli et al. [2] suggest the functional classification criteria of the *International Wheelchair Basketball Federation* (IWBF Table) to classify the functional abilities of users in a range from 1.0 (little or no controlled trunk movement) to 4.5 (normal trunk movement in all directions). Two of the wheelchair users have paraplegia, one classified as 3.0 and one as 4.5. The other wheelchair user has quadriplegia, scoring 2.0, respectively.

We conducted five sessions of participatory design. According to previous studies, we time-marked our sessions to 60 minutes [30]. This time limit aims to avoid fatigue and the pressure under the participants and keep their focus.

Before the beginning of each session, we announced the time limit to all participants.

Every PD session occurred after a wheelchair tennis practice by the participants. Since our participants always wanted to make productive contributions, an effect of an agreed-upon time limit was that participants tried to resolve future discussions timely instead of getting lost in endless arguing.

All sessions were video-recorded to capture the information of the design as a narrative [9, 31]. The application resulted in a reviewed prototype of a gesture-based game. For the artistic assets, we had the support of the Jecripe Project (https://jecripe.wordpress.com/english/).

The role of the participants during the sessions, as "experts of their own lives", included providing information based on their values to nourish the participant's Creative Process. Furthermore, they participated in identifying and prioritizing requirements, evaluating prototypes, and interpreting and discussing collected data. The tasks of our role as researchers are listed below [31]:

(i) Explain the objectives of the design activities in each PD session

(ii) Facilitate discussions among participants

(iii) Document data coming from participants

(iv) Abstract the resulting information in the game elements considering the technical feasibility of their implementation

(v) Discuss the results with the participants taking into account the findings in our previous studies and good practice in participatory design in the literature

*3.1. Session 1: Introducing the Framed Problem.* Our design initially required researchers to pursue an analysis of the population and social impact and used technology for the game to be developed. Our research is detailed in a previous work [6] and resulted in a problem framing: *How to develop a gesture-based game for wheelchair users focusing on their values and social context?* In this session, we introduced the *framed problem* and conducted a conversation to settle the participants. Our objective was to capture relevant elements from values of the participants. The discussion flowed freely, and the participants did not seem to worry about the final goal (the game). The main topics of the conversation were objects or events of interest of the participants, such as the sports that they used to practice and obstacles of their daily life. We defined and conducted a design lasting 60 minutes and with a theme focused on *elements of interest of the participants.* Figure 1 shows a photo of the first session; the meeting format of the other sessions was similar to that one shown in the figure.

As supporting materials for the creative stimulus of the participants, we provided paper, pencils, colored pens, scissors, and glue, following the observations from Pommeranz et al. [30], who investigated how the use of such materials can influence the creativity stimulus during design sessions. Thus, we made such materials available to participants to help them express their ideas. Nevertheless, we did not set specific rules for the use of materials. We noticed that all participants

TABLE 1: Characteristics of the codesigners (participants).

| Label | Role in PD | Age | Sex | IWBF Classification |
|---|---|---|---|---|
| A | Wheelchair User | 26 | Female | 2.0 |
| B | Wheelchair User | 40 | Male | 3.0 |
| C | Wheelchair User | 34 | Male | 4.5 |
| D | Tennis Coach | 58 | Female | 4.5 |
| E | Physiologist | 53 | Female | 4.5 |

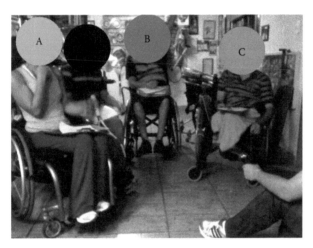

FIGURE 1: Participants A, B, and C during the first PD session: they used paper and pencil to annotate their insights.

adopted the practice of writing their elements of interest as topics on the paper voluntarily. They ignored scissors and glue. We believe that, as the designers were very excited because the session occurred just after their tennis practices and there was a time restriction of 30 minutes, they opted to a strong conversation interaction instead of using manual materials where they would not interact with each other.

The influence of time constraints in the process was evident. The predetermined time span for the session induced the participants to write more elements on paper and faster. The feeling of participating in a game with time constraints made participants worry about optimizing the process. Sometimes, when the conversation involved only a part of the participants, the others used the time to write down more elements. We used the written elements to restore the pace of the conversation when it decreased. During long gaps between interactions, we (the researchers) intervened asking the quietest participant to read aloud the elements that he or she had written and about which we had not yet talked. As a result, the entire session generated data to be analyzed. Therefore, we obtained a satisfactory outcome from this session. However, we noticed that extending the session's time could have led to more information being collected.

To not influence the flow of the conversation, we interacted with participants in rare opportunities. The main interaction took place at the beginning of the session when we explained the framed problem. There were also interactions to keep the pace of the conversation. In that case, we interacted when we perceived a lack of balance in the

discussion, i.e., when one of the participants spoke much more than others. In those situations, we asked the opinion of the quieter participants on the subject at hand. We opted to keep the discussion among wheelchairs A, B, and C and not between able-bodied (and their tennis coaches) D and E [31]. Thus, we took into account but did not voluntarily encourage interactions between participants D and E.

Finally, we realized that the fact that users are aware of our intention to develop a game with the *Kinect* sensor contributed to this topic being often mentioned during the conversation, as observed by Smith et al. [32, 33]. The final goal of the session was to compile valuable information from participants. We outlined the information in the form of a recorded discussion. Afterward, we could work with that information to represent it in a cloud map. We detail that step of the process in the next session. Table 2 summarizes the characteristics of Session 1.

*3.2. Session 2: Cloud Map Building.* Watching the recording of the first session, we analyzed it, transcribing all the main elements that were verbalized during the conversation. We considered as main elements the substantives or verbs that represented relevant aspects to the theme of the conversation. Supported by the visualization software *VOSViwer* [34], we output those elements into a cloud map, highlighting and evidencing the most relevant words from texts. The maps can also represent words that have a close relationship to each other.

During the second PD session, participants B, C, and E (Table 1) attended. We conducted the meeting with those participants and updated the others afterward. In this session, only two from the three researchers participated. We managed to keep the number of participants higher than the number of researchers to allow the participants to feel more comfortable during the sessions [8]. In the session, the participants recommended performing manual changes in the cloud map so that it reflected more accurately the elements that they tried to express. Figure 2 displays the resulting cloud map from this PD session. That map contained information about values and social context of the participants. We used that information in the future sessions to structure relevant *user stories*, commonly employed in Game SCRUM [35] that guided the development of the game. Table 3 summarizes the characteristics of Session 2.

As the codesigners asked to modify the cloud map, we noticed that some values started to arise. For instance, the words in the cloud map (Figure 2) *adrenaline, speed, race,* and *height* were mentioned in the context where the codesigners

TABLE 2: Summary of the characteristics of Session 1.

| Objective | Collect information from the participants to solve the framed problem |
|---|---|
| Format | Design Activity played with the participants and facilitated by researchers |
| Duration | 60 minutes |
| Output | A recorded video with information about the participants |

TABLE 3: Summary of the characteristics of Session 2.

| Objective | Generate and check a document compiling the information (cloud map) |
|---|---|
| Format | Meetings among researchers and participants |
| Duration | Non pre-defined duration |
| Output | A cloud map with the main information recorded in the video of Session 1 |

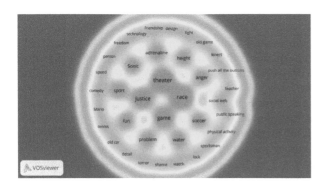

FIGURE 2: Cloud Map generated from information collected in Session 1. The most relevant words are highlighted and located closer to words related to them.

were looking for *empowerment*. While the codesigners were discussing *theater, friendship,* and *justice,* they focused on *noncompetitive* sports. Finally, when talking about *fun, sports, game,* and *physical activity,* they are talking about their *motivation* to engage in diverse activities in their lives. We discuss in detail each of these aspects in Section 5.

*3.3. Session 3: Generating User Stories.* The goal of Session 3 was to combine into user stories the possible aspects of the cloud maps within the given time. The participants randomly read some items in the maps and tried to create sentences with those elements. We suggested that, while forming the sentences, participants kept in mind the essential game elements: mechanics, technology, story, and aesthetics [29]. The stories did not necessarily use the exact words that are in the cloud map. Instead, we noticed that the participants were inspired by the words in the maps to create stories with similar words [36]. For instance, the fact that the words *car* and *adrenaline* were present in the maps led to a discussion about including a *race* in the game. As the codesigners connected the elements, the values emerging in the previous session started to be more evident.

The use of cloud maps showed to be effective for the session. To perform the combinations, participants tended to focus on elements highlighted in the cloud map. Cloud maps evidence elements that were frequently mentioned, which are the most relevant to the users. Therefore, participants

prioritized combinations among the most relevant elements. In this session, we had to intervene as researchers more often than in previous sessions. We realized that, at first, the participants had some difficulties to understand the purpose of the Design Activity. Thus, we provided some examples of combinations to clarify the purpose. We noticed that the participation of at least two researchers in the session was important. While one researcher intervened with examples of combinations, the other mediated the session to guarantee that participants created their combinations.

We observed divergence of views between participant A and the subgroup formed by B and C. B and C proposed user stories directing to a more realistic and serious game, whereas A produced user stories leading to a more recreational and playful game. Regarding the gesture-based aspect of the game, participant A proposed controls by extravagant gestures inspired by dance moves. Participant B demonstrated to be slightly disconcerted in imagining himself executing those kinds of movements. However, participant B discoursed on the importance of the game has an educational aspect for people who need to gain experience in conducting wheelchairs. Participant C agreed with B by nodding his head, while A demonstrated signs of frustration.

Concerning participant values, the conflict appears at least on two levels: first, the question whether the game and its educational dimension should be something serious or something playful or even artistic and, second, the question whether game mechanics should allow or also require a more extrovert expressibility. To include more participants in the discussion and thus give everybody a chance to be heard, we solved this conflict in the next session.

As a result from Session 3, we obtained a database of 42 user stories for the development of the game. We saved the user stories in tables classified into the four basic game elements proposed by Schell [29]: Aesthetics, mechanics, story, and technology. In this study, the stories are sorted in the tables according to their prioritization level, defined in Session 4. We observed that even though user stories related to technology (Table 5) influence other elements of the game [7], the participants produced a lower number of those stories compared to different categories. Keith [35] recommended around 100 user stories for simple games. Nevertheless, as the session got close to its end, the frequency of creating

TABLE 4: Summary of the characteristics of Session 3.

| Objective | Connect the information the cloud map into user stories |
|---|---|
| Format | Design Activity played with the participants and facilitated by researchers |
| Duration | 60 minutes |
| Output | A set of user stories |

TABLE 5: User stories about technology collected from participants during Session 3.

| 1 | As a player, I want to control the character mostly with arm movements. |
|---|---|
| 2 | As a wheelchair user, I do not want to have to move around with the wheelchair to control the game because I want to be able to play the game also in relatively small rooms. |
| 3 | As a player, I do not necessarily want the character of the game to copy my movements, because I want to be able to control it with representations of movements. |

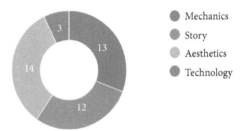

FIGURE 3: Number of suggested user stories by basic elements of games [29].

combinations for the game decreased considerably, and the participants appeared to be tired [32, 33]. Figure 3 relates the number of suggested user stories and the basic game elements. Table 4 displays the summary of the characteristics of Session 3.

*3.4. Session 4: Prioritizing User Stories.* The goal of the fourth PD session was to converge the user stories retrieved in Session 3 into the basic elements for structuring a Concept Prototype of the game. Between the third and fourth sessions, we did not interact with the participants to allow subconscious idea generation, also referenced as the period of *incubation of ideas* of the Creative Process, to improve the quality of the creative outputs [36, 37]. We understood that the session successfully reached its goal because the information received in it was enough to develop the Concept Prototype. The convergence of the collected information in the other sessions marked the illumination event [36] and the transition from the concept to the preproduction phase.

We started the session asking the participants to try visualizing the structure of a game based on the user stories generated in Session 3. The participants remained at the consensus on the game elements that should build in the game. After 15 minutes of discussion, there were some disagreements. The main impasse of the session was the balance between the playful and educational aspects of the game. This question had already appeared in the previous session, during a discussion between the participant A and participants B and C. We intervened by providing printed

versions of the tables with the user stories. We suggested to the participants to decide which stories would be prioritized to minimize the conflict [38]. With the tables at hand, it was easier for the participants to converge their opinions. We understood that such a fact happened because the stories that represented contradictory elements were not eliminated, but attributed with a lower level of prioritization [35]. This prioritization is how we tackled the conflict of the previous session. Table 6 displays a summary of the characteristics of Session 4.

*3.5. The Concept Prototype.* The result of Session 4 was the definition of the Concept Prototype to be developed. Considering the deadline needed for the project, we agreed with the participants which user stories would be implemented for this first functional version of the game. We implemented seven user stories out of 13 about the game mechanics, three of the three about technology, 9 of the 12 about story, and 9 of the 14 about aesthetics. We developed the first version of the game following the directions in the prioritized user stories. We structured the aspects of the game not covered by the user stories based on insights from previous work [6]. In the next subsections, we detail the prototype. Because this is a Concept Prototype, we implemented the main character as male because he reflects a high-performance athlete who is a friend of the codesigners. However, in future versions of the game, we can develop a customizable character to the users.

*3.5.1. Design and Gameplay.* Differently, from the study of Gerling et al. [9], all the participants of our work requested that the main character of the game should be a wheelchair user. Having the main character as a wheelchair user evidenced the motivational value of the game because the players felt more engaged to participate in outdoor activities by watching the character of the game. We managed to create the context and scenarios of the game in a way to involve the character in diverse activities as a wheelchair user. Thus, we divided the game into four stages named *House, Street, Sea,* and *Sky.* The first playable stage is the *House* of the main character. Figure 4 illustrates the possible flow between stages. Starting from the *House,* the player can choose from carrying out activities inside the home or moving to another

TABLE 6: Summary of the characteristics of Session 4.

| Objective | Prioritize the generated user stories |
|---|---|
| Format | Design Activity played with the participants and facilitated by researchers |
| Duration | 60 minutes |
| Output | User stories prioritized in a way that allows the development of the game |

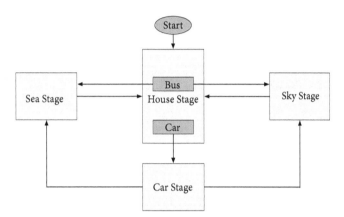

FIGURE 4: Possible flow between stages: the player can choose to go directly to stages *Sea* or *Sky* by taking the bus or drive to them by passing through the *Street* stage.

FIGURE 5: A screen from the developed game with one person playing. The depicted stage is the *House*, where the character of the game explores the scenario to enter the other stages.

stage. Figure 5 displays the scenario of the *House* stage. For selecting the stages, the character can drive a car or take a bus. Thus, the stage *House* works as a *selection menu*. Opting for driving the vehicle, the player enters the *Street* stage. Opting to take the bus, he or she comes directly into the chosen stage.

Except for the *House* stage, the game is essentially multi-player. This aspect encourages interactions of the main player, whom we are assuming is a wheelchair user, with other people around him or her. The game mechanics are similar in the stages *Street* and *Sea*. The player must dodge obstacles while piloting a car and a jet-ski, respectively. The goal of all stages is to travel onto a route and cross a finish line at the end of the stage. At the end of each stage, the game records the players' time-stamp in a ranking that is reproduced on a panel in the *House* stage. The player starts the route with an initial speed. This speed increases as the player go around obstacles

without colliding or go through items in *turbo* mode. Hitting obstacles causes the speed to decrease. Having the speed varying according to how well players move around the stage causes the difficulty of the game to vary according to the skills of the players. Especially in the *Sky* stage, the player rides a paraglider from a starting point until the finish line, but not through a predefined route. The speed does not vary in that stage.

The game aims to produce an encouraging atmosphere to the player. This aspect was a result of our balance between the playful and educational aspects suggested by the participants during the PD process. Players can try the stages various times to improve their scores (playful). As a consequence, players perform more exercises (educational). The game is multiplayer, but noncompetitive. The stage is only finished when both players cross the finish line. The speed is equal for both players during the whole gameplay. For instance, if one player hits an obstacle, the speed for both players decreases. The purpose of this feature is to allow friendly and equal interaction between players. In all stages, when one player is close to the finish line, applause sounds and supporting voices are played. At the end of each stage, the game shows fireworks and celebrating audiences to reward the players. Figure 6 displays the celebration screen after players completing the *Street* stage. In general, the game aims to encourage wheelchair users to practice activities considered obstacles by the community, such as driving a car or riding a jet-ski or a paraglider.

*3.5.2. User Interface.* There were few user stories concerning the technology of the game, so we had few features to define the user interface. Nevertheless, we designed the controls of the Concept Prototype as simple as possible to facilitate

FIGURE 6: Celebration screen after a stage completion.

the engagement and understanding of the participants. The gesture-based interaction for this version of the game prioritized the movement of the arms, including wheelchair users with high or low mobility in the column. We developed the controls equally for all stages as a simulation of handling a steering wheel.

In particular, in the *House* stage, the character speed in the forward plane was controlled by small head movements. In the *Sky* stage, the head movements controlled the height of the character. A forward bend causes that character to move forward, and vice versa. Figure 7 represents the logic for controlling the character.

*3.6. Session 5: Enhancing the Game's Interface Based on Users' Values.* Session 5 was based on the methodology of Sprint Reviewing of the Game SCRUM [35]. Along with the participants, we decided which features of the game could be enhanced with the experience that we acquired. We enhanced game features to increase the playing experience in general. Moreover, we detected with the participants the necessity of including features to evidence their values in the game. At this point, we could represent the game values that emerged during the sessions (*empowerment, noncompetition, and motivation*).

The *empowerment* of the players in the game was mainly symbolized by the explicit representation of the main character as a wheelchair user. In the game, the character handles his wheelchair without any help and is capable of moving to any location. He performs activities that, according to the participants, are considered obstacles to that group of people: taking a bus, driving a car, riding a jet-ski, and a paraglider. For starting the performance of any of the activities, the character steers the wheelchair to the location where the action starts. In that context, we represent the wheelchair as a mean to transition from the game character's home to a more attractive place, rather than a tool to supply a disabled person.

The *noncompetition* value is represented by the fact that succeeding in the levels does not depend on beating the other player. Instead, both players have to cross the finish line to store a record for the level. The participants mutually agreed with this feature. Their objective was to develop a friendly atmosphere for friends and relatives that had suffered a lesion

and were still recovering from a potential trauma of learning how to handle a wheelchair.

The *motivation* value was mentioned by the participants as a necessity of the game working also as an encouragement for players to try to perform the same or similar activities in real life. All the participants agreed that the gesture-based aspects of the game could increase the potential for this value if the required gestures in the game are more similar to the ones used in the real-life activities. It is because, according to our discussion, by repetitively performing similar gestures during the game, there is a better probability of players to feel more confident to perform those gestures in real life.

From the Sprint Review, we concluded that values empowerment and noncompetition were well represented in the game. However, motivation could be better represented with a revision in the gesture inputs. Thus, we decided to modify the user interface so that the required gestures were more similar to the ones in real life. Table 7 summarizes the characteristics of Session 5.

*3.7. The Preproduction Prototype.* We developed the reviewed game during the *preproduction* phase, according to the Game SCRUM's principle [35]. Therefore, we considered it a preproduction prototype. The developed game was named "Wheelchair Jecripe", as a continuity of the works of the Jecripe Project studies [39].

In Sessions 3 and 4, we structured the user stories to guide the game development. Most of the user stories were related to the mechanics, aesthetics, and story of the game. Only three user stories defined the game technology about the gesture inputs (Figure 3). As a consequence of not having focused on the game technology, the features that had to be modified the most in Session 5 were the gesture inputs. According to the participants, the revision of the movements reinforced the motivational aspect of the game. With the new inputs, players performed movements not precisely identical to those that they would do in real life in the activities depicted in the game. Nevertheless, the revised movements are more similar to the real movements than the initial ones. This aspect potentially increases their confidence to enroll in those activities in real life.

As a recommendation from the participants, we switched from hand movements to body movements in the *Street, Sea,* and *Sky* stages: reclining the body to the left (right) makes the character move to the left (right). Specially for the *Sky* stage, players control the character with open arms, imitating the movement of flying. We modified the input movements in the *House* stage so that players could control the character by representing movements of controlling a wheelchair: representing turning the left (right) wheel of the wheelchair makes the character turn to the right (left). Representing turning both wheels to the front while reclining the body to the front moves the character forward. Representing the movement of pulling back with the arms makes the character move back. Figure 8 displays the revised inputs for the game.

The gesture inputs for the *House* sage required a specific mounting setup of the Kinect sensor and a more complex approach for motion capture. Contrary to the other stages,

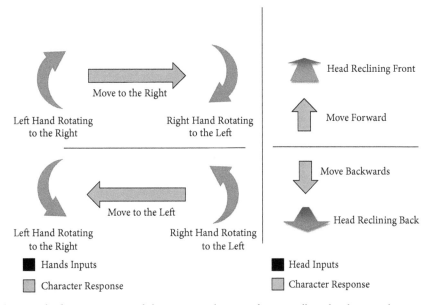

FIGURE 7: Relationship between body movements and the inputs in the game for controlling the character by gestures in the first version of the game.

TABLE 7: Summary of the characteristics of Session 5.

| Objective | Review the developed game with the participants |
|---|---|
| Format | Sprint Review with the participants |
| Duration | Non pre-determined duration |
| Output | A set of refinements to be done into the game |

the gestures in the *House* stage required tracking of body parts in the $z$-axis (Figure 8). For optimized motion capture, the Kinect was placed at a total height from the floor of 2 meters. The distance between the players was 1.5 meters. The defined distances provide better motion captures of the spatial coordinates because it avoided occlusions of the players' body parts in the $z$-axis. Figure 9 illustrates the mounting setup for the revised inputs.

In addition to the revision of the user interface, the participants asked for alternative inputs to control the game's flow. We implemented a pause menu with options to quit the game and return to the *House* stage. At any time in the game, players can lift the left arm and access that menu, in the same way as in other Kinect-based games. As a consequence, the flow among the stages of the game was modified. Figure 10 demonstrates the revised flow of the game.

## 4. Evaluating the Enjoyment of the Game

We analyzed the enjoyment of the game. Thus, we asked some of the participants and other wheelchair users as well as their relatives to play the developed game. To estimate the enjoyment of testers for the game, we evaluated metrics such as learnability, immersion, enjoyment, or fatigue. Then, we compared the player experience of those groups (participants and other wheelchair users and their relatives) for the game. This section presents the experiment and its results. All

testimonials presented in this section were freely translated from Brazilian Portuguese by the authors.

*4.1. Experimental Setup.* We experimented the preproduction prototype of our game with a population of 19 people ($N = 19$), divided into two groups. The first group consisted of four members of the codesigners: two wheelchair users and two able-bodied users, three female and one male, aged 58, 53, 26, and 34.

The second group was the noncodesigners group, with 15 testers. This group contained seven wheelchair users and eight able-bodied users. All the able-bodied users were relatives or colleagues of the wheelchair users. Seven were female, and eight were male. The average age of this group was 32 years old, ranging from 10 to 60 years. Figures 11 and 12 represent the sex and age distributions of the groups.

Figure 13 displays the favorite game genres among the testers. It is possible to see in Figure 13 that, for all the groups, most of the testers prefer games related to sports. We noticed that having the common practice of playing sports increased the expectation among participants for the game. A testimonial of one of the participants before the testing session reflects this fact:

(i) "I like to practice sports, I am really enjoying this project. I am sure it will be of great value to all involved people. Perhaps this game will make me

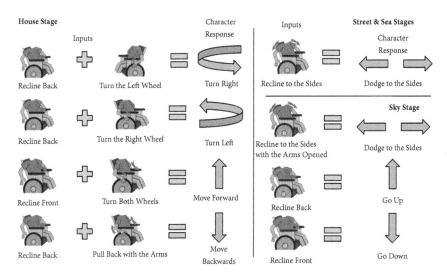

FIGURE 8: Relationship between body movements and the inputs in the game for controlling the character by NUI in the revised version of the game.

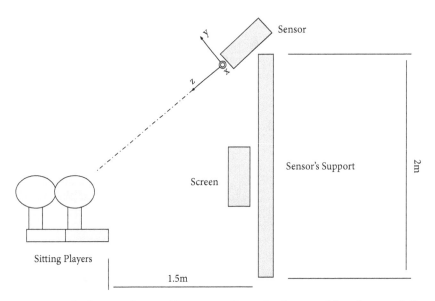

FIGURE 9: The Kinect mounting setup for the revised inputs. The $xyz$ coordinates for the game follow the sensor's direction. This configuration reduces occlusions of body parts.

play more video games." (Translated from Brazilian Portuguese)

The testers filled a pretest questionnaire, played the game from 15 to 20 minutes, and filled a posttest questionnaire. We have also registered testimonials and observations from the testers. We only interrupted the test to provide the first explanation on how to play the game and in the case of software or hardware problems. The experiment had the approval of the *Federal University of ABC's Ethics Committee*. For the testers that did not have physical or cognitive conditions to fill in the questionnaires, we asked their parents to answer the questions. A testimonial from the father of one of the testers reflected that situation:

(i) "I am the father of the child playing the game. The answers of the questionnaires are based on the playing session of my son. He is a ten-year-old wheelchair user with coordination and cognitive limitations. His cerebral palsy is due to a problem during birth. He is a kid of easy comprehension. He communicates trough gestures or communication tablets. He is very interested in electronic games." (Translated from Brazilian Portuguese)

We summarized the user experience questionnaires in Tables 8 and 9. Table 8 shows the pretest questionnaire, which was based on insights from our previous studies [6]. We have formulated the topics in the pretest questionnaire to inquire the player profile of testers. Table 9 displays the posttest questionnaire, also based on related the work of

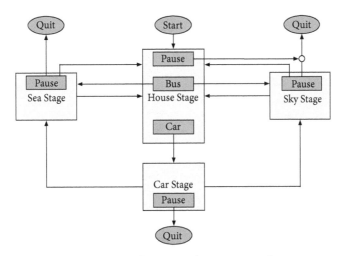

FIGURE 10: Revised flow of the game stages: with the new configuration, players can quit the game or return to the *House* stage at any time during gameplay.

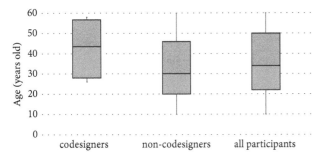

FIGURE 11: Genre distribution among the testers.

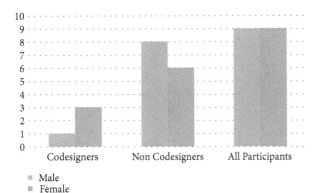

FIGURE 12: Age distribution among the testers.

van der Spek [40]. We have formulated the topics in the posttest questionnaire to inquire the enjoyment of testers on the game. Testers were graded from each topic from the questionnaires from 1 to 10 according to how much they agreed with the information presented on that topic, except for topic 1 from Table 8, where testers informed their classification in the *IWBF Functional Classification* [2].

To generate topics 1 to 11 from Table 9, we employed part of the standardized *ITC Sense of Presence Inventory* [41] that measures the immersion level of testers when experiencing digital media. We formulated our questionnaire following the study of van der Spek [40], who employed the ITC Sense of Presence Inventory to measure the immersion of several testers in different versions of a serious game. Spek's study was able to provide clear conclusions by using the ITC Sense of Presence Inventory since part of the ITC Sense of Presence Inventory is related to engagement and other factors, for instance, physical spaces and negative effects. Thus, the average of topics 1 to 11 from Table 9 formed an index for the immersion caused by the game to players.

In addition, as our game is gesture-based for wheelchair users, we had the necessity of including specific questions related to the movements of the users to infer the tiredness of the users as well as the facility of getting used to the Microsoft Kinect Sensor in our game.

*4.2. Results.* For our analysis of the results, we created boxplots from the questionnaires (Tables 8 and 9) and also considered the testimonials of the testers. Figure 14, for instance, displays the boxplots of the players' immersion level (average of grades resulting from the answers of topics 1 to 11 in Table 9). Each boxplot depicts the results of the codesigners and noncodesigners, individually, and then the results for all testers.

Figure 14 reveals that, even though the developed game was in a prototype stage during the test, most of the testers experienced a satisfying immersion level, close to 9. The outliers in Figure 14 occurred due to the presence of a boy who has cerebral palsy. The boy had a hard time understanding how the game works. This result conforms to the results shown in Figures 15–17. These boxplots show facility of learning how to play, getting used to the sensor, and scoring in the game. Those topics received median grades equal to or higher than 5 for both groups. Testers' testimonials that reflect their player experience are listed below.

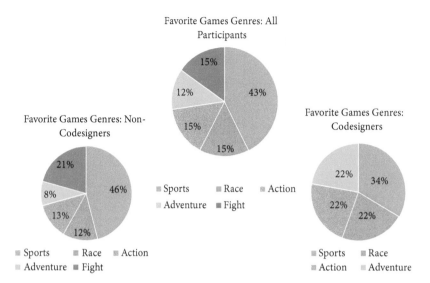

FIGURE 13: Favorite game genres among testers.

TABLE 8: Pretest questionnaire for characterizing the player profiles, translated from Portuguese.

| | |
|---|---|
| 1 | What is my score in the *IWBF Functional Criteria* |
| 2 | I have experience in playing video games |
| 3 | I enjoy playing video games |
| 4 | I have experience in playing video games with NUI |
| 5 | I enjoy playing video games with NUI |

TABLE 9: Posttest questionnaire, translated from Portuguese.

| | |
|---|---|
| 1 | I had the sensation of coming from a journey |
| 2 | I wish my playing experience continued |
| 3 | I remember very well parts of the experience |
| 4 | I felt thrown inside the game |
| 5 | I felt involved with the universe of the game |
| 6 | I lost the notion of time |
| 7 | I enjoyed myself |
| 8 | My experience was intense |
| 9 | I paid more attention to the game than to my thoughts |
| 10 | I felt emotionally involved with the game |
| 11 | The game content was made for me |
| 12 | I felt physically tired after playing |
| 13 | I felt mentally exhausted after playing |
| 14 | I wish movements in the game were more intense |
| 15 | I wish movements in the game were less intense |
| 16 | It was easy to learn how to play |
| 17 | It was easy to get used to the sensor |
| 18 | It was easy to get a good score in the game |
| 19 | The game was fun |

(i) "The game is an important encouragement for inclusion and physical and emotional rehabilitation for people with physical disabilities. It is the great training of balance and coordination." (Translated from Brazilian Portuguese)

(ii) "It was very good to see the excitement of my son when he perceived that he could control and interact with a video game with a simple body movement." (Translated from Brazilian Portuguese)

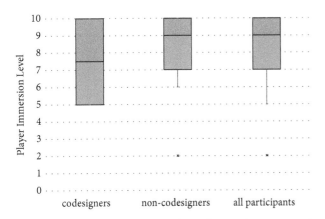

FIGURE 14: ITC score boxplot graphics: the graphs compare the dispersion of results from the immersion level for the codesigners and noncodesigners in the game. The ITC score was formed by the average of grades from topics 1 to 10 of Table 9.

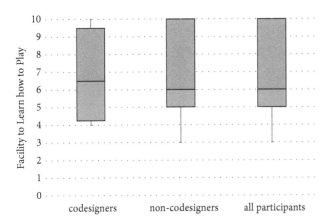

FIGURE 15: Answers from topic 16 of Table 9: this topic measures the facility of users on learning how to play the tested game.

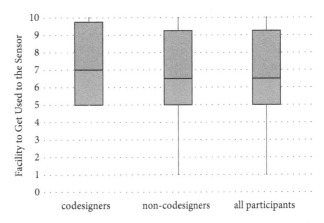

FIGURE 16: Answers from topic 17 of Table 9: this topic measures the facility of users on getting used to the gestures requested in the game.

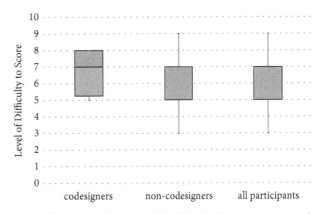

FIGURE 17: Answers from topic 18 of Table 9: this topic measures the facility of users to score in game.

The boxplot in Figure 18 displays the level of enjoyment during the game. This topic received median grades greater than or equal to 8.5. Testers' testimonials that reflect their enjoyment are listed below.

(i) "Playing was very enjoyable and likable. I enjoyed it very much. I had lots of fun and guess that the game will be a success. Congratulations to the dedication and commitment of the involved people." (Translated from Brazilian Portuguese)

(ii) "I enjoyed the game very much!" (Translated from Brazilian Portuguese)

(iii) "The game is amazing for people with disabilities." (Translated from Brazilian Portuguese)

(iv) "The game was delightful! I loved it!" (Translated from Brazilian Portuguese)

Moreover, we noticed that the lower scores to immersion and enjoyment levels (Figures 14 and 18) were frequently related to difficulties in playing the game due to more severe cognitive or physical disabilities of some testers. We display below a testimonial reflecting that scenario.

(i) "It was pleasant. However, in the case of my son, we need something more playful and interactive to capture his attention better. As he does not have body control, he has difficulty to interact with the game. The experience was valuable, though." (Translated from Brazilian Portuguese)

It is possible to see in Figures 19 and 20 that the medians of the answers from topics 12 and 13, which concern physical and mental fatigue levels after playing the game, are higher for the noncodesigners group than for the codesigners group. This result is potentially due to the adjustments of game inputs implemented in Session 5. In that session, codesigners suggested more intense controls, which provided better movements in the game. On the other hand, the noncodesigners with less body control were harmed with the new inputs. In general, Figures 21 and 22 imply that most of the testers from both groups would prefer a game with even more intense movements.

We noticed that, even though the immersion (Figure 14) and enjoyment (Figure 18) evaluations indicated satisfying results, noncodesigners evaluated these dimensions more positively than the codesigners. We believe this is probably due to the expectation that the codesigners group had for

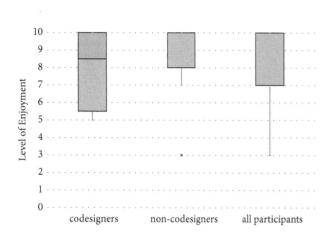

FIGURE 18: Answers from topic 19 of Table 9: this topic measures the enjoyment proportioning the game.

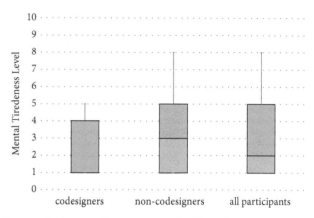

FIGURE 20: Answers from topic 13 of Table 9: this topic measures mental fatigue after playing the game.

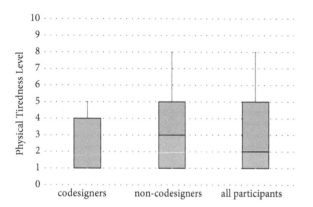

FIGURE 19: Answers from topic 12 of Table 9: this topic measures physical fatigue after playing the game.

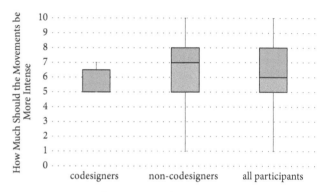

FIGURE 21: Answers from topic 14 of Table 9: this topic measures how much testers would prefer the movements in the game to be more intense.

the game since they participated in its development. Another hypothesis relies on the fact that codesigners had contact with the game along with its design process. Therefore, it was expected that the game would cause less impact on them. We collected testimonials from all testers referring to technical improvements in the game. Those improvements can be implemented in possible future Sprint Reviews. We list the testimonials below.

(i) "I loved participating in the test. I think that the characters could have more intense colors. Congratulations for the initiative. I loved the project." (Translated from Brazilian Portuguese)

(ii) "I liked it. However, some things did not work well in my opinion. The movements in the House scenario, for example, were not easy or practical. Maybe you guys should change the movements in that scenario. In the flying scenario, I did not find the correct route. Maybe it would be easier if I had more lights to follow, like a path. Lights in the arriving lane would be good too. In the Street scenario, the initial velocity was low. Maybe it could start faster." (Translated from Brazilian Portuguese)

(iii) "My son is losing his vision, and the screen was too high; he did not see the game adequately. In our home, where the television is in his eyes' height, he makes better progress. All in all, the game was great, I loved it. It gives players a sensation of freedom. This is very good and interesting. Congratulations for the initiative." (Translated from Brazilian Portuguese)

(iv) "I have an Xbox 360 with a Kinect. This new Kinect is more sensitive than mine; then, I messed up a little bit with the controls." (Translated from Brazilian Portuguese)

(v) "Suggestion of Improvement: Improve the velocity of the vehicles. Improve the Pause Menu that is called up every time we raise the left arm." (Translated from Brazilian Portuguese)

As a final observation, it is relevant to mention that the atmosphere during the tests was pleasant. We often noticed testers laughing and performing game gestures even when not playing the game. The atmosphere allowed even the shyest testers to interact and cooperate with their colleagues. We believe that the fact that we developed a game focused on the values of the users provided a friendly environment. The users seemed to feel comfortable with their representation in the game.

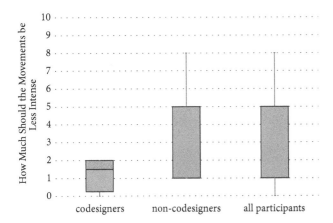

FIGURE 22: Answers from topic 15 of Table 9: this topic measures how much testers would prefer the movements in the game to be less intense.

## 5. Discussion

The participants actively contributed to the data analysis and interpretation, e.g., during the discussion and adaptation of the cloud maps. The researchers participated mainly as facilitators during the sessions. As a consequence, the participants generated a few user stories concerning technology. If the researchers had opted to be more active in the discussions with the participants, perhaps some issues could have been avoided, for instance, the refactoring of the input gestures. However, this could have also led to less freedom of the participants regarding expressing their values.

The design that we applied enabled the participants to influence the design process, e.g., by defining and prioritizing the user stories or by redefining the input gestures. One goal of the design process was to create a game that could improve the quality of life of players by increasing their self-confidence and by encouraging them to conduct the activities portrayed in the game or other sports activities in the physical world. Although it is too early to make assertive claims, testers' testimonials indicate the potential of the game to reach this goal. Regarding the context or user situation, we recruited participants that are already active sports practitioners, in this case, tennis. For future iterations of the design, practitioners of other sports could be included, as well as people who are less active and even practice no sports at all.

The participants contributed to defining, designing, and evaluating aspects of the game mechanics, content, aesthetics, and the base technology. Thus, all participants performed crucial roles during the design process. The base technology was defined by the researchers since the other participants had no expertise in this area. In the remaining areas, they were seen as equal partners and conflicts of different opinions during the design were resolved by open-ended discussions; i.e., the researchers did not try to push through preestablished decisions. Adjustments to the design were made on a smaller scale, i.e., regarding the content of scheduled sessions, e.g., the evaluation and redesigning the gestures. Since the applied design is aligned to the Game SCRUM, major adjustments are also possible, resulting in additional iterations or sprints.

As described in Section 3.2, words in the cloud map originated the user stories, which turned into game features. For each of those user stories, we reflected the values features of the codesigners nonresearchers into the game. Figure 23 describes a summary of how the insights for the game originated from the participatory design meetings, fed the game values, and transformed into the game features that we evaluate in our qualitative analysis. In the qualitative analysis, we were interested in how testers reacted to the game concerning the values it proportioned. In Figure 23, we also linked the testimonials and our observations about the environment's atmosphere during the user tests.

As an example of flow in Figure 23, it is possible to see that words, such as speed and height, originated the *empowerment* value of the game. It happened because, in the context that those words were mentioned during the meetings, the codesigners expressed a need for empowerment. That empowerment was translated into the excitement of testers while playing the game. The testimonial to which we linked the empowerment value exemplifies this fact. Afterward, in other meetings (Section 3.5), we concluded that representing the main character as a wheelchair user could also bring an empowerment value to the wheelchair in the game. Therefore, the empowerment value linked the words speed and height. Furthermore, we also realized the speed could be an essential feature of the game. Together with the codesigners nonresearchers, we decided that controlling the speed was an efficient way to develop the mechanics of the Street and Sea stages. Figure 23 presents the word *speed* is also linked to those stages, as it influenced their design.

We believe that the Creative Process elements aided our work to support the elicitation and discussion of values of the users. We employed the Creative Process concepts into a PD consisting of five segments: (1) a free, recorded conversation, (2) representation of the conversation topics into cloud maps, (3) connection of the elements in the cloud maps into user stories with high significance to user experience, (4) prioritizing of those stories by participants after a period of no workload, and (5) revising the outputs of the stories. Based on such segments, the activities were structured to promote creative and effective participation of the participants. As a consequence, we developed a game that had a satisfying and near homogeneous positive player experience of wheelchair users with different characteristics. Therefore, we believe that the used tools and techniques successfully led us to represent those people's values into the game.

The Game SCRUM concepts were important to manage the design with flexibility for participants to express themselves. We realized that user stories were a simple technique that allowed the participants to express user experience related aspects in a way that could be understood and used by the developers. Moreover, structuring the process on Game SCRUM avoided workload being applied to elements with low value to the game. As a result, we could develop a simple, but effective game. We display a graphical scheme of our design process in Figure 24.

The closest study to ours is the one from Gerling et al. [9] that also addressed the development of gesture-based games for wheelchair users with participatory design. The

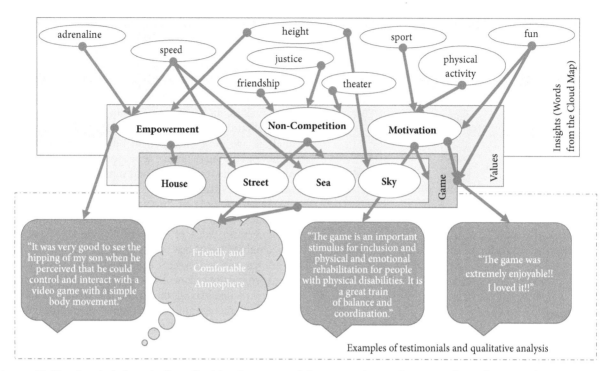

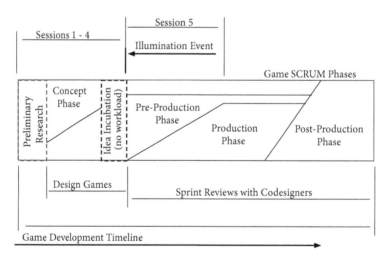

FIGURE 23: Visual analysis from the flow of insights that generated the game and its implication to the qualitative analysis of the game.

FIGURE 24: Flow of the process stages during game development: the framework stages overlap with Game SCRUM phases and Creative Process' events.

main focus of the work of Gerling et al. [9] was to explore with a qualitative analysis the value of gesture-based games for young powered wheelchair users. Different from Gerling et al. [9], we defined the gesture-based interactions during the process of PD. We aimed to provide more flexibility to participants to express their values through the definition of the interaction. Nevertheless, some of the defined movements were not compatible with wheelchair users with more limited body abilities. We also noticed that Gerling et al. [9] and our works represented disabilities of participants in a way that empowered them in the game. However, our representation was explicit, displaying a wheelchair user as the main character. Gerling et al. [9] empowered their characteristics

with implicit features in the game. For both cases, we confirmed that the players had a positive experience with the game. We summarized the main differences concerning the PD process and experimentation that we observed from the present work and the work of Gerling et al. [9] in Table 10.

We detected three main values that emerged during the process and that were "designed into" the preproduction prototype: (1) empowerment of wheelchair users by representing the wheelchair in the game as an apparatus to enroll in interesting activities instead of a tool to supply a particular need, (2) noncompetition in the game to amplify the friendly atmosphere of the game, and (3) motivation in terms of

TABLE 10: Main differences between the present work and its most similar study.

| Characteristic | Gerling et al. [9] | Present Work |
|---|---|---|
| Input device | Kinect V1 | Kinect V2 |
| User Interface | Gestures to control game features defined in previous research [10] and utilized during PD | Gestures to control game features defined during PD |
| Users in PD | Young powered- wheelchair users | Manual wheelchair users with diverse age |
| Representation of disabilities in the game | Implicit | Explicit |
| Main focus of the Experimentation | Explore value of the developed games for a users similar to the participants | Apply and evaluate a process that includes values of wheelchair users in NUI games |
| Main form of Experiments Evaluation | Testimonials from users | Questionnaires and testimonials |
| Number of users in the Experiment | 4 | 19 |

encouraging players to enroll in similar activities in real life. In particular, the (3) motivational value influenced technical aspects of the game. We evidenced this value after a review meeting among participants and performed the necessary changes. The modifications of the game were mainly regarding the user interface. We modified the motion capture inputs so that the required gestures in the depicted activities in the game were more similar to the ones performed in those activities in real life. The new inputs increased the confidence of players to enroll in those activities in real life. That situation reinforced the importance of developing the game through iterations in conformance with an agile process. We learned with the critiques of the first prototype to enhance the prototype in the second iteration.

## 6. Limitations

We applied a method with a determined social niche: manual wheelchair users that practice sports as a hobby. Also, we tested the outcome of the participatory design process, a digital game with NUI, in a testing group formed by wheelchair users and their relatives. It is worth mentioning that we evaluate the outcome, indicating a positive player experience by the testing group. It leads us to observe the effectiveness of the participatory design. However, we are aware of the importance of evaluating another audience.

We acknowledge that the circumstances in which we developed the game and applied the tests influenced the results. Due to schedule restrictions of participants, all the PD sessions took place after their training. As a consequence of the physical exercises, the mood of those codesigners was frequently high. Even though the relaxed atmosphere supported us in conducting meetings with a good flow, we suggest performing potential next sessions in varying situations to get a more diverse input from the participants. Similarly, due to resource constraints, we (the researchers and developers of the game) were responsible for applying the playing tests during the experiments in this study. Even though we focused on being as impartial as possible, potential sympathy created between the participants and us could have influenced the results. In future work, we suggest conducting additional tests and evaluations with evaluators and test subjects unrelated to the design and development team.

We understand that the participatory design process is expansible and flexible. We fundamentally based the process on Game SCRUM. However, we believe that it is possible to adapt the process to be used with different development processes. Examples of variables liable of being explored with different configurations in the current process are the period of each session, time-spacing between sessions, and the frequency and degree of participation of researchers or design experts during sessions in opining about the design of the game. As a next step, researchers can adapt the process to Agile Software Development in general. We also believe that the process has the potential to assist in the development of games for a mixed social audience.

As a final observation, we evidence that we apply the process under an academic approach. We recognize that the process is liable of being applied in any commercial game development. Therefore, we believe that some modifications have to be performed to reach the often tight deadlines of commercial game development projects [35, 42, 43]. As a suggestion of modification, instead of performing five weekly participatory design meetings, researchers can conduct two more extended meetings applying design games. In the first meeting, researchers introduce the framed problem, build the cloud map, and generate the user stories. The second meeting is spaced from the first by one day, so participants have enough time to incubate the idea. In the second meeting, participants prioritize the user stories, build a concept for the prototype, and submit it to critiques. We reinforce that the mentioned time periods are liable of being optimized by experimentation. In particular, the time before the illumination event and the periods of stimulating participants with design objective related content can be critical factors to evaluate.

## 7. Conclusions

In this work, we described a design process for the development of a gesture-based game, where manual wheelchair users (and their stakeholders) acted as participants in the sessions. Values from the participants emerged during the design sessions and were explored for the development of the game. Sessions were aligned to Game SCRUM, employing concepts such as user stories, prioritization, and sprints.

Creative Process elements were also employed to stimulate the emerging of values.

Our study aims to develop a game focused on entertainment that reflects the values of the wheelchair users with the sole purpose of entertainment. With the possibility of reflection of values in an entertainment game, we will be able, in future works, to carry out studies with physical and educational challenges, as continuity of the research described in the current study.

We believe that the game can further be improved based on the results and testimonials retrieved during the experimentation. Even though we understood that the pre-production prototype of the game reached its objective in representing values of the users, it can be adapted to encompass a broader public. Possibly, the next group of people to be involved in the game content are wheelchair users with more limited functional abilities than the users that participated in the development of this study.

## Acknowledgments

We specially thank the *CR Tennis Academy*, the participants of the design process and the evaluation, and the *PARAJE-CRIPE Team* for providing us with artistic assets for the game. We also thank Heiko Hornung for our fruitful discussions about this work. This work was financially supported by Federal University of ABC–UFABC and the Coordination for the Improvement of Higher Education Personnel (CAPES, Brazil) Masters Scholarship. The authors also thank São Paulo Research Foundation (FAPESP, Brazil), proc. No. 2014/11067-1, for the equipment support.

## References

[1] K. Hicks and K. Gerling, "Exploring casual exergames with kids using wheelchairs," in *Proceedings of the 2nd ACM SIGCHI Annual Symposium on Computer-Human Interaction in Play, CHI PLAY 2015*, pp. 541–546, New York, NY, USA, October 2015.

[2] G. Fiorilli, E. Iuliano, G. Aquino et al., "Mental health and social participation skills of wheelchair basketball players: A controlled study," *Research in Developmental Disabilities*, vol. 34, no. 11, pp. 3679–3685, 2013.

[3] P. Paulsen, R. French, and C. Sherrill, "Comparison of mood states of college able-bodied and wheelchair basketball players.," *Perceptual and Motor Skills*, vol. 73, no. 2, pp. 396–398, 1991.

[4] K. M. Gerling, M. R. Kalyn, and R. L. Mandryk, "KINECT wheels," in *Proceedings of the CHI '13 Extended Abstracts on Human Factors in Computing Systems*, pp. 3055–3058, 2013.

[5] D. Wigdor and D. Wixon, *Brave NUI World: Designing Natural User Interfaces for Touch and Gesture*, Elsevier, 2011.

[6] A. G. Szykman, J. P. Gois, and A. L. Brandão, "A Perspective of Games for People with Physical Disabilities," in *Proceedings of the the Annual Meeting of the Australian Special Interest Group for Computer Human Interaction*, pp. 274–283, Parkville, VIC, Australia, December 2015.

[7] K. M. Gerling, C. Linehan, B. Kirman, M. R. Kalyn, A. B. Evans, and K. C. Hicks, "Creating wheelchair-controlled video games: Challenges and opportunities when involving young people with mobility impairments and game design experts," *International Journal of Human-Computer Studies*, vol. 94, pp. 64–73, 2015.

[8] Y. Hutzler, A. Chacham-Guber, and S. Reiter, "Psychosocial effects of reverse-integrated basketball activity compared to separate and no physical activity in young people with physical disability," *Research in Developmental Disabilities*, vol. 34, no. 1, pp. 579–587, 2013.

[9] K. Gerling, K. Hicks, M. Kalyn, A. Evans, and C. Linehan, "Designing movement-based play with young people using powered wheelchairs," in *Proceedings of the 34th Annual Conference on Human Factors in Computing Systems, CHI 2016*, pp. 4447–4458, USA, May 2016.

[10] K. M. Gerling, R. L. Mandryk, M. Miller, M. R. Kalyn, M. Birk, and J. D. Smeddinck, "Designing wheelchair-based movement games," *ACM Transactions on Accessible Computing (TACCESS)*, vol. 6, no. 2, 2015.

[11] B. Friedman, P. Kahn, and A. Borning, "Value Sensitive Design: Theory and Methods," University of Washington technical report 02–12, 2002.

[12] O. S. Iversen, K. Halskov, and T. W. Leong, "Rekindling values in participatory design," in *Proceedings of the the 11th Biennial Participatory Design Conference*, p. 91, Sydney, Australia, November 2010.

[13] G. Cockton, "Value-centred HCI," in *Proceedings of the the third Nordic conference*, pp. 149–160, Tampere, Finland, October 2004.

[14] C. A. Le Dantec, E. S. Poole, and S. P. Wyche, "Values as lived experience," in *Proceedings of the the SIGCHI Conference*, p. 1141, Boston, MA, USA, April 2009.

[15] A. Borning and M. Muller, "Next steps for value sensitive design," in *Proceedings of the SIGCHI Conference on Human Factors in Computing Systems, CHI '12, ACM*, pp. 1125–1134, New York, NY, USA, May 2012.

[16] B. Friedman, "Value-sensitive design," *Interactions*, vol. 3, no. 6, pp. 16–23.

[17] B. Friedman and P. H. Kahn Jr., "The Human-computer, Interaction Handbook," in *Ch. Human Values, Ethics, and Design*, L. Erlbaum, Ed., pp. 1177–1201, L. Erlbaum Associates Inc., Hillsdale, NJ, USA, 2003, http://dl.acm.org/citation.cfm.

[18] G. Cockton, "A development framework for value-centred design," in *Proceedings of the CHI '05 Extended Abstracts on Human Factors in Computing Systems, CHI EA '05, ACM*, pp. 1292–1295, New York, NY, USA, April 2005.

[19] J. Halloran, E. Hornecker, M. Stringer, E. Harris, and G. Fitzpatrick, "The value of values: Resourcing co-design of ubiquitous computing," *CoDesign*, vol. 5, no. 4, pp. 245–273, 2009.

[20] G. Cockton, "Designing worth—connecting preferred means to desired ends," *Interactions*, vol. 15, no. 4, pp. 54–57, 2008.

[21] O. S. Iversen and T. W. Leong, "Values-led participatory design," in *Proceedings of the 7th Nordic Conference on Human-Computer Interaction: Making Sense Through Design, NordiCHI '12, ACM*, p. 468, New York, NY, USA, October 2012.

[22] M. Sicart, *The Ethics of Computer Games*, The MIT Press, 2009.

[23] M. Flanagan, D. C. Howe, and H. Nissenbaum, "Values at play: Design tradeoffs in socially-oriented game design," in

*Proceedings of the SIGCHI Conference on Human Factors in Computing Systems, CHI '05, ACM*, p. 751, New York, NY, USA, April 2005.

[24] A. Kultima and A. Sandovar, "Game design values," in *Proceedings of the 20th International Academic Mindtrek Conference, AcademicMindtrek '16, ACM*, pp. 350–357, New York, NY, USA, October 2016.

[25] M. Flanagan and H. Nissenbaum, *Values at Play in Digital Games*, The MIT Press, 2014.

[26] S. Cuzzort and T. Starner, "AstroWheelie: A wheelchair based exercise game," in *Proceedings of the 12th IEEE International Symposium on Wearable Computers, ISWC 2008*, pp. 113-114, USA, October 2008.

[27] K. Seaborn, J. Edey, G. Dolinar et al., "Accessible play in everyday spaces: Mixed reality gaming for adult powered chair users," *ACM Transactions on Computer-Human Interactions (TOCHI)*, vol. 23, no. 2, 2016.

[28] K. M. Gerling, I. J. Livingston, L. E. Nacke, and R. L. Mandryk, "Full-body motion-based game interaction for older adults," in *Proceedings of the 30th ACM Conference on Human Factors in Computing Systems, CHI 2012*, pp. 1873–1882, USA, May 2012.

[29] J. Schell, *The Art of Game Design: A Book of Lenses*, Morgan Kaufmann Publishers Inc, San Francisco, CA, USA, 2008.

[30] A. Pommeranz, U. Ulgen, and C. M. Jonker, "Exploration of facilitation, materials and group composition in participatory design sessions," in *Proceedings of the 30th European Conference on Cognitive Ergonomics (ECCE '12)*, pp. 124–130, Edinburgh, UK, August 2012.

[31] N. Hendriks, K. Slegers, and P. Duysburgh, "Codesign with people living with cognitive or sensory impairments: a case for method stories and uniqueness," *CoDesign*, vol. 11, no. 1, pp. 70–82, 2015.

[32] S. M. Smith, D. R. Gerkens, J. J. Shah, and N. Vargas-Hernandez, "Empirical studies of creative cognition in idea generation," *Creativity and Innovation in Organizational Teams*, pp. 3–20, 2005.

[33] S. M. Smith and T. B. Ward, "Cognition and the Creation of Ideas," *The Oxford Handbook of Thinking and Reasoning*, pp. 456–474, 2012.

[34] N. J. van Eck and L. Waltman, "Software survey: VOSviewer, a computer program for bibliometric mapping," *Scientometrics*, vol. 84, no. 2, pp. 523–538, 2010.

[35] C. Keith, *Agile Game Development with Scrum*, Pearson Education, 2010.

[36] T. J. Howard, S. J. Culley, and E. Dekoninck, "Describing the creative design process by the integration of engineering design and cognitive psychology literature," *Design Studies*, vol. 29, no. 2, pp. 160–180, 2008.

[37] R. Diluzio and C. B. Congdon, "Infusing the creative-thinking process into undergraduate STEM education: An overview," in *Proceedings of the 5th IEEE Integrated STEM Education Conference, ISEC 2015*, pp. 52–57, USA.

[38] E. Brandt, "Designing exploratory design games: A framework for participation in participatory design?" in *Proceedings of the 9th Conference on Participatory Design, PDC 2006*, pp. 57–66, Italy, August 2006.

[39] A. L. Brandao, L. A. Fernandes, D. Trevisan, E. Clua, and D. Strickery, "Jecripe: how a serious game project encouraged studies in different computer science areas," in *Proceedings of the 2014 IEEE 3rd International Conference on Serious Games*

*and Applications for Health (SeGAH)*, pp. 1–8, Rio de Janeiro, Brazil, May 2014.

[40] E. D. van der Spek, *Experiments in serious game design: a cognitive approach [Ph.D. thesis]*, University of Utrecht, 2011.

[41] J. Lessiter, J. Freeman, E. Keogh, and J. Davidoff, "A cross-media presence questionnaire: The ITC-sense of presence inventory," *Presence: Teleoperators and Virtual Environments*, vol. 10, no. 3, pp. 282–297, 2001.

[42] D. Salah, R. F. Paige, and P. Cairns, "A systematic literature review for agile development processes and user centred design integration," in *Proceedings of the the 18th International Conference*, pp. 1–10, London, England, United Kingdom, May 2014.

[43] M. Brhel, H. Meth, A. Maedche, and K. Werder, "Exploring principles of user-centered agile software development: A literature review," *Information and Software Technology*, vol. 61, pp. 163–181, 2015.

# 4

# Model for Educational Game using Natural User Interface

**Azrulhizam Shapi'i and Sychol Ghulam**

*Faculty of Information Science & Technology, Universiti Kebangsaan Malaysia (UKM), 43600 Bangi, Selangor, Malaysia*

Correspondence should be addressed to Azrulhizam Shapi'i; azrulhizam@ukm.edu.my

Academic Editor: Michela Mortara

Natural User Interface (NUI) is a new approach that has become increasingly popular in Human-Computer Interaction (HCI). The use of this technology is widely used in almost all sectors, including the field of education. In recent years, there are a lot of educational games using NUI technology in the market such as Kinect game. Kinect is a sensor that can recognize body movements, postures, and voices in three dimensions. It enables users to control and interact with game without the need of using game controller. However, the contents of most existing Kinect games do not follow the standard curriculum in classroom, thus making it do not fully achieve the learning objectives. Hence, this research proposes a design model as a guideline in designing educational game using NUI. A prototype has been developed as one of the objectives in this study. The prototype is based on proposed model to ensure and assess the effectiveness of the model. The outcomes of this study conclude that the proposed model contributed to the design method for the development of the educational game using NUI. Furthermore, evaluation results of the prototype show a good response from participant and in line with the standard curriculum.

## 1. Introduction

Serious game has strong potential for learning. It can be used as an innovative tool for constructive teaching approaches in classrooms. However, students usually interact with computer using mouse and keyboard while playing the game. This action gives a negative impact to students while sitting too long staring at the computer screen [1]. A good learning should involve all the senses and limbs to act and react. The appearance of Natural User Interface (NUI) gives a new way on interacting with computer. NUI refers to sensory inputs such as touch, speech, and gesture but goes much further to describe computing. Computing is described as intelligent and contextually aware, with the ability to recognize a person's face, environment and intent, and also emotions and relationships.

Several technologies use NUI for their interfaces such as Microsoft Kinect, Microsoft PixelSens, Leap Motion, and Intel RealSense. For the game context, Microsoft Kinect is most popular than the others. Kinect described as a revolution in the making, because it provides a brand new type of interaction with computers [2]. Motion sensing input device

by Microsoft for the Xbox 360 video game console can capture, track, and decipher body movements such as gestures and voice. In other words, users are not by bound neither keyboards, mouse, nor joysticks and thus have intuitive and virtual experiences with digital contents. In recent years, there are many educational games using Kinect technology making an additional option in the learning market. However, the contents of most Kinect games do not follow the standard curriculum for classroom, so it cannot fully achieve learning objectives. Any media and resources in classroom are more effective when integrated into the curriculum [3].

Kinect technology has potential to enhance classroom interactions, but it largely depends on the development of Kinect software [4]. The effectiveness of the Kinect game depends on the content and how the game is developed. Simply adding a curriculum to the game does not mean they were integrate with it. However, the implementation of Kinect in the classroom has pedagogical constraint that must be considered such as the difficulties in shifting to kinesthetic pedagogical practices and limited understanding of its effect [4]. Therefore, this paper proposes design model guideline for development of NUI game-based on learning.

TABLE 1: Categorization of Kinect games' utilization for educational purposes in various developmental axes.

| Game | Physical development | Cognitive development | Emotional development | Social development |
|---|---|---|---|---|
| Body & Brain Connection | × | × | | |
| Kinect Sport | × | | | × |
| Kinectimals | | | × | × |
| The Fantastic Pets | | | × | × |
| Kinect Adventures | × | | × | × |
| Disneyland Adventures | × | | × | × |
| Sesame Street | | | × | × |
| Kinect Funlabs | | × | | × |

FIGURE 1: Mathematic game, user has to choose the answer by kicking the right ball and complete the equation.

## 2. Objectives

The main objectives of this research are to (1) develop a design model for NUI game-based on learning and demonstrate the model by designing a prototype and (2) evaluate the prototype to ensure it is in line with the standard curriculum. The scope of this research incorporates the following: (1) the subject content selected for this prototype is Science subject for primary school year 3; one game under subtitle "classification" was created and (2) the testing of prototype is done by fifteen students to assess the effectiveness of the proposed model.

## 3. Literature Review

The key in education is how games are used. Simply adding games to a curriculum does not mean they are integrated with it. The students should be involved, through technology, in the learning process in order to (a) be engaged with the theories, (b) acquire knowledge through autonomous and discovery learning, (c) cultivate thinking skills, (d) learn how to learn (metacognition), (e) interact and communicate, and (f) operate as active producers of knowledge [5].

There are several games that use NUI in education, such as Kids Magic Learning. This Kinect game was designed for early childhood education and contain six different games. Each game was accompanied by some specific courses such as physical coordination, instant memory, ability in mathematics, and ability of memorizing vocabulary and speaking including sense of space [6]. Figure 1 shows one example of the games.

Unfortunately, the existing games mostly only be used in teaching basic skills. Research was done to analyze Kinect game existence in the market [7]. This research attempts to categorize the most popular Kinect games. The result was the games that are teaching basic skills such as physical, emotional, cognitive, and social development. Table 1 shows the result of the research. Moreover, the proposed categorization consists an initial approach to these games which are considered necessary in order to conduct future research to investigate what is the impact of Kinect games in students' life exactly.

## 4. Design Model

One of the keys on designing frameworks or models is to identify the core elements and patterns that define the complex structure of what makes a successful video game [8], where the player's main objective is having fun but the real goal of the activities is still the learning experience.

*4.1. Serious Game Elements.* According to Annetta [9] in "The I'6s Model," there are six elements of serious game. These six elements appear in an order of magnitude: identity, immersion, interactivity, increasing complexity, informed teaching, and instructional. Figure 2 illustrates a nest model of the six elements for developing serious game.

*Identity* is ability to capture the player's mind and trick him or her into believing that he or she is in the game environment. In many modern video games, the player's identity is represented through a unique character called an avatar.

*Immersion* is where the players have a higher sense of presence through individual identity, engaged in the content and intrinsically motivated to succeed in the challenge of the game's goal.

*Interactivity* is where the games allow players to be social communicators, whether it is with other players in a multiplayer environment or with the machine. High interactivity refers to a situation in which all the component parts are interconnected and there is feedback between each other.

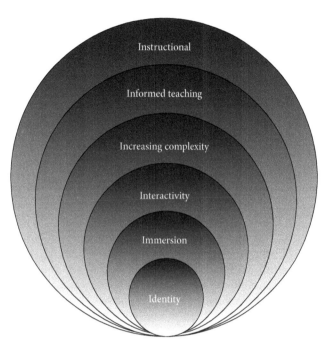

FIGURE 2: Nested elements for educational game.

*Increasing complexity* is where the games have multiple levels. Level provides a platform to increase the complexity of the concept and content of a game.

*Informed teaching* is the feedback and embedded assessments within games. The game should contain a scoring mechanism used to determine the player progress.

*Instructional* is where the game can be used as instruction media. Learning is the goal of any educational endeavor. For games to be instructional, they need to have all of the aforementioned components in addition to the following concepts.

*4.2. NUI Element.* The NUI is defined by three elements [10]:

(i) Enjoyable.

(ii) Leading to skilled practice.

(iii) Appropriate to context.

These elements are joined by "and." NUI must have all of these elements in varying degrees. Games are enjoyable, but unfortunately many of them have nothing to do with NUI. Many training systems (e.g., Mavis Beacon teaches typing) lead to skilled practice but are not NUIs. An ATM is appropriate to context but is not NUI.

*4.3. Curriculum Integration.* The architecture of succeed curriculum integration is when curriculum components are connected and related in a meaningful way to learners [11]. This can be achieved through three fundamental steps (see Figure 3).

*Step 1* (plot a course based on component of present curriculum that can benefit from game-enhanced approaches). This

approach involves the dissection of curriculum into components, for example, if we took an introductory statistic course and dissect it into (1) statistical theory, (2) worked examples, and (3) final component that applies worked example to real world problem. This components dissection further lends to reinforcement of the theoretical underpinnings of the subject matter, as the learner now has a tool that provides a causal approach to the content and its outcomes.

*Step 2* (create an environment of learning flexibility). Learning flexibility removes in-built perceptions, attitude, and belief structures akin with traditional curriculum. So it will change the learners from those who need to be tested to learners whose desire to understand through the causality associated with games play.

*Step 3* (focus initially on subject matter that can be efficiently measured and then expanded). In this step, the focus is on subject matter that can be efficiently measured and then expanded for game-enhanced learning that is critical. The other meaning of this is to apply a systematic approach for game integration by the following:

(1) Removing learning barrier: the virtual wall between learners and academic needs to be sufficiently removed to allow student to perceive their teachers more as coaches than academic stalwarts.

(2) Enable the subject matter: trying something new such as game that enhanced curriculum should include some "Easter egg," that is, hidden messages or clues, which support student to take new direction.

(3) Direct subject matter flow: measure initial subject matter through strategically mapping subject content into specific elements of the game, to enhance the curriculum.

*4.4. Pedagogy.* Pedagogy is the discipline that deals with the theory and practice of education. It also concerns at the study and practice of the best ways to teach. Successful game is a combination of potentially adaptive structures (such as rules) and the delivery time of information. Both of these are relevant when teaching; hence the institute of education argues that using game design theory can inform virtual world pedagogy [12]. Those who adopt this view frequently situate the learning process within a framework of pedagogical theories such as Kolb's experiential learning.

As a theoretical model, experiential learning was first defined by Kolb as "the process whereby knowledge is created through the transformation of experience." According to Kolb's model (see Figure 4), learning is a cyclical process which consists of four main stages. Beginning with a concrete experience, the learner makes observations and reflects on this experience. Based on these reflection, he or she draws conclusions and generalizes on how their new knowledge can be used in other scenarios. Finally, the learner tests these generalizations and hypotheses through experimentations and further experiences [13].

In designing serious games, there are three factors involved, that is, theory; contents; and game design [14]. The

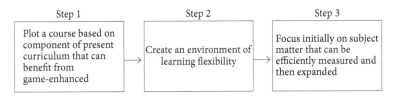

FIGURE 3: Curriculum integration.

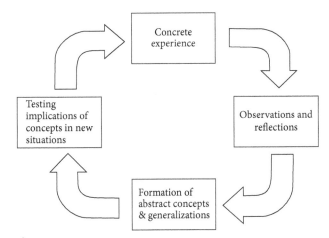

FIGURE 4: Kolb's experiential learning model.

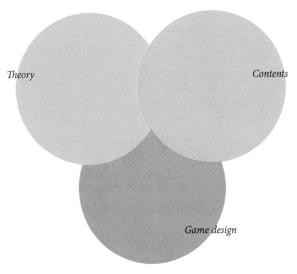

FIGURE 5: A multidisciplinary challenge.

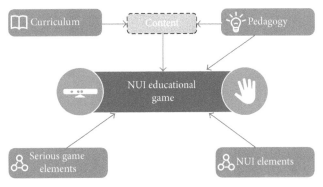

FIGURE 6: NUI educational games model.

between the components of the proposed model in this study can be seen in Figure 6.

NUI educational game should provide a quality content for the target domain that is in line with curriculum and based on pedagogy as a discipline of education. After that, during the development stages, the involvement of six serious game elements and three elements of NUI needs to be ensured.

## 5. Prototype

The prototype was implemented in Unity platform, using C Sharp programming language and Microsoft Kinect as NUI technology platform. It was developed based on the proposed model and the aims are to ensure the effectiveness of the model. Before starting to develop the game, meeting and interview with Science teacher were done to collect the data about curriculum needs.

The fundamental steps of curriculum integration applied on the data to select the content of the game. The selection was based on analysis about students' needs and abilities on the subject. The analysis was conducted by interviewing the teachers. The results of the interview were recorded and classified according to students' interest in learning each title and then assessed in percent. A high percentage indicates high interest in learning the subject. The low percentage is selected as the content of prototype. The results are shown in Table 2.

The next step, selected content must be appropriate to the pedagogical approach. The content of the game must deal with pedagogy to be relevant when used as a teaching tool in classroom. The appropriate methods in teaching and learning Science are a process-oriented approach. This is consistent with Kolb Theory that used experiential learning for its methods. In this prototype, we select subtitle "classification" as a content of the game. Classification is the arrangement of

theory included pedagogy, cognition learning, and behavioral learning. The content is the course that will be the game's content. Game design includes Artificial Intelligence (AI), Human-Computer Interaction (HCI), a User Interface (UI), and programming.

In order to use game as a learning tool, we need to consider three factors that had been mentioned above. Figure 5 describes the relationship between the three factors in the development of serious games. Educational games are identical with serious game. Therefore, the relationship

FIGURE 7: The gestures.

TABLE 2: The result of interview on students' learning interest on each title.

| Number | Title | Percentage |
|---|---|---|
| 1 | The Science Process Skills | 90% |
| 2 | Human Dentition | 90% |
| 3 | Characteristics of Plants | 100% |
| 4 | Water Absorption | 100% |
| 5 | Soil Composition | 100% |

objects, ideas, or information into groups and the members which have one or more characteristics in common. The format of this game is to classify objects based on their characteristics. This format is commonly and widely used in digital games such as puzzle games that use drag-and-drop to collect objects. However, in this study the game structure uses gestures provided by NUI. Users can classify objects by moving their bodies; it will make the game more interesting. The gestures used included raised right hand, lowered right hand, raised left hand, and lower left hand as shown in Figure 7.

This four gestures control the movement of the bridge. The object to be classified across the bridge to get to the classification or characteristics that are across the bridge. Players need to use the gestures to make sure the objects go to the correct classification. Game sketches is shown in Figure 8. Players have to raise their right hand to raise the right bridge and to make it lower, players have to lower their hand. As well as for the left bridge, players can control it using their left hand. This format was designed to ensure that students have the ability to classify object properly and quickly.

The next step was designing the game. Six serious game elements and three elements of NUI should be applied in this step. Figure 9 shows the interface of the game. We developed colorful interface and added sound effects and animation to make the game look more interesting for children.

All elements that have been studied previously should be considered and included into the gameplay for making the game effective and can be used as a learning tool in classroom. Element of *increasing complexity* was used by created three

levels in the game that is easy, medium, and hard. These are different in terms of the number of animals and their walking speed. Figure 10 shows the screenshot of level menu page.

## 6. Testing and Result

Usability testing technique has been used to evaluate the prototype by testing it with 15 students. The purpose of this testing is to identify any usability problems, determine student's satisfaction, and ensure that the prototype is in line with standard curriculum.

The usability testing was conducted using observation and interview method. During the user testing session, researcher and teachers conduct observation while students play the game. Meanwhile, at the same time they also filled out the checklist question regarding game interface.

These questions contain five quality components of usability [15]: learnability (Q1), efficiency (Q2), memorability (Q3), errors (Q4), and satisfaction (Q5) (see Table 3). Then semistructured interviews were conducted after the users testing session was done. The interview was conducted with the teachers to answer a set of question regarding content of the prototype.

The observation result shows that all students can perform the tasks given. Only one student did not pass one part of "error" section (Q4), that is, "menus do not mislead the users." Table 3 shows the observation result.

During interview session, teachers provide the suggestion for improvement of the prototype including the error part that the student encountered during his work. Teachers suggest providing a text in any button on the game interface, so it would not mislead players in their action. Another suggestion is to add voice over to the instructor character on the game. In the term of game content, teachers agreed that the content of prototype is in line with their standard curriculum.

## 7. Conclusion

In commercial circles, we see games pushing the envelope as it relates to such technologies as Microsoft's Kinect and

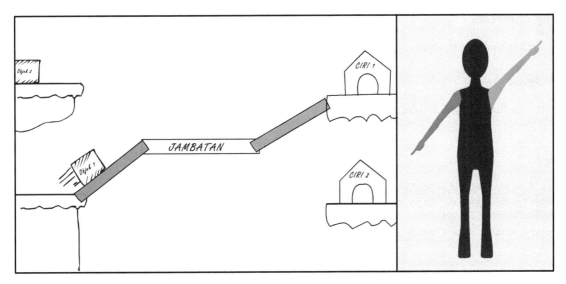

FIGURE 8: The game sketches.

FIGURE 9: A screenshot of the game.

FIGURE 10: A screenshot of menu level page.

TABLE 3: The result of the observation session.

| Item | Question | Yes |
|---|---|---|
| Q1 | (i) Game design is simple and structured | 100% |
| | (ii) Navigations buttons are easy to understand and consistent | 100% |
| | (iii) Game design is natural | 100% |
| Q2 | (i) Fast response to user gestures | 100% |
| | (ii) Efficient in completing the game missions | 100% |
| Q3 | (i) Game instructions help users | 100% |
| | (ii) Color and menu size are appropriate according to function | 100% |
| | (iii) Gestures used is natural | 100% |
| Q4 | (i) Menus do not mislead users | 93.3% |
| | (ii) Background music does not interfere users while playing | 100% |
| Q5 | (i) Game interface in accordance with target users | 100% |
| | (ii) User does not feel pressured while completing the game task | 100% |
| | (iii) The game attracts user | 100% |
| Q6 | (i) Game content is in line with curriculum | 100% |
| | (ii) Content is easily understood | 100% |
| | (iii) User can perform tasks correctly | 100% |

Nintendo's Wii. These games have pushed the boundary in terms of game play, digital storytelling, and graphics without consideration about the content, whether it is suitable for education or not. This study proposed a model for NUI game-based learning to help game developers in designing NUI game. With the existence of this model, hopefully it will support those technologies in processing to be integrated and used as learning tool in classroom. So that it can enhance the classroom interactions, increase the classroom participation, and create opportunities for interaction and discussion to achieve learning goal.

One limitation of this work is that we did not compare our model to other methodologies or frameworks. However, it is our intention to do so, as part of the future work, and we hope other researchers to continue the robust research about NUI educational games.

## Competing Interests

The authors declare that they have no competing interests.

## Acknowledgments

This research was funded by University Grant GUP-2015-004.

## References

[1] A. Shapi'i, N. A. Mat Zin, and A. M. Elaklouk, "A game system for cognitive rehabilitation," *BioMed Research International*, vol. 2015, Article ID 493562, 7 pages, 2015.

[2] "The Kinect revolution," *New Scientist*, vol. 208, no. 2789, p. 5, 2011.

[3] L. D. McManis, *Finding the Education in Educational Technology with Early Learners*, National Association for the Education of Young Children, Washington, DC, USA, 2012.

[4] H. J. Hsu, "The potential of Kinect in education," *International Journal of Information and Education Technology*, vol. 1, no. 5, pp. 365–370, 2011.

[5] M. Kandroudi and T. Bratitsis, "Exploring the educational perspectives of XBOX kinect based video games," in *Proceedings of the 6th European Conference on Games Based Learning (ECGBL '12)*, p. 219, Cork, Ireland, January 2012.

[6] E. H.-k. Wu, C.-W. Liao, S. Huang, C.-N. Chang, Z.-Y. Chen, and J.-R. Yang, "Kids magic learning: kinect-based game learning development and practice," in *Proceedings of the 7th European Conference on Games Based Learning*, 2013.

[7] V. K. Vaishnavi and W. Kuechler, *Design Science Research Methods and Patterns: Innovating Information and Communication Technology*, Auerbach Publications, Taylor & Francis Group, 2008.

[8] D. Cook, "The chemistry of game design," World Wide Web electronic publication, 2007, http://www.gamasutra.com/view/feature/1524/the_chemistry_of_game_design.php.

[9] L. A. Annetta, "The 'I's' have it: a framework for serious educational game design," *Review of General Psychology*, vol. 14, no. 2, pp. 105–112, 2010.

[10] D. Wigdor and D. Wixon, *Brave NUI World Designing Natural User Interfaces for Touch and Gesture*, Morgan Kaufmann, Burlington, Mass, USA, 2011.

[11] S. de Freitas, "New Pedagogical Approaches in Game Enhanced Learning: Curriculum Integration," Idea Group Inc (IGI) United States of America, 2013.

[12] M. Ulicsak and M. Wright, *Game in Education: Serious Games*, Futurelab, Bristol, UK, 2010.

[13] P. Rooney, "A theoretical framework for serious game design: exploring pedagogy, play and fidelity and their implications for the design process," *International Journal of Game-Based Learning*, vol. 2, no. 4, pp. 41–60, 2012.

[14] F. Bellotti, R. Berta, M. Carvalho, and A. De Gloria, "Serious Games Design A Tutorial," 2013.

[15] J. Nielsen, "Usability 101: Introduction to Usability," Nielsen Normal Group, 2015, http://www.nngroup.com/articles/usability-101-introduction-to-usability/.

# 5

# Engagement in Games: Developing an Instrument to Measure Consumer Videogame Engagement and its Validation

**Amir Zaib Abbasi,[1] Ding Hooi Ting,[1] and Helmut Hlavacs[2]**

[1]*Department of Management and Humanities, Universiti Teknologi PETRONAS, Tronoh, Malaysia*
[2]*Research Group Entertainment Computing, University of Vienna, Vienna, Austria*

Correspondence should be addressed to Amir Zaib Abbasi; aamir.zaib.abbasi@gmail.com

Academic Editor: Kok W. Wong

The aim of the study is to develop a new instrument to measure engagement in videogame play termed as consumer videogame engagement. The study followed the scale development procedure to develop an instrument to measure the construct of consumer videogame engagement. In this study, we collected the data in two different phases comprising study 1 ($n = 136$) and study 2 ($n = 270$). We employed SPSS 22.0 for exploratory factor analysis using study 1 respondents to explore the factors for consumer videogame engagement and reliability analysis. Results of EFA resulted with six-factor solution. We further used SmartPLS 3.0 software on study 2 respondents to further confirm the six-factor solution as reflective measurement model on the first-order level, and three second-order formative constructs on the second-order or higher-order level as formative measurement model. Results of the reflective measurement model and formative measurement model evidenced that consumer videogame engagement has strong psychometric properties and is a valid instrument to measure engagement in videogame play. Results also confirmed that consumer videogame engagement is a multidimensional construct as well as a reflective-formative construct. The study is unique in its investigation as it develops an instrument to measure engagement in videogame play which comprises the cognitive, affective, and behavioral dimensions.

## 1. Introduction

The popularity of videogame playing has increased significantly in the last decade [1, 2]. The total consumer's expenditure on games industry has increased to $22.41 billion in 2015 [3]. Videogame playing has the potential to attract millions of individuals worldwide to play [4] and it has become an essential part of our daily lives [5]. Videogame playing causes consumers to get addicted to a videogame [6] which finally leads people to engage in videogame play [7]. This is one of the key characteristics of videogames—it creates engagement in a videogame play [8]. Hence, engagement in videogames has become an important subject of study that needs considerable attention.

Engagement in videogames has been termed as a multidimensional concept [9, 10] which can be associated with a number of other notions, for instance, immersion [4, 7, 11], flow [12], fun [13], enjoyment [14, 15], presence [16], motivations in videogame play [17], arousal [18], game engagement [19], and user engagement [20, 21].

However, several types of research have been conducted in videogame studies to explore and measure engagement in both the qualitative [7, 11, 20] and quantitative manner [4, 5, 19, 21, 22]. Among all the studies, the study by Brown and Cairns [7] was the first study to qualitatively explore the concept of immersion and define a videogame player's experiences. The study results lead to the three main factors, *engagement, engrossment,* and *total immersion,* contributing to the construct of immersion. Another qualitative research by Ermi and Mäyrä [11] has studied the notion of immersion to recognize the essential features of game-play experience. The study came up with a new model of game-play experience called *"SCI model,"* comprising the three dimensions *sensory-immersion, challenge-based immersion,* and *imaginative immersion.* We find that the results of Ermi and Mäyrä's study have similarities with the definition of immersion given by Brown and Cairns, for instance; imaginative immersion is similar to the state of engrossment and total immersion while challenge-based immersion and sensory-immersion refer to the dimension of engagement in Brown and Cairns' study.

Jennett et al. [4] expanded the study of [7] to measure the concept of immersion quantitatively. Their study developed an instrument to measure the subjective experience of videogame play based on the dimensions of *gameflow, cognitive-absorption,* and *presence* and named it game-experience questionnaire or GEQ. Brockmyer et al. [19] have developed another scale named game engagement questionnaire or GEQ using a combination of four constructs, *flow, presence, absorption,* and *immersion,* to measure a player's engagement in videogames. Again, this study has used almost similar dimensions that were earlier used by [4]. In a similar vein, a recent study by Procci [23] has reviewed the model of the game engagement [19]. The author of the study discussed three dimensions such as *flow, immersion,* and *presence* of the game engagement questionnaire [19] to measure the subjective experience of videogame play. However, the absorption construct is more or less similar to the flow dimension, which makes the measurement less popular. According to Procci [23], a newly revised construct of game engagement comprises the dimensions *flow, presence, involvement,* and *immersion* that can be applied to examine the subjective experience of videogame play.

In previous literature, there is another available scale which was used to measure user experience in video games labeled user-engagement scale [24] that comprised of six factors—*aesthetic appeal, novelty, focused attention, felt involvement, perceived usability,* and *endurability (i.e., a user's overall experience)* [21]. The study applied the user engagement in videogame setting [24], but the structure of factors was not consistent with the original definition. The authors have also developed another scale to measure engagement in videogame learning with the combination of flow theory and cognitive load theory [22].

Hitherto, the current study has addressed past studies that have examined the past measurements of engagement scale and found that there is a critical need to develop and use engagement scale to examine player's engagement or subjective experience in videogame play. Critical review of prior studies indicates that few studies have used almost similar dimensions *flow, presence,* and *absorption* to examine the subjective experience of videogame play and measured player engagement in video games [4, 19, 23]. These studies have not properly conceptualized and operationalized the term engagement and immersion in their studies. Rather, these studies have just discussed that the constructs *flow, presence, absorption,* and *immersion* are related to immersion which can be used to measure the construct of immersion and game engagement. Besides, measurements were mainly focusing on quantifying the subjective experience of videogame play.

Secondly, several studies have stated that engagement in a videogame is a multidimensional construct [5, 9, 10, 22, 24, 25]. Among these studies, Cheng et al. [5] try to capture the meaning of engagement on a second-order construct when other studies did not analyze the concept of higher-order construct. The problem with the study by Cheng et al. [5] is that the authors have studied this construct as a reflective-reflective model. However, after critically reviewing the article, we believe that the authors have wrongly specified the construct of game immersion as a reflective-reflective model; rather, the game immersion construct seems to be a reflective-formative model. This conclusion was drawn by reviewing the following studies [26, 27] which have discussed the important decision rules for specifying the construct as reflective or formative. The following studies have precisely discussed the decision rules [26, 27]. The first rule is to look at the nature of the construct whether the latent construct is existing or formed. The second rule is to look at the direction of causality between the items and latent construct; if it is reflective, the causality is from construct to items, if it is formative then the causality is from items to the construct. The third rule is to look at the characteristics of items used to measure the construct such that if it is reflective, then the items should have a shared common theme, items are exchangeable, and deleting or adding an item does not change the meaning of the construct, whereas, if the construct is formative, items do not share a common theme, items are not replaceable, and deleting or adding an item changes the conceptual meaning of the construct.

This can be evidenced from the study [5] that, on the first order, all these dimensions of engagement *(attraction, time investment,* and *usability), engrossment (emotional attachment, decreased perceptions),* and total immersion *(presence* and *empathy)* are reflectively measured as these dimensions have causality from the construct to items and each dimension has a common-shared theme with interchangeable items, whereas, on the second-order constructs, these dimensions such as attraction, time investment, and usability *(engagement),* emotional attachment, decreased perceptions *(engrossment),* and presence and empathy *(total immersion)* should be measured formatively, where authors of the study [5] have neglected the importance of using formative construct, because engagement is collectively formed with the following dimensions *(attraction, time investment,* and *usability),* while engrossment is jointly made up by these dimensions *(emotional attachment, decreased perceptions)* and total immersion is together built with the following factors *(presence* and *empathy).* Besides, these dimensions have causality from the dimension itself to the higher level, dimensions do not share a common theme, dimensions are not interchangeable, and deleting any dimension can cause a variation on higher-order construct of game immersion. On this basis, game immersion construct should be considered a reflective-formative model than a reflective-reflective model.

Thirdly, past studies have given much importance to psychological dimensions *immersion, flow, presence, involvement,* and *absorption* to measure engagement in videogames

[4, 12, 19, 22, 23]. However, these studies have not considered the importance of behavioral dimensions to measure a player's engagement in videogame play.

Hence, the current study considers the limitations of previous studies and intends to first conceptualize and operationalize the notion of engagement in videogame playing as consumer videogame engagement. Accordingly, the study aims to develop a new scale comprising both the psychological and behavioral dimensions to measure the construct of consumer videogame engagement. Moreover, the aim of the study is to validate the new scale *consumer videogame engagement* among the videogame consumers.

## 2. Literature Review

The present study reviews past researches that have mainly defined engagement and developed an instrument for measuring engagement in videogame studies.

*2.1. Definitions of Engagement and Its Related Constructs Used in Videogames.* Engagement has acquired a significant attention in several studies [19–22, 24]. Among these studies, the research by O'Brien and Toms [20] has qualitatively defined engagement as *"a value of user-experience that is dependent on numerous dimensions, comprising aesthetic appeal, novelty, usability of the system, the ability of the user to attend to and become involved in the experience and the user's overall evaluation of the salience of the experience."* However, other studies have explained the notion of engagement with other theoretical constructs; for instance, flow, presence, immersion and absorption [19], presence, immersion, involvement and flow [23], cognitive and affective dimensions [22], focused-attention, perceived usability, aesthetics, and satisfaction [24] introduced a motivational model of videogame engagement that includes *autonomy, competence,* and *relatedness* [17].

Another definitional construct that has often used interchangeably with engagement is *immersion* [28]. Both engagement and immersion constructs have been investigated by these studies [4, 5, 19, 23] to examine the subjective experience as well as player's engagement in videogame play. Among these studies, the following researches [4, 19, 23] have used almost common dimensions of *flow, presence,* and *immersion* to quantify the subjective experience and engagement in videogame play.

*2.2. Existing Questionnaires on Immersion and Engagement in Videogames.* A large number of studies have put their efforts on developing and measuring the construct of immersion [4, 5] and engagement [19, 22, 24]. A study by Jennett et al. [4] was the first research to study the construct of immersion to describe the subjective experience in videogame play as game engagement. The construct of immersion [4] was developed with the help of three main theoretical constructs, *flow, presence,* and *cognitive-absorption,* which are commonly used to define engaging experiences. However, this study has ignored to differentiate these constructs *flow* and *immersion* in their study questionnaire labeled game immersion questionnaire.

However, a study by Brockmyer et al. [19] has addressed this gap by introducing the distinct position of these constructs *flow* and *immersion* in the study questionnaire called *game engagement questionnaire.* The study has used the term *game engagement* rather than *game immersion* to measure the subjective experience in videogame play. According to this study, game engagement is "a general sign of game-involvement." To measure game engagement in videogame play, the study has developed a game engagement questionnaire by considering such theoretical constructs *absorption, presence, immersion,* and *flow.* These theoretical constructs can be conceptualized as *"a progression of ever deeper-engagement in videogame-playing."* Recently, a study by [23] has revisited the game engagement model in which the author has revised the game engagement model which was originally given by [19]. The author has identified that absorption is principally a flow. Therefore, it is better to exclude "absorption" from the game engagement model. Furthermore, the author has introduced the *"involvement"* dimension and termed it as R-GEM *(revisited game engagement model).*

Extant reviews of literature illustrate that few studies have developed a scale for measuring engagement through a *user-engagement scale* [24], or *immersion* by the game immersion questionnaire [5]. Among these studies, Cheng et al. [5] have developed a game immersion questionnaire by immersion theory [7]. According to these studies [5, 7], immersion comprises of the three phases—*engagement, engrossment,* and *total immersion.* The study by O'Brien and Toms [21] has applied the definition of user engagement [20] to operationalize and develop the construct of user engagement. The user-engagement scale was originally developed to measure engagement in an online shopping environment by [21]. Recently, this scale was also used in the context of a videogame by [24] who found that only the four factors-*focused-attention, perceived usability, aesthetics,* and *satisfaction* have passed through the EFA test, while the remaining factors have been deleted. However, the factor structure of the user-engagement scale was not consistent with the original measurement scale proposed by [21] which comprised of six factors such as *aesthetics, focused-attention, felt-involvement, novelty, endurability,* and *perceived usability.* The same authors [22] have also measured engagement with a combination of cognitive load theory and flow theory.

To date, past studies have only considered psychological constructs to measure the subjective experience and player engagement in videogame play [4, 5, 19, 22, 23]. However, these studies are limited to measure the construct of game engagement with both psychological and behavioral dimensions. These studies [4, 19, 22, 23] have not properly conceptualized and operationalized the construct of game engagement in their studies, while some studies have wrongly specified the model [5, 24]; for instance, according to Wiebe et al. [24], the user-engagement scale is a multidimensional construct, but they measured on a unidimensional level and authors have ignored investigating it on a multidimensional level or higher-order level. In a similar vein, another study by Cheng et al. [5] has also miss-specified the construct of immersion as a reflective-reflective model. Rather, the construct of immersion is a reflective-formative model and should be dealt with carefully.

This study considers the limitations of past studies and takes an opportunity to properly conceptualize and operationalize the construct of engagement in videogame play as consumer videogame engagement. Furthermore, the objective of this study is to validate the construct of consumer videogame engagement on a multidimensional level; it first measures the first-order construct as reflective measurement model, also known as Mode A type of analysis, and evaluates the second-order construct as formative measurement model called Mode B type of analysis in SEM-PLS.

## 3. Conceptualization of Consumer Videogame Engagement

This study aims to conceptualize the notion of engagement in videogames as *consumer videogame engagement*. This study follows the definition of engagement given by [29–31] to conceptualize the concept of consumer videogame engagement as *"engagement is a multidimensional construct which is subject to a context-specific expression of relevant cognitive, emotional, and behavioral dimensions."* Moreover, Hollebeek [31] has further added that engagement is a process which is revealed as a result of two-way communications between the engagement-subject (consumer/customer) and a particular engagement-object such as a product, service, or a brand, which leads to generating consumer engagement states *(cognitive, affective,* and *behavioral)*. Following the above stated definition, this study conceptualizes consumer videogame engagement as *"a psychological state that triggers due to two-way interactions between the consumer and videogame product, which generates different level of consumer engagement states (cognitive, affective and behavioral)"* [32].

## 4. Scale Development and Validation of Consumer Videogame Engagement

This study adopts the scale development procedure suggested by [33, 34] to operationalize and develop a scale for the construct of consumer videogame engagement. The scale development process involves the four main steps as in the following part: step one is to generate items for samples, step two involves first-time data collection and instrument-purification, and step three comprises second-time data collection and performs the reanalysis. Finally, step four is to determine the scale of consumer videogame engagement on multidimensional level and the following part explains the four steps.

*A Flow Chart of Scale Development Process [33, 34]*

Item generation:

  (i) Specify domains of consumer videogame engagement

  (ii) Literature review

  (iii) Content validity

Data collection (Study 1) and purification of measures:

  (i) Coefficient of alpha

  (ii) Exploratory factor analysis

   Data collection (Study 2) and reanalysis of measures

  (i) Coefficient of alpha

  (ii) Confirmatory factor analysis

  (iii) Construct validity

### 4.1. Step One: Item Generation

*4.1.1. Operationalization or Specifying Domains of the Construct "Consumer Videogame Engagement".* According to the scale development procedure [33, 34], the research should be specific in defining the construct—what needs to be included or excluded in the construct. Accordingly, this study defines consumer videogame engagement as *"a psychological state that triggers due to two-way interactions between the consumer and video-game product, which generates different level of consumer engagement states (cognitive, affective and behavioral)."* This study is mainly interested in measuring consumer videogame engagement regarding consumer's cognitive, affective, and behavioral engagement in videogame playing.

Besides, Churchill Jr. [33] has suggested some techniques *(literature review, experience-surveys, focus-groups, and interviews)* that can be applied to generate initial scale items. This study applies an extensive literature review approach to get a list of scale items. According to the literature review process suggested by [33], it has been discussed that a study should clearly explain how the variable is defined and how many factors/dimensions it has.

Through conducting an in-depth literature review, this study concludes that consumer videogame engagement is a multidimensional construct that comprises the three engagement states *cognitive, affective, and behavioral*. These three engagement states are further categorized into two subdimensions, for instance, conscious attention and absorption as dimensions of cognitive engagement, while dedication and enthusiasm represent affective engagement. Lastly, interaction and social interaction together refer to the state of behavioral engagement.

This study compiles the measurement scales as already reported in the literature which is specifically relevant to the following dimensions: conscious attention, absorption (cognitive engagement), dedication, enthusiasm (affective engagement), social interaction, and interaction (behavioral engagement). The items on the following dimensions such as conscious attention, six items (items 1 to 6) from [35], item 7 from [36], and item 8 from [24] are adapted. For the absorption dimension, this study adapts the scale from [37], whereas the measurement items for dedication are organized as item 1 from [38] and item 2 to item 7 from [39] and the scale items of enthusiasm are adapted from the study of [35]. However, the items of social connection such as item 1 to item 4 from [35] and remaining items 5, 6, and 7 from [40] are adapted. Finally, the scale items on the interaction dimension are adapted as item 1 to item 5 from [37]. In this phase, the study has generated 39 items that together measure the overall construct of consumer videogame engagement [32]. Next, this study performs the content validity on the generated 39 items.

*4.1.2. Content Validity.* According to [41], *content validity is a subjective but systematic assessment of how sound the domain content of a construct is explained by its indicators.* This study has invited 4 Ph.D. students and two experts specializing in Marketing to first evaluate the content of consumer videogame engagement and the relevance of 39 measurement items, second to assess the relevance of a dimension and its measuring items, and lastly to check the wording of the item content. Based on their comments and recommendations, this study revised and corrected certain items [32]. Following this procedure, the overall scale of consumer videogame engagement has satisfied the prerequisite of content validity.

*4.2. Study One: First-Time Data Collection and Purification.* To further purify the instrument of consumer videogame engagement, this study has collected data from teenage students and analyzes the data through internal consistency analysis and exploratory factor analysis. The reason behind the selection of teenage students is teenage students are considered the main population in studying videogame-consumption behavior, because they are not merely the first-generation of *"home-based"* console videogame-players such as *"Nintendo, Sega-Genesis, and Sony-PlayStation,"* but they are yet labeled as enthusiastic videogame-players today [42].

This study has applied a multistage sampling technique to collect the study subjects. According to [43], multistage sampling technique involves the replication of two fundamental steps; step one is listing, and the other is sampling. Initially, this study has generated a list of four main states *(Penang, Selangor, Johor, and Perak)* of Malaysia. Next, it has randomly selected one state *(Perak)* from the list of four main states of Malaysia. From the Perak state, this study has obtained a list of intuitions both colleges and universities from the following source *(http://www.malaysiauniversity.net)*. From this list, the study has randomly selected one public University and one private University. Within each selected university, the teenage students aged 16–19 of foundation/diploma and 1st year undergraduate programs were invited to participate in the survey. In the case of public university, the diploma students of these two faculties *(faculty of architecture, planning and survey and faculty of arts and design)* were randomly selected to participate in the study survey, while, in the private university, this study has randomly selected the foundation and 1st year undergraduate students of these faculties *(IT and Engineering stream)*.

During the phase of data collection, the study questionnaire has been distributed and collected in the classroom setting under the presence of a lecturer. In total, this study has distributed 205 questionnaires in both universities, out of which 165 questionnaires were returned with a response rate of 0.81%. Out of 165 questionnaires, this study left with 136 valid cases after deleting the missing values. The demographic

TABLE 1: Demographic profile of respondents.

| | Sample 1 (N = 136), % EFA | Sample 2 (N = 270), % CFA |
|---|---|---|
| Gender | | |
| Male | 55.1 | 63.3 |
| Female | 44.9 | 36.7 |
| Age (years) | | |
| 15-16 | 0 | 1.1 |
| 17-18 | 16.2 | 19.6 |
| 19 | 83.8 | 79.3 |
| Ethnicity | | |
| Malay | 88.2 | 38.1 |
| Chinese | 10.3 | 50.0 |
| Indian | 1.5 | 11.9 |
| Education | | |
| Secondary school student | 3 | 11.5 |
| Diploma/foundation student | 109 | 28.9 |
| Fresh undergraduate student | 24 | 59.6 |
| Frequency of videogame play | | |
| Everyday | 33.1 | 39.6 |
| Once a week | 19.1 | 20.4 |
| A few times a week | 47.8 | 40.0 |
| Average daily hours of videogame play | | |
| 1–4 hrs/daily | 66.9 | 71.5 |
| Above 4–8 hrs/daily | 30.1 | 24.1 |
| Above 8–12 hrs/daily | 2.2 | 2.6 |
| More than 12 hrs/daily | .7 | 1.9 |

*Answers generated in multiple response setting (percent of cases means each percentage is out of 100)*

| | | |
|---|---|---|
| Most genre of videogames played | | |
| Action | 68.4 | 64.4 |
| Adventure | 64.0 | 60.4 |
| Arcade | 39.7 | 30.7 |
| Shooter | 58.1 | 54.8 |
| Role-playing | 39.7 | 47.0 |
| Fighting | 55.9 | 47.0 |
| Strategy | 60.3 | 58.1 |
| Sports game | 45.6 | 34.8 |
| Racing | 60.3 | 45.2 |
| Casual | 22.1 | 22.6 |
| Children' entertainment | 14.0 | 11.1 |
| Family entertainment | 22.8 | 14.8 |
| Flight | 14.0 | 14.4 |
| Other videogames/genre | 8.1 | 6.7 |
| Most common platform for videogame players | | |
| Personal computer | 81.6 | 78.5 |
| Dedicated gaming console | 43.4 | 23.7 |
| Smartphone | 70.6 | 66.7 |
| Wireless device | 20.6 | 22.6 |
| Dedicated handheld device | 8.1 | 8.1 |
| Others | .7 | 0 |

profile of the respondents for data collection one (sample 1 N = 136) and data collection two (sample 2 N = 270) is given in Table 1.

TABLE 2: Exploratory factor analysis (sample 1 $N$ = 136).

| | | Six-Factors extracted based on Eigen values | | | | | | Cronbach's alpha |
| --- | --- | --- | --- | --- | --- | --- | --- | --- |
| | | 1 | 2 | 3 | 4 | 5 | 6 | |
| Conscious attention (Eigen value = 10.949) | ConAtten2 | .863 | | | | | | 0.893 |
| | ConAtten1 | .854 | | | | | | |
| | ConAtten3 | .779 | | | | | | |
| | ConAtten4 | .760 | | | | | | |
| | ConAtten5 | .696 | | | | | | |
| Enthusiasm (Eigen value = 2.579) | Enthusi6 | | .907 | | | | | 0.861 |
| | Enthusi2 | | .772 | | | | | |
| | Enthusi3 | | .755 | | | | | |
| | Enthusi5 | | .635 | | | | | |
| | Enthusi1 | | .598 | | | | | |
| Interaction (Eigen value = 1.818) | Interact4 | | | .837 | | | | 0.877 |
| | Interact5 | | | .801 | | | | |
| | Interact3 | | | .779 | | | | |
| | Interact2 | | | .715 | | | | |
| | Interact1 | | | .606 | | | | |
| Absorption (Eigen value = 1.630) | Absorp3 | | | | .857 | | | 0.863 |
| | Absorp2 | | | | .820 | | | |
| | Absorp1 | | | | .815 | | | |
| | Absorp6 | | | | .729 | | | |
| | Absorp5 | | | | .663 | | | |
| Dedication (Eigen value = 1.141) | Dedicate2 | | | | | .797 | | 0.834 |
| | Dedicate4 | | | | | .793 | | |
| | Dedicate3 | | | | | .784 | | |
| | Dedicate5 | | | | | .608 | | |
| | Dedicate7 | | | | | .413 | | |
| Social connection (Eigen value = 1.084) | SocialCon3 | | | | | | .871 | 0.787 |
| | SocialCon2 | | | | | | .830 | |
| | SocialCon1 | | | | | | .788 | |

The next section has analyzed the collected data on the basis of internal consistency analysis also known as reliability analysis and exploratory factor analysis.

*4.2.1. Purification: Exploratory Factor Analysis (EFA) and Reliability Analysis.* The data were further analyzed through exploratory factor analysis using the *promax* rotation to drop the number of items and explore the factors for consumer videogame engagement. The items were dropped on having a loading lower than 0.40 on single factor as well as on their associated cross-loadings [44]. In total we had generated 39 items for consumer videogame engagement, but out of 39 items, we loaded 34 items to explore the factors for consumer videogame engagement. The remaining 5 items were used for redundancy analysis as discussed in the later stage and out of 5 items; only 3 items were better capturing the whole construct of consumer videogame engagement.

The result of factor analysis is shown in Table 2. Table 2 resulted with six-factor solution based on Eigen values as suggested by [45]. This study further examined the reliability of the construct which should be more than 0.70 as mentioned

by [46] and Table 2 showed that all dimensions had reliability of more than .70 which means the construct met the criteria of reliability assessment.

*4.3. Study Two: Second-Time Data Collection and Reanalysis of the Measurement Construct.* Study two also followed the same procedure of multistage sampling technique. The only difference is that this study has extended the survey from two universities to 5 institutions. This time, the study has distributed around 365 questionnaires in five institutions, out of which the study has successfully collected 300 questionnaires with a response rate of 82%. After treating the missing values, the study was left with 270 valid responses and the demographic details of the respondents were given in Table 1. In the next section, we analyzed the confirmatory factor analysis and other validity tests on using sample 2 comprising 270 respondents.

*4.3.1. Analysis.* SEM-PLS *(structural equation modeling-partial least squares)* was employed to validate the measurement construct of consumer videogame engagement because

TABLE 3: Confirmatory factor analysis and construct validity (convergent and discriminant validity) Sample 2 ($N = 270$).

| Construct scale | Item | Convergent validity | | CR | Cronbach's alpha |
|---|---|---|---|---|---|
| | | Loadings | AVE | | |
| Conscious attention | Con.Atten1 | 0.854 | 0.72 | 0.93 | 0.91 |
| | Con.Atten2 | 0.864 | | | |
| | Con.Atten3 | 0.841 | | | |
| | Con.Atten4 | 0.854 | | | |
| | Con.Atten5 | 0.840 | | | |
| Absorption | Absorp1 | 0.735 | 0.61 | 0.89 | 0.84 |
| | Absorp2 | 0.728 | | | |
| | Absorp3 | 0.832 | | | |
| | Absorp5 | 0.802 | | | |
| | Absorp6 | 0.808 | | | |
| Dedication | Dedicate2 | 0.832 | 0.64 | 0.90 | 0.86 |
| | Dedicate3 | 0.849 | | | |
| | Dedicate4 | 0.819 | | | |
| | Dedicate5 | 0.821 | | | |
| | Dedicate7 | 0.678 | | | |
| Enthusiasm | Enthusi1 | 0.756 | 0.65 | 0.90 | 0.86 |
| | Enthusi2 | 0.846 | | | |
| | Enthusi3 | 0.837 | | | |
| | Enthusi5 | 0.813 | | | |
| | Enthusi6 | 0.768 | | | |
| Social connection | Social.Con1 | 0.895 | 0.75 | 0.90 | 0.84 |
| | Social.Con2 | 0.850 | | | |
| | Social.Con3 | 0.857 | | | |
| Interaction | Interact1 | 0.819 | 0.68 | 0.91 | 0.88 |
| | Interact2 | 0.808 | | | |
| | Interact3 | 0.873 | | | |
| | Interact4 | 0.821 | | | |
| | Interact5 | 0.792 | | | |

consumer videogame engagement has both reflective and formative constructs [47]. This study has further employed SEM-PLS, which is currently used by many academics as it delivers a robust way to analyze the survey data [47]. Moreover, PLS has less restriction on sample size and data distribution, and it has the potential to measure the measurement model and structural model simultaneously [39]. The current study is mainly on scale validation. Therefore, structural model assessment is not applicable. The next section follows the measurement model.

*4.3.2. Measurement Model.* The construct of consumer videogame engagement is a multidimensional construct, which comprises the reflective-formative model. For a reflective measurement model, this study involves the estimation of internal consistency, convergent validity, and discriminant validity, whereas the evaluation of the measurement model of a formative construct follows different guidelines such as testing of multicollinearity, indicator weights, and redundancy analysis.

*4.3.3. Evaluation of Reflective Measurement Model.* Initially, a reflective measurement model was assessed for its convergent validity. Convergent validity was measured through factor loadings greater than 0.60 [48], composite reliability desirable at 0.70, and average variance extracted that should be at least 0.50 [41, 49]. The results in Table 3 claimed that all standards of convergent validity were met, whereas factor loadings were more than 0.60, and composite reliability and Cronbach's alpha were greater than 0.70, while AVE of all constructs exceeded the critical value 0.50.

*4.3.4. Discriminant Validity.* Discriminant validity of reflective constructs was evaluated through newly introduced method called Heterotrait-Monotrait ratio of correlations [50]. The criterion to evaluate the discriminant validity is to assess the HTMT value; if it exceeds the HTMT value of 0.85, then there is an issue of discriminant validity. According to Table 4, all the values passed the critical value of HTMT.85 which represents that discriminant validity is not a problem.

TABLE 4: Discriminant validity Heterotrait-Monotrait (HTMT).

|                    | Absorption | Conscious attention | Dedication | Enthusiasm | Interaction | Social connection |
|--------------------|------------|---------------------|------------|------------|-------------|-------------------|
| Absorption         |            |                     |            |            |             |                   |
| Conscious attention| 0.67       |                     |            |            |             |                   |
| Dedication         | 0.70       | 0.83                |            |            |             |                   |
| Enthusiasm         | 0.81       | 0.71                | 0.74       |            |             |                   |
| Interaction        | 0.57       | 0.60                | 0.64       | 0.66       |             |                   |
| Social connection  | 0.41       | 0.57                | 0.49       | 0.55       | 0.62        |                   |

TABLE 5: Evaluation of formative constructs (full collinearity, weights, and $T$-value).

| Construct | Measurement model | Items | Weights | VIF | $T$-values | $P$ values |
|-----------|-------------------|-------|---------|-----|------------|------------|
| Cognitive engagement | Formative | ConsAtten | 0.72 | 1.54 | 7.33 | 0.00 |
|           |                   | Absorption | 0.39 | 1.54 | 3.24 | 0.00 |
| Affective engagement | Formative | Dedication | 0.48 | 1.671 | 4.90 | 0.00 |
|           |                   | Enthusiasm | 0.62 | 1.671 | 6.35 | 0.00 |
| Behavioral engagement | Formative | Interaction | 0.76 | 1.399 | 10.86 | 0.00 |
|           |                   | Social connection | 0.36 | 1.399 | 4.16 | 0.00 |

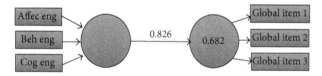

FIGURE 1: The result of redundancy analysis/convergent validity is shown.

*4.3.5. Evaluation of Formative Measurement Model.* This study has assessed the three criteria for the evaluation of formative measurement model as suggested by [41]. The first criterion to assess the convergent validity is the redundancy analysis. To do redundancy analysis in this study, the formative constructs were loaded on an exogenous latent variable named *"consumer videogame engagement"* predicting endogenous latent-variable labeled *"global measure"* that comprises the three reflective items. The path coefficient between the two constructs is desired to be at least 0.80 as recommended by [41]. The results indicated that the path coefficient between consumer videogame engagement and global measure was 0.826 as shown in Figure 1, which was higher than the threshold value and thus demonstrating that the formative constructs have achieved the convergent validity.

Additionally, this study has assessed the second criterion to check the collinearity issues in the formative constructs. The study found that there is no multicollinearity issue because of all values as shown in Table 3 are below the threshold value of 5 as suggested by [41]. The third criterion is to check the significance of the indicator weights on the

designated second-order formative constructs. If indicator weights are significant then formative construct fulfills the criteria to be in the construct [41] and this study assessed the significance of indicator weights as shown in Table 5 and found that all formative constructs were highly significant at 0.00 level.

## 5. Discussion

The present study discussed the concept of engagement in videogame studies and also debated on previous scales of engagement in videogame literature. We reviewed each of the engagement scale and discussed its limitations and issues. We also discussed that previous measurements were limited to measure engagement from these theoretical constructs *immersion, flow, presence, involvement, and absorption*, which were more related to player's psychological engagement (cognitive engagement) in videogame playing. However, another psychological dimension such as affective engagement and behavioral dimension was largely ignored to apply in examining the player's engagement in digital game playing. Therefore, we took this opportunity to develop a new scale coined as consumer videogame engagement that had both psychological (cognitive and affective) and behavioral dimensions. To develop a scale for consumer videogame engagement, we applied the definition of consumer engagement that is generally defined as follows: engagement is a multidimensional construct which is subject to a context-specific expression of relevant cognitive, emotional, and behavioral dimensions. So, we adapted this definition in videogame context and defined the construct of consumer videogame engagement as it is a psychological state that triggers due to two-way interactions between the consumer and videogame product, which generates different level of consumer engagement states (cognitive, affective, and behavioral). On the basis of consumer videogame engagement definition, we applied the scale development approach to develop a scale for consumer videogame engagement. During the validation process, we extracted a six-factor solution for consumer videogame engagement. We further analyzed the six-factor solution for the evaluation for reflective measurement model and then, we also assessed the six factors on their designated second-order construct such as cognitive, affective, and behavioral engagement for the evaluation of formative measurement model on second-order or higher-order level. We found that consumer videogame engagement is a multidimensional and valid source for capturing player's engagement in terms of both psychological (cognitive and affective engagement) and behavioral engagement. The newly developed and validated scale provides a better tool to assess engagement in videogame playing as it covers three aspects of player's engagement in game playing such as player's cognitive, affective, and behavioral engagement.

This study has several contributions and enhanced the studies of [4, 5, 19, 22–24] which have been particularly conducted on engagement in videogame studies. For instance, this research is first among videogame studies that have considered both psychological and behavioral dimensions to measure the construct of consumer videogame engagement. Secondly, the construct of consumer videogame engagement has been properly conceptualized as a multidimensional construct comprising cognitive, affective, and behavioral dimensions and accordingly developed a scale for measuring consumer videogame engagement. Thirdly, the scale of consumer videogame engagement has been validated as a reflective-formative model such as being reflective on the first-order and formative on the second-order. The results of the study have met both the criteria that have been suggested for the assessment of reflective and formative measurement model.

This study first conceptualized the definition of consumer videogame engagement and developed the scale for consumer videogame engagement. The data were collected in two phases. EFA and CFA were conducted to validate the scale of consumer videogame engagement. We further analyzed the consumer videogame engagement on the multidimensional level and results showed that consumer videogame engagement is a multidimensional and a reflective-formative construct.

## Competing Interests

The authors declare that they have no competing interests.

## References

[1] A. Z. Abbasi, D. H. Ting, and H. Hlavacs, "Proposing a new conceptual model predicting consumer videogame engagement triggered through playful-consumption experiences," in *Entertainment Computing—ICEC 2016: 15th IFIP TC 14 International Conference, Vienna, Austria, September 28–30, 2016, Proceedings*, vol. 9926 of *Lecture Notes in Computer Science*, pp. 126–134, Springer, Berlin, Germany, 2016.

[2] J. Takatalo, J. Häkkinen, J. Kaistinen, and G. Nyman, "User experience in digital games: differences between laboratory and home," *Simulation & Gaming*, vol. 42, no. 5, pp. 656–673, 2011.

[3] Entertainment Software Association, *Essential Facts about the Computer and Video Game Industry*, Entertainment Software Association, Washington, DC, USA, 2015.

[4] C. Jennett, A. L. Cox, P. Cairns et al., "Measuring and defining the experience of immersion in games," *International Journal of Human-Computer Studies*, vol. 66, no. 9, pp. 641–661, 2008.

[5] M.-T. Cheng, H.-C. She, and L. A. Annetta, "Game immersion experience: its hierarchical structure and impact on game-based science learning," *Journal of Computer Assisted Learning*, vol. 31, no. 3, pp. 232–253, 2015.

[6] S. Rigby and R. M. Ryan, *Glued to Games: How Video Games Draw Us in and Hold Us Spellbound: How Video Games Draw Us in and Hold Us Spellbound*, ABC-CLIO, 2011.

[7] E. Brown and P. Cairns, "A grounded investigation of game immersion," in *Proceedings of the Conference on Human Factors in Computing Systems (CHI '04)*, pp. 1297–1300, Vienna, Austria, April 2004.

[8] N. Whitton, "Game engagement theory and adult learning," *Simulation & Gaming*, vol. 42, no. 5, pp. 596–609, 2011.

[9] M. Filsecker and M. Kerres, "Engagement as a volitional construct: a framework for evidence-based research on educational games," *Simulation & Gaming*, vol. 45, pp. 450–470, 2014.

[10] H. Schonau-Fog and T. Bjorner, "'Sure, I would like to continue': a method for mapping the experience of engagement in video games," *Bulletin of Science, Technology & Society*, vol. 32, no. 5, pp. 405–412, 2012.

[11] L. Ermi and F. Mäyrä, "Fundamental components of the gameplay experience: analysing immersion," in *Worlds in Play: International Perspectives on Digital Games Research*, vol. 37, p. 2, 2005.

[12] J. Chen, "Flow in games (and everything else)," *Communications of the ACM*, vol. 50, no. 4, pp. 31–34, 2007.

[13] R. Koster, *Theory of Fun for Game Design*, O'Reilly Media, Sebastopol, Calif, USA, 2013.

[14] D. K. Mayes and J. E. Cotton, "Measuring engagement in video games: a questionnaire," in *Proceedings of the 45th Annual Meeting of Human Factors and Ergonomics Society*, pp. 692–696, Minneapolis, Minn, USA, October 2001.

[15] W. IJsselsteijn, W. Van Den, C. Hoogen et al., "Measuring the experience of digital game enjoyment," in *Proceedings of the 6th International Conference on Methods and Techniques in Behavioral Research, Measuring Behavior*, pp. 88–89, Maastricht, the Netherlands, August 2008.

[16] A. McMahan, "Immersion, engagement and presence," *The Video Game Theory Reader*, vol. 67, p. 86, 2003.

[17] A. K. Przybylski, C. S. Rigby, and R. M. Ryan, "A motivational model of video game engagement," *Review of General Psychology*, vol. 14, no. 2, pp. 154–166, 2010.

[18] N. Ravaja, T. Saari, M. Salminen, J. Laarni, and K. Kallinen, "Phasic emotional reactions to video game events: a psychophysiological investigation," *Media Psychology*, vol. 8, no. 4, pp. 343–367, 2006.

[19] J. H. Brockmyer, C. M. Fox, K. A. Curtiss, E. McBroom, K. M. Burkhart, and J. N. Pidruzny, "The development of the Game

Engagement Questionnaire: a measure of engagement in video game-playing," *Journal of Experimental Social Psychology*, vol. 45, no. 4, pp. 624–634, 2009.

[20] H. L. O'Brien and E. G. Toms, "What is user engagement? A conceptual framework for defining user engagement with technology," *Journal of the American Society for Information Science and Technology*, vol. 59, no. 6, pp. 938–955, 2008.

[21] H. L. O'Brien and E. G. Toms, "The development and evaluation of a survey to measure user engagement," *Journal of the American Society for Information Science and Technology*, vol. 61, no. 1, pp. 50–69, 2010.

[22] D. Sharek and E. Wiebe, "Measuring video game engagement through the cognitive and affective dimensions," *Simulation & Gaming*, vol. 45, pp. 569–592, 2014.

[23] K. C. Procci, *The subjective gameplay experience: an examination of the revised game engagement model [Ph.D. thesis]*, University of Central Florida Orlando, Orlando, Fla, USA, 2015.

[24] E. N. Wiebe, A. Lamb, M. Hardy, and D. Sharek, "Measuring engagement in video game-based environments: investigation of the user engagement scale," *Computers in Human Behavior*, vol. 32, pp. 123–132, 2014.

[25] C. Silpasuwanchai, X. Ma, H. Shigemasu, and X. Ren, "Developing a comprehensive engagement framework of gamification for reflective learning," in *Proceedings of the 11th ACM SIGCHI Conference on Designing Interactive Systems (DIS '16)*, pp. 459–472, ACM, Brisbane, Australia, June 2016.

[26] T. Coltman, T. M. Devinney, D. F. Midgley, and S. Venaik, "Formative versus reflective measurement models: two applications of formative measurement," *Journal of Business Research*, vol. 61, no. 12, pp. 1250–1262, 2008.

[27] S. Petter, D. Straub, and A. Rai, "Specifying formative constructs in information systems research," *MIS Quarterly*, vol. 31, no. 4, pp. 623–656, 2007.

[28] G. Hookham, K. Nesbitt, and F. Kay-Lambkin, "Comparing usability and engagement between a serious game and a traditional online program," in *Proceedings of the Australasian Computer Science Week Multiconference (ACSW '16)*, Canberra, Australia, February 2016.

[29] R. J. Brodie, L. D. Hollebeek, B. Jurić, and A. Ilić, "Customer engagement: conceptual domain, fundamental propositions, and implications for research," *Journal of Service Research*, vol. 14, no. 3, pp. 252–271, 2011.

[30] R. J. Brodie, A. Ilic, B. Juric, and L. Hollebeek, "Consumer engagement in a virtual brand community: an exploratory analysis," *Journal of Business Research*, vol. 66, no. 1, pp. 105–114, 2013.

[31] L. D. Hollebeek, "Demystifying customer brand engagement: exploring the loyalty nexus," *Journal of Marketing Management*, vol. 27, no. 7-8, pp. 785–807, 2011.

[32] A. Z. Abbasi, D. H. Ting, and H. Hlavacs, "A revisit of the measurements on engagement in videogames: a new scale development," in *Proceedings of the International Conference on Entertainment Computing*, pp. 247–252, Vienna, Austria, September 2016.

[33] G. A. Churchill Jr., "A paradigm for developing better measures of marketing constructs," *Journal of Marketing Research*, vol. 16, no. 1, pp. 64–73, 1979.

[34] S.-H. Tsaur, C.-H. Yen, and Y.-T. Yan, "Destination brand identity: scale development and validation," *Asia Pacific Journal of Tourism Research*, pp. 1–14, 2016.

[35] S. D. Vivek, S. E. Beatty, V. Dalela, and R. M. Morgan, "A generalized multidimensional scale for measuring customer engagement," *The Journal of Marketing Theory and Practice*, vol. 22, no. 4, pp. 401–420, 2014.

[36] H. Qin, P.-L. P. Rau, and G. Salvendy, "Measuring player immersion in the computer game narrative," *International Journal of Human-Computer Interaction*, vol. 25, no. 2, pp. 107–133, 2009.

[37] K. K. F. So, C. King, and B. Sparks, "Customer engagement with tourism brands: scale development and validation," *Journal of Hospitality & Tourism Research*, vol. 38, no. 3, pp. 304–329, 2014.

[38] W. B. Schaufeli, M. Salanova, V. González-romá, and A. B. Bakker, "The measurement of engagement and burnout: a two sample confirmatory factor analytic approach," *Journal of Happiness Studies*, vol. 3, no. 1, pp. 71–92, 2002.

[39] C. M. K. Cheung, X.-L. Shen, Z. W. Y. Lee, and T. K. H. Chan, "Promoting sales of online games through customer engagement," *Electronic Commerce Research and Applications*, vol. 14, no. 4, pp. 241–250, 2015.

[40] E. Kemp, "Engaging consumers in esthetic offerings: conceptualizing and developing a measure for arts engagement," *International Journal of Nonprofit and Voluntary Sector Marketing*, vol. 20, no. 2, pp. 137–148, 2015.

[41] J. Hair, G. T. Hult, C. M. Ringle, and M. Sarstedt, *A Primer on Partial Least Squares Structural Equation Modeling (PLS-SEM)*, Sage, Thousand Oaks, Calif, USA, 2013.

[42] D. Lee and R. LaRose, "A socio-cognitive model of video game usage," *Journal of Broadcasting and Electronic Media*, vol. 51, no. 4, pp. 632–650, 2007.

[43] A. S. Acharya, A. Prakash, P. Saxena, and A. Nigam, "Sampling: why and how of it," 2013.

[44] J. K. Ford, R. C. Maccallum, and M. Tait, "The application of exploratory factor analysis in applied psychology: a critical review and analysis," *Personnel Psychology*, vol. 39, no. 2, pp. 291–314, 1986.

[45] H. F. Kaiser, "The application of electronic computers to factor analysis," *Educational and Psychological Measurement*, vol. 20, no. 1, pp. 141–151, 1960.

[46] J. F. Hair, W. C. Black, B. J. Babin, R. E. Anderson, and R. L. Tatham, *Multivariate Data Analysis*, vol. 6, Prentice Hall, Upper Saddle River, NJ, USA, 2006.

[47] J. F. Hair, C. M. Ringle, and M. Sarstedt, "PLS-SEM: indeed a silver bullet," *Journal of Marketing Theory and Practice*, vol. 19, no. 2, pp. 139–152, 2011.

[48] W. W. Chin, "How to write up and report PLS analyses," in *Handbook of Partial Least Squares*, pp. 655–690, Springer, 2010.

[49] C. Fornell and D. F. Larcker, "Evaluating structural equation models with unobservable variables and measurement error," *Journal of Marketing Research*, vol. 18, no. 1, pp. 39–50, 1981.

[50] J. Henseler, C. M. Ringle, and M. Sarstedt, "A new criterion for assessing discriminant validity in variance-based structural equation modeling," *Journal of the Academy of Marketing Science*, vol. 43, no. 1, pp. 115–135, 2015.

# 6

# Mining Experiential Patterns from Game-Logs of Board Game

**Liang Wang,**[1] **Yu Wang,**[1] **and Yan Li**[2]

[1]*School of Computer Science and Technology, Hebei University, Baoding 071000, China*
[2]*School of Mathematics and Information Science, Hebei University, Baoding 071002, China*

Correspondence should be addressed to Liang Wang; wangl@hbu.cn

Academic Editor: Hanqiu Sun

In board games, game-logs record past game processes, which can be regarded as an accumulation of experience. Similar to a real person, a computer player can gradually increase its skill by learning from game-logs. Therefore, the game becomes more interesting. This paper proposes an extensible approach to mine experiential patterns from increasing game-logs. The computer player improves its strategies by utilizing these growing patterns, just as it acquires experience. To evaluate the effect and performance of the approach, we designed a sample board game as a test platform and elaborated an experiment consisting of a series of tests. Experimental results show that our approach is effective and efficient.

## 1. Introduction

Gaming is one of the main intellections in our daily life. To some extent, gaming shows the wisdom of humankind more directly. Artificial intelligence for games (Game AI) is an important subfield of AI research. The current generations of computer games offer an interesting testbed for Game AI [1]. Meanwhile, applying AI techniques to game design will make the games more interesting. The research of Game AI plays an important role in promoting the development of the computer game industry.

Board game is one of the earliest objects that AI focused on [2, 3]. By contrast with other types of games, board games reflect human's intelligence more purely and thus attract the interest of AI researchers [4, 5]. At first, researchers concentrated on the algorithm design about the chess road searching and the chess manual matching and made some important progresses. John von Neumann presented the Minimax algorithm in 1920s [6]. Shannon [2] proposed the game tree searching algorithm with his chess program in 1950. Knuth and Moore deeply analyzed the alpha-beta pruning algorithm in 1958 [7]. Then, studies on AI in board games were widely launched [8–13]. Many contests of board games between machines and real persons showed the advances in AI research [14–16]. Recently, researchers find that game-logs (game records) cover a lot of important and interesting knowledge. Chen et al. [17] proposed an approach to abstract expert knowledge from annotated Chinese chess game records. GO game records are used for the life and death predicting, the pattern acquisition, and the pattern matching [18–20]. Esaki and Hashiyama [21] carried out some experiments to extract human players' strategies from the game records of Shogi. Weber and Mateas [22] used a data mining approach to process game-logs for the strategy prediction. Takeuchi et al. [23] presented a way of evaluating game tree search methods by game records. Moreover, Wender [24] expounded how to use data mining and machine learning techniques to analyze the game-logs in his project.

The common design of board games is to factitiously set the difficulty level on an invincible computer player, but this way is just a simulation. However, human players often expect a computer player to act and think as a real person rather than a superman. Game-logs in a board game are considered as cumulative experience, which will become richer and more effective with the increase of game times. With the accumulation of the experience, computer players can gradually enhance their intelligence level, just like human beings. Data mining techniques can be used to extract experience from game-logs. Nevertheless, there are few works on this topic.

In this paper, an approach is presented to mine experiential patterns from the growing game-logs of a sample board game. The computer player can learn from these patterns to improve its intelligence naturally. Firstly, a Chinese checkers game was designed as a test platform for collecting game-logs and launching empirical studies. Then, series of algorithms based on a sequence-tree were proposed to mine experiential patterns from game-logs. These patterns included Experience Rules, Key States, and Checker Usage. Finally, the mined patterns were applied back to the test platform, and then a series of experimental tests was elaborated to verify the effectiveness and performance of our approach.

Experimental results demonstrate that our approach is effective and efficient and easy to be transplanted to fit for other types of games.

## 2. Methods

The application of the experiential pattern mining requires two basic conditions listed below.

(i) The computer players of a game have the minimum ability to play the game correctly without any experiential pattern.

Doing so ensures that the game can run properly in the initial stage.

(ii) There are sufficient and valid game-logs to make the pattern mining task runnable.

Only when the number of game-logs reaches a certain size can the regularity hidden in them appear. In addition, our purpose is to make computer players learn from human players' strategies. So, these game-logs should be from human players' games.

To satisfy the above conditions, we designed a simplified Chinese checkers game as a test platform to provide the basic move algorithms and collect the game-logs. Subsequent sections cover the following topics in detail:

(a) the concepts concerned with the game and the mining algorithms;

(b) the algorithms for mining experiential patterns;

(c) the methods for applying experiential patterns to the game.

*2.1. Key Concepts.* The traditional Chinese checkers game has flexible gameplay (see [25] for more details). In this work, the game was simplified to be more convenient for experimenting (the design details are provided in Appendix). The key concepts used in the following sections are briefly explained below.

*(i) Checker.* The checker means the position used to put pieces on the chessboard. Each checker has its own coordinate.

*(ii) Checkers-State.* The checkers-state describes all the checkers on the chessboard and can be traversed to get or update the information of every checker.

*(iii) Piece.* Each player holds ten pieces. The coordinate of a piece is dependent on the current position of the piece.

*(iv) Pieces-State.* Pieces-states are used to store the coordinates of pieces. A pieces-state is a set that consists of several subsets. The number of the subsets depends on how many players are there in the game. Each subset contains ten elements, which correspond to the ten pieces of a player. For 2-player mode, there are two subsets, called the active side (SAS) and the passive side (SPS), respectively.

*(v) Game-Log.* During gaming, once a piece moves a step, the test platform will save the corresponding pieces-state to a game-log. The pieces-states in a game-log are sorted by their creation time. Hence, a game-log is a sequence of pieces-states. Separate XML files are used to store the game-logs.

*(vi) Experiential Pattern.* Experiential patterns are mined from game-logs and easily used by computer players. In this work, we considered three kinds of experiential patterns, including Experience Rule, Key State, and Checker Usage.

An Experience Rule is similar to an if-then rule. If pieces-state $PS_a$ appears, then the player should achieve the pieces-state $PS_b$ by moving a piece. The rule can be represented as $PS_a \rightarrow PS_b$, where $PS_a$ is called last state and $PS_b$ next state.

Key States are a group of particular pieces-states. They appear in victor games frequently and thus indicate some good game situation. By algorithm designing, one can help the computer player in approaching these Key States. Furthermore, approaching the Key States may also promote the applying of some Experience Rules, because some Key States may just be the last states or the next states.

Checker Usage describes the usage of a checker and is denoted by $CU$. The $CU$ of a checker can be calculated by

$$CU_C = \begin{cases} \dfrac{FC\_Count_C}{N}, & N > 0 \\ 1, & N = 0, \end{cases} \quad (1)$$

where $CU_C$ represents the $CU$ of checker $C$, $FC\_Count_C$ holds the times that $C$ has been used as the falling checker, and $N$ stores the number of game-logs in database.

*2.2. Mining Experiential Patterns.* By using some traditional move algorithms, the computer player may figure out the best move within several rounds. However, being subject to the computing capability of the computer and the requirement of game runtime, the computer player is hard to make more skillful moves or longer layouts. Humans improve their chess skill by accumulating the playing experience. A computer player can simulate this process to study experience from humans' excellent games and thus make the moves more strategic. The three experiential patterns introduced in Section 2.1 are mined from the game-logs generated in the games of human-human mode. The data mining process is run in server-side, and its workflow is shown in Figure 1.

TABLE 1: Attributes of the *PiecesState*.

| Attribute name | Description | Data type | Restrictions |
|---|---|---|---|
| ID | The ID of pieces-state. | Big integer | Unique, nonnull |
| SAS_0 | The coordinate of the first piece in active side. | Coordinate | Nonnull |
| SAS_1 | The coordinate of the second piece in active side. | Coordinate | Nonnull |
| ⋮ | ⋮ | ⋮ | ⋮ |
| SAS_9 | The coordinate of the tenth piece in active side. | Coordinate | Nonnull |
| SPS_0 | The coordinate of the first piece in passive side. | Coordinate | Nonnull |
| SPS_1 | The coordinate of the second piece in passive side. | Coordinate | Nonnull |
| ⋮ | ⋮ | ⋮ | ⋮ |
| SPS_9 | The coordinate of the tenth piece in passive side. | Coordinate | Nonnull |
| Count | The times this pieces-state appeared in victor games. | Big integer | Nonnull |

TABLE 2: Attributes of the *PiecesStateSequence*.

| Attribute name | Description | Data type | Restrictions |
|---|---|---|---|
| ID | The ID of the sequence. | Big integer | Unique, nonnull |
| SequenceStr | Sequential string. | Long text | Nonnull |

TABLE 3: Attributes of the *CheckerUsage*.

| Attribute name | Description | Data type | Restrictions |
|---|---|---|---|
| ID | Serialized ID | Big integer | Unique, nonnull |
| c | The coordinate of the falling checker | Coordinate | Nonnull |
| Times | The usage of the falling checker | Big integer | Nonnull |

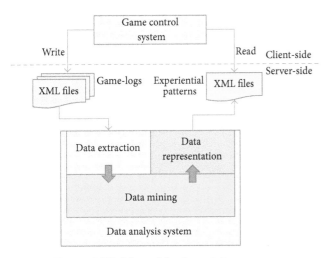

FIGURE 1: Workflow of the data mining process.

As shown in Figure 1, the data mining process consists of three phases, including data extraction, data mining, and data representation.

*2.2.1. Data Extraction.* Each game makes a single game-log file, and this will generate lots of XML files stored in server-side. These XML files are not suitable to be the direct data source of data mining. Therefore, the sequential data with consistent format needs to be extracted from game-logs and stored in database first.

Three data entities, *PiecesState*, *PiecesStateSequence*, and *CheckerUsage*, are used to format the game-logs. Their attributes are, respectively, shown in Tables 1, 2, and 3. The pieces-states in *PiecesState* are distinct, and each of them has a unique ID. The sequences in *PiecesStateSequence* are

repeatable, and each of them corresponds to a game-log. The tuples in *CheckerUsage* have the same number as the checkers on the chessboard.

Algorithm 1 describes the process of data extraction.

In Algorithm 1, lines (29)–(37) add a win/loss mark to the nondraw game and use minus to mark the pieces-states created by the loss player. Lines (38)–(41) combine all the PiecesState IDs from the same game into a single sequential string.

*2.2.2. Data Mining.* Experiential pattern mining means finding useful patterns from a large number of sequences composed of pieces-states. The types of these patterns include but are not limited to those mentioned in Section 2.1. Mining the Experience Rules, which are the most important experiential patterns in this work, is an objective of sequential pattern mining. Sequential pattern mining is a topic of data mining concerned with finding statistically relevant patterns between data examples where the values are delivered in a sequence [26]. In this field, many efforts of mining sequential patterns have been devoted to developing efficient algorithms, such as *GSP* [27], *SPADE* [28], *CloSpan* [29], *PrefixSpan* [30], and *MEMISP* [31]. In recent years, researchers have paid more attention to the applied research of sequential pattern mining as discussed elsewhere [32–36].

In this section, we describe the methods for mining the three kinds of experiential patterns explained in Section 2.1.

*Experience Rule.* Experience Rules describe the experience of the human players most directly. The problem of mining Experience Rules can be described as follows. Let $S$ be

**Procedure** *DataExtraction*
**Input:**
    *statesD*, the data table of PiecesState in database.
    *files*: the XML files of game-logs.
**Output:** Non.
**Method:**
(01) **let** *stateIds* be the set of PiecesState ids;
(02) **let** *file* be a file of game-log;
(03) **let** *statesF* be the set of the pieces-states extracted from game-logs;
(04) **let** *newStateId* be the new PiecesState id;
(05) **while** *files*.empty == **false do**
(06)    *file* = *files*.**getOne**(); //Read a game-log.
(07)    Extract the pieces-states from *file*, and save them to *statesF*;
(08)    Extract the game result from *file*, and save it to *result*;
(09)    **for** $i = 0$ **to** *statesF*.length $- 1$ **do**
(10)      //Get the sequence of ids of PiecesState.
(11)      *ifFound* = **false**;
(12)      Update the *times* field of CheckerUsage with *statesF*[*i*].
(13)      **for** $j = 0$ **to** *statesD*.length $- 1$ **do**
(14)        **if equal**(*statesF*[*i*], *statesD*[*j*].state) **then**
(15)         *stateIds*.**add**(*statesD*[*j*].id);
(16)         *isFound* = **true**;
(17)         count += result;
(18)         **break**;
(19)        **endif**
(20)      **endfor**
(21)      **if** *isFound* == **false then**
(22)        Insert *statesF*[*i*] into PiecesState;
(23)        count = result;
(24)        Save the new id to *newStateId*.
(25)        *stateIds*.**add**(*newStateId*);
(26)        *statesD*.**add**(*newStateId*, *statesF*[*i*]);
(27)      **endif**
(28)    **endfor**
(29)    **if** *result* != 0 **then**
(30)      $k = 1$;
(31)      **if** *result* == $-1$ **then**
(32)        $k = 0$;
(33)      **endif**
(34)      **for** $n = 0$ **to** *stateIds*.length $- 1$ **do**
(35)        *stateIds*[*n*] *= $(-1)$ ^ $((i - k) \% 2)$;
(36)      **endfor**
(37)    **endif**
(38)    *sequenceString* = *stateIds*[0];
(39)    **for** $p = 0$ **to** *stateIds*.length $- 1$ **do**
(40)      *sequenceString* += (":" + *stateIds*[*p*]);
(41)    **endfor**
(42)    Insert *sequenceString* into PiecesStateSequence;
(43)    **delete**(*file*); //Delete the current game-log.
(44) **endwhile**

ALGORITHM 1: *DataExtraction*.

a set of items, where each item is a sequence of pieces-states. Given a minimum support threshold *minSupport*, the aim is to find out all the consecutive binary subsequences (CBSSs) whose frequency is not less than *minSupport*. Each CBSS consists of two pieces-states that are consecutive in the original sequence, and this can be regarded as a constraint in data mining. In this paper, an algorithm based on pattern-growth is proposed for mining CBSSs. This algorithm uses a sequence-tree (see Figure 2) as the data structure to load all the sequences in database. The sequence-tree is different from the FP-tree [37] of frequent pattern mining, and we do not have to scan database previously to obtain the supports

**Procedure** *SequenceTreeCreation*
**Input**: *sequencesD*, the data table of PiecesStateSequence in database.
**Output**: *root*, the root node of the sequence-tree.
**Method**:
(01) **let** *stateIds* save the ids of PiecesState;
(02) *root* = **new** *Node*(*value* = 0, *branches* = null);
(03) **for** *i* = 0 **to** *sequencesD*.length − 1 **do**
(04)　　*stateIds* = *sequencesD*[*i*].sequenceStr.**split**(":");
(05)　　//Eliminate redundant pieces-state of stateIds.
(06)　　**for** *j* = *stateIds*.length − 1 **to** 2 **do**
(07)　　　**for** *k* = *j* − 2 **to** 0 **by** 2 **do**
(08)　　　　**if** *stateIds*[*j*] ==*stateIds*[*k*] **then**
(09)　　　　　*stateIds*.**delete**(*k* + 1, *j*);
(10)　　　　　*j* = *k*;
(11)　　　　**endif**
(12)　　　**endfor**
(13)　　**endfor**
(14)　　*node* = *root*;
(15)　　**for** *m* = 1 **to** *stateIds*.length − 1 **do**
(16)　　　**if** *node*.value == 0 **then**
(17)　　　　*node*.value = |*stateIds*[0]|;
(18)　　　**endif**
(19)　　　*isFound* = **false**;
(20)　　　**if** *node*.branches != **null then**
(21)　　　　**for** *n* = 0 **to** *node*.branches.length − 1 **do**
(22)　　　　　**if** *node*.branches[*n*].next.value == |*stateIds*[*m*]| **then**
(23)　　　　　　*node*.branches[*n*].weight += (*stateIds*[*m*]/|*stateIds*[*m*]|);
(24)　　　　　　*node* = *node*.branches[*n*].next;
(25)　　　　　　*isFound* = **true**;
(26)　　　　　　**break**;
(27)　　　　　**endif**
(28)　　　　**endfor**
(29)　　　**endif**
(30)　　　**if** *isFound* == **false then**
(31)　　　　*branch* = **new** *Branch*(
(32)　　　　　*weight* = *stateIds*[*m*]/|*stateIds*[*m*]|,
(33)　　　　　*next* = **new** *Node*(*value* = |*stateIds*[*m*]|, *branches* = **null**)
(34)　　　　);
(35)　　　　*node*.branches.**add**(*branch*);
(36)　　　　*node* = *node*.branches[*node*.branches.length − 1].next;
(37)　　　**endif**
(38)　　　//Merge the nodes of same values.
(39)　　　*BranchShifting*(*root*, *node*);
(40)　　**endfor**
(41) **endfor**
(42) **return** *root*;

ALGORITHM 2: *SequenceTreeCreation*.

of every pieces-state. Algorithm 2 describes the procedure of creating a sequence-tree.

In Figure 2, *value* stores the ID of the pieces-state, *weight* represents the support of the related CBSS, and *next* stores the linkage pointing to the next node.

On a certain player's perspective, if two same pieces-states appear, the moves between the two pieces-states will become noneffective interference data. Eliminating these data will reduce the unnecessary data analyses and improve the reliability of mining results (see lines (05)–(13) in Algorithm 2).

Not all the frequent CBSSs are good, since some of them may be from losing games. The support count of a CBSS denoted by *suppCount* can be calculated by

$$suppCount = posSuppCount - negSuppCount, \quad (2)$$

where *posSuppCount* is the support count of the CBSS generated in winning games and *negSuppCount* in losing games.

By means of the win/loss mark, the *suppCount* of each CBSS has been calculated during the process of creating the sequence-tree. Hence, the weight of each branch is

```
Procedure BranchShifting
Input:
    root, the root node of the sequence-tree.
    node, the pointer that points to the current node.
Output:
    Updated node.
    isShifted, the result of shifting.
Method:
(01) if node.value == root.value then
(02)    node = root;
(03)    return true;
(04) else
(05)    if root.branches == null then
(06)       return false;
(07)    else
(08)       for i = 0 to root.branches.length − 1 do
(09)          if BranchShifting(root.branches[i].next, node) == true then
(10)             return true;
(11)          endif
(12)       endfor
(13)       return false;
(14)    endif
(15) endif
```

ALGORITHM 3: *BranchShifting*.

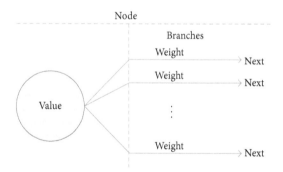

FIGURE 2: Data structure of a node on the sequence-tree.

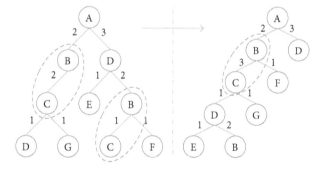

FIGURE 3: Branch shifting. The two pairs of nodes B-C marked with dotted circles on the left tree should be merged together, and their branch weights should be added up too. The right tree is the result of this branch shifting.

equal to the *suppCount* of the relevant CBSS. Moreover, the same pairs of nodes are not allowed to appear on the same sequence-tree; otherwise the *suppCount* values will be incomputable (as illustrated in Figure 3). To solve this problem, the algorithm for shifting branches is designed (see Algorithm 3).

To obtain the frequent CBSSs, the following formula is given:

$$supp = \frac{suppCount}{totalSeqs} \times 100\%, \qquad (3)$$

where *supp* denotes the support of a CBSS and *totalSeqs* denotes the total number of the sequences in database. Given a *minSupport*, the frequent CBSSs are those whose supports are not less than *minSupport*. All the frequent CBSSs can be found out by traversing the sequence-tree only once, and the script to do so is shown in Algorithm 4.

In Algorithm 4, the structure of the object SequentialPattern is shown in Figure 4. The found CBSSs will serve as the data source for selecting Experience Rules.

*Key State.* Given a threshold percentage *minFreq*, Key States are those pieces-states of the frequencies not less than *minFreq*. The frequency (denoted by *freq*) of a pieces-state can be calculated by

$$freq = \frac{count}{N} \times 100\%, \qquad (4)$$

where $N$ stores the total number of sequences in database and *count* denotes the occurrence number of the pieces-state in the net winning games. The value of *count* is figured out

```
Procedure CBSSFinding
Input:
    minSupport, the minimum support threshold.
    root, the root node of the sequence-tree.
    total: the total number of sequences.
    sps, the set of the found CBSSs.
Output:
    Updated sps.
Method:
(01) let supp be the support of a CBSS;
(02) let sp be the instance of SequentialPattern;
(03) if root.branches == null then
(04)    return;
(05) endif
(06) for i = 0 to root.branches.length − 1 do
(07)    supp = root.branches[i].weight/total;
(08)    if supp ≥ minSupport then
(09)       sp = new SequentialPattern();
(10)       sp.premise = root.value;
(11)       sp.result = root.branches[i].next.value;
(12)       sp.support = supp;
(13)       sps.add(sp);
(14)    endif
(15)    CBSSFinding(minSupport, root.branches[i].next, total, sps);
(16) endfor
```

ALGORITHM 4: *CBSSFinding*.

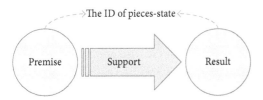

FIGURE 4: The structure of SequentialPattern.

during the process of data extraction (see lines (17) and (23) in Algorithm 1).

In respect of threshold selection, adjusting *minFreq* dynamically in accordance with the number of Experience Rules can make the Key States more efficient.

*Checker Usage.* This pattern can be calculated by formula (1), in which the $FC\_Count_C$ is figured out during the process of data extraction (see line (12) in Algorithm 1).

*2.2.3. Data Representation.* In this phase, the main task is to make the mined experiential patterns recognizable to the computer player. The experiential pattern here mainly refers to Experience Rule. The following format is used to represent an Experience Rule:

$$premise \longrightarrow result : support. \qquad (5)$$

According to the data structure of the Experience Rule, the process of data representation can be described as follows. Replace the IDs, which denote the last states or next states of

Experience Rules, with the corresponding pieces-states, and then write these pieces-states to an XML file in server-side.

However, the mined patterns may not be all reliable. For example, given a *minSupport*, the obtained Experience Rules are as follows:

$$PS_a \longrightarrow PS_b : 15\% \qquad PS_a \longrightarrow PS_c : 13\%$$
$$PS_a \longrightarrow PS_d : 17\%. \qquad (6)$$

That is, one last state has multiple next states. When pieces-state $PS_a$ appears, it is clearly reliable to select the pieces-state $PS_d$, which is of the highest *support*. Hence, the reliability selection should be done before data presentation. Algorithm 5 shows this process.

*2.3. Applying Experiential Patterns.* The way of applying experiential patterns depends on the specific gameplay. In this section, we give a computer player's strategy as shown in Figure 5 and then explain how to apply the mined experiential patterns to the actual game.

In the course of the game, the computer player uses Experience Rules first. Algorithm 6 demonstrates the procedure of matching Experience Rules.

When there are no available Experience Rules, the computer player will automatically approximate a certain Key State. Doing so can promote the formation of some good game situation and may activate some Experience Rules. Obviously, the approached Key State is the nearest pieces-state after the current one. So, all of the Key States are sorted

```
Procedure ReliabilitySelection
Input:
    minSupport, the minimum support threshold.
    total: the total number of sequences.
    sequencesD, the data table of PiecesStateSequence in database.
Output:
    sps, the set of reliable Experience Rules.
Method:
(01) root = CreatSequenceTree(sequencesD);
(02)    CBSSFinding(minSupport, root, total, sps);
(03) for i = 0 to sps.length − 2 do
(04)   for j = i + 1 to sps.length − 1 do
(05)     if sps[i].premise == sps[j].premise then
(06)       if sps[i].support < sps[j].support then
(07)         sps.delete(i);
(08)         i − −;
(09)         break;
(10)       else
(11)         sps.delete(j);
(12)         j − −;
(13)       endif
(14)     endif
(15)   endfor
(16) endfor
```

ALGORITHM 5: *ReliabilitySelection*.

by their occurrence time. Let $PS_a$ and $PS_b$ be two different pieces-states. Their order is defined below.

*Definition 1.* Assume that $PS_a \neq PS_b$. If $PS_a \cdot SAS \geq PS_b \cdot SAS$ and $PS_a \cdot SPS \geq PS_b \cdot SPS$, then $PS_a$ is behind $PS_b$, which can be expressed as $PS_a \geq PS_b$.

The concept of dissimilarity (denoted by *Diss*) is used to represent the closeness between two pieces-states. The *Diss* between $PS_a$ and $PS_b$ is equal to the least moves from $PS_a$ to $PS_b$. The less the value of *Diss*, the closer the two pieces-states. For calculating *Diss*, the following definitions are given.

*Definition 2.* Let $P$ be a piece and let $PS$ be a set of pieces-states. If the coordinate of $P$ is included in $PS$, then $P$ belongs to $PS$, which can be expressed as $P \in PS$.

*Definition 3.* Let $C_a$ and $C_b$ be two checkers, $(x_a, y_a)$ and $(x_b, y_b)$ their coordinates, respectively, and $x_a + y_a \geq x_b + y_b$. Then, the minimal number of steps for a move from $C_a$ to $C_b$ is called move distance from $C_a$ to $C_b$ and denoted by $MD_{ab}$, which can be calculated by

$$MD_{ab} = \varphi(x_a - x_b) + \varphi(y_a - y_b), \quad (7)$$

where the function $\varphi$ is defined as

$$\varphi(x) = \begin{cases} x, & x \geq 0 \\ 0, & x < 0. \end{cases} \quad (8)$$

*Definition 4.* Let $P_a$ and $P_b$ be two pieces, $C_a$ and $C_b$ their checkers, respectively, $PS_a$ and $PS_b$ two pieces-states,

$P_a \in PS_a \cdot SIS$, and $P_b \in PS_b \cdot SIS$. Then, the minimal number of steps for a move from $C_a$ to $C_b$ is called the Distance in Active Side between $P_a$ and $P_b$, which is denoted by $DAS_{ab}$. Similarly, one can define the Distance in Passive Side between $P_a$ and $P_b$, which is denoted by $DPS_{ab}$.

Algorithm 7 demonstrates the calculation of the distance between two pieces.

Let $PS_a$ and $PS_b$ be two pieces-states. According to Definitions 2–4, the dissimilarity matrices between $PS_a$ and $PS_b$ are defined as follows:

$$\begin{aligned} DissMatrixAS &= \begin{bmatrix} DAS_{00} & \cdots & DAS_{09} \\ \vdots & \ddots & \vdots \\ DAS_{90} & \cdots & DAS_{99} \end{bmatrix} \\ DissMatrixPS &= \begin{bmatrix} DPS_{00} & \cdots & DPS_{09} \\ \vdots & \ddots & \vdots \\ DPS_{90} & \cdots & DPS_{99} \end{bmatrix}, \end{aligned} \quad (9)$$

where *DissMatrixAS* is defined on the active side and *DissMatrixPS* on the passive side. Then, the *Diss* between two pieces can be calculated by

$$Diss = \min\left( \sum_{a=0}^{9} \sum_{b=0}^{9} DAS_{ab} X_{ab} + \sum_{a=0}^{9} \sum_{b=0}^{9} DPS_{ab} Y_{ab} \right), \quad (10)$$

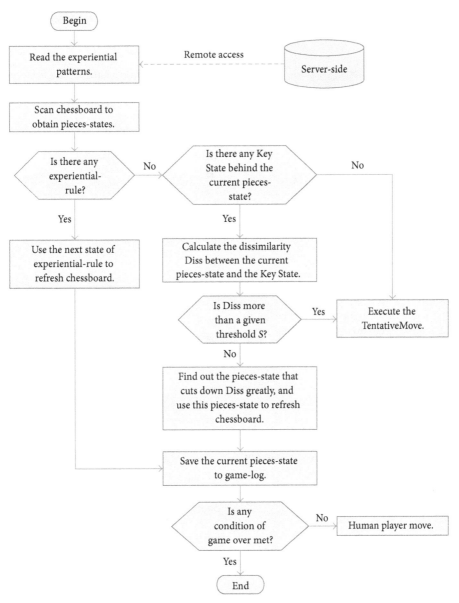

FIGURE 5: Strategy of the computer player.

where $X_{ab}$ and $Y_{ab}$ satisfy the following conditions, respectively:

$$\sum_{a=0}^{9} X_{ab} = 1$$

$$\sum_{b=0}^{9} X_{ab} = 1$$

$$a, b = 0, 1, 2, \ldots, 9$$

$$X_{ab} = 0, 1,$$

$$\sum_{a=0}^{9} Y_{ab} = 1$$

$$\sum_{b=0}^{9} Y_{ab} = 1$$

$$a, b = 0, 1, 2, \ldots, 9$$

$$Y_{ab} = 0, 1.$$

$$(11)$$

It follows that the calculation of the *Diss* between pieces is a typical assignment problem in linear programming. This problem can be solved by *Hungarian* algorithm as discussed by Edmonds [38].

When there are no Key States behind the current pieces-state or the *Diss* between the nearest Key State and the current pieces-state is more than a given threshold, the computer

```
Procedure ExperienceRuleMatching
Input:
    PS, the current pieces-state.
    ERs: the set of Experience Rules.
Output:
    nextPS, the next pieces-state.
Method:
(01) for each er in ERs do
(02)    if PS == er.last then
(03)        nextPS = er.next;
(04)        break;
(05)    else
(06)        nextPS = null;
(07)    endif
(08) endfor
```

ALGORITHM 6: *ExperienceRuleMatching.*

TABLE 4: Data records of the test in human-computer mode without any experiential pattern.

| Tester | Gts | Role | Wts | Anrs | Wr (%) |
|---|---|---|---|---|---|
| 00 | 15 | OffP | 5 | 45 | 33.33 |
| 00 | 15 | DefP | 4 | 42 | 26.67 |
| 01 | 15 | OffP | 5 | 47 | 33.33 |
| 01 | 15 | DefP | 3 | 45 | 20.00 |
| 02 | 15 | OffP | 4 | 44 | 26.67 |
| 02 | 15 | DefP | 1 | 40 | 6.67 |
| 03 | 15 | OffP | 3 | 45 | 20.00 |
| 03 | 15 | DefP | 2 | 41 | 13.33 |
| 04 | 15 | OffP | 4 | 42 | 26.67 |
| 04 | 15 | DefP | 4 | 47 | 26.67 |
| 05 | 15 | OffP | 4 | 44 | 26.67 |
| 05 | 15 | DefP | 1 | 40 | 6.67 |
| 06 | 15 | OffP | 6 | 49 | 40.00 |
| 06 | 15 | DefP | 4 | 42 | 26.67 |
| 07 | 15 | OffP | 2 | 37 | 13.33 |
| 07 | 15 | DefP | 2 | 36 | 13.33 |
| 08 | 15 | OffP | 6 | 45 | 40.00 |
| 08 | 15 | DefP | 3 | 45 | 20.00 |
| 09 | 15 | OffP | 5 | 45 | 33.33 |
| 09 | 15 | DefP | 2 | 40 | 13.33 |

Note: Gts: game times; Role: role of the computer player; Wts: winning times of the computer player; Anrs: average number of the rounds per game; and Wr: winning rate of the computer player.

player will execute a tentative move algorithm named *TentativeMove*, which was designed based on the traditional alpha-beta pruning algorithm [7] (see Appendix for more details). Moreover, the pattern Checker Usage is one of the parameters of *TentativeMove*.

## 3. Results and Discussions

In order to evaluate the effect and performance of our proposed approach, we conducted an experiment on our designed test platform mentioned in Section 2. The experiment contains a series of tests. To maintain the objectivity of the experiment, we chose the same group of testers, who are ten experienced human players.

*3.1. Test in Human-Computer Mode without any Experiential Patterns.* Each tester played against the computer player for 30 games, serving as offensive player (OffP) and defensive player (DefP) alternately. The computer player was only allowed to use *TentativeMove* using a default value of Checker Usage as the parameter. A total of 300 game-logs in this test were recorded. The test results are shown in Table 4.

Furthermore, we observed the performance of our algorithms by using the parameter ATMC (the average time for each move of the computer player). A script embedded into the program was used to calculate the response time of the computer player during testing and give the value of ATMC in the end. In this test, the value of ATMC was 5.85 s (s = seconds).

*Descriptions of Effects.* (a) The computer player has the ability to play correctly; (b) the winning rate of the computer player in competition with every tester is not more than a half; (c) the computer player spends a little long time to move a piece.

*Discussions.* (a) Condition (i) mentioned at the beginning of Section 2 is satisfied by the TentativeMove algorithm; (b) the moves driven by TentativeMove may not be optimal due to the error of its evaluation function and the restraint

of searching depth, which affects the winning rate of the computer player; (c) TentativeMove has a deeper recursion depth. As the game goes on, the checkers to be searched in each recursive layer will increase rapidly, which degrades the performance of TentativeMove.

*3.2. Test in Human-Human Mode for Collecting Game-Logs.* Each tester played with all the others for 30 games, serving as OffP and DefP alternately. A total of 1350 game-logs in this test were recorded. This satisfied condition (ii) mentioned at the beginning of Section 2. Subsequently, additional tests in human-computer mode were performed to select the appropriate *minSupport* and *minFreq*. These tests were similar to those in Section 3.1, and the results are shown in Table 5. Finally, the experiential pattern mining program was executed with the selected *minSupport* and *minFreq*. As a result, we gained 528 Experience Rules and 575 Key States, and the Checker Usage of every checker was updated in real time.

As shown in Table 5, when *minSupport* was 2% and *minFreq* was 1%, the crest value of *Auep* was reached, which meant the mined experiential patterns were better utilized.

*3.3. Test in Human-Computer Mode with Experiential Patterns.* The test plan here was the same as that in Section 3.1, except for the applying of the experiential patterns obtained in the test mentioned in Section 3.2. The results are shown in Table 6, and the comparison with the test results in Section 3.1

**Procedure** *PiecesDistanceCalculation*

**Input**:

    *PS*, the current pieces-state.

    $P_a$, piece $P_a$.

    $P_b$, piece $P_b$.

**Output**:

    *Dab*, the distance between $P_a$ and $P_b$.

**Method**:

(01) **let** *CS* be the checkers-state;

(02) **let** *vAllFC* be a vector to store the falling checkers of every layer.

(03) //The maximum distance between $P_a$ and $P_b$.

(04) Calculate the move distance *MDab*;

(05) **if** *MDab* == 0 **or** *MDab* == 1 **or** *MDab* == 2 **then**

(06)    //If MDab is less than 3, there is no less distance.

(07)    **return** *MDab*;

(08) **endif**

(09) **for** $i = 0$ **to** 9 **do**

(10)    $CS[PS \cdot SAS[i] \cdot x][PS \cdot SAS[i] \cdot y] = 1;$

(11)    $CS[PS \cdot SPS[i] \cdot x][PS \cdot SPS[i] \cdot y] = -1;$

(12) **endfor**

(13) *FindVirtualFallingCheckers*(0, *CS*, $P_a \cdot x$, $P_a \cdot y$, **true**, *vAllFC*, 0);

(14) *isBreak* = **false**; //Denotes the end of searching.

(15) *Dab* = *MDab*; //The distance in the worst case.

(16) **for each** *allFC* **in** *vAllFC* **do**

(17)   **for each** *c* **in** *allFC* **do**

(18)     **if** *allFC*.index == (*MDab* − 1) **then**

(19)      *isBreak* = **true**; **break**;

(20)     **endif**

(21)     **if** $c \cdot x == P_b \cdot x$ **and** $c \cdot y == P_b \cdot y$ **then**

(22)      *Dab* = *allFC*.index + 1; *isBreak* = **true**;

(23)      **break**;

(24)     **endif**

(25)     **if** *allFC*.index == (*MDab* − 2) **then break**; **endif**

(26)     *FindVirtualFallingCheckers*(0, *CS*, $c \cdot x$, $c \cdot y$, **true**, *vAllFC*, *allFC*.index + 1);

(27)   **endfor**

(28)   **if** *isBreak* == **true then break**; **endif**

(29) **endfor**

(30) **return** *Dab*;

(31) //Search the virtual falling checkers of specified checkers.

(32) **Function** *FindVirtualFallingCheckers*(*d*, *CS*, *x*, *y*, *isFirstStep*, *vAllFC*, *index*)

(33) **begin**

(34)   **for** $i = 3$ **to** $-3$ **do**

(35)     **if** $i == -d$ **then continue**; **endif**

(36)     **if** $i == 0$ **then continue**; **endif**

(37)     Search the next jumping falling checker $(x', y')$ in direction *i* of checker $(x, y)$.

(38)     **if** $(x', y')$ exists **then**

(39)      *vAllFC*[*index*].***add***(**new** *Coordinate*$(x', y')$);

(40)      *FindVirtualFallingCheckers*(3, *CS*, $x'$, $y'$, **false**, *vAllFC*, *index*);

(41)     **else if** the piece on $(x', y')$ is of own side **then**

(42)      *FindVirtualFallingCheckers*(3, *CS*, $x'$, $y'$, **true**, *vAllFC*, *index* + 1);

(43)     **else**

(44)      **if** *isFirstStep* == **true then**

(45)       *vAllFC*[*index*].***add***(**new** *Coordinate*$(x', y')$);

(46)      **endif**

(47)     **endif**

(48)   **endfor**

(49) **end**

ALGORITHM 7: *PiecesDistanceCalculation*.

TABLE 5: Data records of the additional tests for selecting thresholds. A total of 1650 game-logs were used as the data source.

| Gts | Ms (%) | Mf (%) | Ner | Nks | Anep | Auep (%) |
|---|---|---|---|---|---|---|
| 15 | 10 | 5 | 113 | 160 | 4 | 1.47 |
| 15 | 8 | 4 | 275 | 323 | 11 | 1.84 |
| 15 | 6 | 3 | 386 | 421 | 15 | 1.86 |
| 15 | 4 | 2 | 460 | 512 | 19 | 1.95 |
| **15** | **2** | **1** | **528** | **575** | **26** | **2.36** |
| 15 | 1 | 0.5 | 582 | 649 | 26 | 2.11 |
| 15 | 0.5 | 0.25 | 638 | 691 | 27 | 2.03 |
| 15 | 0.25 | 0.125 | 690 | 743 | 28 | 1.95 |

Note: Gts: game times; Ms: minSupport; Mf: minFreq; Ner: number of Experience Rules; Nks: number of Key States; Anep: average number of experiential patterns used in each game; and Auep: average usage of experiential patterns per game.

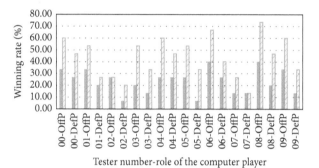

Tester number-role of the computer player

▨ Winning rates of the computer player not using experiential pattern
▨ Winning rates of the computer player using experiential patterns

FIGURE 6: Comparison of the winning rates of the computer player.

is illustrated in Figure 6. In this test, the value of ATMC was 0.93 s.

*Descriptions of Effects.* (a) Figure 6 shows that, by using experiential patterns, the computer player has increased its winning rates in most of the games at different degrees; (b) the average number of the rounds per game has increased; (c) the value of ATMC has declined dramatically.

*Discussions.* (a) The effectiveness of experiential patterns will become more obvious with the increase of game-logs, and this will give the human players an impression that the computer player is learning from the experience; (b) in a few games such as 02-OffP and 07-DefP shown in Figure 6, although the computer player's winning rates are not increased, the average number of the rounds per game is greatly raised (see the lines with bold font shown in Table 6). The testers obviously feel the improvement of the computer player's chess skill; (c) if the Experience Rules exist, the computer player will match and use them first. Compared with TentativeMove, the pattern matching algorithm is of linear complexity and consumes less time (see Algorithm 6).

*3.4. Test in Computer-Computer Mode.* In this test, we set two computer players. One could use the experiential patterns

TABLE 6: Data records of the test in human-computer mode with experiential patterns.

| Tester | Gts | Role | Wts | Anrs | Wr (%) |
|---|---|---|---|---|---|
| 00 | 15 | OffP | 9 | 51 | 60.00 |
| 00 | 15 | DefP | 7 | 51 | 46.67 |
| 01 | 15 | OffP | 8 | 52 | 53.33 |
| 01 | 15 | DefP | 4 | 54 | 26.67 |
| **02** | **15** | **OffP** | **4** | **56** | **26.67** |
| 02 | 15 | DefP | 3 | 50 | 20.00 |
| 03 | 15 | OffP | 8 | 51 | 53.33 |
| 03 | 15 | DefP | 5 | 49 | 33.33 |
| 04 | 15 | OffP | 9 | 54 | 60.00 |
| 04 | 15 | DefP | 7 | 52 | 46.67 |
| 05 | 15 | OffP | 8 | 52 | 53.33 |
| 05 | 15 | DefP | 5 | 48 | 33.33 |
| 06 | 15 | OffP | 10 | 56 | 66.67 |
| 06 | 15 | DefP | 6 | 50 | 40.00 |
| 07 | 15 | OffP | 4 | 48 | 26.67 |
| **07** | **15** | **DefP** | **2** | **51** | **13.33** |
| 08 | 15 | OffP | 11 | 52 | 73.33 |
| 08 | 15 | DefP | 7 | 52 | 46.67 |
| 09 | 15 | OffP | 9 | 52 | 60.00 |
| 09 | 15 | DefP | 5 | 50 | 33.33 |

Note: Gts: game times; Role: role of the computer player; Wts: winning times of the computer player; Anrs: average number of the rounds per game; and Wr: winning rate of the computer player.

TABLE 7: Data records of the test in computer-computer mode. The computer player using experience patterns is denoted by CP1 and the other by CP2.

| Player | Wts | Anep | ATMC (s) | Wr (%) |
|---|---|---|---|---|
| CP1 | 56 | 26 | 0.91 | 93.33 |
| CP2 | 4 | 0 | 5.77 | 6.67 |

Note: Wts: winning times; Anep: average number of experiential patterns used in each game; ATMC: value of ATMC; and Wr: winning rate.

and the other could not. They took turns to serve as OffP and played with each other for 30 games. The results are shown in Table 7.

*Description of the Effect.* The computer player using experience patterns has a great advantage in winning rate and ATMC.

*Discussion.* Experiential patterns can help the computer player in making more strategic moves; still, we are aware of four losing games of CP1 (as shown in Table 7). This indicates that some of the experiential patterns may not be really good. However, the invalid patterns will die out with the growth of game-logs.

*3.5. Comparative Analysis on the Algorithms of Pattern Mining.* A sequence database consists of sequences of ordered elements, and these elements contain some unordered items. The common objectives of the previous works [27–31] are

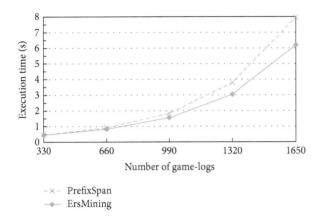

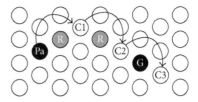

FIGURE 8: Single-piece-jump. Pa can jump to C1, C2, and C3.

FIGURE 7: Performance of the two algorithms on a given data set. *ErsMining* denotes the set of algorithms, including *Sequence-TreeCreation*, *BranchShifting*, *CBSSFinding*, and *ReliabilitySelection*, for mining Experience Rules.

to find the interesting relations between these items. In this work, however, the pattern mining algorithms aim at finding only the frequent CBSSs in the game-logs. This can be considered as a special case of the sequential pattern mining on a sequence database. For ease of comparison, we implemented the traditional algorithm *PrefixSpan* and added some restraints to make it fit for mining in our game-logs. These restraints were (a) setting length of each subsequence to 2 and (b) setting size of each element to 1. The comparative results are shown in Figure 7.

Here the minSupport was set to 2%, and the given data set contained 1,650 sequences (i.e., game-logs), 155,100 elements (i.e., pieces-states). Figure 7 indicates that our algorithms compared with *PrefixSpan* are more efficient.

*3.6. Discussion on the Using of Game-Logs.* Previous works [17–24] mainly discuss the methods of extracting expert knowledge from game records. The extracted knowledge is commonly used to construct a game agent of high intelligence. Differently, our work aims at helping a computer player in learning from growing game-logs, acquiring human's experience, and gradually becoming more skillful. It is a practical approach to make the game more fascinating. Furthermore, by satisfying the two conditions mentioned at the beginning of Section 2, any board game can utilize this approach after a minor adjustment. And this shows the extensibility of our approach.

## 4. Conclusions

In this paper, a novel approach is proposed to mine experiential patterns from the game-logs of board game. Those experiential patterns can be utilized to improve the intelligence of a computer player. This approach makes computer players learn from human's experience progressively during gaming and become more experienced with the increase of game-logs. This will make the game more interesting. We conducted an experiment on our designed test platform of Chinese checkers game, and the results demonstrate that our approach is effective, efficient, and extensible.

Nevertheless, our approach still needs improvements from several aspects, such as the following:

(i) designing algorithms to automatically adjust the parameters *minSupport* and *minFreq*;

(ii) optimizing the related algorithms to improve their access performance for a huge sequence-tree;

(iii) researching the fast matching problem in massive experiential patterns;

(iv) developing the approach for online analysis of game-logs;

(v) looking for more experiential patterns making games interesting.

## Appendix

*(1) Rules and Data Structures.* The rules and data structures used for programming are described as follows.

(i) Only use the 2-player mode.

(ii) Move rules: there are two move rules, shift and jump. The shift means moving a single piece one step in any direction to an adjacent empty checker. The jump here means single-piece-jump, which is the simplest and most usual rule. An example of single-piece-jump is shown in Figure 8.

(iii) Checker: a computer can get the complete appearance of a game by scanning all the checkers on the chessboard. A checker has three properties including *color*, *position*, and *status*. The *color* stores a hexadecimal number to represent the color of the piece on the checker. The *position* stores the coordinate of the checker. The *status* uses the values of 1, −1, and 0 to describe who is on the checker.

(iv) Chessboard: for the convenience of programming, the chessboard is designed to fit for 2-player mode. That means the other four useless star corners on traditional chessboard are cut out (as illustrated in Figure 9).

We used a coordinate system to locate the positions on the chessboard. This coordinate system is unfixed and has an included angle of 60°. Players have their own frames of axes with the same form (as shown in Figure 10). This design has two advantages. First,

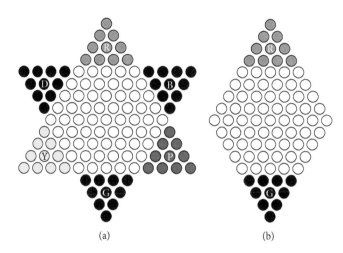

FIGURE 9: Chessboard. (a) The traditional chessboard. (b) The simplified chessboard without the useless star corners.

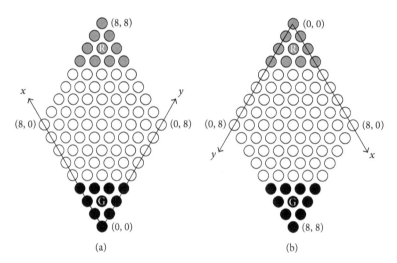

FIGURE 10: Unfixed coordinate system. The frames of axes in (a) and (b) are used by green and red player, respectively.

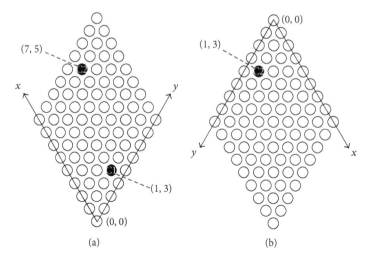

FIGURE 11: Every checker has two coordinates due to different frames of axes. For example, checkers C1 in (a) and C2 in (b) have the same coordinate. The two coordinates of checker C2 are (7, 5) and (1, 3), respectively.

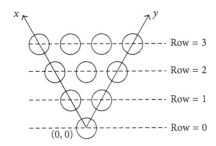

FIGURE 12: Parameter row.

the space of the coordinate system is utilized sufficiently. Secondly, the coordinate discrepancy between checkers is eliminated naturally.

Unavoidably, the unfixed coordinate system causes a checker to have dual coordinates (as shown in Figure 11).

To solve this problem, it is necessary to consider one of the two frames of axes as the reference, which is called normal frame of axes (NFoA). The other one called reverse frame of axes (RFoA) can be converted to the NFoA with

$$(x, y) \begin{cases} x = 8 - x' \\ y = 8 - y'. \end{cases} \quad (A.1)$$

In formula (A.1), $(x, y)$ and $(x', y')$ are the coordinates in NFoA and RFoA, respectively.

(v) Row: the *row* means the vertical distance from current checker to the origin of the coordinate system (as illustrated in Figure 12). For checker $C(x, y)$, the following equation holds:

$$row = C \cdot x + C \cdot y. \quad (A.2)$$

(vi) FD: the *FD* represents the distance moved forward by a piece. It can be calculated by

$$FD = rowFC - rowSC, \quad (A.3)$$

where *rowFC* is the row of the falling checker and *rowSC* is the row of the starting checker. For example, if a player moves a piece from (1, 3) to (5, 6) in one step, then the *FD* of this move is 7 (as illustrated in Figure 13). Note that the *FD* is negative when moving a piece backward.

(vii) Checkers-state: the checkers-state is an integer two-dimensional array. The subscripts and values of the checkers-state represent the coordinates and statuses of the corresponding checkers, respectively.

(viii) Piece: it is time consuming to scan all the 81 checkers at runtime. But on the contrary, there are only 20 pieces in a game. Scanning these pieces is efficient. The piece has the same properties as the checker.

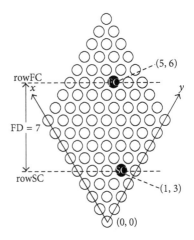

FIGURE 13: Parameter FD.

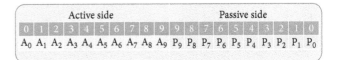

FIGURE 14: Logical expression of the pieces-state.

(ix) Pieces-state: a pieces-state is a special set consisting of two subsets; one is active side and the other is passive side. Each subset has ten elements representing the coordinates of pieces as illustrated in Figure 14. In active side, the coordinates belong to the pieces of the player whose last move has led to this pieces-state. These pieces are sorted by their row values in ascending order (sorted by $y$-axis when they are in the same row). The situation in passive side is just the opposite.

The pieces-state can be formally defined as follows:

$$Pieces\text{-}state = \{SAS, SPS\}$$

SAS

$= \{A_n \mid A_n \text{ is the coordinate of piece } n \text{ in active side,}$

$\quad n \in [0, 9]\}$

SPS

$= \{P_n \mid P_n \text{ is the coordinate of piece } n \text{ in passive side,}$

$\quad n \in [0, 9]\}. \quad (A.4)$

By using formula (A.1), a pieces-state in RFoA can be easily transposed to that in NFoA.

*(2) Gameplay.* A set of computer programs is designed to control the gameplay and save the game-logs automatically. For different purposes, the game provides three play modes described as follows.

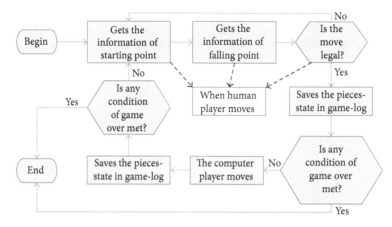

FIGURE 15: Gameplay of the human-human mode.

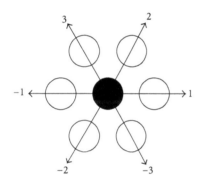

FIGURE 16: Searching directions.

TABLE 8: The calculations in different directions.

| Direction ID | Coordinate of current position | Coordinate of the next position |
|---|---|---|
| 3 | $(x, y)$ | $(x + 1, y)$ |
| 2 | $(x, y)$ | $(x, y + 1)$ |
| 1 | $(x, y)$ | $(x - 1, y + 1)$ |
| −1 | $(x, y)$ | $(x + 1, y - 1)$ |
| −2 | $(x, y)$ | $(x, y - 1)$ |
| −3 | $(x, y)$ | $(x - 1, y)$ |

surrounding directions. So, the term searching direction is defined (as illustrated in Figure 16).

The features of searching direction are listed below.

(i) There is no direction 0.

(ii) The IDs of opposite directions can be changed to each other by picking minus.

(iii) The checkers in a certain direction can be found by adjusting the coordinates. Table 8 shows the calculations in every direction.

According to the three features, all checkers can be traversed recursively.

The solution to Problem 2 is described in Algorithm 9.

To solve Problem 3, we provide an algorithm based on the traditional alpha-beta pruning method (see Algorithm 10).

In Algorithm 10, the evaluation function is formally defined as follows:

$$\text{evaf}\,(FD, CU, FC\_Incre),\qquad(A.5)$$

where $CU$ denotes the Checker Usage of the falling checker and $FC\_Incre$ denotes the number of increased legal falling checkers arising out of a move. Negative $FC\_Incre$ means that the number of falling checkers has decreased. Then, a simple evaluation function is given below:

$$\text{eva} = (FD + FC\_Incre) * (1 + CU).\qquad(A.6)$$

(i) Human-human mode: this mode is mainly used to collect the experience from humans. All the players in this mode are real persons.

(ii) Computer-computer mode: this mode is only used for carrying out experiments. All the players in this mode are controlled by the computer programs.

(iii) Human-computer mode: in this mode, a human player is allowed to play against the computer player, and the game-logs are also collected. This mode is in charge of effect analysis.

Taking the human-human mode as an example, the gameplay is shown in Figure 15. And the other two play modes can be designed in a similar way.

In the gameplay, there are three problems to be solved.

*Problem 1.* It is to find out all the falling checkers related to the specified starting checker.

*Problem 2.* It is to determine the legality of a move.

*Problem 3.* It is to make the computer player have the ability to move spontaneously.

The solution to Problem 1 is described in Algorithm 8.

In Algorithm 8, $d$ denotes the searching direction. According to the game rules, a piece can be moved in six

**Procedure** *FindFallingCheckers*

**Input**:
    $d$, the direction that will be searched in.
    $PS$, the specified pieces-state.
    $x$, the $x$-coordinate of starting checker.
    $y$, the $y$-coordinate of starting checker.
    $isFS$, whether it is the first step.
    $allFC$: the array for collecting falling checkers.
**Output**: Updated *allFC*.
**Method**:
(01) **for** $i = 3$ **to** $-3$ **do**
(02)   //Don't search the repeated falling checker.
(03)   **if** $i == -d$ **then continue**; **endif**
(04)   //Don't search the direction 0.
(05)   **if** $i == 0$ **then continue**; **endif**
(06)   Search the next jumping falling checker $(x', y')$ in direction $i$ of checker $(x, y)$.
(07)   **if** $(x', y')$ exists **then**
(08)     *allFC*.**add**(**new** *Coordinate*$(x', y')$);
(09)     *FindFallingCheckers*$(3, PS, x', y', allFC, $**false**$)$;
(10)   **else**
(11)     **if** $isFS == $**true then**
(12)       *allFC*.**add**(**new** *Coordinate*$(x', y')$);
(13)     **endif**
(14)   **endif**
(15) **endfor**
(16) **return** *allFC*;

ALGORITHM 8: *FindFallingCheckers*.

**Procedure** *LegalityDetermination*

**Input**:
    $PS$, the initial pieces-state.
    $cSC$: the coordinate of starting checker.
    $cFC$: the coordinate of falling checker.
**Output**:
    **True** means legal, and **false** not legal.
    Updated *PS*.
**Method**:
(01) **let** $CS$ be the checkers-state;
(02) **for** $i = 0$ **to** 9 **do**
(03) //Initialize the checkers-state from pieces-state.
(04)   $CS[PS{\cdot}SAS[i]{\cdot}x][PS{\cdot}SAS[i]{\cdot}y] = 1$;
(05)   $CS[PS{\cdot}SPS[i]{\cdot}x][PS{\cdot}SPS[i]{\cdot}y] = -1$;
(06) **endfor**
(07) *FindFallingCheckers*$(0, CS, cSC{\cdot}x, cSC{\cdot}y, allFC, $**true**$)$;
(08) **for each** *Coordinate* **in** *allFC* **do**
(09)   **if** $cFC == $*Coordinate* **then**
(10)     Update $PS$ with $cSC$ and $cFC$;
(11)     **return true**;
(12)   **endif**
(13) **endfor**
(14) **return false**;

ALGORITHM 9: *LegalityDetermination*.

**Procedure** *TentativeMove*
**Input**:
    *steps*, the steps will be searched.
    *PS*: the initial pieces-state.
    *isFL*: whether it is the first level of recursion.
**Output**:
    *maxEva*: the maximum value of evaluation.
**Method**:
(01) **let** *allFC* be the set of falling checkers' coordinates;
(02) **let** *cSC* be the coordinate of starting checker;
(03) **let** *cFC* be the coordinate of falling checker;
(04) **let** *CS* be the checkers-state;
(05) **let** the elements of *CS* be equal to 0;
(06) **for** $i = 0$ **to** 9 **do**
(07)   //Obtain the checkers-state from pieces-state.
(08)   $CS[PS \cdot SAS[i] \cdot x][PS \cdot SAS[i] \cdot y] = 1$;
(09)   $CS[PS \cdot SPS[i] \cdot x][PS \cdot SPS[i] \cdot y] = -1$;
(10) **endfor**
(11) *maxEva* = **−Infinity**;
(12) *steps* - -;
(13) **for** $i = 0$ **to** 9 **do**
(14)   //Evaluate all moves by Depth First Search.
(15)   *copyCS* = **clone**(*CS*);
(16)   **FindFallingCheckers**(0, *copyCS*, $PS \cdot SAS[i] \cdot x$, $PS \cdot SAS[i] \cdot y$, *allFC*, **true**);
(17)   **for each** *FC* **in** *allFC* **do**
(18)     $FD = (FC \cdot x + FC \cdot y) - (PS \cdot SAS[i] \cdot x + PS \cdot SAS[i] \cdot y)$;
(19)     Calculate *FC_Incre*;
(20)     Query *CU*;
(21)     $thisEva = (FD + FC\_Incre) * (1 + CU)$;
(22)     **if** *steps* > 0 **and** *isFL* == **true then**
(23)       *copyPS* = **clone**(*PS*);
(24)       Update *copyPS* with $PS \cdot SAS[i]$ and *FC*.
(25)       **PiecesStateTransposition**(*copyPS*);
(26)       *thisEva* = *thisEva* − **TentativeMove**(*Steps*, *copyPS*, **false**);
(27)     **endif**
(28)     **if** *thisEva* > *maxEva* **then**
(29)       *maxEva* = *thisEva*;
(30)       *cSC* = $PS \cdot SAS[i]$;
(31)       *cFC* = *FC*;
(32)     **endif**
(33)   **endfor**
(34) **endfor**
(35) **if** *isFL* == **true then**
(36)   Update *PS* with *cSC* and *cFC*;
(37) **else if** *steps* > 0 **then**
(38)   *copyPS* = **clone**(*PS*);
(39)   Update *copyPS* with $PS \cdot SAS[i]$ and *FC*;
(40)   **PiecesStateTransposition**(*copyPS*);
(41)   *maxEva* = *maxEva* − **TentativeMove** (*Steps*, *copyPS*, **false**);
(42) **endif**
(43) **return** *maxEva*;

ALGORITHM 10: *TentativeMove*.

Formula (A.6) is based on the following reasons:

the longer the forward distance, the better the move;

the more the generated falling checkers, the better the move;

the higher the Checker Usage of the falling checker, the better the move.

To reduce the error of the evaluation function and ensure its execution efficiency, an appropriate value of *steps* is given. During these steps, a computer player alternately enacts both sides' players to move, and the evaluation values of every move are recorded. Then, the algorithm calculates the difference of the sum of evaluation values between its own side and the opponent's and selects the move with the maximum difference. Through testing, we set *steps* to 11 and obtained effect preferably.

# Acknowledgments

This work is supported by the Scientific Research Foundation of Hebei Education Department (Grant no. Z2012147), the Natural Science Foundation of Hebei Province (Grant no. F2014201100), and the Soft Science Research Program of Hebei Province (Grant no. 14450318D).

# References

[1] A. El Rhalibi, K. W. Wong, and M. Price, "Artificial intelligence for computer games," *International Journal of Computer Games Technology*, vol. 2009, Article ID 251652, 3 pages, 2009.

[2] C. E. Shannon, "Programming a computer for playing chess," *Philosophical Magazine*, vol. 41, no. 7, pp. 256–275, 1950.

[3] A. M. Turing, "Computing machinery and intelligence," *Mind*, vol. 59, no. 49, pp. 433–460, 1950.

[4] A. L. Samuel, "Some studies in machine learning using the game of checkers," *International Business Machines Corporation*, vol. 3, pp. 211–229, 1959.

[5] A. L. Samuel, "Some studies in machine learning using the game of checkers II—recent progress," *IBM Journal of Research and Development*, no. 11, pp. 601–617, 1967.

[6] T. H. Kjeldsen, "John von Neumann's conception of the minimax theorem: a journey through different mathematical contexts," *Archive for History of Exact Sciences*, vol. 56, no. 1, pp. 39–68, 2001.

[7] D. E. Knuth and R. W. Moore, "An analysis of alpha-beta pruning," vol. 6, no. 4, pp. 293–326, 1975.

[8] J. R. Slagle and R. C. T. Lee, "Application of game tree searching techniques to sequential pattern recognition," *Communications of the ACM*, vol. 14, no. 2, pp. 103–110, 1971.

[9] J. Pearl, "Asymptotic properties of minimax trees and game-searching procedures," *Artificial Intelligence*, vol. 14, no. 2, pp. 113–138, 1980.

[10] R. L. Rivest, "Game tree searching by min/max approximation," *Artificial Intelligence*, vol. 34, no. 1, pp. 77–96, 1987.

[11] L. W. Li and T. A. Marsland, "Probability-based game tree pruning," *Journal of Algorithms*, vol. 11, no. 1, pp. 27–43, 1990.

[12] M. Levene and T. I. Fenner, "The effect of mobility on minimaxing of game trees with random leaf values," *Artificial Intelligence*, vol. 130, no. 1, pp. 1–26, 2001.

[13] Y. Björnsson and T. A. Marsland, "Learning extension parameters in game-tree search," *Information Sciences*, vol. 154, no. 3-4, pp. 95–118, 2003.

[14] Wikipedia, English Draughts, 2014, http://en.wikipedia.org/wiki/English_draughts.

[15] W. Saletan, "Chess Bump: The Triumphant Teamwork of Humans and Computers," May 2007, http://www.slate.com/articles/health_and_science/human_nature/2007/05/ches-s_bump.html.

[16] Wikipedia, Logistello, 2014, http://en.wikipedia.org/wiki/Logistello.

[17] B. N. Chen, P. Liu, S. C. Hsu, and T. S. Hsu, "Abstracting knowledge from annotated Chinese-chess game records," in *Computers and Games*, vol. 4630 of *Lecture Notes in Computer Science*, pp. 100–111, Springer, Berlin, Germany, 2007.

[18] E. C. D. van der Werf, M. H. M. Winands, H. J. van den Herik, and J. W. H. M. Uiterwijk, "Learning to predict life and death from Go game records," *Information Sciences*, vol. 175, no. 4, pp. 258–272, 2005.

[19] Z.-Q. Liu and Q. Dou, "Automatic pattern acquisition from game records in GO," *The Journal of China Universities of Posts and Telecommunications*, vol. 14, no. 1, pp. 100–105, 2007.

[20] S. J. Yen, T. N. Yang, J. C. Chen, and S. C. Hsu, "Pattern matching in GO game records," in *Proceedings of the 2nd International Conference on Innovative Computing, Information and Control (ICICIC '07)*, p. 297, Kumamoto, Japan, September 2007.

[21] T. Esaki and T. Hashiyama, "Extracting human players' shogi game strategies from game records using growing SOM," in *Proceedings of the International Joint Conference on Neural Networks (IJCNN '08)*, pp. 2176–2181, IEEE, Hong Kong, June 2008.

[22] B. G. Weber and M. Mateas, "A data mining approach to strategy prediction," in *Proceedings of the IEEE Symposium on Computational Intelligence and Games (CIG '09)*, pp. 140–147, IEEE, Milano, Italy, September 2009.

[23] S. Takeuchi, T. Kaneko, and K. Yamaguchi, "Evaluation of game tree search methods by game records," *IEEE Transactions on Computational Intelligence and AI in Games*, vol. 2, no. 4, pp. 288–302, 2010.

[24] S. Wender, *Data Mining and Machine Learning with Computer Game Logs*, Project Report, University of Auckland, Auckland, New Zealand, 2007.

[25] Wikipedia, "Chinese checkers," August 2014, http://en.wikipedia.org/wiki/Chinese_checkers.

[26] N. R. Mabroukeh and C. I. Ezeife, "A taxonomy of sequential pattern mining algorithms," *ACM Computing Surveys*, vol. 43, no. 1, article 3, 2010.

[27] R. Srikant and R. Agrawal, "Mining sequential patterns: generalizations and performance improvements," in *Advances in Database Technology—EDBT '96*, vol. 1057 of *Lecture Notes in Computer Science*, pp. 1–17, Springer, Berlin, Germany, 1996.

[28] M. J. Zaki, "SPADE: an efficient algorithm for mining frequent sequences," *Machine Learning*, vol. 42, no. 1-2, pp. 31–60, 2001.

[29] X. Yan, J. Han, and R. Afshar, "CloSpan: mining closed sequential patterns in large databases," in *Proceedings of the 3rd SIAM International Conference on Data Mining*, pp. 166–173, SIAM, San Francisco, Calif, USA, 2003.

[30] J. Pei, J. Han, B. Mortazavi-Asl et al., "Mining sequential patterns by pattern-growth: the prefixspan approach," *IEEE Transactions on Knowledge and Data Engineering*, vol. 16, no. 11, pp. 1424–1440, 2004.

[31] M. Y. Lin and S. Y. Lee, "Fast discovery of sequential patterns by memory indexing," in *Data Warehousing and Knowledge Discovery*, vol. 2454 of *Lecture Notes in Computer Science*, pp. 150–160, Springer, Berlin, Germany, 2002.

[32] R.-F. Hu, L. Wang, X.-Q. Mei, and Y. Luo, "Fault diagnosis based on sequential pattern mining," *Computer Integrated Manufacturing Systems*, vol. 16, no. 7, pp. 1412–1418, 2010.

[33] G. Yilmaz, B. Y. Badur, and S. Mardikyan, "Development of a constraint based sequential pattern mining tool," *The International Review on Computers and Software*, vol. 6, no. 2, pp. 191–198, 2011.

[34] S. Dharani, J. Rabi, N. Kumar, and Darly, "Fast algorithms for discovering sequential patterns in massive datasets," *Journal of Computer Science*, vol. 7, no. 9, pp. 1325–1329, 2011.

[35] H.-J. Shyur, C. Jou, and K. Chang, "A data mining approach to discovering reliable sequential patterns," *Journal of Systems and Software*, vol. 86, no. 8, pp. 2196–2203, 2013.

[36] G.-C. Lan, T.-P. Hong, V. S. Tseng, and S.-L. Wang, "Applying the maximum utility measure in high utility sequential pattern mining," *Expert Systems with Applications*, vol. 41, no. 11, pp. 5071–5081, 2014.

[37] J. Han, J. Pei, and Y. Yin, "Mining frequent patterns without candidate generation," *ACM SIGMOD Record*, vol. 29, no. 2, pp. 1–12, 2000.

[38] J. Edmonds, "Paths, trees, and flowers," *Canadian Journal of Mathematics*, vol. 17, pp. 449–467, 1965.

# 7

# A Dynamic Platform for Developing 3D Facial Avatars in a Networked Virtual Environment

**Anis Zarrad**

*Department of Computer Science and Information Sciences, Prince Sultan University, Riyadh 11586, Saudi Arabia*

Correspondence should be addressed to Anis Zarrad; anis.zarrad@gmail.com

Academic Editor: Michela Mortara

Avatar facial expression and animation in 3D collaborative virtual environment (CVE) systems are reconstructed through a complex manipulation of muscles, bones, and wrinkles in 3D space. The need for a fast and easy reconstruction approach has emerged in the recent years due to its application in various domains: 3D disaster management, virtual shopping, and military training. In this work we proposed a new script language based on atomic parametric action to easily produce real-time facial animation. To minimize use of the game engine, we introduced script-based component where the user introduces simple short script fragments to feed the engine with a new animation on the fly. During runtime, when an embedded animation is required, an xml file is created and injected into the game engine without stopping or restarting the engine. The resulting animation method preserves the real-time performance because the modification occurs not through the modification of the 3D code that describes the CVE and its objects but rather through modification of the action scenario that rules when an animation happens or might happen in that specific situation.

## 1. Introduction

There is a growing interest in online collaborative virtual environment (CVE) applications. CVE applications are as a distributed 3D graphic application where multiple users can interact and collaborate. Each player in the VE is represented by a 3D body called an avatar [1], which allows the players to see, interact with, and hear each other. Many successful applications are already launched in educational, social, gaming, commercial, virtual shopping, and training simulations.

Today, the growth of game engines is accelerating, and the development of VE applications continues to increase. Therefore, there is a need for new approaches that handle VE runtime extensibility requirements without a complex manual initialization and engine restarting. Such a requirement is vital for critical virtual environmental applications like military training, emergency preparedness scenarios, and E-shopping. The integration of the avatars' face animation as an on the fly feature will complicate the task and require an important amount of work for qualified artists with a strong knowledge in facial anatomy.

The ability to change an application without having to stop it is an important nonfunctional requirement for 3D CVEs especially if they are to be used as disaster management systems, which should be available around the clock. In CVE, changes in the CVE requirements are driven by changes in the game engine and are time-consuming. Broadly, 3D objects and avatars' faces may change in various ways to give the users a visual display about the actions that are being applied to the objects or embed animation modeling into an avatar according to the constantly changing situation during a disaster. Traditionally, any modifications to the virtual environment system require collaborative effort from graphic designers and 3D programmers to develop the required new scenario and then stop and restart the engine to reflect the new modification in the VE. Due to its complexity, we focus here on avatar facial animations. Several research studies on 3D disaster management have been used to model human behavior and offer true-to-life VE. However, there is still a lack of studies that can easily present avatar animation in emergent situations [2–5] and in real time without stopping the engine. Therefore, 3D modifications can be very time-consuming and costly.

The challenge that the 3D game engine had to deal with is the change of the avatars behavior during the game scenario. We propose a framework that implements a modular architecture based on atomic simulation concepts to manage both the virtual environment content and avatars behavior in dynamic environments and guarantee continuity during runtime. The proposed game engine is designed to separate the language used to implement the game from the game scenario and offer flexibility and simplicity to the user when modification is required. We integrate a scripting story interpreter component in the game engine to control and manage avatar face animation changes. We found that using an eXtensible Virtual Environment Markup Language (XVEML) as a general-purpose of event-based state machine language can make the development easier and faster during the runtime and discharge designers and professionals' programmers.

The XVEML provides hierarchical structure content for simulation description, objects behaviors, and avatar facial animation. We choose MPEG-4 Facial Animation Parameters (FAP) for avatar facial animation [6, 7]. We used VRML to define the avatars' face because VRML provides a standardized functionality and is also aligned with the MPEG-4 standard [2]. We adopt two script levels called *Class* and *Instance* for fast creation of large-scale VE applications. In the *Class* level we incorporate the atomic simulation [8] concept to model all possible simulation scenarios. In the *Instance* level, we incorporate the atomic behavior and action concepts to manage entities behavior and avatars' facial animation. Two types of state machines can be distinguished in our system—those modeling avatars and entities (mainly avatars' facial expression) and those modeling the simulation scenario. Consequently, two script files called Scenario Simulation XML (SCXML) and Instance XML (IXML) are generated automatically and independently based on each state machine modeling. The use of two separate scripting levels offers more flexibility to our solution and allows simulation flow, object specifications, and avatar behavior to be managed independently.

In BIM (building information modeling) [5] a significant number of developer and graphic designers are needed to represent human behavior in a real-time game environment for fire evacuation to conduct effective information interaction between the building and the avatars. Many previous studies have completely discarded avatars' behavior and animation [3, 9] concepts. In 3D disaster management applications, the avatar behavior is necessary to offer full realism for effective interpersonal communication on a level of richness interchangeable with face-to-face interactions.

Game engine systems have recently been in the popular press. Before the appearance of game engine technologies [10–12], most systems were developed as virtual reality systems to handle specific task such as NPSNET [13], DIVE [1], and SPLINE [14]. Thus, any modification requires a hard change in the programming environment and architecture. As game engine technology matures and becomes more flexible to 3D environments, programming skills remain a concern and can hamper the development of complex environments. Existing programming approaches such as

VRML [4], OpenGL [15], X3D [16], and MPEG-4 [2] can build CVE applications. However, most of them cannot provide native support for such systems. Consequently, extensibility action requires complete loading of the CVE application into memory before the modification occurs.

The remainder of the paper is organized into five main sections. In Section 2, we provide some related works. An overall system architecture is presented in Section 3. Section 4 describes the novelty in our proposed approach to build and/or extend a VE application as avatar facial expression during runtime. In Section 5 we propose a firefighter case study. An overview of the proposed XVEML language is given in Section 6. An extensity scenario example is provided in Section 7. Section 8 describes the modular architecture used in our system and prototype implementation. We conclude with a discussion and future direction of system development.

## 2. Related Works

CVEs are increasingly attractive especially in education, entertainment, simulation, and many others. Today, the research tendency leans towards easy and rapid runtime without having intensive programming skills.

Most game engines use the Unity engine [10], the Unreal engine [17, 18], Gamebryo engine [12], CryEngine [19], and Software's Source engine [11]. However, these are limited to specific tasks, and their features are coupled with proposed game characteristics. Thus, any extension or change that adopts a new feature in the application requires a game engine restart. Such systems are promising platforms as long as they serve a specific application without extensions. In addition, only professional programmers can modify the virtual environments within games because they are complex. Choosing an adequate game engine depends on the goal, platform, and speed with which changes are needed.

Wang et al. [5] developed a BIM game based on virtual reality to provide real-time fire evacuation guidance. However, modification is static and limited, which means that it cannot dynamically change the 3D content according to a constantly changing situation during a fire emergency. In addition, a significant number of developers are needed to design and implement this system. In [20], the authors introduced a fire-training simulator to allow trainees to experience a realistic fire scenario and assess different rescue plans in a graphic environment. Representations of human behavior are completely ignored in the implemented case studies. This influences the validity and the true-to-life concept of the VE. Cao et al. [21] presented complex real-time facial recognition using 3D shape regression. The animation algorithm uses a set of training data generated from 2D facial images. System accuracy is improved when the captured image and training data are increased. This requires considerable data to process and may lead to failure in real time.

Before game engine, virtual environments were developed using dedicated systems to implement a specific scenario. Some of the most well-known former systems are DIVE [1], MASSIVE [22], NPSNET [13], SPLINE [14], and

VLNET [23]. They focus on particular applications to reduce the overall implementation complexity. The problem stems from the fact that systems are strongly coupled in terms of implementation. Consequently, any modifications in the application require modifications in the supporting architecture because the complexity is due to a combination of the internal architecture and specific application functionalities.

Zarraonandia et al. [24] described a 3D virtual environment to improve the learning of airport emergency protocols. Each user plays a different role in a particular emergency situation. The idea is based on replication and does not reflect a real context. In [25], the authors proposed a solution to help specialists and decision makers better understand, analyze, and predict natural disasters to reduce damage and save lives. One important factor that is not taken into consideration is the dynamic behavior of the disaster. System interruption is required to adopt new scenarios.

To support extensibility, several approaches have been implemented. Magerko and Laird [26] used a microkernel-based architecture to separate the system elements from the kernel to add, remove, and modify during runtime. Unfortunately, this highly accredited approach incurs a great deal of complexity particularly in terms of facilitating communication between components written in different languages. Also, extensibility requires an intensive knowledge of programming language. Oliveira et al. [9] developed a Java Adaptive Dynamic Environment (JADE) based on the Java architecture. It consists of a lightweight cross platform kernel that permits system evolution during runtime. The adoption of JADE does not provide an efficient solution to problems from extending CVE applications.

In [3, 27], the authors developed a Virtual Environment Markup Language (VEML) based on the nonlinear story concept defined by Szilas [28] to build and/or extend CVE applications. This model allows story progress during the simulation, which is implemented independently of the 3D environment programming. In [3], a repetitive atomic simulation was modeled in response to similar events. For example, in virtual shopping, the Real Madrid FC store may run many sales around the year (every game). To control this situation, VE manager will send a VEML script file to all participating clients whenever a sale event is set. Thus, by transferring many descriptions, the files regularly impact the network bandwidth. Also, any change in the script file must be done manually. This may lead to unplanned atomic simulation and the loss of realistic appearances of the application.

Many other systems have adopted script language technology to design avatar facial and body gesture animations. The Virtual Human Markup Language (VHML) [28] is an independent XML-based language used in MPEG-4 applications which encapsulates a markup language dedicated to body animation (BAML). Perlin and Goldberg [29] describe an IMPROV system using a high-level script language for the creation of real-time behavior with nonrepetitive gestures. Arafa et al. [30] describe an avatar markup language AML based on XML to encapsulate text to speech as well as facial and body animations in a unified manner with appropriate synchronization. The main concern in the proposed work is the complexity implementation that requires realistic avatar facial animation. Furthermore, their supporting architectures are typically designed to handle only avatar behaviors. As a result, it is difficult to apply any relevant code from a particular system and adapt it to our target system. In addition, implementation and change in the code are done manually and require a change in the supporting structure.

## 3. System Architecture

This work is a part of a funding project from a Research and Translation Center (RTC) in Riyadh, Saudi Arabia. The goal of the project is the design and implementation of a complete 3D collaborative virtual environment application for disaster management. It is important to have a believable 3D virtual environment to prepare a rescue scenario with an acceptable response time whenever there is a need. Having such system with a 3D representation of current situation as input is very helpful for police, military, and medical staff in order to let them react properly with an appropriate effort management when they arrive to the accident site.

The overall scenario can be described as follows: once deployed sensors in the monitored area detect a fire disaster or crowded zone, a protocol for gathering data like location and severity is set. The data is sent to the central location through a communication mechanism between sensor node and central station. Many robots are sent to the accident site to investigate site and send more details to the central station. Based on the received data, a new 3D representation is created to closely reflect the reality.

Depending on the situation, a rescue plan is established using the IA mechanism to give workers (firefighters, police, etc.) the quickest access with improved response. Rescue implementation will vary according to the work situations, the equipment used, and the victim's condition. An implemented rescue plan is governed by the on-site rescue plan. In this work we focus only on the avatars facial behavior during the runtime to reflect the real situation described in the sensors data. The overall system architecture is presented in Figure 1. Three layers are identified: (1) the WSN layer, (2) the 3D virtual environment server layer, and (3) the client side 3D player.

Initial 3D representation of the VE is preloaded into the server for quick access and modeling. We focus only on the game engine components implemented in the 3D server layer to manage facial animation changes in the VE when there is a need for requirements adjustment. Wireless sensors protocols and the artificial intelligence (AI) mechanism to establish the rescue plan are out of the paper scope. Engine architecture is detailed in Section 8.

The implementation of the main game engine components in the server side offers the user the freedom to use any device (desktop, mobile devices, etc.) when operating the system.

## 4. Proposed Approach

In addition to advancing our understanding of the factors that contribute to the 3D disaster management application

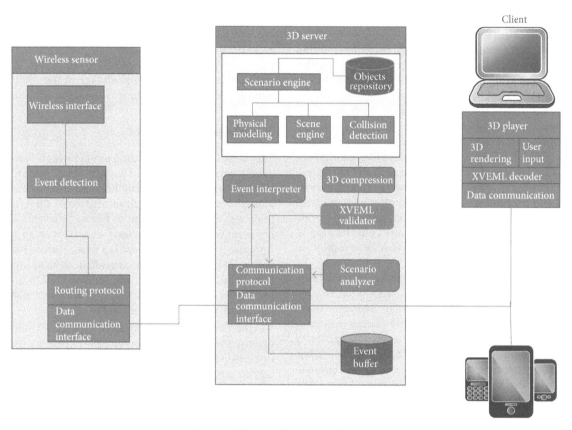

FIGURE 1: The overall system architecture.

platforms, the results are useful for other applications such as military training and virtual shopping via an automatic scenario for face expression adaptation. Disaster management is a dynamic and delicate environment where many events can occur suddenly in real life. They must be reflected in the 3D environment to enable better performance in live exercises and real incidents.

In our previous work [3], we described a script language through the concept of atomic simulations. The resulting file language is generated manually and emphasizes the simulation scenario and completely ignores the avatars' facial animations and objects' behaviors. In this way, the file generation process becomes tedious, and the scenario becomes complex. The number of avatars participating in the VE is very large.

In conclusion, a lack of facile tools limits freelance developers. Thus, our goal was to overcome the complexity of established modeling tools by combining them with the concept of atomic behaviors. Our methodology models the avatars and objects separately from the simulation execution scenario to consider the importance of the avatars' behavior.

*4.1. State Machines Modeling.* We propose to design the entire virtual environment simulation scenario and its entities (avatars facial animations, 3D geometric objects, and their behaviors) through the state machine theory. We use a branching graph story [31] incorporated with atomic model concepts. Through atomic modeling, we mean both atomic

simulation and atomic action including avatar facial animation and object behavior. We use an atomic simulation similar to [8]. Atomic avatar facial animation is a primitive state that cannot be divided further. It is needed for building complex facial expressions, for example, talking with the head moving. Each atomic model runs as a distinct process to facilitate the modification. As a result, the user and designer can make any modifications in the simulation scenario without affecting the facial animations and vice versa. The branching graph takes the form of directed graph containing nodes and arcs between nodes. In this approach, we define chapters as a set of atomic simulations, and a node denotes a chapter. Some nodes exist outside the simulation graph to denote the planned set of avatars facial animation in a specific chapter and can be activated by precondition rule-based or without any incoming transition.

We denote $E_{i,\text{avj}}$ as a facial animation expression for a designed avatar with ID avj:

$$i \in \{\text{"Happy", "Frightened", "Stressed", "Neutral"}\}. \quad (1)$$

Each chapter can be designed through a state machine which is defined as a set:

$$A = \{S, E, T, S_0, F\}, \quad (2)$$

where $S$ is a set of finite states, $E$ is an alphabet, $T$ is a transition function $T : S \times E \rightarrow S$, $S_0$ is initial states, and $F$ is final states.

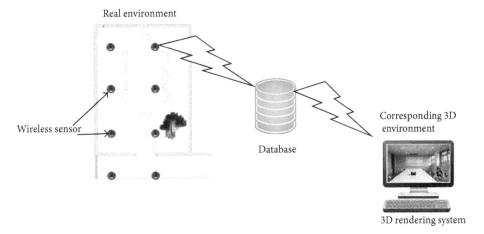

Real environment

Wireless sensor

Database

Corresponding 3D environment

3D rendering system

FIGURE 2: Fire scenario in meeting room.

*4.2. Script Languages.* The proposed script language is retrieved directly from the state machines as output. Two separate script files are generated to make the VE extensibility procedure more rapid and easy in large-scale VE systems as follows:

(i) The first script language file is called Scenario Simulation XML (SCXML) and it is used to model the scenario simulation (scene description and objects) and predefined avatar facial animation; it is class modeling. This file is less susceptible to changes. However, when any modification has to be reported to the scenario (delete a chapter, add a new chapter, etc.) or to the facial animation (define a new avatar expression and modify an expression), it can be done easily through our state machines. A new script language will be generated and will be injected to the environment. Moreover, the modified script is uploaded into the VE application during the runtime without the need to stop the application.

(ii) The second script language file is called Instance XML (IXML). Here, all the object properties are set to defined values: 3D geometry objects specifications, avatar representation (ID, type, etc.), and the assigned facial animation for a specific avatar. For example, avatar 2 will be happy at time point 00:00 in chapter X. This script language is a class instance for a given scenario.

Clearly the use of two separate modeling ideas is very promising because the VE changes are more frequent in objects and avatar behaviors rather than the simulation scenario. Thus, there is no need to modify our entire VE when the 3D object behavior or avatar facial animation needs to be changed.

## 5. Case Study: Firefighters Emergency Preparedness Scenario

To better understand the impetus of our proposed approach, we illustrate a true-to-life firefighter emergency preparedness

scenario in a meeting room that is used for training purpose. The overall scenario is presented in Figure 2.

Wireless sensors are deployed in the monitoring area (meeting room, real environment). An initial 3D environment covering the monitored area is loaded in the server priorly. When sensors detect a fire situation in this real environment, many events are collected and are sent back to a central database.

A rendering protocol is used to modify the initial 3D environment in order to visualize the detailed live representation in the meeting room and everything that is going on within the target environment including the new events such as fire and smoke.

To deal with the fire disaster, many human resources are involved including firefighters, fire truck drivers, police officers, and ambulance services. The Emergency Service (ES) receives an emergency call from a witness reporting a fire disaster somewhere in the city. ES informs the closest fire station (FS) having sufficient efforts. In addition we may inform ambulance service and police in case there are injuries. Players take the role of witnesses, firefighters, police officers, and medical staff to deal with the fire. Based on the fire density we may need to call two fire stations. Table 1 shows the story structure.

When the game begins, the fire location is not known. FS1 has higher effort than FS2. For simplicity, effort is measured based on the number of firefighters. The game initializations are as follows: the number of fire stations is 2 (FS1 and FS2), the number of firefighters in FS1 is 5, the number of firefighters in FS2 is 3, the number of medical staff is 2, and the number of policemen is 2.

After defining the simulation scenario and its chapters as described in Table 1, we modeled the complete scenario using a state machine. Each chapter is modeled separately using a state machine concept. Every state has a label, which will help us to determine, at any moment, in which state of which chapter our scenario is. Some states are blocking because they need a specific external event. For example, the state "*PrepareEquipment*" in chapter 3 is waiting for the event "3000" (an event can be modeled as a simple OS signal),

TABLE 1: Fire scenario.

| Chapters | Chapter details |
| --- | --- |
| 1 | *Fire scene* |
| 1.1 | Observe scene by witness, witness face expression: *frightened* |
| 1.1.2 | Get location info |
| 1.1.3 | Estimate the fire density |
| 1.2 | Call emergency center, witness face expression: *stress* |
| 2 | *Emergency center* |
| 2.1 | Ask the closet fire station (FS) |
| 2.1.1 | FS1 identified |
| 2.1.1.1 | Firefighters availability indicates weak efforts |
| 2.1.1.2 | Firefighters availability indicates good efforts |
| 2.1.1.3 | Firefighters availability indicates excellent efforts |
| 2.1.2 | FS2 identified |
| 2.1.2.1 | Firefighters availability indicates weak efforts |
| 2.1.2.2 | Firefighters availability indicates good efforts |
| 2.1.2.3 | Firefighters availability indicates excellent efforts |
| 2.2 | Call the police center |
| 2.3 | Call the ambulance service |
| 3 | *Fire station (one selected)* |
| 3.1 | Prepare equipment |
| 3.1.1 | Firefighter inside the trucks, firefighters face expression: *stressed (all)* |
| 3.2 | Move to location |
| 3.3 | Manage the fire |
| 3.3.1 | Set equipment |
| 3.3.2 | Deal with the fire |
| 3.3.2.1 | FS1.AV1, FS1.AV2 evacuate people, face expression: *happy* |
| 3.3.2.2 | FS1.AV3, FS1.AV4 extinct fire, face expression: *frightened* |
| 3.3.2.3 | FS1.AV5 control equipment, face expression: *stressed* |
| 4 | *Fire station (two selected)* |
| 4.1 | Prepare equipment |
| 4.1.1 | Firefighter inside the trucks |
| 4.2 | Move to location |
| 4.3 | Manage the fire |
| 4.3.1 | Set equipment |
| 4.3.2 | Deal with the fire |
| 4.3.2.1 | FS2.AV1 evacuate people, face expression: *happy* |
| 4.3.2.2 | FS2.AV2 extinct fire, face expression: *frightened* |
| 4.3.2.3 | FS2.AV3 control equipment, face expression: *stressed* |
| 5 | *Police service arrives* |
| 5.1 | Clean the area |
| 5.1.1 | Control the local traffic |
| 5.1.2 | Secure the fire site |
| 5.2 | Investigate the area |
| 5.2.1 | Ask witness, witness face expression: *stressed* |
| 6 | *Ambulance service arrives* |
| 6.1 | Manage evacuated people, staff face expression: *stressed (all)* |
| 6.1.1 | Injuries identified, staff face expression: *compassionate (all)* |
| 6.1.1.1 | Provide first-aid on site |
| 6.1.1.2 | Transport to hospital |
| 6.1.2 | No injuries identified, staff face expression: *happy (all)* |
| 7 | *Fire extinct* |
| 7.1 | By FS1, firefighters face expression: *happy (all)* |
| 7.2 | By FS2, firefighters face expression: *happy (all)* |
| 7.3 | By FS1 and FS2, firefighters face expression: *happy (all)* |

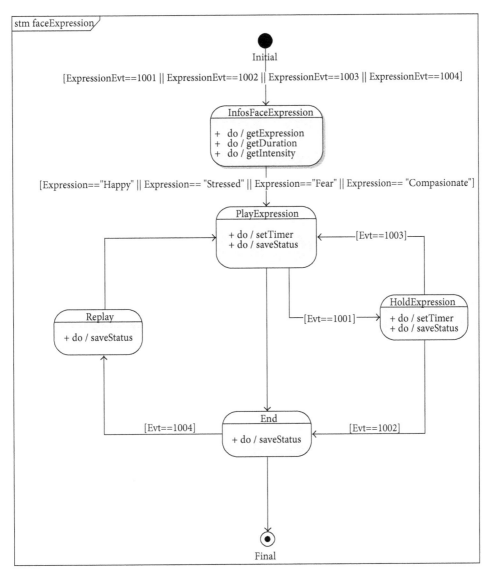

FIGURE 3: Avatars face animation modeling.

which will be emitted by a state in another chapter as shown in Figure 3.

In this scenario, we focus on the avatars facial animation expressions. The avatar dynamically changes his behavior to reflect the surrounding situation in the virtual environment depending on the current situation and what is being executed.

In Figure 3, we present facial animation modeling. Any facial animation is defined with specific attributes such as a file name describing the animation type and two parameters, duration and start time. Duration is used to define the duration of the animation (e.g., happy for 25 seconds). Start time parameters are used to define when the animation should start.

It is important to notice that any animations can be planned for a replay when there is a need without the involvement of a VE designer in each replay. Such modeling offers

a better solution especially for an application that requires regular modifications. For example, doctor should be happy when meeting patient in E-health application or during end of year sale in E-shopping application where many red sale signs should be integrated into the 3D E-shopping.

## 6. Markup Language VEXML

In this section we explore the syntax and elements of the proposed XVEML language. Algorithms 1 and 2 show screenshots of the language. It is composed principally of SCXML and IXML. The root tag <XVEML> marks the beginning and end of the script.

*6.1. Syntax and Simulation Scenario.* Algorithm 1 gives an overview of our SCXML script language file. The original file has been relieved of some irrelevant tags. The resulting script

```
<?xml version="1.0" encoding="UTF-8"?>
<XVEML>
<connector xmi:idref="EAID_11A4687E_B5B3_451e_95F1_0CAF77327D4D">
<source xmi:idref="EAID_85BFDD36_7149_43b8_8F62_7A0EBE5D338F">
<model ea_localid="54" type="State" name="MoveToLocation"/>
</source>
  <target xmi:idref="EAID_9F1539F4_2DF9_40db_8FE5_0E6F7B8EB2AB">
  <model ea_localid="55" type="State" name="ExtinctFire"/>
  </target>
<labels mt=" [Expression==1]"/>
  </connector>
<connector xmi:idref="EAID_42C7882B_A52A_4a2e_A03B_63DC132DFBAD">
<source xmi:idref="EAID_E5E29AA8_0921_444f_9666_EC47340F9417">
<model ea_localid="53" type="State" name="PrepareEquipment"/>
</source>
  <target xmi:idref="EAID_85BFDD36_7149_43b8_8F62_7A0EBE5D338F">
  <model ea_localid="54" type="State" name="MoveToLocation"/>
  </target>
<labels/>
</connector>
  <connector xmi:idref="EAID_82DBB96D_4094_4428_AD2C_0EE4C8848FC5">
  <source xmi:idref="EAID_C0E3E4C7_ECED_48d3_9478_0E4720678FC9">
  <model ea_localid="52" type="StateNode" name="Initial"/>
</source>
  <target xmi:idref="EAID_E5E29AA8_0921_444f_9666_EC47340F9417">
  <model ea_localid="53" type="State" name="PrepareEquipment"/>
</target>
<labels mt=" [Evt==3000 || Evt==4000]"/>
</connector>
</XVEML>
```

ALGORITHM 1: SCXML script file.

language is organized as set of "connectors" which mean two states: "Source" and "Target." Each state is defined by its name and its ID. An extra tag "Label" is used when there is a transition from "Source" to "Target" that meets some prerequisite conditions.

The root tag <AFSL> marks the beginning and the end of Avatar Facial Script Language. It accepts four attributes: avatar face ID (*unique reference ID for the 3D face to be animated*), file path (*the path for animated file used in the animation*), start time (*the time where the animation must start*), and description (*describes the animation*).

Expressions tag has two subelements <TTS> or text to speech and <Expression>. There may be many Expressions and only one <TTS>; text to speech cannot be overlapped. The Tag TTS accepts three attributes: start time (starting time of the animation), fab file (file used to generate the Facial Animation Parameters FAP output), and Audio File (file used to generate the audio output of the text to be spoken). Expression may or may not overlap.

Each <Expression> has a start time, repeat number (to specify the number of repeats in need, otherwise default value 0), pause time (when a repeat is needed, we specify the pause time between consecutive expressions), and animation description. We choose this scheme to define expressions using a set of distinct expression to allow the designer to

add as many expressions as desired from the FAP database. However, only one TTS is allowed in Expressions to control the overlapping.

## 7. Extensibility Mechanism at Runtime

Changing and/or extending the existing VE application during the runtime must be done easily and smoothly. Most systems require extensive programming activities and collaboration with different professional to manipulate the extended action. The dual modeling of our VE application allows us to rapidly and easily prevent any changes in the VE simulation during modeling. For example, as shown in Figures 2 and 3, if we need to modify the simulation scenario by dropping chapter B from the global scenario, we have to modify the corresponding state machine by removing chapter B and then automatically generate the new SCXML file. Consequently, when the simulation scenario changes, it must be followed by instances modification. Thus, there is a need to generate a new IXML file as well. On the contrary, any modifications in instance models do not require a modification in the class model. Such an approach makes code that would otherwise be mitigated and challenging to modify simple, easy, and accessible to novices. In addition, the challenges of developing SCXML and IXML script codes

```
<IXML>
<xmi:Extension extender="...">
<declaration>
<Object name= "AV1" file = "Firefighter.mp4" manager= "Keyboard"/>
<Expression name = "Happy" File = "Happy.mp4"/>
<TTS start="t2" fab_file ="ABS" wav_file="SS" Text="Text to speak">
</declaration>>
<elements>
<element xmi:idref="EAID_...2C38" xmi:type="uml:State" name="ControlEquipment" scope="public">
<EAModel.scenario>
<EAScenario name="Expression ( FS1.AV5, &quot;Stressed&quot;, StartTime = 12, Duration=30,
Intensity= &quot;Medium&quot;) " type="Alternate"../>
</EAModel.scenario>
</element>
<element xmi:idref="EAID_...7E34" xmi:type="uml:State" name="EvacuatePeople" scope="public">
  <EAModel.scenario>
<EAScenario name="Expression ( FS1.AV1, &quot;Happy&quot;, StartTime = 12, Repeat = n,
PauseTime= p, Duration=40, Intensity= &quot;Low&quot;) />
<EAScenario name="Expression ( FS1.AV2, &quot;Happy&quot;, StartTime = 32, Duration=40,
Intensity= &quot;Low&quot;) " type="Alternate" />
</EAModel.scenario>
</element>
<element xmi:idref="EAID_...B2AB" xmi:type="uml:State" name="ExtinctFire" scope="public">
......
</element>
<element xmi:idref="EAID_...338F" xmi:type="uml:State" name="MoveToLocation" scope="public">
  <EAModel.scenario>
<EAScenario name="MoveTo(FS1.AV1,&quot;&quot;)" type="Simple" weight="1,00"
subject="EAID_...338F" xmi:id="EAID_...C3AD"/>
....
</EAModel.scenario>
</element>
<element xmi:idref="EAID_...9417" xmi:type="uml:State" name="PrepareEquipment" scope="public">
<EAModel.scenario>
<EAScenario name="Expression ( FS1.AV1, &quot;Stressed&quot;, StartTime = 12, Duration=30,
Intensity= &quot;Low&quot;) " type="Alternate"../>
.....
</EAModel.scenario>
</element>
<element xmi:idref="EAID_...056A" xmi:type="uml:StateNode" name="Final" scope="public">
<extendedProperties tagged="0" package_name="Chapter3_4"/>
</element>
<element xmi:idref="EAID_...8FC9" xmi:type="uml:StateNode" name="Initial" scope="public">
<extendedProperties tagged="0" package_name="Chapter3_4"/>
</element>
</elements>
  </xmi:XMI>
</IXML>
```

ALGORITHM 2: IXML script file.

for execution in large-scale VE application can completely avoid limitations in traditional development processes. The resulting files are sent to all users participating in the VE during runtime without interrupting the system.

In addition, there is a need to manipulate existing avatars in the dropped chapter to guarantee in a natural and realistic way the developed application. Two approaches can be proposed: managing the singleton manually by directly changing the avatar attributes in the objects' repository database or

creating specific state machines (migration state machine) that will remove the avatars from the ghost chapter B to any other chapter.

## 8. Game Engine Architecture and Prototype Implementation

The proposed architecture is specifically designed to bridge the gap between extending the 3D VE during runtime and

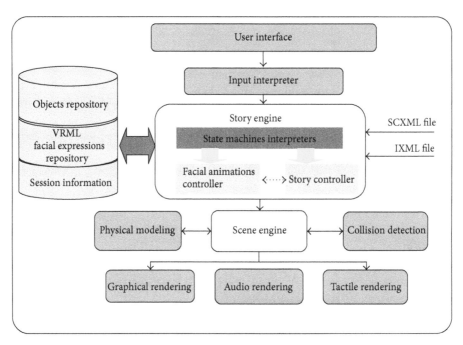

FIGURE 4: Proposed game engine architecture.

FIGURE 5: Face animation control.

the system functionality interruption. We use modular architecture to facilitate the integration and the management of new components and offer qualities to the developed system. In client side architecture, the model as well as animations engines are web-based, and animation results can be viewed locally in the end user browser. Figure 4 shows the detailed proposed architecture.

The low level architecture deals with the extensibility at runtime and is composed of the following:

(a) Message controller: it acts as an entry point to receive a message from the server side and identifies the set of message that can be accepted.

The high-level architecture is composed of the following:

(a) User interface: it is composed of GUI and VRML viewer. *GUI* stands for the graphical user interface

of the system to transmit the user's commands such as the following: modify the scene content or add avatar face animation. *VRML viewer* visualizes the virtual environment content and the VRML avatars' face animations.

(b) Story engine: it is the main component in this architecture. It models the simulation scenario of the proposed system and avatar facial behavior through the state machine concept. This component is composed principally of the following.

(i) *State Machines Interpreter*. In a classic case, this module will get in its input only once from a SCXML file (the scenario story). It models the states and transitions and manages all possible transitions through the defined states. There are several examples of the IXML file, which represent one instance for the given scenario. Also, this module is responsible for the validation of the files using a parser.

(ii) *Story Controller*. This is a component responsible for converting the SCXML into commands for the story engine.

(iii) *Face Animation Controller*. It is a component responsible for managing the IXNML file and performing core functionalities of the execution of facial animations.

(c) Conflict detection: it will address the conflict issue in facial animation such as when two animations cannot be combined (happy expression and angry expression).

(d) VRML faces expressions and animation database: it contains a description of a face. Each facial object

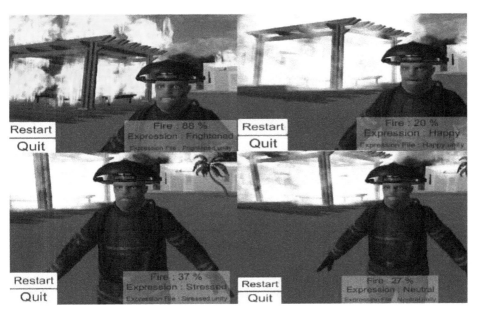

FIGURE 6: Firefighter face animation.

is implemented as a VRML transform node, which describes shapes and other properties. This also has all new facial animations created during the simulation.

Avatars participating in this scenario are modeled with four animations: frightened, stressed, neutral, and happy depending on the situation context.

The XVEML file is first written by serializing the expression data. We then write into the file using the standard C# IO functions:

```
var serializer = new XmlSerializer(typeof
(xExpressionList));

var stream = new FileStream
("ExpressionList.xml", FileMode.Create);

serializer.Serialize(stream,
expressionList);
```

Figure 5 shows the firefighter face modeling and the animation control features. We used sixteen features marked as black dots on the face. Texturing was done using Photoshop.

For easy facial animation we adapt the Rigging Process [32]. We have built a "Custom Controller" for every feature to get a real avatar emotion in the Face Animation Controller module. Figure 6 shows four animations (frightened, happy, neutral, and stressed) depending on the fire density in the actual scene. The corresponding XML file structure is as in Algorithm 3.

When fire density becomes low, the firefighter changes his expression to happy. The State Machine Interpreters module communicates events to the Face Animation Controller to be reflected on the firefighter face. Appropriate face expression file is loaded for rendering.

```
<ExpressionList>
  <Expression>
   <Firefighter_ID>1</Firefighter_ID>
   <ExpressionName>Frightened</ExpressionName>
   <ExpressionFile>Frightened</ExpressionFile>
        <Parameters>
         .......
        </Parameters>
</Expression>
<Expression>
   <Firefighter_ID>2</Firefighter_ID>
   <ExpressionName>Stressed</ExpressionName>
   ...............
  </Expression>
<Expression>
   <Firefighter_ID>2</Firefighter_ID>
   <ExpressionName>Happy</ExpressionName>
    <Parameters>
         <Replay value="No" >
         <Start value="10">
         .....
    </Parameters>
</Expression>
</ExpressionList>
```

ALGORITHM 3

## 9. Conclusions

In this work, we present a new architecture to develop and extend VE applications with facial modeling without game engine interruption during runtime. This approach offers benefits to human life especially when used for critical actions that require an immediate update like E-health and military training applications.

We describe our game scenario as a nonlinear story using state machine concepts. Avatars and object behaviors are modeled separately to offer more flexibility and robustness when updates are required. The script file describing facial animation is retrieved directly from the state machine module and injected on the fly in the game engine. Generated scripts can be reused and customized to fit a wide range of other virtual environment applications such as military training, E-learning, E-shopping, and E-health. However, the system still has some limitations for further improvement in the validation process about facial features in complex scene.

## Acknowledgments

The author would like to acknowledge the support of Research and Translation Center (RTC) in Prince Sultan University, Saudi Arabia. This work was supported by Grant no. GP-CCIS-2013-11-10 from Research and Translation Center.

## References

[1] O. Hagsand, "Interactive MUVEs in the DIVE system," *IEEE Computer*, vol. 3, no. 1, pp. 30–39, 1996.

[2] Information Technology—Coding of audio-visual objects—Part 1: Systems, ISO/IEC JTC 1/SC 29/WG 11-14496-1, 2000.

[3] A. Boukerche, R. Duarte, R. Araujo, L. Andrade, and A. Zarrad, "A novel solution for the development of collaborative virtual environment simulations in large scale," in *Proceedings of the 9th IEEE International Symposium on Distributed Simulation and Real Times (DS-RT '05)*, pp. 86–97, Montreal, Canada, October 2005.

[4] VRML Homepage, 2012, http://www.w3.org/MarkUp/VRML/.

[5] B. Wang, H. Li, Y. Rezgui, A. Bradley, and H. N. Ong, "BIM based virtual environment for fire emergency evacuation," *The Scientific World Journal*, vol. 2014, Article ID 589016, 22 pages, 2014.

[6] J. Noh and U. Neumann, "A survey of facial modeling and animation techniques," Tech. Rep. 99-705, USC, 1998.

[7] I. S. Pandzic and R. Forchheimer, *MPEG-4 Facial Animation: The Standard, Implementation and Applications*, John Wiley & Sons, New York, NY, USA, 2002.

[8] A. Boukerche, D. D. Duarte, and R. B. de Araujo, "A language for building and extending 3D virtual web-based environments," in *Proceedings of the 2th Latin American Web Congress and the 10th Brazilian Symposium on Multimedia and the Web (WebMedia-LA-Web '04)*, pp. 114–116, IEEE, Ribeirão Preto, Brazil, October 2004.

[9] M. Oliveira, J. Crowcroft, and M. Slater, "Component framework infrastructure for virtual environments," in *Proceedings of the 3rd International Conference on Collaborative Virtual Environments (CVE '00)*, pp. 139–146, ACM, San Francisco, Calif, USA, September 2000.

[10] Unity, http://www.unity3d.com.

[11] Valve Software, Source engine, 2015, http://source.valvesoftware.com/.

[12] Emergent Game Technologies, Gamebryo, 2015, http://www.gamebryo.com/gamebryo.php.

[13] M. R. Macedonia, M. J. Zyda, D. R. Pratt, P. T. Barham, and S. Zeswitz, "NPSNET: a network software architecture for large scale virtual environments," *Presence: Teleoperators and Virtual Environments*, vol. 3, no. 4, pp. 265–287, 1994.

[14] SPLINE Homepage, http://www.merl.com/projects/spline/.

[15] OpenGL Homepage, 2015, http://www.opengl.org.

[16] Web3D, 2012, http://www.web3d.org.

[17] T. Sweeney, *Unreal Script Language Reference*, 1998, http://unreal.epicgames.com/UnrealScript.htm.

[18] Epic Games. Epic games' unreal development kit eclipses 50,000 users in one week, 2015, http://www.udk.com/udk50k.

[19] CryEngine, 2015, http://www.crytek.com/cryengine.

[20] A. Ren, C. Chen, and Y. Luo, "Simulation of emergency evacuation in virtual reality," *Tsinghua Science and Technology*, vol. 13, no. 5, pp. 674–680, 2008.

[21] C. Cao, Y. Weng, S. Lin, and K. Zhou, "3D shape regression for real-time facial animation," *ACM Transactions on Graphics*, vol. 32, no. 4, article 41, 2013.

[22] S. Benford and L. Fahlén, "A spatial model of interaction in large virtual environments," in *Proceedings of the Third European Conference on Computer-Supported Cooperative Work 13–17 September 1993, Milan, Italy ECSCW '93*, pp. 109–124, Springer, Berlin, Germany, 1993.

[23] S. Pandžić, K. Tolga, L. Elwin, N. Thalmann, and D. Thalmann, "A flexible architecture for virtual humans in networked collaborative virtual environments," in *Proceedings of the Eurographics*, pp. 177–188, Budapest, Hungary, 1997.

[24] T. Zarraonandia, M. R. R. Vargas, P. Díaz, and I. Aedo, "A virtual environment for learning aiport emergency management protocols," in *Human-Computer Interaction. Ambient, Ubiquitous and Intelligent Interaction*, vol. 5612 of *Lecture Notes in Computer Science*, pp. 228–235, Springer, Berlin, Germany, 2009.

[25] L. Hashemi Beni, M. A. Mostafavi, and J. Pouliot, "3D dynamic simulation within GIS in support of disaster management," in *Geomatics Solutions for Disaster Management*, Lecture Notes in Geoinformation and Cartography, pp. 165–184, Springer, Berlin, Germany, 2007.

[26] B. Magerko and J. E. Laird, "Building an interactive drama architecture," in *Proceedings of the 1st International Conference on Technologies for Interactive Digital Storytelling and Entertainment*, pp. 24–26, Darmstadt, Gemany, 2003.

[27] A. Zarrad and A. Bensefia, "A novel approach to develop large-scale virtual environment applications using script-language," in *Proceedings of the 9th International Conference on Innovations in Information Technology (IIT '13)*, pp. 169–174, Abu Dhabi, United Arab Emirates, March 2013.

[28] N. Szilas, "IDtension: a narrative engine for interactive drama," in *Proceedings of the 1st International Conference on Technologies for Interactive Digital Storytelling and Entertainment (TIDSE '03)*, Göbel, Ed., Fraunhofer IRB, Darmstadt, Germany, March 2003.

[29] K. Perlin and A. Goldberg, "Improv: a system for scripting interactive actors in virtual worlds," in *Proceedings of the Computer Graphics Conference (SIGGRAPH '96)*, pp. 205–216, ACM Press, August 1996.

[30] Y. Arafa, K. Kamyab, S. Kshirsagar, N. Magnenat-Thalmann, A. Guye-Vuille, and D. Thalmann, "Avatar markup language," in *Proceedings of the 8th Eurographics Workshop on Virtual Environments (EWVE '02)*, pp. 109–118, Barcelona, Spain, May 2002.

[31] M. O. Riedl and R. M. Young, "From linear story generation to branching story graphs," *IEEE Computer Graphics and Applications*, vol. 26, no. 3, pp. 23–31, 2006.

[32] I. Baran and J. Popovi, "Automatic rigging and animation of 3D characters," in *Proceedings of the International ACM Conference on Computer Graphics and Interactive Techniques (SIGGRAPH '07)*, San Diego, Calif, USA, August 2007.

# 8

# Enhancing Video Games Policy based on Least-Squares Continuous Action Policy Iteration: Case Study on StarCraft Brood War and Glest RTS Games and the 8 Queens Board Game

**Shahenda Sarhan, Mohamed Abu ElSoud, and Hebatullah Rashed**

*Computer Science Department, Faculty of Computers and Information, Mansoura University, Mansoura 35516, Egypt*

Correspondence should be addressed to Shahenda Sarhan; shahenda_sarhan@yahoo.com

Academic Editor: Manuel M. Oliveira

With the rapid advent of video games recently and the increasing numbers of players and gamers, only a tough game with high policy, actions, and tactics survives. How the game responds to opponent actions is the key issue of popular games. Many algorithms were proposed to solve this problem such as Least-Squares Policy Iteration (LSPI) and State-Action-Reward-State-Action (SARSA) but they mainly depend on discrete actions, while agents in such a setting have to learn from the consequences of their continuous actions, in order to maximize the total reward over time. So in this paper we proposed a new algorithm based on LSPI called Least-Squares Continuous Action Policy Iteration (LSCAPI). The LSCAPI was implemented and tested on three different games: one board game, the 8 Queens, and two real-time strategy (RTS) games, StarCraft Brood War and Glest. The LSCAPI evaluation proved superiority over LSPI in time, policy learning ability, and effectiveness.

## 1. Introduction

An agent is anything that can be viewed as perceiving its environment through sensors and acting in that environment through actuators as in Figure 1, while a rational agent is the one that does the right thing [1].

However, agents may have no prior knowledge on what the right or optimal actions are. To learn the best action selection the agent needs to explore the state-action search space and, from the rewards provided by the environment, the agent can calculate the true expected reward when selecting an action from a state.

Reinforcement learning (RL) is learning what the agent can do and how to map situations to actions in order to maximize the numerical reward signal. Reinforcement learning assists agents to discover which actions yield the most reward and the most punishment after trying them through trial-and-error and delayed reward. Reinforcement learning concentrated more on finding a balance between exploration

of anonymous areas and exploitation of its current knowledge [2–4].

Batch reinforcement learning (BRL) is a subfield of dynamic programming (DP) [4, 5] based reinforcement learning that recently has immensely grown. Batch RL is mainly used, where the complete amount of learning experience, usually a set of transitions sampled from the system, is fixed and given a priori. The learning system concern then is to derive an optimal policy out of the given batch of samples [6–8]. So batch reinforcement learning algorithms aim to achieve the utmost data efficiency through saving experience data to make an aggregate batch of updates to the learned policy [7, 8].

Figure 2 classifies different batch RL algorithms based on interaction perspectives into offline and online algorithms. The offline algorithms are also known as pure batch algorithms that mainly work offline on a fixed set of transition samples as Fitted Q Iteration (FQI) [9, 10], Kernel-Based Approximate Dynamic Programming (KADP) [11, 12], and

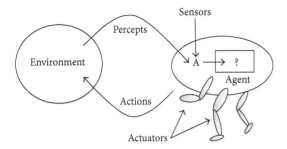

FIGURE 1: Agent-environment interaction [18].

Least-Squares Policy Iteration (LSPI) [13–15], while online algorithms comprised pure online algorithms, semibatch algorithms, and growing batch algorithms as Neural Fitted Q Iteration (NFQ) [16] that depends on making an aggregate update for several transitions and storing and reusing the experiences after making this update.

Different problems had been solved using BRL based on the RL agents' ability to learn without expert supervision. Game playing problem is one of major areas where BRL represented a magical solution for determining the best policy to be applied in a game. This often depends on a number of different factors, as the space of possible actions is too large for an agent to reason about directly, while still meeting real-time constraints. To cover this many states, using a standard rule based approach would mean specifying a large number of hard coded rules. BRL cuts out this need to manually specify rules, as agents learn simply by playing the game. For example, in backgammon game, agent can be trained by playing against other human player or even other RL agent [7].

As we mentioned obtaining the optimal policy [17] (decision-making function which represents a mapping from states to actions) the game can apply is a major key in evaluating game performance through game-human interaction. The problem arises here as all games especially games with large space of possible actions as real-time strategy (RTS) games and board games suffer through finding the optimal policy and thus the best action. As almost all algorithms count only for discrete states, discrete actions, or continuous states, discrete actions while agents are in such a setting have to learn from the consequences of their continuous actions, in order to maximize the total reward over time. So the researchers in this paper proposed an algorithm based on LSPI considering continuous actions, which we called Least-Squares Continuous Actions Policy Iteration (LSCAPI). The LSCAPI was applied and tested using three game genres: StarCraft Brood War, Glest, and 8 Queens.

This paper is organized as follows. Section 2 covers a brief review of video games concentrating on RTS games and board games. In Section 3, the proposed Least-Squares Continuous Actions Policy Iteration (LSCAPI) algorithm is described in detail. Section 4 comprises the testing of LSCAPI on some real cases. In Section 5 the simulation results and discussion are introduced and in Section 6 the implantation of LSCAPI. Finally Section 7 outlines our conclusions.

## 2. Background

*2.1. Board Games.* Board games are the most known and mostly played games over centuries. A board game is a game that involves pieces moved or placed on a board, according to a set of rules. Moves in board games may depend on pure strategy or only pure chance as the rolling dice, or both; in all cases expert opponents can achieve their aims [20].

Earlier board games were represented as a battle between two armies with no rules except points, while modern board games basically relied on defeating opponent players in terms of counters, winning position, or points entitlement thus relying on rules. Many board [21] games as Tic-Tac-Toe [22], chess, and Chinese chess (checker) had a long history in machine learning researches. Trinh et al. in [23] discussed the application of temporal-difference-learning in training a neural network to play a scaled-down version of Chinese chess.

Runarsson and Lucas in [24] studied and likened the temporal difference learning (TDL) using the self-play gradient-descent method and coevolutionary learning, using an evolution strategy for acquiring position evaluation for small Go boards. The two approaches are compared with the hope of gaining a greater insight into the problem of searching for optimal strategies.

Wiering et al. in [25] used reinforcement learning algorithms that can learn a game position evaluation function through learning the backgammon game. They examine three different methods for training games: learning by self-play, learning by playing against an expert program, and learning from viewing experts play against themselves.

And Block et al. in [26] proposed a chess engine which proved that reinforcement learning in combination with the classification of board state leads to a notable improvement, when compared with other engines that only use reinforcement learning, such as Knight-Cap.

Skoulakis and Lagoudakis in [27] demonstrated the efficiency of the LSPI agent over the TD agent in the classical board game of Othello/Reversi. They presented a learning approach based on LSPI algorithm that focuses on learning a state-action evaluation function. The key advantage of the proposed approach is that the agent can make batch updates to the evaluation function with any collection of samples, can utilize samples from past games, and can make updates that do not depend on the current evaluation function since there is no bootstrapping.

Finally Szubert and Jaskowski in [28] employed three variants of temporal difference learning to acquire action value, state value, and after-state value functions for evaluating player moves through puzzle game 2048. To represent these functions they adopt n-tuple networks, which have recently been successfully applied to Othello and Connect 4 board games.

*2.1.1. 8 Queens.* The 8 Queens puzzle is a context of the N-Queens problem where eight chess queens are placed on an 8 × 8 chessboard [29]. Any of the queens must not attack any of the others, so that no two queens share the same row, column, or diagonal as in Figure 3.

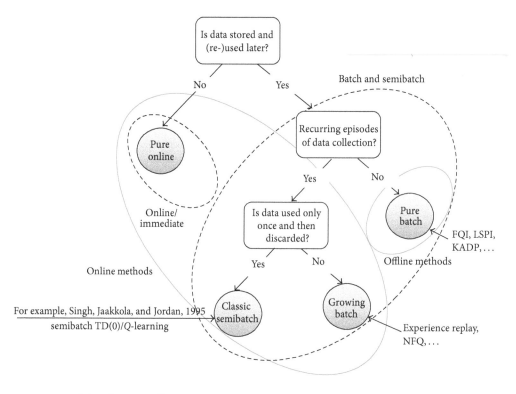

FIGURE 2: Classification of batch versus nonbatch algorithms [7].

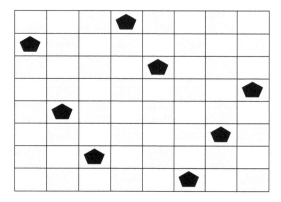

FIGURE 3: 8 Queens [19].

Many algorithms had been proposed for solving 8 Queens as in Lim and Son [30], who applied the Q-learning as a problem solving algorithm for the N-Queens and compared it with the traditional existing methods for solving N-Queens problem.

*2.2. Real-Time Strategy Games.* Real-time Strategy (RTS) games are a subgenre of strategy games where players need to build an economy and military power in order to defeat their opponents. In RTS games players race and struggle against enemy factions by harvesting resources scattered over a terrain and producing buildings and units and help one another in order to set up economies, improve their

technological skill and level, and win battles, until their enemies are extinct [31–34]. The better the balance you get among economy, technology, and army, the more the chances you have to win RTS games [34].

Marthi et al. in [35] applied hierarchical reinforcement learning in a limited RTS domain. This approach used reinforcement learning augmented with prior knowledge about the high-level structure of behavior, constraining the possibilities of the learning agent and thus greatly reducing the search space.

Gusmao in [36] considered the problem of effective and automated decision-making in modern real-time strategy games through the use of reinforcement learning techniques. The researcher proposed a stable, model-based Monte Carlo method assuming that models are imperfect, reducing their influence in the decision-making process. And its effectiveness is further improved by including a novel online search procedure in the control policy.

Leece and Jhala in [37] presented a simplified game that mimics spatial reasoning aspects of more complex games, while removing other complexities through analyzing the effectiveness of classical reinforcement learning for spatial management in order to build a detailed evaluative standard across a broad set of opponent strategies. The authors also demonstrated the potentiality of knowledge transfer to more complex games with similar components.

In 2015, Sethy et al. [38] proposed reinforcement learning algorithm based on Q-learning and SARSA with the generalized reward function to train agents. The proposed model

FIGURE 4: Glest RTS game.

FIGURE 5: StarCraft Brood War RTS game.

was evaluated using Battle City RTS game proving superiority over the state of the art in enhancing agent learning ability.

### 2.2.1. Glest.

Glest is an open source 3D real-time strategy game, where the player can have armies of two different factions, tech, and magic. Tech mainly included warriors and mechanical devices, while magic relied on mages and summoned creatures in the battlefield [34, 39]. In Glest warriors fight by weapons and mangonel, while magicians cast spells and magic forces as shown in Figure 4. The final goal for both factions is to extinct all enemy units, finish the episode, or die.

Glest actions are structured in three levels. The first consists of primitive low-level actions, such as modifications of basic variables that describe low-level microstates. In the second level of actions, grouped primitive actions form a more abstract task or rule. There are thirteen different rules in Glest as Worker Harvest, Return Base, Massive Attack, Add Tasks, Produce Resource Producer, Build One Farm, Produce, Build, Upgrade, and Repair [33, 39, 40].

The third level represents a strategy tactic level, grouping second-level actions-rules with respect to the timer of the game. Each second-level action-rule is associated with a certain time interval. Depending on the module of the timer a certain rule will be picked up and applied by the tactic of the game within the rule's interval [40].

Glest has four main variables: Kills, Units, Resources, and Timer. Each state is characterized by the values of the four variables, where "Kills" refers to the number of kills that the player has achieved, "Units" counts the units the player has produced, "Resources" are the resources the player had harvested, and finally "Timer" counts the game time units.

Every variable is connected with some related actions except for "Timer"; its only role is to count time. "Units" is connected with Build One Farm, Produce, Build, Upgrade, Expand, and Repair actions, while "Kills" is connected with Scout Patrol, Return Base, Massive Attack, and Add Tasks. Finally "Resources" are connected with Worker Harvest, Refresh Harvester, and Produce Resource Producer.

Glest recently attracts the attention of different researchers as in 2009 Dimitriadis [33] investigated the design of reinforcement learning autonomous agents that learn to play Glest RTS game through interaction with the game itself. He used the well-known SARSA and LSPI algorithms to learn how to choose among different high-level

strategies with the purpose of winning against the embedded AI opponent, while Aref et al. in 2012 proposed a new model called (REAL-SEE) for exchanging opponent experiences among real-time strategy game engines of Glest [34].

### 2.2.2. StarCraft Brood War.

StarCraft Brood War shown in Figure 5 is an expansion pack released in 1998 for the award-winning real-time strategy game StarCraft. Brood War gameplay remains fundamentally unchanged from that of StarCraft but with new difficult campaigns, map tilesets, music, extra units for each race, upgraded advancements, and less practical rushing tactics where missions are no longer entirely linear [41, 42]. Through the Brood War a single agent can make high-level strategic decisions as attacking an opponent or creating a secondary base and mid-level decisions as deciding what buildings to build [42, 43].

Brood War has gained popularity as a test bed for research as it exhibits all of the issues concerning most interested AI research areas in RTS environments including pathfinding, planning, spatial and temporal reasoning, and opponent modeling. Also Brood War has a huge number of online game replays that have been used as the case base for case-based reasoning (CBR) systems to analyze opponent strategies [42, 43].

In 2012, Wender and Watson introduced an evaluation of the suitability of Q-learning and SARSA reinforcement learning algorithms to perform the task of micromanaging combat units in the StarCraft Brood War RTS game [44], while in 2014 Siebra and Neto proposed a modeling approach for the use of SARSA in enabling the computational agents evolving their combat behavior according to actions of opponents to obtain better results in later battles [45].

## 3. Least-Squares Continuous Actions Policy Iteration (LSCAPI)

Reinforcement learning and video games have a long beneficial conjoint history as games are fruitful fields for testing reinforcement learning algorithms. In any application of reinforcement learning, the choice of algorithm is just one of many factories that determined success or failure. The choice of the algorithm is not even the most significant factor. The choice of representation, formalization, the encoding of domain knowledge, and setting of parameters can all have great influence.

**Input:** discount factor $\gamma$
$\phi_i \colon X \rightarrow R, i = 1, \ldots, N, \psi_j \colon U, j = 0, 1, 2, \ldots, M_P$
(1) $l \leftarrow 0$, initialize policy $h_0$
(2) measure initial state $x_0$
(3) **for** step $k = 0, 1, 2, \ldots$ **do**
(4) $u_k = \phi^T(x, \overline{u})\theta_l, \psi = 1$; a uniform random action in $U, \psi = -1$
(5) apply $u_k$, measure state $x_{k+1}$, and reward $r_{k+1}$
(6) start LSTD-Q policy evaluation
$\qquad \Gamma_0 \leftarrow 0, \Lambda_0 \leftarrow 0, z_0 \leftarrow 0$
(7) $\Gamma_{k+1} \leftarrow \Gamma_k + \phi(x_k, u_k)\phi^T(x_k, u_k)$
(8) $\Lambda_{k+1} \leftarrow \Lambda_k + \phi(x_k, u_k)\phi^T(x_{k+1}, h(x_{k+1}))$
(9) $z_{k+1} \leftarrow z_k + \phi(x_k, u_k)r_{k+1}$
(10) finalize policy evaluation
$$\frac{1}{k+1}\Gamma_{k+1}\theta_l = \gamma\frac{1}{k+1}\Lambda_{k+1}\theta_l + \frac{1}{k+1}z_{k+1}$$
(11) policy improvement
$$h_{l+1}(x) \leftarrow u_L + (u_H - u_L)\frac{1 + \text{argmax}_{\overline{u}}\phi^T(x, \overline{u})\theta_l}{2} \forall x$$
(12) **until** $h_{l+1}$ is a satisfactory
(13) $l \leftarrow l + 1$
(14) **end for**
**Output:** $\widehat{h^*} = h_{l+1}$

ALGORITHM 1: Offline Least-Squares Continuous Actions Policy Iteration.

In this research the researchers proposed an offline pure batch algorithm based on the Least-Squares Policy Iteration algorithm. Least-Squares Policy Iteration is a relatively new, model-free, approximate policy iteration algorithm for control. It is an offline, off-policy batch training method that exhibits good sample efficiency and offers stability of approximation [13–15].

Least-Squares Policy Iteration evaluates policies using the least-squares temporal difference for Q-functions (LSTD-Q) and performs exact policy improvements. To find the Q-function of the current policy, it uses a batch of transition samples, with LSTD-Q, to compute the parameter vector. Then, an improved policy in this Q-function is determined, to find the Q-function of the improved policy and so on [5]. Most releases of LSPI use discrete actions although for control problems; continuous actions are needed. As systems need to be stabilized, any discrete action may cause unneeded chattering of the control action.

The idea of LSCAPI as described in Algorithm 1 concentrates on solving discrete action problem through comparing actions to get the largest Q-value action to be applied. But first scalar control actions $U$ are considered to deal with the actions as a continuous action chain where $(U = [u_L, u_H])$.

A new parameter for evaluating actions other than state parameters is proposed called orthogonal polynomials $\Psi$. $\Psi$ is evaluated by two values $\{-1, 1\}$ considering if the action is selected for applying in the game through the current step or not. Fitted action is evaluated by 1 where the engine will return the true value that was used to compute the policy. The other value is $-1$ where the action is discarded and a new action is selected from the action space $U$.

As soon as the fitted action is selected the LSTD-Q [13] function evaluates the policy by creating parameter $\theta$ from the input transition using the selected fitted action.

Finally the difference between the previous and the new selected actions is calculated and stored with the new action as in (1). This step optimizes the needed storage space for actions by only storing the difference between actions not the actions themselves:

$$\widehat{Q}(x, u) = \sum_{j=0}^{M_P} \psi_j(\overline{u}) \sum_{i=1}^{N} \overline{\phi}_i(x) \theta_{[i, j+1]},$$

$$\widehat{Q}(x, u) = \phi^T(x, \overline{u})\theta. \tag{1}$$

## 4. Testing LSCAPI on Real Cases

For more explanation the LSCAPI algorithm was tested on 8 Queens, Glest, and StarCraft Brood War games and implemented using Microsoft visual studio 2013 C# engine.

*4.1. 8 Queens.* Through this section the proposed algorithm will be used for solving the 8 Queens problem and tracing each step separately. But first there are some assumptions to clarify:

(i) $X$ is the states in the game which are eight states (eight rows).

(ii) $U$ is the actions which are continuous as every state has a chain of actions for it.

(iii) $N = 8$ considering $8 \times 8$ board and $M_P = 64$ which represents the probability of actions that the 1st queen can be taken on the board.

*(i) 1st Queen.* As clarified in Figure 6, the first queen will be set randomly on the first row of the board, where the initial state $\phi_1 = s_0 = 1$ indicates that $s_0$ is in row 8 and in column

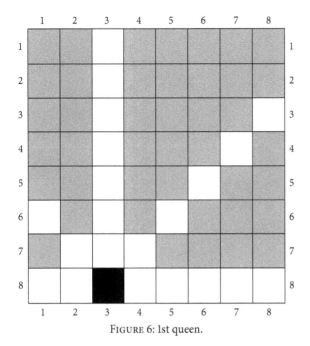

FIGURE 6: 1st queen.

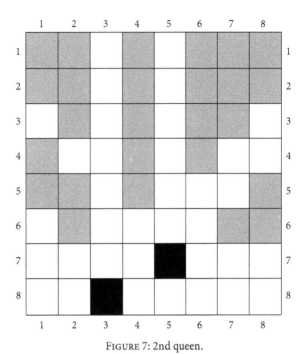

FIGURE 7: 2nd queen.

3 ($j = 3$). The probability [row, column] of the 1st queen is $(8, 3)$, which indicates that the action for placing the 1st queen in column 3 is taken.

*(ii) 2nd Queen.* After placing the 1st queen, the probability of actions for the second queen is $M_P = 42$, eliminating the probabilities that other queens could be on the same row, column, or diagonals. In the current state a matrix of continuous actions will be initiated holding the five available probabilities of actions $[(7, 1); (7, 5); (7, 6); (7, 7); (7, 8)]$ that the second queen could take in the next row.

Through applying LSCAIP, the value of $\psi$ will be set to $-1$ if action $(7, 1)$ is selected as it increases the probability of having pairs of attacking queens and set to 1 if the action $(7, 5)$ is selected as it provides more possible actions to take. Based on LSCAPI the action with the higher $Q$-function $(7, 5)$ will be selected. State $\phi_2 = s_1 = 2$ means that $s_1$ is in row 7 and in column 5 ($j = 5$). So the action with the largest $Q$-function was to place the queen in position $(7, 5)$ as shown in Figure 7.

*(iii) 3rd Queen.* After placing the 2nd queen, we will move to the next state, the third row, having 26 probabilities of actions to place the 3rd queen on board and only 3 probabilities of actions in the continuous actions matrix $[(6, 2); (6, 7); (6, 8)]$. The previous steps will be repeated from state 2 to select the action with the higher $Q$-function indicating the action generating more possible positions on the board to place the 4th queen. As in Figure 8, the 3rd queen will be placed on position $(6, 2)$, where state $\phi_3 = s_2 = 3$ means that $s_2$ is in row 6 and column 2.

The same is done in the next five states to get the policy of the game and solve the problem by placing the eight queens in their true places without errors as shown in Figures 9, 10, 11, 12, and 13.

Table 1 describes some of the other solutions generated by LSPI and LSCAPI for the 8 Queens game.

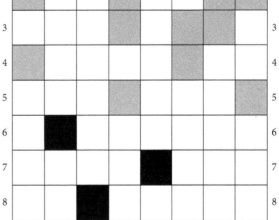
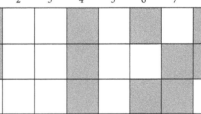

FIGURE 8: 3rd queen.

The performance of any action in the chain is measured based on the number of nonattacking queens. The minimum is equal to zero where all queens attack each other. The maximum is 28 where there are no attacking queens. The performance is calculated based on (2) to determine the fitness of the action compared to alternative actions:

$$P_A = \frac{\text{No. of Non-attacking pairs}}{\text{No. of pairs}}. \qquad (2)$$

Table 2 represents the performance evaluation of actions taken by LSCAPI in case 1 $\{6, 3, 7, 2, 8, 5, 1, 4\}$. Every row has

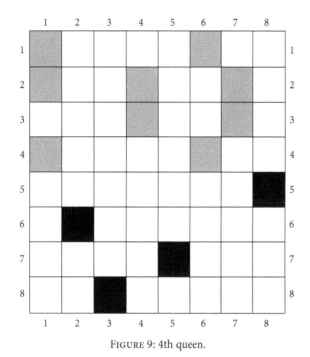

FIGURE 9: 4th queen.

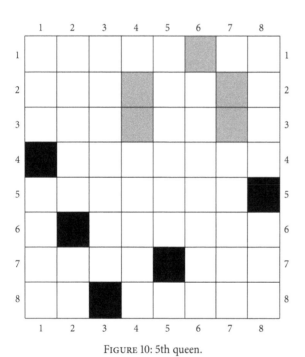

FIGURE 10: 5th queen.

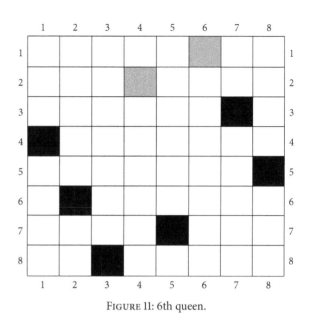

FIGURE 11: 6th queen.

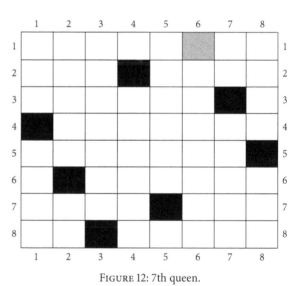

FIGURE 12: 7th queen.

chain of fitted actions evaluated by (2). Notice that if two fitted actions have the same values, the fitted one is chosen depending on the previous chosen actions. Table 3 represents the performance evaluation of discrete actions taken by LSPI.

It is noticed that the case performance achieved by LSCAPI is higher than the case performance achieved by LSPI from which we can also determine that actions selected by LSCAPI are much better than LSPI that finally produce better game performance.

TABLE 1: Problem solution using LSPI versus LSCAPI.

| Cases | Problem solution | | | | | | | |
|-------|---|---|---|---|---|---|---|---|
|       | 1 | 2 | 3 | 4 | 5 | 6 | 7 | 8 |
| LSCAPI | | | | | | | | |
| Case 1 | 5 | 1 | 8 | 6 | 3 | 7 | 2 | 4 |
| Case 2 | 6 | 3 | 7 | 2 | 8 | 5 | 1 | 4 |
| Case 3 | 5 | 7 | 2 | 6 | 3 | 1 | 8 | 4 |
| Case 4 | 4 | 2 | 5 | 8 | 6 | 1 | 3 | 7 |
| Case 5 | 5 | 3 | 1 | 6 | 8 | 2 | 4 | 7 |
| LSPI | | | | | | | | |
| Case 1 | 2 | 7 | 5 | 8 | 1 | 4 | 6 | 3 |
| Case 2 | 5 | 2 | 8 | 1 | 4 | 7 | 3 | 6 |
| Case 3 | 6 | 3 | 1 | 8 | 4 | 2 | 7 | 5 |
| Case 4 | 7 | 4 | 2 | 5 | 8 | 1 | 3 | 6 |
| Case 5 | 1 | 7 | 5 | 8 | 2 | 4 | 6 | 3 |

TABLE 2: LSCAPI case (1).

| State (row) | Action performance inside the chain (column) | | | | | | | |
|---|---|---|---|---|---|---|---|---|
| 8 | 0 | 0 | 0 | **4** | 0 | 0 | 0 | 0 |
| 7 | **1/21** | 0 | 0 | 0 | 0 | 0 | 0 | 0 |
| 6 | 0 | 0 | 0 | 0 | **1/21** | 0 | 0 | 0 |
| 5 | 0 | 0 | 0 | 0/21 | 0 | 0 | 0 | **2/21** |
| 4 | 0 | **3/21** | 0 | 3/21 | 0 | 0 | 0 | 0 |
| 3 | 3/21 | 0 | 0 | 0 | 4/21 | 0 | **5/21** | 0 |
| 2 | 3/21 | 5/21 | **6/21** | 2/21 | 0 | 0 | 0 | 6/21 |
| 1 | 0 | 0 | 0 | 0 | 0 | **6** | 0 | 0 |
| | 1 | 2 | 3 | 4 | 5 | 6 | 7 | 8 |
| Total performance = 18/21 = 0.857 | | | | | | | | |
| Problem | 6 | 4 | 5 | 2 | 1 | 5 | 6 | 4 |
| Solution | 6 | 3 | 7 | 2 | 8 | 5 | 1 | 4 |

TABLE 3: LSPI case (1).

| State (row) | Action performance inside the chain (column) | | | | | | | |
|---|---|---|---|---|---|---|---|---|
| 8 | 0 | 0 | 0 | 0 | 0 | **6** | 0 | 0 |
| 7 | 0 | 0 | **0/23** | 0 | 0 | 0 | 0 | 0 |
| 6 | **1/23** | 0 | 0 | 0 | 0 | 1/23 | 0 | 0 |
| 5 | 0 | 0 | 0 | 0 | 0 | 0 | 0 | **2/23** |
| 4 | 0 | 0 | 0 | 0 | **4/23** | 0 | 0 | 3/23 |
| 3 | 4/23 | **4/23** | 0 | 0 | 0 | 2/23 | 0 | 3/23 |
| 2 | 3/23 | 5/23 | 3/23 | **6/23** | 3/23 | 0 | 0 | 0 |
| 1 | 0 | 0 | 0 | 0 | 0 | 0 | **7** | 0 |
| | 1 | 2 | 3 | 4 | 5 | 6 | 7 | 8 |
| Total performance = 17/23 = 0.739 | | | | | | | | |
| Problem | 7 | 8 | 2 | 5 | 8 | 1 | 6 | 3 |
| Solution | 7 | 4 | 2 | 5 | 8 | 1 | 3 | 6 |

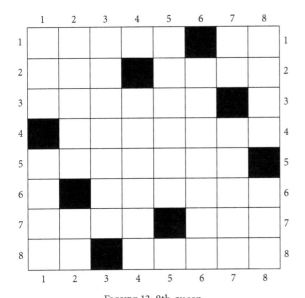

FIGURE 13: 8th queen.

TABLE 4: LSCAPI three towers case.

| Game | | | | | | |
|---|---|---|---|---|---|---|
| Available actions | AT | B | MA | P | PRP | WH |
| Actions priority | | | | | | |
| State 1 | PRP | MA | B | AT | P | 0 |
| | *Kills* = 250 *Units* = 200 *Resources* = 1100 | | | | | |
| State 2 | PRP | MA | B | WH | 0 | 0 |
| | *Kills* = 900 *Units* = 850 *Resources* = 3000 | | | | | |
| Player | | | | | | |
| Available actions | AT | B | MA | P | PRP | WH |
| Actions priority | | | | | | |
| State 1 | WH | PRP | B | MA | AT | P |
| | *Kills* = 150 *Units* = 200 *Resources* = 400 | | | | | |
| State 2 | PRP | WH | MA | B | P | 0 |
| | *Kills* = 300 *Units* = 300 *Resources* = 800 | | | | | |

*4.2. Glest.* The evaluation of LSCAPI in Glest is a bit different than in 8 Queens as in Glest the LSCAPI works on improving the game engine policy against the player. The researchers in evaluating LSCAPI in Glest concentrated on three parameters $\Delta kills$, $\Delta Units$, and $\Delta resources$ as in Table 4, where $\Delta kills$, $\Delta Units$, and $\Delta resources$ represent the gained or lost knights, units, and resources as a result of moving from state $S_i$ to $S_{i+1}$ (executing an action).

In LSCAPI algorithm we will get action for a state not as discrete but as continuous chain of actions. Every action in a chain has the value of polynomial 1 or −1 not as a calculation but only for selecting the fittest action in this state. Using continuous chain will improve efficiency of the game and speed it up. The LSCAPI arranges the most fitted action then the next action and so on based on priority. It saves time to select the fitted action and enhance performance. Fitted actions are evaluated by the most reward resulting from them.

In Table 4 a sample case of Glest game called three towers was introduced. LSCAPI arranges the available actions in a priority continuous chain. This method helps to get the actions with the higher performance in less time.

In this case the available actions were Add Tasks (AT), Build (B), Massive Attack (MA), Produce (P), Produce Resource Producer (PRP), and Worker Harvest (WH). These actions are arranged based on their priority; the action with a high priority will be in the beginning of the chain and so on until the only fitted actions that will be used in state are complete.

In "game" state 1 the priority of continuous actions chain is (PRP, MA, B, AT, P); we use only five actions from the six input actions in this case with the shown reward. In state 2 we use only four actions of them, while in player the priority chain of actions in state 1 includes all of the input actions and in state 2 it includes only five of them.

Meanwhile in the tower of souls case as in Table 5 the available actions were Produce Resource Producer, Build One Farm, Refresh Harvest, Massive Attack, Return Base, and Upgrade.

In game state 1 the priority of continuous actions chain is (MA, PRP, RH, RB, and BOF); we use only five actions from the six input actions in this case with the shown reward. In

TABLE 5: LSCAPI tower of souls case.

| Game | | | | | |
|---|---|---|---|---|---|
| Available actions | PRP | BOF | RH | MA | RB | Up |
| Actions priority | | | | | |
| State 1 | PRP | MA | BOF | Up | RB | 0 |
| | *Kills* = 350 *Units* = 300 *Resources* = 1700 | | | | |
| State 2 | MA | PRP | Up | RB | 0 | 0 |
| | *Kills* = 1300 *Units* = 950 *Resources* = 5000 | | | | |
| Player | | | | | |
| Available actions | PRP | BOF | RH | MA | RB | Up |
| Actions priority | | | | | |
| State 1 | MA | PRP | RH | RB | BOF | 0 |
| | *Kills* = 200 *Units* = 150 *Resources* = 900 | | | | |
| State 2 | PRP | RB | BOF | MA | Up | 0 |
| | *Kills* = 500 *Units* = 400 *Resources* = 2300 | | | | |

state 2 we use only four actions of them, while in player the priority chain of actions, as in the table, in state 1 includes all of the input actions and in state 2 it includes only five of them. Finally the calculations of the reward function to evaluate the action selection mechanism are based on

$$\text{reward} = \Delta\,(\text{kills}) + \Delta\,(\text{units}) + \Delta\,(\text{resources}) \quad [33], \quad (3)$$

where

$$\Delta\,(\text{kills}) = \big[\text{kills (agent new state)}$$
$$- \text{kills (agent old state)}$$
$$- \text{kills (enemy new state)}$$
$$- \text{kills (enemy old state)}\big] \times 100 \quad [33],$$

$$\Delta\,(\text{units}) = \big[\text{units produced (agent new state)}$$
$$- \text{units produced (agent old state)}$$
$$- \text{units produced (enemy new state)}$$
$$- \text{units produced (enemy old state)}\big] \times 50 \quad [33], \quad (4)$$

$$\Delta\,(\text{resources}) = \big[\text{resources (agent new state)}$$
$$- \text{resources (agent old state)}$$
$$- \text{resources (enemy new state)}$$
$$- \text{resources (enemy old state)}\big] \quad [33].$$

Table 6 demonstrates an example for calculating reward function, based on the values obtained from the number of kills, units, and resources in each two consecutive states as in (3). The reward values support the superiority of the LSCAPI over LSPI with a reasonable difference.

*4.3. StarCraft Brood War.* The StarCraft Brood War applied the same case form as Glest, so we will just concentrate on the calculations of the reward function. The reward function of

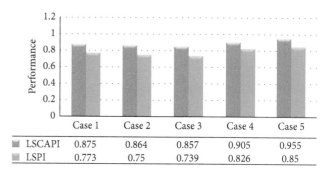

| | Case 1 | Case 2 | Case 3 | Case 4 | Case 5 |
|---|---|---|---|---|---|
| LSCAPI | 0.875 | 0.864 | 0.857 | 0.905 | 0.955 |
| LSPI | 0.773 | 0.75 | 0.739 | 0.826 | 0.85 |

FIGURE 14: LSPI versus LSCAPI generated solution cases performance.

Brood War is representing the difference between the damage done by the agent and the damage received by the agent in each two consecutive states, to evaluate the action selection mechanism as in

$$\text{Reward}_{t+1} = \sum_{i=1}^{m} \Big(\big(\text{enemy\_unit\_health}_{i_t}$$
$$- \text{enemy\_unit\_health}_{i_{t+1}}\big) - \big(\text{agent\_unit\_health}_{i_t} \quad (5)$$
$$- \text{agent\_unit\_health}_{i_{t+1}}\big)\Big) \quad [42].$$

Table 7 demonstrates an example for calculating the reward of agent in case of applying the LSPI and the SARSA (already applied in the StarCraft Brood War engine) action selection mechanisms, through the Protoss versus Zerg Case. This case included four ground units, Probe, Dragon, Drone, and Larva, considering that Drone and Larva units belong to Zerg which represents the game agent, while Probe and Dragon units belong to Protoss which represents the game enemy.

We can notice that the reward values in the Brood War are within the range of [0, 1] which is much smaller in range than Glest. Also from the table it is cleared that the reward of the agent resulting from applying actions supported by LSCAPI is much higher than the agent reward in case of SARSA.

## 5. LSCAPI Implementation

The LSCAPI was implemented using Microsoft visual studio 2013 C# and packaged to the Glest and StarCraft Brood War games engines while the 8 Queens was a fully standup application based on LSPI and LSCAPI.

## 6. Results and Discussion

*6.1. 8 Queens.* The overall performance of 5 different solutions generated by the LSCAPI and LSPI is calculated through the implementation and shown in Figure 14 from which we can detect that the LSCAPI generated actions and solutions that achieved better performance against opponents than LSPI which also indicates better policy through the game.

Meanwhile in Figure 15 the time taken by each one of these solutions through LSPI and LSCAPI is presented. It is

TABLE 6: Three towers case.

| | LSCAPI | | | | |
|---|---|---|---|---|---|
| | State 1 (old) | | State 2 (new) | | Reward |
| Evaluation metrics | Game (agent) | Player (enemy) | Game (agent) | Player (enemy) | |
| Kills | 250 | 150 | 900 | 300 | 20,000 |
| Units | 200 | 200 | 850 | 300 | 7,500 |
| Resources | 1100 | 400 | 3000 | 800 | 70 |
| | | *Total reward* | | | *Reward* = 27,570 |
| | LSPI | | | | |
| | State 1 (Old) | | State 2 (New) | | Reward |
| Evaluation metrics | Game (agent) | Player (enemy) | Game (agent) | Player (enemy) | |
| Kills | 300 | 100 | 700 | 120 | 18,000 |
| Units | 200 | 152 | 660 | 240 | 3,400 |
| Resources | 2500 | 200 | 4000 | 300 | 100 |
| | | *Total reward* | | | *Reward* = 21,500 |

TABLE 7: Protoss versus Zerg Case.

| | LSCAPI | | | | |
|---|---|---|---|---|---|
| | State 1 (old) | | State 2 (new) | | Reward |
| Evaluation metrics | Zerg (agent) | Protoss (enemy) | Zerg (agent) | Protoss (enemy) | |
| Drone units health | 0.85 | | 0.6 | | |
| Larva units health | 0.95 | | 0.8 | | 0.2 |
| Probe units health | | 0.85 | | 0.65 | |
| Dragon units health | | 0.9 | | 0.5 | |
| | SARSA | | | | |
| | State 1 (old) | | State 2 (new) | | Reward |
| Evaluation metrics | Zerg (agent) | Protoss (enemy) | Zerg (agent) | Protoss (enemy) | |
| Drone units health | 0.65 | | 0.5 | | |
| Larva units health | 0.65 | | 0.6 | | 0.08 |
| Probe units health | | 0.9 | | 0.85 | |
| Dragon units health | | 0.85 | | 0.58 | |

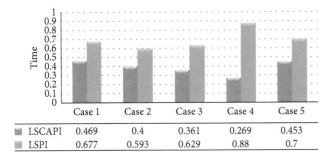

| | Case 1 | Case 2 | Case 3 | Case 4 | Case 5 |
|---|---|---|---|---|---|
| LSCAPI | 0.469 | 0.4 | 0.361 | 0.269 | 0.453 |
| LSPI | 0.677 | 0.593 | 0.629 | 0.88 | 0.7 |

FIGURE 15: LSPI versus LSCAPI solution generating time.

noticed from Figure 15 that LSCAPI not only generated policies that achieved a higher performance, but also generated them in less time as in case 4 solution of LSCAPI where the performance reaches 0.905 in 0.269 seconds while in LSPI case 4 performance only reached 0.28 in 0.88 seconds which is nearly the triple of the time needed to generate the LSCAPI solution.

Table 8 demonstrates the number of generated solutions by LSPI and LSCAPI in 10 different simulation attempts and the time taken by each attempt. The LSCAPI in attempt 4 generated 34 different arrangements of the 8 Queens in 9.16 seconds while LSPI generated only 10 solutions in 8.8 seconds.

Finally we can assure that LSCAPI achieved a really obvious superiority over LSPI generating more accurate solutions in less time which leads to better policies through game solving.

*6.2. GLEST.* To evaluate Glest, the reward of the agent in cases under consideration generated by LSPI and LSCAPI was calculated based on (3) and listed in Table 9 demonstrating that LSCAPI achieved much higher rewards to agents after performing the selected actions by LSCAPI which leads to better policies through facing opponents. For example, LSCAPI achieved 15000 in case 8 while LSPI selected actions only achieved 8500 which is nearly the half.

As we also can see from Table 9, LSCAPI cases with higher reward are associated with less number of used actions. This means that the reward has an inverse relationship with the number of used actions so that when the number of actions decreases the reward increases and vice versa.

TABLE 8: Number of solutions and their time generated by LSCAPI versus LSPI.

| Simulation attempts | LSCAPI | | LSPI | |
|---|---|---|---|---|
| | Number of solutions | Time in seconds | Number of solutions | Time in seconds |
| 1 | 22 | 10.31 | 13 | 08.80 |
| 2 | 22 | 08.80 | 15 | 08.89 |
| 3 | 25 | 09.03 | 14 | 08.81 |
| 4 | 34 | 09.16 | 10 | 08.80 |
| 5 | 20 | 09.06 | 12 | 08.39 |
| 6 | 25 | 09.05 | 13 | 08.79 |
| 7 | 31 | 09.35 | 19 | 08.85 |
| 8 | 25 | 08.99 | 17 | 09.15 |
| 9 | 24 | 09.03 | 16 | 08.45 |
| 10 | 35 | 09.18 | 12 | 08.64 |

TABLE 9: Reward function calculations of LSCAPI versus LSPI.

| Cases | LSCAPI algorithm | | | LSPI algorithm |
|---|---|---|---|---|
| | Used actions | Ratio | Reward | Reward |
| 1 | 20/24 | 0.833 | 27,570 | 21,500 |
| 2 | 19/24 | 0.792 | 30,010 | 25,000 |
| 3 | 16/24 | 0.667 | 33,000 | 26000 |
| 4 | 21/24 | 0.875 | 18,000 | 13,000 |
| 5 | 23/24 | 0.958 | 12,000 | 8,500 |
| 6 | 22/24 | 0.917 | 14,530 | 11,500 |
| 7 | 20/24 | 0.833 | 29,000 | 22,000 |
| 8 | 22/24 | 0.917 | 15,000 | 8,500 |
| 9 | 21/24 | 0.875 | 17,000 | 14,000 |
| 10 | 22/24 | 0.917 | 15,700 | 13,000 |
| 11 | 22/24 | 0.917 | 14,000 | 12,000 |

TABLE 10: Agent reward calculations of LSCAPI versus SARSA.

| Cases | Agent reward in case of LSCAPI | Agent reward in case of SARSA |
|---|---|---|
| 1 | 0.8 | 0.45 |
| 2 | 0.65 | 0.37 |
| 3 | 0.67 | 0.58 |
| 4 | 0.73 | 0.6 |
| 5 | 0.71 | 0.66 |
| 6 | 0.88 | 0.65 |
| 7 | 0.83 | 0.56 |
| 8 | 0.75 | 0.44 |
| 9 | 0.68 | 0.53 |
| 10 | 0.72 | 0.47 |

Finally Figure 16 presents the game army score achieved by LSCAPI policy learning against the score achieved by learning LSPI policy through the Duel scenario which is a medium difficulty level scenario. LSCAPI and LSPI policy scores were evaluated in 15 test games played taking into account that each policy game testing is played after every 10 games of learning.

Figure 16 clarified that game army using LSCAPI policy achieved much higher score than that achieved by LSPI, which means that LSCAPI really helps the game agents to efficiently face opponents and defeat them.

*6.3. StarCraft Brood War.* To evaluate Brood War, the reward function of the agent in the cases under consideration generated by LSCAPI and SARSA was calculated and listed in Table 10. The rewards values from Table 10 illustrated that LSCAPI achieved superiority over SARSA concerning the agent rewards, leading to better policies through facing opponents as in case 8, where LSCAPI achieved 0.75 as an agent reward value while SARSA action only achieved 0.44.

Finally Figure 17 presents the game army score achieved by LSCAPI policy learning against the score achieved by SARSA through the Terran scenario 1 which is a medium

difficulty level scenario. LSCAPI and SARSA policy scores were evaluated in 15 test games played taking into account that each policy game testing is played after every 10 games of learning.

Figure 17 illustrated that LSCAPI achieved much higher scores through the 15 test games than those achieved by SARSA. Also we can notice that SARSA score values increase with a decreasing rate which finally turned into a fixed value whatever the number of trials. On the other side LSCAPI score values grow with an increasing rate indicating that the learning rate is increasing based on the increasing states of agent rewarding as a result of better actions selection. From all of the foregoing, we can assure that LSCAPI represents a real help to the game engines to easily and efficiently face opponents and defeat them.

## 7. Conclusions and Future Work

Mapping from states to actions is the base function of game engine to face and react towards opponent, which is known as game policy. In this paper, we had studied the impact of batch reinforcement learning on enhancing game policy and proposed a new algorithm named Least-Squares Continuous Actions Policy Iteration (LSCAPI). The LSCAPI algorithm relied on LSPI considering handling continuous

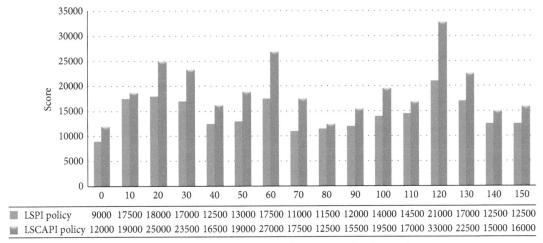

| | 0 | 10 | 20 | 30 | 40 | 50 | 60 | 70 | 80 | 90 | 100 | 110 | 120 | 130 | 140 | 150 |
|---|---|---|---|---|---|---|---|---|---|---|---|---|---|---|---|---|
| ■ LSPI policy | 9000 | 17500 | 18000 | 17000 | 12500 | 13000 | 17500 | 11000 | 11500 | 12000 | 14000 | 14500 | 21000 | 17000 | 12500 | 12500 |
| ■ LSCAPI policy | 12000 | 19000 | 25000 | 23500 | 16500 | 19000 | 27000 | 17500 | 12500 | 15500 | 19500 | 17000 | 33000 | 22500 | 15000 | 16000 |

FIGURE 16: LSPI versus LSCAPI policy score on Duel scenario.

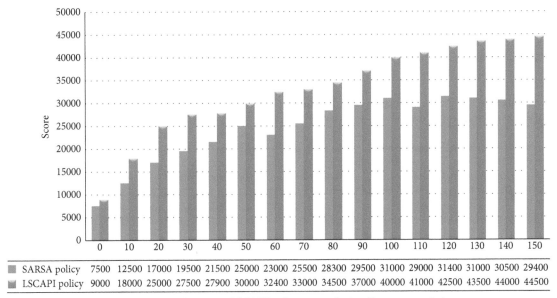

| | 0 | 10 | 20 | 30 | 40 | 50 | 60 | 70 | 80 | 90 | 100 | 110 | 120 | 130 | 140 | 150 |
|---|---|---|---|---|---|---|---|---|---|---|---|---|---|---|---|---|
| ■ SARSA policy | 7500 | 12500 | 17000 | 19500 | 21500 | 25000 | 23000 | 25500 | 28300 | 29500 | 31000 | 29000 | 31400 | 31000 | 30500 | 29400 |
| ■ LSCAPI policy | 9000 | 18000 | 25000 | 27500 | 27900 | 30000 | 32400 | 33000 | 34500 | 37000 | 40000 | 41000 | 42500 | 43500 | 44000 | 44500 |

FIGURE 17: SARSA versus LSCAPI policy scores during Terran scenario 1.

actions through a tradeoff between available actions and electing the action that scores higher reward to the game agent.

LSCAPI was tested on two different types of games: board games represented in 8 Queens and RTS games represented in Glest and StarCraft Brood War open source games. The proposed algorithm was evaluated based on the agent reward values, scores, time, and number of generated solutions. The evaluation result indicated that LSCAPI achieved better performance, time, policy, and agent learning ability than original LSPI.

In the future we plan to pursue testing LSCAPI on more complicated games as chess and poker to check its impact on game policy especially that the nonplaying character in these two games heavily relies on the game policy.

## References

[1] S. Russell and P. Norvig, *Artificial Intelligence: A Modern Approach*, Pearson, 3rd edition, 2009.

[2] E. Kok, *Adaptive reinforcement learning agents in RTS games [M.S. thesis]*, Utrecht University, Utrecht, The Netherlands, 2008, Thesis number INF/SCR-07-73.

[3] R. Sutton and A. Barto, *Reinforcement Learning: An Introduction*, MIT Press, Cambridge, Mass, USA, 1998.

[4] F. Guenter, M. Hersch, S. Calinon, and A. Billard, "Reinforcement learning for imitating constrained reaching movements," *Advanced Robotics*, vol. 21, no. 13, pp. 1521–1544, 2007.

[5] L. Busoniu, R. Babuska, B. De Schutter, and D. Ernst, *Reinforcement Learning and Dynamic Programming Using Function Approximators*, CRC Press, New York, NY, USA, 2010.

[6] M. Riedmiller, T. Gabel, R. Hafner, and S. Lange, "Reinforcement learning for robot soccer," *Autonomous Robots*, vol. 27, no. 1, pp. 55–73, 2009.

[7] S. Lange, T. Gabel, and M. Riedmiller, "Batch reinforcement learning," in *Reinforcement Learning: State of the Art*, M. Wiering and M. van Otterlo, Eds., Springer, 2011.

[8] S. Kalyanakrishnan and P. Stone, "Batch reinforcement learning in a complex domain," in *Proceedings of the 6th International Joint Conference on Autonomous Agents and Multiagent Systems (AAMAS '07)*, pp. 650–657, ACM, New York, NY, USA, May 2007.

[9] D. J. Lizotte, M. Bowling, and S. A. Murphy, "Linear fitted-q iteration with multiple reward functions," *The Journal of Machine Learning Research*, vol. 13, no. 1, pp. 3253–3295, 2012.

[10] A. Antos, R. Munos, and C. Szepesvari, "Fitted Q-iteration in continuous action-space MDPs," in *Advances in Neural Information Processing Systems 20*, pp. 9–16, MIT Press, Cambridge, Mass, USA, 2008.

[11] X. Xu, H. Zhang, B. Dai, and H.-G. He, "Self-learning path-tracking control of autonomous vehicles using kernel-based approximate dynamic programming," in *Proceedings of the International Joint Conference on Neural Networks (IJCNN '08)*, pp. 2182–2189, Hong Kong, June 2008.

[12] X. Xu, C. Lian, L. Zuo, and H. He, "Kernel-based approximate dynamic programming for real-time online learning control: an experimental study," *IEEE Transactions on Control Systems Technology*, vol. 22, no. 1, pp. 146–156, 2014.

[13] M. Lagoudakis and R. Parr, "Model-free least-squares policy iteration," in *Advances in Neural Information Processing Systems 14 (NIPS 2001)*, 2001.

[14] M. G. Lagoudakis and R. Parr, "Least-squares policy iteration," *The Journal of Machine Learning Research*, vol. 4, pp. 1107–1149, 2003.

[15] L. Buşoniu, A. Lazaric, M. Ghavamzadeh, R. Munos, R. Babuška, and B. De Schutter, "Least-squares methods for policy iteration," in *Reinforcement Learning*, vol. 12 of *Adaptation, Learning, and Optimization*, pp. 75–109, Springer, Berlin, Germany, 2012.

[16] M. Riedmiller, "Neural fitted Q iteration—first experiences with a data efficient neural reinforcement learning method," in *Machine Learning: ECML 2005*, Springer, Porto, Portugal, 2005.

[17] B. King, A. Fern, and J. Hostetler, "On adversarial policy switching with experiments in real-time strategy games," in *Proceedings of the 23rd International Conference on Automated Planning and Scheduling (ICAPS '13)*, pp. 322–326, Rome, Italy, June 2013.

[18] 2015, https://johnbaps.wordpress.com/2014/03/20/intelligent-agents-in-artificial-intelligence/.

[19] 2014, http://cs.smith.edu/~thiebaut/transputer/chapter9/chap9-4.html.

[20] I. Ghory, "Reinforcement learning in board games," Tech. Rep., Computer Science Department, Bristol University, Bristol, UK, 2004.

[21] M. Genesereth, N. Love, and B. Pell, "General game playing: overview of the AAAI competition," *AI Magazine*, vol. 26, no. 2, 2005.

[22] P. Ding and T. Mao, *Reinforcement Learning in Tic-Tac-Toe Game and Its Similar Variations*, vol. 1, Thayer School of Engineering at Dartmouth College, Hanover, NH, USA, 2009.

[23] T. B. Trinh, A. S. Bashi, and N. Deshpande, "Temporal difference learning in Chinese Chess," in *Tasks and Methods in Applied Artificial Intelligence*, vol. 1416 of *Lecture Notes in Computer Science*, pp. 612–618, Springer, Berlin, Germany, 1998.

[24] T. P. Runarsson and S. M. Lucas, "Coevolution versus self-play temporal difference learning for acquiring position evaluation in small-board go," *IEEE Transactions on Evolutionary Computation*, vol. 9, no. 6, pp. 628–640, 2005.

[25] M. Wiering, J. Patist, and H. Mannen, "Learning to play board games using temporal difference methods," Tech. Rep. UU-CS-2005-048, Institute of Information and Computing Sciences, Utrecht University, 2007.

[26] M. Block, M. Bader, E. Tapia et al., "Using reinforcement learning in chess engines," *Research in Computing Science*, vol. 35, pp. 31–40, 2008.

[27] I. E. Skoulakis and M. G. Lagoudakis, "Efficient reinforcement learning in adversarial games," in *Proceedings of the IEEE 24th International Conference on Tools with Artificial Intelligence (ICTAI '12)*, vol. 1, pp. 704–711, IEEE, Athens, Greece, November 2012.

[28] M. Szubert and W. Jaskowski, "Temporal difference learning of N-tuple networks for the game 2048," in *Proceedings of the IEEE Conference on Computational Intelligence and Games (CIG '14)*, pp. 1–8, IEEE, Dortmund, Germany, August 2014.

[29] G. Schrage, "The eight queens problem as a strategy game," *International Journal of Mathematical Education in Science and Technology*, vol. 17, no. 2, pp. 143–148, 1986.

[30] S. Lim and K. Son, "The improvement of convergence rate in n-queen problem using reinforcement learning," *International Journal of Information Technology*, vol. 11, no. 5, pp. 52–60, 2005.

[31] 2014, http://en.wikipedia.org/wiki/Real-time_strategy.

[32] M. Buro, "Real-time strategy gaines: a new AI research challenge," in *Proceedings of the 18th International Joint Conference on Artificial Intelligence (IJCAI '03)*, pp. 1534–1535, August 2003.

[33] K. Dimitriadis, *Reinforcement Learning in Real Time Strategy Games Case Study on the Free Software Game Glest*, Department of Electronic and Computer Engineering, Technical University of Crete, Chania, Greece, 2009.

[34] M. Aref, M. Zakaria, and S. Sarhan, "Real-time strategy experience exchanger model [real-see]," *International Journal of Computer Science Issues*, vol. 8, no. 3, supplement 1, pp. 360–368, 2011.

[35] B. Marthi, S. Russell, and D. Latham, "Writing stratagus-playing agents in concurrent ALisp," in *Proceedings of the 19th International Joint Conference on Artificial Intelligence (IJCAI '05)*, pp. 67–71, Edinburgh, Scotland, 2005.

[36] A. Gusmao, *Reinforcement learning in real-time strategy games [M.S. thesis]*, Aalto School of Science, Department of Information and Computer Science, 2011.

[37] M. Leece and A. Jhala, "Reinforcement learning for spatial reasoning in strategy games," in *Proceedings of the 9th AAAI Conference on Artificial Intelligence and Interactive Digital Entertainment (AIIDE '13)*, pp. 156–162, October 2013.

[38] H. Sethy, A. Patel, and V. Padmanabhan, "Real time strategy games: a reinforcement learning approach," *Procedia Computer Science*, vol. 54, pp. 257–264, 2015.

[39] 2014, http://glest.org/en/index.php.

[40] 2014, http://glest.org/en/techtree.php.

[41] K. Efthymiadis and D. Kudenko, "Using plan-based reward shaping to learn strategies in starcraft: broodwar," in *Proceedings of the IEEE Conference on Computational Intelligence in Games (CIG '13)*, pp. 1–8, IEEE, August 2013.

[42] S. Wender and I. Watson, "Applying reinforcement learning to small scale combat in the real-time strategy game StarCraft: Broodwar," in *Proceedings of the IEEE International Conference on Computational Intelligence and Games (CIG '12)*, pp. 402–408, Granada, Spain, September 2012.

[43] J. Eriksson and D. Ø. Tornes, *Learning to play starcraft with case-based reasoning: investigating issues in large-scale case-based*

*planning [Master of Science in Computer Science]*, Department of Computer and Information Science, Norwegian University of Science and Technology, Trondheim, Norway, 2012.

[44] S. Wender and I. Watson, "Applying reinforcement learning to small scale combat in the real-time strategy game StarCraft:Broodwar," in *Proceedings of the IEEE International Conference on Computational Intelligence and Games (CIG '12)*, pp. 402–408, IEEE, Granada, Spain, September 2012.

[45] C. Siebra and G. Neto, "Evolving the behavior of autonomous agents in strategic combat scenarios via SARSA reinforcement learning," in *Proceedings of the 13th Brazilian Symposium on Computer Games and Digital Entertainment (SBGAMES '14)*, pp. 115–122, Porto Alegre, Brazil, November 2014.

# 9

# MEnDiGa: A Minimal Engine for Digital Games

**Filipe M. B. Boaventura and Victor T. Sarinho**

*State University of Feira de Santana, Feira de Santana, BA, Brazil*

Correspondence should be addressed to Filipe M. B. Boaventura; fmbboaventura@gmail.com

Academic Editor: Michael J. Katchabaw

Game engines generate high dependence of developed games on provided implementation resources. Feature modeling is a technique that captures commonalities and variabilities results of domain analysis to provide a basis for automated configuration of concrete products. This paper presents the Minimal Engine for Digital Games (MEnDiGa), a simplified collection of game assets based on game features capable of building small and casual games regardless of their implementation resources. It presents minimal features in a representative hierarchy of spatial and game elements along with basic behaviors and event support related to game logic features. It also presents modules of code to represent, interpret, and adapt game features to provide the execution of configured games in multiple game platforms. As a proof of concept, a clone of the *Doodle Jump* game was developed using MEnDiGa assets and compared with original game version. As a result, a new *G-factor* based approach for game construction is provided, which is able to separate the core of game elements from the implementation itself in an independent, reusable, and large-scale way.

## 1. Introduction

Game engines allow game developers to reuse significant portions of key software components [1]. A game engine is defined as "extensible software that can be used as the foundation for many different games without major modification" [1] and represents "the collection of modules of simulation code that do not directly specify the game's behavior (game logic) or game's environment (level data)" [2].

Although game engines are reusable across multiple game projects, they generate high dependence of the game on implementation resources provided by the chosen engine [3]. Referring collectively to game logic, object model, and game state elements as *G-factor*, BinSubaih and Maddock [3] provided a service-oriented based architecture able to separate the core of game objects from the implementation itself and to support the game portability among game engines.

As an attempt to identify commonalities and variabilities in the digital game domain, Sarinho and Apolinário [4] proposed the *Narrative, Entertainment, Simulation*, and *Interaction* (NESI) feature model. It is a feature-based approach capable of representing the *G-factor* according to game concepts found in the literature. Sarinho and Apolinário also

proposed the *GameSystem, DecisionSupport*, and *SceneView* (GDS) feature model [5], which is based on game features that describe generic configurations and behavioral aspects found on game implementation resources identified in the literature. GDS was also used as a reference model to a proposed generative approach of digital games, showing as a result the feasibility of using features in the production of concrete digital games [5].

Although NESI and GDS models represent digital games without relying on the structure of game engines, the large number of proposed features became a difficulty in the design of small and casual games such as platform, quiz, or maze games [6]. This difficulty was confirmed during the production of the *SimplifiedPacMan* version [5] using Feature-based Environment for Digital Games (FEnDiGa) [7], a game production environment based on a combined representation of NESI and GDS features via Object Oriented Feature Modeling (OOFM) approach [8].

This paper presents the *Minimal Engine for Digital Games* (MEnDiGa), an extensible collection of representative classes based on a simplified set of NESI and GDS features that can be used as the foundation for small and casual games without major modification. MEnDiGa also provides a collection of modules of code for the interpretation and adaptation processes of represented features that do not directly specify the game's behavior or game's environment.

This paper is organized as follows. Section 2 describes important papers related to game domain engineering and game feature modeling. Section 3 presents the proposed MEnDiGa feature model and the resulting framework [9] with representative classes and modules of code. Section 4 describes the development steps to provide a *Doodle Jump* clone using MEnDiGa assets. Section 5 presents the software metrics analysis for *Doodle Jump* game versions. Finally, Section 6 presents the conclusions and future work of this project.

## 2. Related Work

Many types of reusable approaches have been applied in game development in recent years. They can simplify and accelerate the production of gaming systems, focusing on game modeling artifacts, digital game components, game product lines, and reusable aspects in game development, for example.

Considering the usage of software components on game development, Folmer [10] stated that developers could reuse specific game components to reduce the cost of building games. Folmer [10] also proposed a Reference Architecture for digital games as an attempt to possibly identify areas of reuse.

Zhang and Jarzabek [11] proposed the RPG Product Line Architecture (RPG-PLA), a group of common and variable features of four distinct RPG games. As a result, any of the original RPGs as well as similar ones could be derived from feature configurations interpreted by the RPG-PLA.

Albassam and Gomaa [12] proposed the use of Software Product Lines (SPL) in the video games domain. They have built a feature dependency model to describe the variability in multiplatform video games (such as different input/output devices, user interface, and CPU) and a variable component-based SPL suited for any video game in the product line.

Furtado et al. [13] proposed an improvement of the Sharp-Ludus project [14], replacing the previous ad hoc approach with a customized DSM approach called Domain-Specific Game Development. In this approach, feature models are used to improve the domain vocabulary and to help the identification of specific subdomains of the SPL domain.

Müller [15] presented the DGiovanni project, an open-source multiagent architecture for building interactive dramas. It makes use of ontologies to support the creation of different stories and to feed the system with story-related information.

Finally, Machado et al. [16] proposed a generic representation to model virtual agents in digital games. It allows the implementation of adaptable behaviors for game agents according to different features of the game environment. Agents are modeled using a linear combination of different variables, which are used to represent specific game features.

## 3. The Minimal Engine for Digital Games (MEnDiGa)

This section presents the proposed MEnDiGa feature model, based on a simplified collection of NESI and GDS features, and the resulting framework, based on representative classes and modules of code able to work with MEnDiGa features. Together, they can configure, represent, perform, and adapt feature specifications of digital games according to *G-factor* portability for distinct game platforms.

*3.1. MEnDiGa Feature Model.* Originally presented by Kang et al. [17] as part of the Feature Oriented Domain Analysis (FODA), feature modeling allows the identification of system properties during the domain analysis. According to them, a feature model represents "the *standard* features of a family of systems in the domain, and the relationships between them," and features are "aspects or characteristics of a domain which are visible to the user."

Following the feature modeling perspective to identify similarities or differences between the products of a product line [18], MEnDiGa presents digital games as collections of three main features: *Spatial*, *Behavior*, and *Observer* (Figure 1).

Regarding the *Spatial* feature, it is a collection of *Node* features that represent the elements of the game. *Spatial* feature can be also an *Environment* feature with a collection of *Location* features. Each *Node* feature contains a *CurrentLocation* feature to determine its current position in a game. Each *Node* feature also has a *BoundingVolume* feature to delimit the collision detection space. *Node* features can also contain *AudioNode*, *GraphicNode*, and *PhysicsNode* features, like *SceneNode* feature from GDS model [5].

The *AudioNode* feature represents information about sound effects to be used later in a digital game. It holds the path to an audio file that contains the desired sound effect or background music. *AudioNode* can also contain information about the state of the audio file and its play mode (*normal* or *looping*).

*GraphicNode* feature represents configurations related to the graphical modeling of a certain *Node* feature. As a simple *Text* feature, it holds information about the font and the alignment to draw a string. As a *Sprite* feature, it holds information related to how a texture, or even a region of a texture, should be rendered. Various regions of the same texture can be used to compose animations. As a *Camera* feature, it contains information about the *viewport* of a *Spatial*.

The *PhysicsNode* feature contains the physical attributes of a *Node* feature, such as its *density*, *mass*, and *restitution* coefficient. It also allows the setting of some constraints for physical simulation, such as the amount of *gravity* that acts on the *Node* feature and whether it is *solid* or not.

*Element* features are specializations of *Node* features. They contain one or more *Property* features represented with identifier *names* and representative *values* (*Speed*: 50 m/s; *Life*: 2 lives). An *Element* that is responsible for user *Behaviors* is defined as a *Player* feature. *Player* behaviors (*Jump* and *Crouch*, for instance) are related to default commands

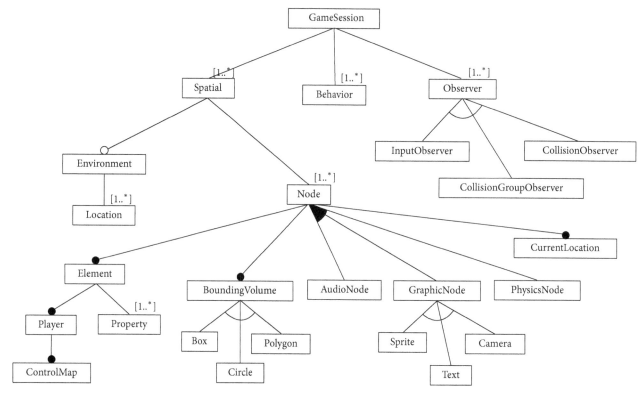

FIGURE 1: MEnDiGa feature diagram.

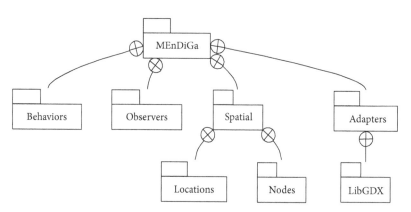

FIGURE 2: Package diagram of the MEnDiGa framework.

(*MOVE_UP, MOVE_DOWN*, etc.) defined on its *ControlMap* feature.

*Observer* features are responsible for performing *Behavior* features according to the evaluation of monitored resources. For instance, an *InputObserver* feature can be set to evaluate the command activation from an input device, executing the related *Behavior* feature of the *Player* after firing it. As another example, a *CollisionObserver* feature can trigger the execution of an *IncreaseScoreBehavior* feature when the *Player* collides with an item or execute a *LoseLifeBehavior* feature when it collides with an enemy.

*3.2. MEnDiGa Framework.* According to Czarnecki [19], a proposed feature model can be used to define a set of classes

capable of configuring various software systems. It is the project stage of a software domain [20], whose objective is to represent a feature value in each instantiated class based on a derived framework from the associated feature model.

In this sense, a collection of classes was proposed to represent, interpret, and adapt feature configurations derived from MEnDiGa feature model. The resulting framework was organized according to the following list of packages and classes (Figures 2 and 3):

(i) *Spatials:* represents the collection of spaces and game elements using *Spatial, Environment*, and *Node* classes

(ii) *Nodes:* defines specializations and internal components of the *Node* class, such as *AudioNode, GraphicNode, BoundingVolume, Element*, and *Player* classes

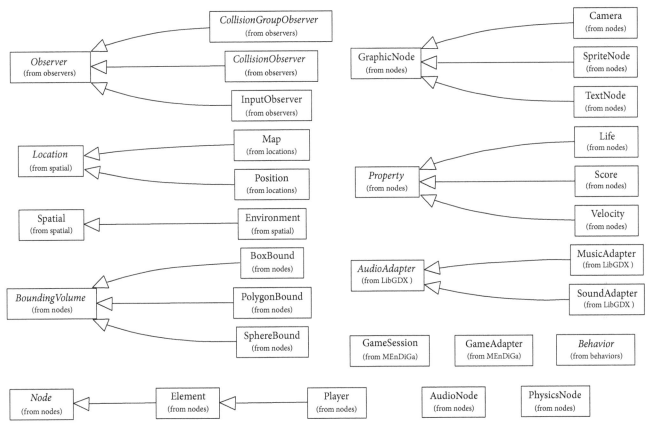

FIGURE 3: Classes and type hierarchies of the MEnDiGa framework.

(iii) *Locations:* defines internal components of an *Environment* using *Location*, *Map*, and *Position* classes

(iv) *Behaviors:* defines the abstract class *Behavior* able to be specialized in actions to be performed by a game

(v) *Observers:* defines abstract structures (*Observer*, *InputObserver*, *CollisionObserver*, and *CollisionGroupObserver*) to handle fired events in a game

(vi) *Adapters:* declares concrete classes able to render MEnDiGa objects in distinct game platforms

As the main class of the MEnDiGa framework, *GameSession* (Figure 3) has the responsibility of integrating the *Spatial*, *Observer*, and *Behavior* objects derived from the proposed MEnDiGa features. The *Spatial* object contains a collection of *Node* instances, such as *AudioNode*, *GraphicNode*, *PhysicsNode*, *BoundingVolume*, and *Location* instances. The *Element* class extends the *Node* class, including a collection of *Property* instances represented in a *HashMap* structure. The *Player* class has been defined as an *Element* subclass. It contains a control map with a collection of *Behavior* instances related to player commands. The *Environment* class was also defined as a *Spatial* specialization. It contains a collection of *locations* objects such as *Map* and *Position* instances (the game space).

For each *Observer* instance, there is a collection of *Behavior* instances. They are executed according to the *Observer* evaluation approach programmed for each possible event of a game. Each *Behavior* instance is programmed to execute a determined game action, modifying attributes in *Node* instances and changing the current *Spatial* instance of the *GameSession* instance in each renderization cycle of the game.

Considering the *adapters* classes, they are responsible for the execution of the instantiated MEnDiGa objects using implementation resources of a chosen game platform. For each worked game platform, a new set of adaptation classes is modeled only once for the first game, allowing the *G-factor* portability of other MEnDiGa games for the same game platform.

## 4. Case Study: A Doodle Jump Clone

A clone of the Doodle Jump game was developed to demonstrate the feasibility of producing games with MEnDiGa assets. The MEnDiGa version is based on a Doodle Jump clone called Super Jumper, developed using the LibGDX game framework [21]. Designed to faithfully reproduce the Super Jumper version, the MEnDiGa clone was developed using the same textures and audio files from the original game. It also presents a similar set of features in comparison with the original game.

This section presents an explanation of the Super Jumper development process, showing the necessary configuration, implementation, and adaptation steps to provide a MEnDiGa game. For the configuration step, it illustrates some identified Super Jumper features according to proposed MEnDiGa

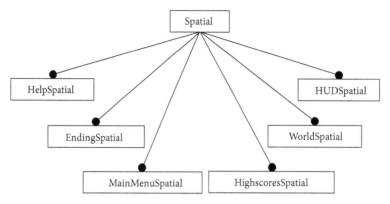

FIGURE 4: *Spatial* subfeatures for the Super Jumper game.

feature model. The implementation step presents developed classes and source codes based on designed MEnDiGa framework which represent structural and dynamics aspects of the Super Jumper game. Finally, the adaptation step describes developed classes able to interpret MEnDiGa objects and perform the Super Jumper game execution using LibGDX resources.

*4.1. Super Jumper Configuration.* According to Super Jumper game, the players must guide Bob (the playable character) to the end of the level. Bob must bounce on platforms to reach the castle, at the top of the game world. Along the way, Bob can collect coins for points and hit springs to jump higher. There are also obstacles, such as crumbling platforms and flying squirrels. The game ends in victory when Bob reaches the castle or defeat if he collides with a squirrel or falls of a platform.

For the MEnDiGa version, each screen of the Super Jumper game is represented using *Spatial* configurations, where each one holds an appropriate set of *Node* features. A *Position* feature contains the Cartesian coordinates of a *Node* instance, and it is used to locate nodes in a *Spatial* feature. *Position* also holds depth information used to define the overlapping between images on *Spatial*. Figure 4 illustrates this descriptive mapping among Super Jumper game elements and *Spatial* subfeatures for the Super Jumper game.

Figure 5 shows the *Spatial* configuration of the main menu screen. Each option in the main menu, as well as any clickable object in the game, is represented using *Node* features. These clickable nodes hold an appropriate *GraphicNode* feature (*Sprite* or *Text*), as well as a rectangular *BoundingVolume* feature to determine the clickable area. *BackgroundNode* and the *TitleNode* features are simply placeholders for the background and title of the game.

Figure 6 also shows the game world represented by the *WorldSpatial* feature. This spatial configuration contains *Node* features that build the game level as a whole. Since platforms and squirrels need the *speed* property, *Platform* and *Squirrel* subfeatures of the *Element* feature are used to represent them. *Bob*, the *Player* character represented as a feature, also contains a property for holding *score* information.

Stationary objects such as *Coins, Springs*, and the *Castle* are modeled as subfeatures of the *Node* feature.

When *Bob* reaches the *Castle* at the end of the level, the *EndingSpatial* feature is used to display the game's ending. Figure 7 shows *Bob* and the *Princess* having a conversation in front of the *Castle*. The *MessageNode* feature contains the *GraphicNode* feature responsible for displaying the line of the dialog. Clicking anywhere on the screen will advance to the next message or return the game to the main menu when the last message is displayed.

Regarding the support of MEnDiGa game events, there is a series of collision events among the Super Jumper game elements and the *Player* feature itself that must be monitored. Figure 8 illustrates some *Observer* features configured to be responsible for this collision detection and player monitoring during the game execution. There are also *Observers* features dedicated to monitoring interactions with the user interface components, such as clicks on the screen and button press.

The actions responsible for changing *Spatial* feature values are represented using *Behavior* features, such as *Player* commands (MOVE_UP, MOVE_LEFT, etc.) or game dynamics (increase/decrease score, win/lose game, etc.). Figure 9 presents some of these *Behavior* features, showing game dynamics that were implemented in the MEnDiGa version. It is noteworthy that *Observer* features will activate such *Behavior* features upon confirmation of a monitored event (ex.: *BUTTON1_PRESS → JUMP*).

*4.2. Super Jumper Implementation.* By the definition of Super Jumper game features, the next step consists of representing the Super Jumper configuration according to the MEnDiGa framework hierarchy. In this sense, *Node* subclasses are used to represent the characteristics of *Spatial* components, such as starting *Position*, *Element* properties, and *GraphicNode* instances.

In case of *Sprite* objects used to represent *GraphicNode* instances in the game, it is necessary to define the desired region of the image that will be shown. If this information is omitted, the whole image will be used. For each selected region in the image, it will contain subregions called *frames*, where each one will have the size set on the *SpriteNode* constructor (Algorithm 1). Each frame can be referenced using an

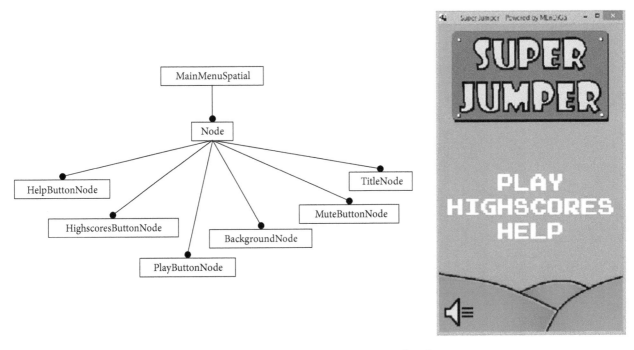

Figure 5: Main menu screen and respective *Spatial* configuration.

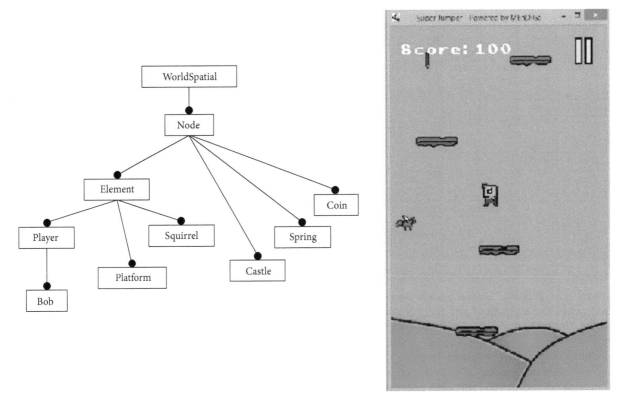

Figure 6: Spatial configuration of the gameplay screen.

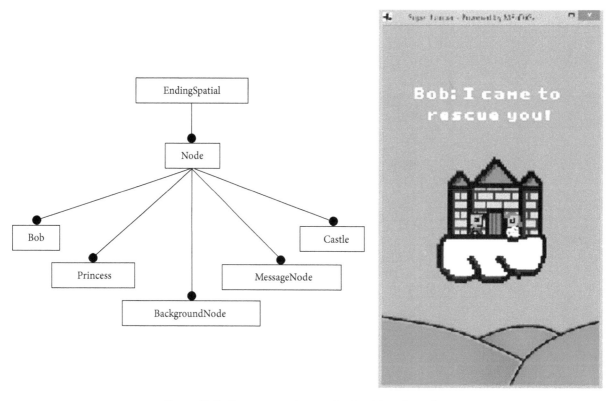

FIGURE 7: Ending screen and respective *Spatial* configuration.

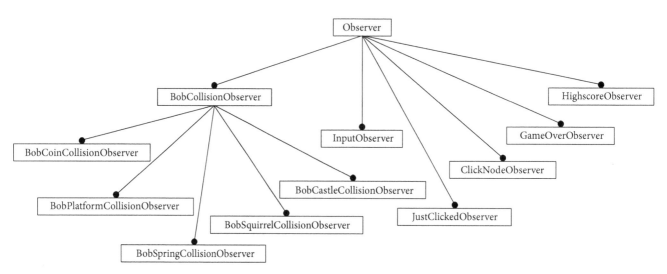

FIGURE 8: *Observer* subfeatures for the Super Jumper game.

index number (Figure 10). Animations are composed using selected frames to be rendered and their respective *frame delay* value (the amount of time that a frame will remain on the screen).

Regarding Super Jumper game dynamics, the *SuperJumperGame* class extends the *GameSession* class to "configure" the game (Algorithm 2). This class is programmed to instantiate *AudioNode* feature values, initial game observers to start the game, and respective game behaviors to perform

the game initialization. After this, the *SuperJumperGame* executes the *ChangeToMainMenuScreen* behavior (Algorithm 2) to prepare the *MainMenuSpatial* (Figure 5) to be displayed and start up the game.

When the player selects the *"Play"* option on the created main menu, the *ClickNodeObserver* instance executes *ReadyGame* behaviors (Figure 9). *ReadyGame*, in turn, executes the *GenerateLevel* behavior, which is responsible for creating and randomly placing the platforms, springs, coins, and

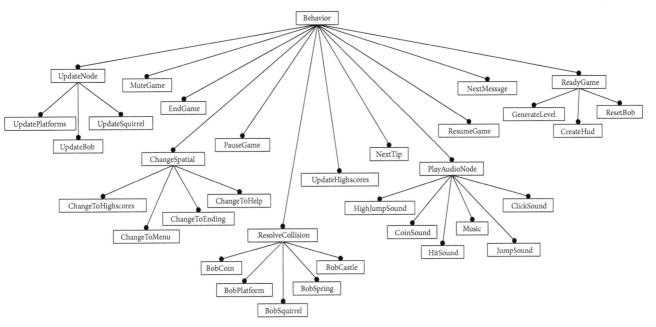

FIGURE 9: *Behavior* subfeatures for the Super Jumper game.

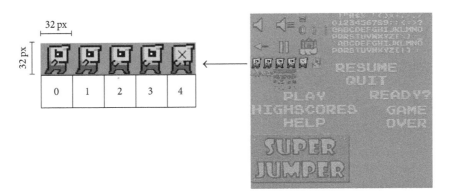

FIGURE 10: The highlighted region is extracted from the texture, according to the *GraphicNode* configuration.

```
// Create the graphic node
SpriteNode graphicNode = new SpriteNode("bob", // sprite name
        "res/superjumper/items.png", // source file path
        32, 32); // width and height of a single frame within the sheet
// Select a rectangular region of the texture
graphicNode.setRegion(0, 128, // Upper left corner position
        160, 32); // region width and height
// Defining animations
graphicNode.defineAnimation("jump", // Animation name
        new int[]{0,1},0.2f,          // Animations frame and frame delay
        PlayMode.LOOP_NORMAL);        // Play mode
graphicNode.setCurrentAnimation("jump"); // Set "jump" as the current animation
graphicNode.setScale(1/32f); // Set the scale as 32 pixels per game unit
this.addGraphicNode(graphicNode); // Add the sprite to the node
```

ALGORITHM 1: Setting up the *GraphicNode* of the playable character.

```
public class SuperJumperGame extends GameSession {
    public static enum GameState {RUNNING, PAUSED, READY, WIN}
    private GameState gameState;
    private AudioNode[] audioNodes;
    public SuperJumperGame() {
        // Configuring AudioNodes
        this.audioNodes = new AudioNode[] {
                new AudioNode("coinSound", "res/superjumper/coin.wav"), // ···
                new AudioNode("gameMusic", "res/superjumper/music.mp3") };
        // Configuring Observers
        this.addObserver(new CheckForNewHighScore(this));
        this.addObserver(new CheckGameOver(this));
        // Configuring Behaviors
        this.addBehavior("changeToMenu", new ChangeToMainMenuScreen(this));
        this.addBehavior("generateLevel", new GenerateLevel(this));
        this.addBehavior("createHud", new CreateHud(this));
        this.addBehavior("resetBob", new ResetBob());
        this.addBehavior(GameState.RUNNING.toString(), new UpdateRunning(this));
        this.addBehavior("endGame", new EndGame(this));
        this.addBehavior("playClickSound", new PlayClickSound(this));
    }
    public void initialize() {
        this.getBehavior("changeToMenu").execute(); // load the game menu
        this.getAudioNode(MUSIC).setState(State.PLAYING);
    }
    public void update(float deltaTime) {
        // Perform the current Running Behavior if the game still running
        if (this.gameState.equals(GameState.RUNNING)) {
            this.getBehavior(this.gameState.toString()).execute(deltaTime);
        }
    } // ···
```

ALGORITHM 2: Partial description of the *SuperJumperGame* class.

squirrels on the *WorldSpatial* instance. With the *WorldSpatial* populated, *ReadyGame* behavior calls the *ResetBob* behavior, putting the *Bob* object in the initial state before inserting it into the *WorldSpatial* instance. The *CreateHud* behavior is executed next, creating the *HUDSpatial* instance that holds the necessary *Node* instances for the *Head-Up Display*. *ReadyGame* behavior also sets the observers and behaviors required for the gameplay, such as the *InputObserver* instance to control *Bob*, the game collision observers and related behaviors, the behaviors to update node values during the gameplay, and the game observers to check for high score updates and game over events.

*UpdateNode* behaviors (Figure 9) are also executed for each generated frame in the game. They update the state of dynamic game elements based on defined game configurations and player inputs. The *UpdateSquirrel* and the *UpdatePlatform* behaviors are set to change the *Position* of *Squirrel* and *Platform* instances according to their *speed Property* value. If a *Platform* instance is set to crumble, the *UpdatePlatform* behavior is responsible for updating the countdown timer for the platform destruction. *UpdateBob* behavior changes the player *Position* using *gravity* and *horizontal speed* values. *UpdateHighscore* behavior is activated by the *HighscoresObserver* when the game ends after falling down the

screen or hitting an enemy/castle, changing the score ranking if the player has enough points.

*BobCollisionObserver* instances are responsible for evaluating collision events among the player character and each *Node* instance in *WorldSpatial*. They fire appropriate *ResolveCollision* behaviors (Figure 9) if the player's *BoundingVolume* intersects another *Node* instance. Some of these observers only trigger collisions on specific situations. For example, *Bob* instance can pass through *Spring* and *Platform* objects from below, but *ResolveCollision* behaviors must be performed if *Bob* hits them from above.

*Bob/Coin* collisions destroy the collided *Coin* instance and increase the *score Property* value. Collisions between *Bob* instance and the *Platform* or *Spring* instances increase its jumping *speed*. However, hitting a *Platform* instance may cause it to crumble, destroying it after a crumbling animation is complete. Hitting a *Squirrel* will trigger the *EndGame* behavior, showing a *"Game Over"* message on the *HUDSpatial* instance as *Bob* goes down through the screen. After clicking anywhere on the screen when the game is over, it will notify the *JustClickedObserver* instance to trigger the *ChangeToMainMenuScreen* behavior. Hitting the *Castle* instance will trigger the *ChangeToEndingScreen* behavior, completing the play through.

*4.3. Super Jumper Adaptation.* In a similar strategy to FEn-DiGa [7], the next and final step consists of applying Super Jumper instances to use MEnDiGa adapters. Such adaptation classes establish an integration pattern between game configurations with implementation resources of a chosen game platform.

LibGDX has been used in this project as a target game engine to provide MEnDiGa adapter classes. It is an open-source framework which presents good market acceptance to produce multiplatform Java games. Among LibGDX available adapters, *SpatialRenderer*, *GraphicNodeRenderer*, and *InputAdapter* should be highlighted.

For each *Spatial* instance on the *SuperJumperGame*, a *SpatialRenderer* needs to be created. It is responsible for loading and rendering specified settings of each *GraphicNode* object available in a *Spatial*. It also follows the rendering order of the *GraphicNode* instances according to the informed depth (*z*-axis of the *Position*) on each *Node* instance.

For each *GraphicNode* instance to be rendered, a specific *GraphicNodeRenderer* object is created based on the *GraphicNode* type. *TextNodeRenderer* uses the information on a *Text GraphicNode* instance to set up LibGDX's Bitmap Font utilities, loading an image file containing the glyphs and a font file to provide image characters. *SpriteNodeRenderer* uses the information stored on a *Sprite GraphicNode* instance to load the desired image file as a LibGDX *Texture* object. This texture is split and its frames are stored in an array, allowing the image usage as shown in Figure 10. In the adaptation process, the animation information defined in the *GraphicNode* instance is used to create *Animations*, LibGDX objects capable of managing *Sprite* animations.

The *InputAdapter* is the class responsible for notifying the *InputObserver* about input events. It implements the *InputProcessor*, an interface provided by LibGDX to receive input events from the keyboard, touchscreen, or mouse. The *InputAdapter* has an *adaptedControlMap* structure that makes the correspondence among *Player* commands (MOVE_LEFT, MOVE_RIGHT, etc.) and the LibGDX constants for input keys. If the pressed/released key corresponds with some *Player* command, the *InputAdapter* notifies the fired/released command to the *InputObserver* that performs the appropriate *playerBehavior* according to the configured game dynamics.

*SuperJumperLibGDX* performs the final adaptation among MEnDiGa assets and the LibGDX engine. It implements the *ApplicationListener* interface of the LibGDX, which contains the methods called during the game lifecycle such as *create* and *render*. *SuperJumperLibGDX* overrides the *create* method to instantiate *SuperJumperGame* and the other needed *adapters* during the application launching. Associations among *Observer* instances of the *SuperJumperGame* and the package *adapter* (*InputAdapter*, for instance) are also configured during the creation of the *SuperJumperLibGDX*. The *render* method is also being overridden to continually *draw* the respective *SpatialRenderer* and evaluate monitoring aspects of *Observer* instances.

In the end, after the *SuperJumperLibGDX* execution, LibGDX starts the initialization, rendering and updating processes of adapted MEnDiGa assets, displaying as a result the configured Super Jump game to be played. As MEnDiGa is an open-source project, more details about the LibGDX adaptation process can be found at https://bitbucket.org/fmbboaventura/mendiga (master branch).

## 5. Super Jumper Metrics Analysis

According to Pressman [22], product metrics help software engineers to visualize the design of the software, focusing on specific and measurable attributes of software engineering artifacts. In order to perform a comparative analysis and evaluate the quality of the produced digital game, a set of software metrics was collected from the original Super Jumper version and the respective cloned MEnDiGa version.

Table 1 presents the collected OO metrics of both games using the Eclipse Metrics plugin [23]. It provides metrics calculation and dependency analysis according to *Number of Classes, Number of Attributes, Number of Methods, Number of Static Attributes, Number of Static Methods, Number of Packages, Number of Overridden Methods, Average Number of Parameters, Total Lines of Code, Average Lines of Code per Method, Abstractness (A), Afferent Coupling (Ca), Efferent Coupling (Ce), Instability (I), Normalized Distance from Main Sequence (Dn), Lack of Cohesion of Methods (LOCOM), Average Nested Block Depth, Cyclomatic Complexity, Weighted Methods per Class (WMC)*, and *Depth of Inheritance Tree (DIT)*.

*Number of Classes, Number of Attributes, Number of Methods, Number of Static Attributes, Number of Static Methods, Number of Packages, Number of Overridden Methods, Average Number of Parameters, Total Lines of Code*, and *Average Lines of Code per Method* are simple and straightforward metrics, with a detailed explanation about them being unnecessary. *Abstractness (A)* represents the ratio of the number of abstract classes and interfaces to the total number of classes in the selected scope. It varies from zero to one, with $A = 0$ indicating a completely concrete solution and $A = 1$ indicating a completely abstract solution. *Afferent Coupling (Ca)* indicates the number of classes outside of the selected package which depend on the classes inside the package [24]. It also indicates the level of responsibility of the given package. *Efferent Coupling (Ce)* indicates the number of classes inside a package which depend on classes from other packages [24]. *Instability (I)* is obtained using $Ce/(Ca + Ce)$. It indicates the level of instability of a package, where $I = 0$ indicates a completely stable package and $I = 1$ a completely unstable package [24]. *Normalized Distance from Main Sequence (Dn)* is calculated using $|(A + I) - 1|$. It measures how far away a package is from the idealized line $A + I = 1$, called the Main Distance [24]. The distance should be close to zero for packages with a good balance between stability and abstractness. *Lack of Cohesion of Methods (LOCOM)* is calculated using $(M - \text{sum}(MF)/F)(M - 1)$, where $M$ is the number of methods in the class, $F$ is the number of fields, $MF$ is the number of methods accessing a particular field of the class, and $\text{sum}(MF)$ is the sum of $MF$ over all fields of the class. As a measure of the cohesiveness of a class, this metric is calculated using the Henderson-Sellers method [25]. A low LOCOM indicates a cohesive class, while a LOCOM close to 1 indicates lack of

TABLE 1: OO metrics from original Super Jumper and cloned MEnDiGa version.

| Metric property | Original Super Jumper | Cloned MEnDiGa version |
|---|---|---|
| *Abstractness (A)* | 0,107 | 0,042 |
| *Afferent Coupling (Ca)* | 14,8 | 2 |
| *Depth of Inheritance Tree (DIT)* | 2,231 | 1,87 |
| *Efferent Coupling (Ce)* | 13 | 17 |
| *Instability (I)* | 0,41 | 0,895 |
| *Lack of Cohesion of Methods (LOCOM)* | 0,023 | 0,267 |
| *Cyclomatic Complexity* | 1,576 | 2,18 |
| *Average Lines of Code per Method* | 7,129 | 7,57 |
| *Average Nested Block Depth* | 1,242 | 1,6 |
| *Normalized Distance from Main Sequence (Dn)* | 0,483 | 0,064 |
| *Number of Attributes* | 44 | 90 |
| *Number of Classes* | 65 | 23 |
| *Number of Methods* | 131 | 94 |
| *Number of Overridden Methods* | 43 | 18 |
| *Number of Packages* | 5 | 1 |
| *Average Number of Parameters* | 0,856 | 0,64 |
| *Number of Static Attributes* | 41 | 72 |
| *Number of Static Methods* | 1 | 6 |
| *Total Lines of Code* | 1912 | 1310 |
| *Weighted Methods per Class (WMC)* | 208 | 218 |

cohesion. *Average Nested Block Depth* indicates the average number of nested code blocks in the selected scope. Too many nested blocks lead to a more complex and less readable solution.

*Cyclomatic Complexity* is used to identify the complexity of a piece of code based on the amount of execution flows [26]. It is the number of independent paths in the source code and it is calculated for methods only. High values of this metric imply a complex solution that can be difficult to understand. *Weighted Methods per Class (WMC)* is the sum of the complexity of all methods in the selected class [27] (for this work, the measure of complexity of methods is Cyclomatic Complexity). Classes with high WCM tend to be complex and hard to reuse. *Depth of Inheritance Tree (DIT)* is the maximum length from the class to the root of the inheritance tree [27]. Hierarchies of classes with high DIT can contribute to reuse because the deeper classes in the hierarchy inherit more methods. However, very deep trees tend to be more complex because there are more classes and methods involved [27].

Analyzing the obtained metric results, it is possible to verify the following:

(i) *Normalized Distance from Main Sequence (Dn), Afferent Coupling (Ca), Efferent Coupling (Ce),* and *Instability (I)* show strong game dependency of the cloned version to MEnDiGa structures in contrast with original game version.

(ii) *Abstractness (A), Depth of Inheritance Tree, Total Lines of Code, Number of Methods, Number of Static Methods, Average Number of Parameters, Number of Packages, Number of Classes,* and *Number of Overridden Methods* metrics confirm the structural simplification of the cloned version in comparison with the original version, despite a higher *Number of Attributes* and *Number of Static Attributes*.

(iii) *Average Lines of Code per Method, Average Nested Block Depth, Cyclomatic Complexity,* and *Weighted Methods per Class (WMC)* indicate a small increment in the complexity of game production with MEnDiGa.

(iv) *Lack of Cohesion of Methods (LOCOM)* presents a higher result in MEnDiGa version, something that can be explained due to *Behavior* and *Observer* classes created to configure and monitore other classes instead of itself.

## 6. Conclusions and Future Work

This paper presented MEnDiGa, a game engine proposal based on the simplification of the NESI and GDS feature models. For this, MEnDiGa provides a minimal collection of necessary features capable of designing small and casual games. MEnDiGa also provides an implementation framework that can be configured and performed according to game designer intentions. Together, these MEnDiGa artifacts are able to realize the *G-factor* portability followed by NESI and GDS models and provide a product line solution capable of building *G-factor* based games in large scale.

Regarding the game platform portability, MEnDiGa assets were implemented and adapted to be interpreted using LibGDX game engine. Per FEnDiGa results [7] and by the production of respective adapter classes, it is possible to affirm that MEnDiGa structure is capable of being extended to additional Java game engines, such as jMonkeyEngine [28], JGame [29], and GTGE [30]. For other game platforms based on different types of programming languages, such as Unreal Engine 4 [31] that uses C++, it is necessary to reimplement MEnDiGa classes to the respective support language. To facilitate this conversion process among game engines based on distinct programming languages, a common XML specification of MEnDiGa games will be defined in the future for generative [5] and interpretive [7] game development approaches.

Regarding the production of games from interactive GUIs, game platforms with graphical support environment such as Unity [32], Godot [33], and Scratch [34] have been widely used to produce digital games. However, it is important to reinforce the fact that important game engines still use the API programming approach to implement the game logic for designed games, such as PixiJS [35] and Panda3D [36]. As described in this paper, MEnDiGa follows the traditional API programming approach to implement desired behaviors, define observer criteria, and "configure" classes of the proposed MEnDiGa framework. In the future, a graphical support environment for MEnDiGa will be developed to allow the visual configuration of a future XML representation of MEnDiGa games.

Moreover, regarding the complexity and variability in the production of digital games, dedicated game platforms for specific game categories [6], such as RPG Maker [37] and Adventure Game Studio [38], have been well accepted in digital game productions. MEnDiGa in its current modeling does not include specific game domains resources, being focused on providing generic elements available in casual and small games. To improve MEnDiGa as a dedicated game platform, it is necessary to define features and classes able to represent game structures of specific game categories, such as menus, HUDs, user interfaces, game rules, and game elements. The provided collection of dedicated features and classes will be able to produce casual games for specific game categories in a highly reusable way, evolving MEnDiGa consequently to the status of product line for specific game domains in the future.

Finally, clone implementation of the Doodle Jump game using MEnDiGa assets was also demonstrated in this paper. As an equivalent example of casual games available today, the developed clone game has similar mechanics, dynamics, and aesthetics characteristics [39] in comparison to the original Super Jumper version. It is an important verification/validation step of this project as an attempt to show the feasibility of MEnDiGa assets in the generation of concrete digital games. Some OO metrics were also collected from the original Super Jumper and cloned MEnDiGa version. By comparison, they confirm that, with a simpler structure and a small increase in complexity, MEnDiGa allows the configuration of digital games from a core structure that follows the *G-factor* concept of game portability across distinct game platforms.

## Acknowledgments

The authors acknowledge the Foundation for Research Support of the State of Bahia (FAPESB) for granting a scholarship to the graduate and coauthor Filipe M. B. Boaventura during the development of a preliminary proposal of this work [40].

## References

[1] G. Jason, *Game Engine Architecture*, CRC Press, 2009.

[2] M. Lewis and J. Jacobson, "Games engines in scientific research," *Communications of the ACM*, vol. 45, no. 1, p. 21, 2002.

[3] A. BinSubaih and S. Maddock, "Game Portability Using a Service-Oriented Approach," *International Journal of Computer Games Technology*, vol. 2008, Article ID 378485, 7 pages, 2008.

[4] V. Sarinho and A. Apolinário, "Feature Model Proposal for Computer Games Design," in *Proceedings of the VII Brazilian Symposium on Computer Games and Digital Entertainment*, pp. 54–63, 2008.

[5] V. T. Sarinho and A. L. Apolinário, "A generative programming approach for game development," in *Proceedings of the 8th Brazilian Symposium on Games and Digital Entertainment (SBGAMES' 09)*, pp. 83–92, Rio de Janeiro, Brazil, October 2009.

[6] M. Wolf, *The Medium of the Video Game*, University of Texas Press, Tex, USA, 2002.

[7] V. T. Sarinho, A. L. Apolinário Jr., and E. S. Almeida, "A feature-based environment for digital games," in *Proceedings of the 10th International Conference on Entertainment Computing (ICEC' 12)*, vol. 7522, pp. 518–523, Springer, Berlin, Germany, 2012.

[8] V. Sarinho and A. Apolinário, "Detailing the UML Profile of the OOFM Technique," in *Proceedings of the 3rd Brazilian Workshop on Model Driven Development (WB-DSDM' 12)*, vol. 8, pp. 25–32, 2012.

[9] E. Fayad, C. Schmidt, and R. Johnson, *Building Application Frameworks Object-Oriented Foundations of Framework Design*, John Wiley Sons, 1999.

[10] E. Folmer, "Component based game development: a solution to escalating costs and expanding deadlines?" in *Proceedings of the 10th International ACM SIGSOFT Symposium Component-Based Software Engineering (CBSE' 07)*, vol. 4608, Springer, Berlin, Germany, 2007.

[11] W. Zhang and S. Jarzabek, "Reuse without Compromising Performance: Industrial Experience from RPG Software Product Line for Mobile Devices," in *Proceedings of the 9th International Conference on Software Product Lines (SPLC' 05)*, vol. 3714 of *Lecture Notes in Computer Science*, pp. 57–69, Springer, Berlin, Gemany, 2005.

[12] E. Albassam and H. Gomaa, "Applying software product lines to multiplatform video games," in *Proceedings of the 2013 3rd International Workshop on Games and Software Engineering: Engineering Computer Games to Enable Positive, Progressive Change (GAS' 13)*, pp. 1–7, San Francisco, CA, USA, May 2013.

[13] A. W. B. Furtado, A. L. M. Santos, and G. L. Ramalho, "Sharp-Ludus revisited: From ad hoc and monolithic digital game DSLs to effectively customized DSM approaches," in *Proceedings of the Compilation of The Co-Located Workshops on DSM'11, TMC'11, AGERE! 2011, AOOPES'11, NEAT'11, & VMIL'11*, pp. 57–62, ACM, Portland, Oregon, USA, October 2011.

[14] A. W. B. Furtado and A. L. M. Santos, "Using domain-specific modeling towards computer games development industrialization," in *Proceedings of the 6th OOPSLA Workshop on Domain-Specific Modeling (DSM' 06)*, October 2006.

[15] V. M. Müller, "An open source architecture for building interactive dramas," in *Proceedings of the 10th Brazilian Symposium on Computer Games and Digital Entertainment (SBGames' 11)*, pp. 89–100, Salvador, Brazil, November 2011.

[16] M. C. Machado, G. L. Pappa, and L. Chaimowicz, "Characterizing and modeling agents in digital games," in *Proceedings of the XI Brazilian Symposium on Computer Games and Digital Entertainment*, pp. 26–33, 2012.

[17] K. Kang, S. Cohen, J. Hess, W. Novak, and S. Peterson, "Feature-oriented domain analysis (FODA): feasibility study," Tech. Rep., Software Engineering Institute, Pa, USA, CMU/SEI-90-TR-21, 1990.

[18] M. Antkiewicz and K. Czarnecki, "FeaturePlugin: feature modeling plug-in for eclipse," in *Proceedings of the 004 OOPSLA Workshop on Eclipse Technology eXchange*, pp. 67–72, Vancouver, British Columbia, Canada, October 2004.

[19] K. Czarnecki, "Overview of generative software development," in *Proceedings of Unconventional Programming Paradigms (UPP)*, vol. 3566 of *Lecture Notes in Computer Science*, pp. 326–341, Springer, Berlin, Germany, 2004.

[20] D. A. Beuche and M. A. Dalgarno, "Software product line engineering with feature models," *Methods & Tools*, vol. 14, no. 4, pp. 9–17, 2006.

[21] LibGDX, "Desktop/Android/BlackBerry/iOS/HTML5 Java game development framework," http://libgdx.badlogicgames.com.

[22] R. Pressman, *Engenharia de Software: Uma Abordagem Profissional*, McGraw-Hill, 7th edition, 2011.

[23] Eclipse Metrics Plugin, http://metrics.sourceforge.net/.

[24] R. Martin, "OO Design Quality Metrics An Analysis of Dependencies," in *Proceedings of the in Proceedings of the Workshop Pragmatic and Theoretical Directions in Object-Oriented Software Metrics (OOPSLA '94)*, 1994.

[25] B. Henderson-Sellers, *Object-Oriented Metrics: Measures of Complexity*, Prentice Hall, 1996.

[26] T. J. McCabe, "A complexity measure," *IEEE Transactions on Software Engineering*, vol. SE-2, no. 4, pp. 308–320, 1976.

[27] S. R. Chidamber and C. F. Kemerer, "A Metrics Suite for Object Oriented Design," *IEEE Transactions on Software Engineering*, vol. 20, no. 6, pp. 476–493, 1994.

[28] jMonkeyEngine, A cross-platform game engine for adventurous Java developers, http://jmonkeyengine.org/.

[29] JGame - a Java/Flash game engine for 2D games, http://www.13thmonkey.org/~boris/jgame/.

[30] GTGE, Golden T Game Engine - Game Programming for Java Programmer, http://goldenstudios.or.id/products/GTGE/.

[31] Unreal, Unreal Engine 4, https://www.unrealengine.com/what--is-unreal-engine-4.

[32] Unity, Unity 3D Game Engine, https://unity3d.com.

[33] Godot, https://godotengine.org/.

[34] Scratch, "Imagine, Program, Share", https://scratch.mit.edu/.

[35] PixiJS, PixiJS v4 - The HTML5 Creation Engine, http://www.pixijs.com/.

[36] Panda3D, Free 3D Game Engine, https://www.panda3d.org/.

[37] RPG Maker, https://en.wikipedia.org/wiki/RPG_Maker.

[38] Adventure Game Studio - AGS, https://www.adventuregame-studio.co.uk/.

[39] R. Hunicke, M. Leblanc, and R. Zubek, "MDA: A formal approach to game design and game research," in *Proceedings of the AAAI-04 Workshop on Challenges in Game AI*, pp. 1–5, July 2004.

[40] V. T. Sarinho and F. M. B. Boaventura, "Uma Proposta de Motor de Jogos Baseado em um Conjunto Simplificado de Features de Jogos Digitais," in *Anais da ERBASE - Escola de Computação Bahia-Alagoas-Sergipe*, pp. 1–10, 2014.

# 10

# RAGE Architecture for Reusable Serious Gaming Technology Components

**Wim van der Vegt,**[1] **Wim Westera,**[1] **Enkhbold Nyamsuren,**[1] **Atanas Georgiev,**[2] **and Iván Martínez Ortiz**[3]

[1]*Open University of the Netherlands, Valkenburgerweg 177, 6419 AT Heerlen, Netherlands*
[2]*Sofia University "St. Kliment Ohridski", Boulevard Tzar Osvoboditel 15, 1504 Sofia, Bulgaria*
[3]*Complutense University of Madrid, Avenida de Séneca 2, 28040 Madrid, Spain*

Correspondence should be addressed to Wim Westera; wim.westera@ou.nl

Academic Editor: Michael Wimmer

For seizing the potential of serious games, the RAGE project—funded by the Horizon-2020 Programme of the European Commission—will make available an interoperable set of advanced technology components (software assets) that support game studios at serious game development. This paper describes the overall software architecture and design conditions that are needed for the easy integration and reuse of such software assets in existing game platforms. Based on the component-based software engineering paradigm the RAGE architecture takes into account the portability of assets to different operating systems, different programming languages, and different game engines. It avoids dependencies on external software frameworks and minimises code that may hinder integration with game engine code. Furthermore it relies on a limited set of standard software patterns and well-established coding practices. The RAGE architecture has been successfully validated by implementing and testing basic software assets in four major programming languages (C#, C++, Java, and TypeScript/JavaScript, resp.). Demonstrator implementation of asset integration with an existing game engine was created and validated. The presented RAGE architecture paves the way for large scale development and application of cross-engine reusable software assets for enhancing the quality and diversity of serious gaming.

## 1. Introduction

The potential of nonleisure games (serious games) in industry, health, education, and the public administration sectors has been widely recognised. An increasing body of evidence is demonstrating the effectiveness of games for teaching and training [1]. While instructional scientists consider motivation as a main driver for effective learning [2–5], games are capable of amplifying the players' motivation by hooking and absorbing them in such a way that they can hardly stop playing [6]. This motivational power of games is ascribed to their dynamic, responsive, and visualised nature, which goes along with novelty, variation, and choice, effecting strong user involvement and providing penetrating learning experiences [6]. In addition, serious games allow for safe experimentation in realistic environments, stimulate problem ownership by

role adoption, and allow for learning-by-doing approaches, which support the acquisition of tacit and contextualised knowledge [7]. Nevertheless, the complexity of serious game design may hamper the games' effectiveness [8]. In particular the subtle balance between game mechanics and pedagogical power is not self-evident [9]. Also, various authors [1, 10] note that many studies fail to evaluate the educational effectiveness of serious games in a rigorous manner and they call for more randomised controlled trials (involving comparisons between an experimental group and a control group) for increased scientific robustness. Still, the potential of games for learning is widely recognised, stimulating serious game development as a new branch of business.

For various reasons, however, seizing this potential has been problematic. The serious game industry displays many features of an emerging, immature branch of business: being scattered over a large number of small independent players, weak interconnectedness, limited knowledge exchange, absence of harmonising standards, a lot of studios creating their localised solutions leading to "reinventing the wheel," limited specialisations, limited division of labour, and insufficient evidence of the products' efficacies [11, 12]. Still, conditions for a wider uptake of serious games are favourable. PCs, game consoles, and handheld devices have become low-priced commodities as are to a lesser extent advanced tools for game creation and the associated graphics design and media production.

In order to enhance the internal cohesion of the serious game industry sector the RAGE project (http://rageproject .eu/), which is Europe's principal research and innovation project on serious gaming in the Horizon-2020 Programme, makes available a diversity of software modules (software assets) for developing serious games easier, faster, and more cost-effectively. The pursued software assets cover a wide range of functionalities particularly tuned to the pedagogy of serious gaming, for example, in player data analytics, emotion recognition, stealth assessment, personalisation, game balancing, procedural animations, language analysis and generation, interactive storytelling, and social gamification. Game developers could then simply add the required assets to their project without the need to do all the programming themselves. For example, the stealth assessment asset would allow the game development team to easily incorporate diagnostic functionality that provides metrics for the progressive mastery of knowledge and skills, based on the tracking and processing of the players' behavioural patterns in the game.

Importantly, the creation of the game software assets is not an isolated technical endeavour, but instead it is positioned as a joint activity of multiple stakeholders represented in the RAGE consortium. In the consortium computer scientists and IT developers are working together with serious game developers, educational researchers, education providers, and end-users to make sure that the new technology components are practical and usable and create added pedagogical value. To this end the architecture presented in this paper is used for supporting the easy integration of assets in a set of serious games that will be developed in the project. The games and the assets included will be empirically tested for their effectiveness in large scale pilots with end-users. Hence, one of the major technical challenges of RAGE is to ensure interoperability of the software assets across the variety of game engines, game platforms, and programming languages that game studios have in use. The incorporation of the software assets should be as easy as possible (e.g., "plug-and-play"), without enforcing specific standards or systems as to avoid principal adoption barriers. In addition, the software assets should allow for being grouped together into more complex aggregates, for example, combining an emotion recognition asset with a game-balancing asset. That is, the assets should comprise a coherent, component-based system that supports data interoperability between its elements.

This paper takes a technical perspective by describing and validating the RAGE software architecture that aims to accommodate the easy integration and reuse of such interoperable software assets in existing game platforms.

The RAGE architecture particularly addresses the structure and functioning of client-side assets. Since exactly client-side assets are supposed to be fully integrated in the game engine, noncompliance issues of assets are likely to occur client-side. This paper will explain the basic requirements and the proposed solution. It presents the proofs of concept that have been created for validating the RAGE architecture in four different programming languages, and it describes how the concrete technical issues encountered in these proofs were overcome.

## 2. Related Work

There are various existing efforts in promoting reusability in both serious games and leisure games. The Unity Asset Store (https://www.assetstore.unity3d.com/) is an example of a successful online marketplace for game objects. Most of the objects are media objects (e.g., terrains, audio, buildings, and weapons), but an increasing number of software modules (e.g., analytics, cloud backend, and game AI) are becoming available. Unfortunately, most of the software objects can only be reused in the Unity game engine. Various other online platforms offer reusable game objects, for instance, the Guru asset store (https://en.tgcstore.net/), Game Salads (http://gshelper.com/), GameDev Market (https://www.gamedev-market.net/), Unreal Marketplace (https://www.unrealengine.com/marketplace), and Construct 2 (https://www.scir-ra.com/store), but their main focus is on user-interface objects and templates.

At a more abstract level Folmer [13] proposed a reference architecture for games. The architecture consists of several layers, such as game interface layer and domain specific layer, and it identifies reusable components within each layer. A similar idea proposed by Furtado et al. [14] describes a software product line-based approach for creating reusable software modules specific to a particular (sub)domain of games. These modules include domain specific reference architectures and languages. The current paper, however, is little concerned with defining a reusability framework for the entire process of game development. Instead, it proposes a "reference architecture" for a particular niche within serious game development that covers enhanced pedagogical functionality. Consequently, while attempting to simplify the reuse of pedagogical components, the RAGE architecture interferes as little as possible with established game development processes.

A recent reusability framework targeting serious games [15, 16] relies on a service-oriented architecture (SOA). Within this framework, domain independent features commonly used in serious games are encapsulated into components and implemented as services. SOA offers several advantages such as decoupling from implementation details and a high degree of reusability. However, the SOA approach goes with several limitations, for instance, the requirement of being constantly online, diminished flexibility such as customisation and configuration of services by service consumers, reduced system performance due to additional overheads associated with SOA, and network calls.

A more versatile reference architecture is needed to ensure seamless interoperability of the software assets across different game engines, game platforms, and programming languages, while the limitations of SOA should be avoided as much as possible.

## 3. Starting Points

*3.1. The Asset Concept.* The idea of making available a set of software assets seems to neglect the fact that the productive reuse of software requires the software to be complemented with installation guides, metadata, product manuals, tutorials examples, documentation, and many other things. For describing these elements we will comply with the W3C ADMS Working Group [17] by referring to the term "asset." Assets are not limited to software but are considered abstract entities that reflect some "intellectual content independent of their physical embodiments" [17] or even more abstractly, an asset would be "a solution to a problem" [18]. Not every asset includes software: indeed, the Unity Asset Store offers a variety of solutions, either media assets, such as 3D-objects, audio, textures, or particle systems, or software assets such as editor extensions, game AI, and physics engines.

The RAGE assets discussed in this paper are software assets. They may contain either a source code file or a compiled program file and may contain various other artefacts (cf. Figure 1).

The software artefact inside the asset is called "Asset Software Component." For being able to retrieve an asset from a wide variety of assets that are stored in an asset repository (the RAGE asset repository), it contains machine-readable metadata. In addition to keyword classifiers and asset descriptions the metadata include information about versions, asset dependencies, and programming language used among other things. The asset may include various additional artefacts that are not to be compiled (tutorials, manuals, licences, configuration tools, authoring tools, and other resources). While the constituents of the asset are stored separately in the RAGE repository, the asset can be packaged for distribution.

In the rest of this paper we will interchangeably use the term "Asset Software Component" and the term "asset" (as a shorthand notation) for indicating the software module that is to be linked or integrated with the game.

*3.2. Basic Requirements.* For being able to fulfil the ambition of the RAGE project to create an interoperable set of advanced game technology assets that can be easily used by serious game studios we have expressed the following basic requirements.

*3.2.1. Interoperability between Assets.* Since game developers may want to group multiple assets into more complex aggregates, data storage of assets to be used in their games and data exchange between assets should be well-defined.

*3.2.2. Nomenclature.* When creating a new asset, asset developers should not replicate functionalities of existing assets but instead should be able to exploit these. This requires a consistent approach to nomenclature of variable names, objects, and methods to be used across the whole set of assets, so that correct calls and references can be made.

*3.2.3. Extendibility.* The architecture should be robust over extending the set of assets with new assets. Developers may want to create new assets and add these to the existing set of assets. For allowing new assets to interact with existing ones, the interoperability conditions should be preserved.

*3.2.4. Addressing Platform and Hardware Dependencies.* Different hardware (e.g., game consoles) and operating systems may require different technical solutions. Browsers, actually the pairing of browsers and operating systems, display an even wider diversity with respect to browser brands, settings, and versions. This suggests that the programming for web browsers should be conservative as to avoid browser version issues as much as possible. Hence, direct access to the game user interface and/or operating system should be avoided.

*3.2.5. Portability across Programming Languages.* Using only well-established software patterns in RAGE would increase the portability as there will be valid existing code available from the start. Nevertheless, portability across different programming languages may be affected by the different nature and execution modes of the supported languages, for instance, interpreted languages such as JavaScript versus compiled languages as C++, C#, and Java. Also multithreading versus single threading could hamper code portability.

*3.2.6. Portability across Game Engines.* The implementation of an asset in a supported programming language should be portable across different game engines and possibly even across hardware platforms and operating systems as much as possible. For this it is important to rely on the programming language's standard features and libraries to maximise the compatibility across game engines. Assets could thus delegate the implementation of required features to the actual game engine, for example, the actual storage of run-time data: as the game engine knows where and how data can be stored, assets could delegate the actual storage operation to the game engine and need not have their own stores.

*3.2.7. Minimum Dependencies on External Software Frameworks.* The usage of external software frameworks (such as jQuery or MooTools for JavaScript) should be avoided as much as possible because of their potential interference with the game engine code. Also namespace conflicts may readily occur when external frameworks were used.

*3.2.8. Quality Assurance.* For preserving the integrity of an ever-growing system of assets basic quality assurance requirements will be needed. With respect to coding RAGE assets require a consistent rather than mandatory coding style and expect documentation on class level or method level in order to accommodate debugging and maintenance. The inclusion of well-established software patterns and compliance with

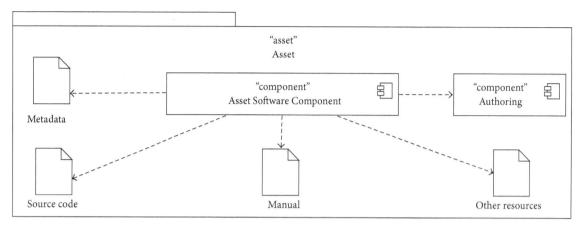

FIGURE 1: Exemplary layout of a RAGE asset.

(subsets of) existing standards in order to minimise overheads should have priority. Namespaces (or modules) should be used to prevent name conflicts between RAGE assets and game engine code.

*3.2.9. Overall Simplicity.* Software complexity should be avoided as to preserve practicability and maintainability. Preferably, assets should address only core functionality, which is in accordance with good practices of software development. Therefore, as a general starting point, the architecture and the integration points should be as simple as possible.

## 4. Component-Based Design and Development

Since RAGE assets are positioned as being used as reusable software components (plug-and-play), we adopt a component-based development approach (CBD) [19, 20]. In accordance with CBD, the RAGE asset architecture defines a component model for creating a reusable asset. The component model conforms to common norms of CBD, which are summarised as follows:

(i) A component is an independent and replaceable part of a system that fulfils a distinct function [20, 21]. Following this norm, it is assumed that an asset provides a game developer with access to a concrete functionality that produces added value. For RAGE this added value will ideally (but not exclusively) be within the context of learning and teaching.

(ii) A component provides information hiding and serves as a black box to other components and technologies using it [22, 23]. In accordance with this norm a game developer does not need to know how a particular functionality was implemented in the asset.

(iii) A component communicates strictly through a predefined set of interfaces that guard its implementation details [20, 21, 24]. Within the context of RAGE, it is assumed that a minimal intervention from a game developer is needed to integrate assets with a game engine.

Various existing CBD frameworks are available such as Enterprise JavaBeans [25] and CORBA [26]. However, we have chosen not to use these for several reasons. Although these frameworks simplify component integration and management, cross-platform support is still an issue. For example, Enterprise JavaBeans is limited to the Java platform. While CORBA is a language independent framework, mapping between different languages using an interface-definition language remains problematic. More critically, these frameworks are overly general and complex, which makes them unsuitable for addressing needs specific to the domain of serious game development. For example, game engines are de facto standard platforms for component control and reusability in game development, which creates a direct conflict with EJB or CORBA. For these and other reasons, existing CBD frameworks find very limited adoption in game development. RAGE will offer a less centralised approach by including a lightweight control component in the form of an AssetManager that is designed to complement game engines rather than take over their functionalities. The AssetManager is discussed in more detail later in this paper.

## 5. RAGE Architectural Design

*5.1. Client-Side Assets versus Server-Side Assets.* Assets can be positioned both client-side and server-side. Figure 2 sketches the general layout of an asset-supported game system.

On the client-side the player has access to a run-time game (game engine). The game may incorporate client-side assets that provide enhanced functionality. On the server-side a game server may be supported by server-side assets. Server-side assets may either be integrated with the game server or reside on remote servers.

Client-side assets should be preferred when frequent and direct interactions with the game engine on the local computer are required or when results should be immediately available. As a general guideline any processing that can be done client-side, for example, the processing of temporary, local data, should in fact be done client-side, as to reduce external communications as much as possible. However, when extensive processing is required, for

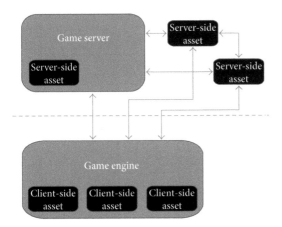

FIGURE 2: Distributed architecture of client-side assets and server-side assets supporting a game.

example, for speech recognition, a server-side asset would be appropriate in order to avoid poor game performance, for example, reduced frame rate or reduced game responsiveness. Obviously, assets that collect and process population data (learning analytics) and assets that require real time synchronisation across multiple remote players need to be server-side as well.

Communications between the game engine and the various servers are readily based on the http protocol, for example, REST and SOAP. On the client-side all assets are fully integrated with the game engine. This allows for direct interface methods, thus avoiding the impediments of SOA. The principal architectural challenges are on the client-side. The easy and seamless integration of multiple collaborating client-side assets as well as the portability of assets across multiple game engines, platforms, and programming languages requires a sound overall component architecture. This client-side architecture will be elaborated in the next sections.

*5.2. Programming Languages.* Given the wide variety of computer programming languages full portability of assets across programming languages will not be possible. It is inevitable to condense the spectrum of covered programming languages to those languages that are mostly used for creating games. This mainly holds for client-side code which is highly dictated by the game engine used, while server-side solutions are able to manage more diversity. For a start RAGE assets will be developed supporting two core code bases: C# (for desktop and mobile games) and HTML5/JavaScript (for browser games), which are predominant products of compiled languages and interpreted languages, respectively. According to a survey among European game studios [27] the most popular programming language is C# (71%), followed by C++ (67%), JavaScript (48%), objective C (33%), and Java (33%), which is quite similar to the latest Redmonk programming languages rankings [28]. The growth of C# has accelerated significantly since 2014, when Microsoft released its .NET core framework as open source, supporting any operating system and pushing the multiplatform nature of C#. Major game engines or multiplatform tools (e.g.,

Unity/Xamarin) use C# as their core language. C++ is still being used a lot, but it is more complex than C# or Java and often relies on platform-dependent constructs. With respect to browser-based games HTML5/JavaScript is considered a de facto standard. However, for overcoming the lack of strictness of JavaScript the RAGE project has adopted TypeScript (http://www.typescriptlang.org/) instead as the primary development language, which directly translates into JavaScript. TypeScript is used as a superclass of JavaScript that adds static typing, which can be used by integrated development environments and compilers to check for coding errors.

*5.3. The Asset Software Component's Internal Structure.* Figure 3 displays the UML class diagram of the Asset Software Component.

The classes, interfaces, and objects will be explained below. Code and detailed documentation of the asset implementation proofs are available on the GitHub repository at https://github.com/rageappliedgame. In particular we refer the C# version (https://github.com/rageappliedgame/asset-proof-of-concept-demo_CSharp), the TypeScript version (https://github.com/rageappliedgame/asset-proof-of-concept-demo_TypeScript), the JavaScript version (https://github.com/rageappliedgame/asset-proof-of-concept-demo_JavaScript), the C++ version (https://github.com/rageappliedgame/asset-proof-of-concept-demo_CPlusPlus), and the Java version (https://github.com/rageappliedgame/asset-proof-of-concept-demo_Java).

*5.3.1. IAsset.* The IAsset class, which is defined as an interface, provides the abstract definition of the Asset Software Component including the fields, properties, and methods required for its operations and communications.

*5.3.2. BaseAsset.* BaseAsset implements the set of basic functionalities following the definitions provided by IAsset. Moreover, BaseAsset exposes standardised interfaces that delegate the storage of component's default settings and runtime data used by the component to the game engine.

*5.3.3. ISettings.* In accordance with the abstract definition in the IAsset interface this interface ensures that every Asset Software Component has the basic infrastructure for managing a unique component ID, type, settings, version information, and so forth.

*5.3.4. BaseSettings.* This class realises the ISettings interface. It serves as a base class for the component's configuration settings.

*5.3.5. IBridge.* IBridge provides a standardised interface that allows the component to communicate with external technologies such as the game engine or a remote service.

*5.3.6. ClientBridge.* This bridge realises the IBridge interface. It mediates the direct communication from an Asset Software Component to the game engine (for calls from the game

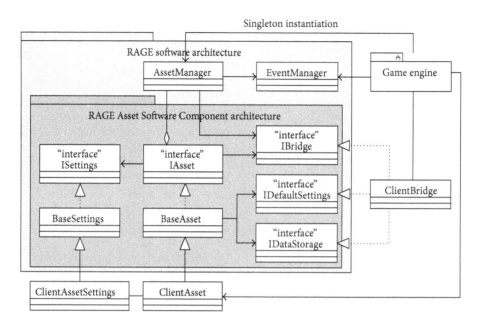

FIGURE 3: Class diagram reflecting the internal structure of an Asset Software Component.

engine to the component mediation is not required). In addition, ClientBridge may implement additional interfaces like IDataStorage via polymorphism. Thus, the same bridge object may provide the component with more specialised functionalities, such as allowing it to retrieve default settings from the game engine.

*5.3.7. IDefaultSettings.* The IDefaultSettings interface delegates the management of component's default settings to the game engine. It can be used when configuration parameters are stored in an external file rather than being hard-coded in a BaseSettings subclass.

*5.3.8. IDataStorage.* The IDataStorage interface delegates the management of run-time data used by the component to the game engine. It can be implemented to access a local file or to query a database.

*5.3.9. AssetManager.* The AssetManager takes over the management of multiple RAGE assets during both compile-time and run-time. The game engine instantiates all necessary assets and creates a singleton of the AssetManager that simplifies the tracking of all instantiated assets. The Asset-Manager covers the registration of the assets used by the game, it locates the registered assets on request, and it offers some common methods and events that may be used by the assets, for example, requesting the name and type of the game engine. The AssetManager is discussed in more detail in the next section.

*5.3.10. EventManager.* Alternatively, indirect (multicast) communication between various elements is also possible via the EventManager that is initialised by the AssetManager.

The RAGE asset architecture can thus be summarised as follows:

(i) The IAsset class defines the requirements for the RAGE asset as a reusable software component.

(ii) For game developers the implementation details of an Asset Software Component are hidden by a set of interfaces.

(iii) Likewise, the implementation details of an external technology are shielded for the Asset Software Component by one or more interfaces, for example, the storage of asset data in the game engine through IDataStorage, which is implemented on a bridge.

(iv) The architecture supports various means of communication, for example, between assets, via the bridge interfaces, or via the EventManager.

*5.4. The AssetManager.* As indicated above, the AssetManager is the coordinating agent for the management of multiple RAGE assets. Obviously, the AssetManager complies with the singleton pattern as only one coordinating agent is needed. The AssetManager covers the registration of all Asset Software Components that are used by the game engine. For achieving this it should expose methods to query this registration so that each Asset Software Component is able to locate other components and link to these. For avoiding duplicate code in each Asset Software Component the AssetManager could also be the provider of basic services that are relevant for all assets, such as the game engine's heartbeat, which indicates the game's proper operation, or user login/logout info for assets that need a user model. It centralises the code and requires only a single interaction point with the game engine. These data could be broadcast and transferred to Asset Software Components that have sub-scribed themselves for this event. Likewise, the AssetManager could also coordinate the link between the Asset Software Component and its data storage (which in fact requires reference to the game engine, because an Asset Software Component would not have storage capacity by itself).

*5.5. Asset Communication.* Asset Software Components need to communicate with the outside world, for instance, for receiving input from a user or game engine, for sending the results of their calculations to the game engine, for making web calls to query server-based services, or for linking up with other RAGE assets. For allowing an Asset Software Component (or its subcomponents) to communicate with the outside world, well-defined interfaces are needed. A set of standard software patterns and coding practices are used for accommodating these communications. These include the "Publish/Subscribe" pattern, the "bridge" pattern, Asset Method calls, and web services (cf. Table 1).

The various communication modes will be briefly explained below.

*5.5.1. Asset Software Component's Methods.* Each Asset Soft-ware Component may dynamically communicate with any other asset in the environment. This capability is enabled through registration by the AssetManager. An Asset Software Component can query the AssetManager for other Asset Software Components by referring to either a unique ID and/or a class name. Once the requested Asset Software Component is encountered, a direct communication can be established between two components without the need for further mediation by the AssetManager.

*5.5.2. Bridges.* For allowing an Asset Software Component to call a game engine method the bridge software pattern [29] is used, which is platform-dependent code exposing an interface. The game engine creates a bridge and registers it either at a specific asset or at the AssetManager. The BaseAsset then allows an Asset Software Component easy access to either one of these bridges to further communicate with the game engine. Overall, the bridge pattern is used to mediate a bidirectional communication between the Asset Software Component and the game engine while hiding game engine's implementation details. Additionally, polymorphism is used by allowing a bridge to implement multiple interfaces. The Asset Software Component may identify and select a suitable bridge and use its methods or properties to get the pursued game data.

*5.5.3. Web Services.* Communication through web services assumes an online connection to a remote service. Web services allow an Asset Software Component to call a ser-vice from the game engine by using a bridge interface. In principle, an Asset Software Component may not implement the communication interface itself and instead may rely on the adapters provided by the game engine [30]. Such approach would remove the asset's dependency on specific communication protocols used by remote services, thereby

TABLE 1: Communication modes of client-side assets.

| Client-side requests | Communication modes |
|---|---|
| Asset to asset | These communications require a once-only registration of the Asset Software Component at the AssetManager: (i) Publish/Subscribe (ii) Asset Method call |
| Asset to game engine | With bridge: (i) Web services (e.g., outside world) (ii) Game engine functionality (iii) Hardware, operating system Without bridge: (i) Publish/Subscribe |
| Game engine to asset | (i) Asset Method calls (ii) Publish/Subscribe |

allowing a greater versatility of the asset. Within the RAGE project automatic coupling with services will be supported by using the REST communication protocol [31]. When a service is unavailable, for example, when the game system is offline, the interface should be able to receive a call without processing it or acting on it. It is reminded here that server-side communications as indicated before in Figure 2 can all be implemented as web services.

*5.5.4. Publish/Subscribe.* Communications can also be ar-ranged using the Publish/Subscribe pattern, which supports a 1-N type of communication (broadcasting). An example would be the game engine frequently broadcasting player performance data to multiple assets. The RAGE architec-ture allows for including Publish/Subscribe patterns where both Asset Software Components and the game engine can be either publishers or subscribers. The Publish/Subscribe pattern requires an EventManager, which is a centralised class that handles topics and events. The EventManager is initialised by the AssetManager during its singleton instan-tiation. Once initialised, either an asset or the game engine can use the EventManager to define new topics, (un)subscribe to existing topics, or broadcast new events. According to the Publish/Subscribe design pattern, subscribers do not have knowledge of publishers and vice versa. This allows an asset to ignore implementation details of a game engine or other assets. Additionally, this mode of communication is more suitable for asynchronous broadcasting to multiple receivers than the bridge-based communication, which realises bilat-eral communications only.

*5.5.5. Composite Communications.* The basic patterns ex-plained above enable composite communication modes, which are composed of multiple stages. For instance, Asset Software Components may use the game engine as an intermediate step for their mutual communications, by using bridges, web services, or the Publish/Subscribe pattern. Also the AssetManager may act as a communication mediator. Once registered at the AssetManager, an Asset Software Component could use the AssetManager's set of commonly used methods and events in order to minimise the number of the game engine interaction points. In many cases it is more efficient to implement widely used functionality in the AssetManager than implementing it in every individual asset.

# 6. Technical Validation

For the technical validation of the RAGE architecture a basic software asset has been developed for all four of the selected programming languages. This basic Asset Software Component included all elementary operations and patterns, for example, registration, save, load, and log. The assets should meet the following test requirements:

(1) Once created, the Asset Software Components should induce the creation of a single AssetManager, which enables the components' self-registration.

(2) The AssetManager should be able to locate Asset Software Components and generate the associated versions and dependency reports.

(3) Asset Software Components should be able to directly connect through a method call.

(4) Asset Software Components should be able to call game engine functionality. The bridge code between the Asset Software Components and the game engine should provide some basic interfaces, such as simple file i/o and access to web services.

(5) The Publish/Subscribe pattern should allow Asset Software Components to both broadcast and subscribe to broadcasts, for example, transferring an object.

(6) The system should support multiple interactions, for example, a dialog system.

(7) The system should check for (default) settings and their serialisation to XML (for C#) and should be able to include default settings at compile-time.

Tested implementation of the basic asset in all four programming languages can be found on GitHub (https://github .com/rageappliedgame). All implementation proved to meet the specified requirements. Yet, a number of language-dependent issues were encountered (and solved) that deserve further attention. In addition, the Unity game engine was used as an integration platform for the C# asset version. A number of engine dependent issues were identified and solved as well.

## 6.1. Issues in C#

*Characters.* First, since Windows and OS X have different directory separator characters, forward slash (/) and backslash (\), respectively, portability fails. Problems can be avoided, however, by using the Environment class in C# that dynamically returns the correct separator rather than using hard-coded separators. Second, the Mono version used in

Unity (v5.2) silently turns UTF-8 XML into UTF-16 during parsing, leading to problems during deserialisation of version info. This issue can be bypassed by omitting the parsing procedure and directly serialising the XML files.

*Debugging.* First, Mono's Debug.WriteLine method does not offer a syntax format such as String.Format. In order to obtain formatted diagnostic output messages during asset development, the String.Format method must be used explicitly. Second, debugging in Unity needs a different format of the debug symbol files generated during compilation with Visual Studio. Mono provides a conversion tool for this. Third, the pdb-to-mdb debug symbol converter of Unity (v5.2) cannot convert debug symbols created by Visual Studio 2015. A workaround is using Visual Studio 2013 or patch and recompile this utility. Finally, Mono and .Net display slight differences in the method names that are used for diagnostic logging. This problem can be solved easily by using the bridge for supplying the actual logging methods.

*Compilation.* In Unity the assemblies with embedded resources (i.e., RAGE Asset Software Components have their version data and localisation data embedded) cannot be compiled as upon compilation Unity automatically removes the embedded resources. The resources can be compiled with Visual Studio though, whereupon they can still be used in the Unity engine.

## 6.2. Issues in TypeScript/JavaScript

*Characters.* TypeScript and JavaScript rely on using a forward slash (/) directory separator on all platforms (Windows uses the backslash but allows using a forward slash). As TypeScript/JavaScript code will mainly be used for web-based games and will not try to access local files, this issue will be of little practical significance.

*Interfaces.* TypeScript implements interfaces but uses these only at compile-time for type checking. The resulting JavaScript is not capable of checking the existence of an interface as such. For allowing the asset to select the bridge to be used, the asset should instead check for the interface method that needs to be called.

*Settings.* During deserialisation of JSON data into asset settings JavaScript will only restore the data but will not recreate the methods present in the class. As a consequence computed properties will fail. A workaround is either to avoid using the methods and/or the computed values or to copy the restored data into a newly created settings instance.

## 6.3. Issues in Java

*Characters.* Because of the different directory separator characters in Windows and OS X, forward slash (/) and backslash (\), respectively, portability fails. Problems can be avoided by using the File.separator field, which dynamically returns the correct separator, instead of using hard-coded separators.

*Properties.* Java does not support the properties concept of C# and TypeScript but relies on naming conventions instead (get/set methods).

*Default Values.* Java has no standard implementation for default value attributes. As a consequence default values have to be applied in the constructor of the settings subclasses.

### 6.4. Issues in C++

*Characters.* Also in C++ portability across Windows and OS X is hampered by the different directory separator characters. Problems can be avoided by creating conditional code for preprocessor directives that provide hard-coded separators tuned to the platform of compilation.

*Properties.* C++ does not support the concept of properties. Instead it relies on naming conventions (get/set methods).

*Default Values.* Like Java, C++ has no standard implementation for default value attributes, so default values have to be applied in the constructor of the settings subclasses.

*Singleton.* During testing the new C++ 2013 singleton syntax led to crashes in Visual Studio, so it had to be replaced with a more traditional double-checked locking pattern.

*Web Services.* Although web service calls, for example, with REST or SOAP, are a well-established approach to client-server communications and other remote communications, problems may arise because of slight semantic differences on different platforms. For instance, the popular JSON data format embedded in the web service protocols may suffer from this ambiguity, in particular with respect to the symbols of decimal separator, thousands separator, list separator, quote, data-time formats, null versus undefined, character encoding (e.g., UTF-8), prohibited characters in filenames, the line feed, and carriage return. XML-converted data are less sensitive to these issues.

## 7. In Conclusion

In this paper we have reported the design of the RAGE architecture, which is a reference architecture that supports the reuse of serious gaming technology components across different programming languages, game engines, and game platforms. An asset would offer a standardised interface that can be directly implemented by a game engine (via the bridge pattern) or it uses the asset's event manager for a Publish/Subscribe event. Proofs of concept in four principal code bases (C#, Java, C++, and TypeScript/JavaScript) have validated the RAGE architecture. In addition, the C# implementation of the test asset was successfully integrated in the Unity game engine, which demonstrates the practicability and validity of the RAGE asset architecture. The RAGE project will now start to develop up to 30 dedicated serious gaming assets and use these in customer-driven serious games projects. RAGE will make these assets available along with a large volume of high-quality knowledge resources on

serious gaming through a self-sustainable delivery platform and social space. This platform aims to function as the single entry point for different stakeholders from the serious gaming communities, for example, game developers, researchers from multiple disciplines, online publishers, educational intermediaries, and end-users. RAGE thus aims to contribute to enhancing the internal cohesion of the serious games industry sector and to seizing the potential of serious games for teaching, learning, and various other domains.

## Competing Interests

The authors declare that they have no competing interests.

## Acknowledgments

This work has been partially funded by the EC H2020 project RAGE (Realising an Applied Gaming Ecosystem), http://www.rageproject.eu/, Grant Agreement no. 644187.

## References

[1] T. M. Connolly, E. A. Boyle, E. MacArthur, T. Hainey, and J. M. Boyle, "A systematic literature review of empirical evidence on computer games and serious games," *Computers & Education*, vol. 59, no. 2, pp. 661–686, 2012.

[2] J. M. Keller, "Development and use of the ARCS model of motivational design," *Journal of Instructional Development*, vol. 10, no. 3, pp. 2–10, 1987.

[3] J. M. Keller, "First principles of motivation to learn and e3-learning," *Distance Education*, vol. 29, no. 2, pp. 175–185, 2008.

[4] R. M. Ryan and E. L. Deci, "Self-determination theory and the facilitation of intrinsic motivation, social development, and well-being," *American Psychologist*, vol. 55, no. 1, pp. 68–78, 2000.

[5] D. I. Cordova and M. R. Lepper, "Intrinsic motivation and the process of learning: beneficial effects of contextualization, personalization, and choice," *Journal of Educational Psychology*, vol. 88, no. 4, pp. 715–730, 1996.

[6] W. Westera, "Games are motivating, aren't they? Disputing the arguments for digital game-based learning," *International Journal of Serious Games*, vol. 2, no. 2, pp. 3–17, 2015.

[7] M. Polanyi, *The Tacit Dimension*, University of Chicago Press, Chicago, Ill, USA, 1966.

[8] W. Westera, R. J. Nadolski, H. G. K. Hummel, and I. G. J. H. Wopereis, "Serious games for higher education: a framework for reducing design complexity," *Journal of Computer Assisted Learning*, vol. 24, no. 5, pp. 420–432, 2008.

[9] S. Arnab, T. Lim, M. B. Carvalho et al., "Mapping learning and game mechanics for serious games analysis," *British Journal of Educational Technology*, vol. 46, no. 2, pp. 391–411, 2015.

[10] C. Linehan, B. Kirman, S. Lawson, and G. Chan, "Practical, appropriate, empirically-validated guidelines for designing educational games," in *Proceedings of the ACM Annual SIGCHI Conference on Human Factors in Computing Systems (CHI '11)*, pp. 1979–1988, ACM, Vancouver, Canada, May 2011.

[11] J. Stewart, L. Bleumers, J. Van Looy et al., *The Potential of Digital Games for Empowerment and Social Inclusion of Groups at Risk of Social and Economic Exclusion: Evidence and Opportunity for*

*Policy*, Joint Research Centre, European Commission, Brussels, Belgium, 2013.

[12] R. García Sánchez, J. Baalsrud Hauge, G. Fiucci et al., "Business Modelling and Implementation Report 2," GALA Network of Excellence for Serious Games, 2013, http://www.galanoe.eu.

[13] E. Folmer, "Component based game development-a solution to escalating costs and expanding deadlines?" in *Component-Based Software Engineering*, pp. 66–73, Springer, Berlin, Germany, 2007.

[14] A. W. B. Furtado, A. L. M. Santos, G. L. Ramalho, and E. S. De Almeida, "Improving digital game development with software product lines," *IEEE Software*, vol. 28, no. 5, pp. 30–37, 2011.

[15] M. B. Carvalho, F. Bellotti, J. Hu et al., "Towards a service-oriented architecture framework for educational serious games," in *Proceedings of the 15th IEEE International Conference on Advanced Learning Technologies (ICALT '15)*, pp. 147–151, IEEE, Hualien, Taiwan, July 2015.

[16] M. B. Carvalho, F. Bellotti, R. Berta et al., "A case study on service-oriented architecture for serious games," *Entertainment Computing*, vol. 6, pp. 1–10, 2015.

[17] M. Dekkers, *Asset Description Metadata Schema (ADMS)*, W3C Working Group, 2013, http://www.w3.org/TR/vocab-adms/.

[18] Object Management Group, *Reusable Asset Specification, Version 2.2*, 2005, http://www.omg.org/spec/RAS/2.2/.

[19] F. Bachmann, L. Bass, C. Buhman et al., *Volume II: Technical Concepts of Component-based Software Engineering*, Carnegie Mellon University, Software Engineering Institute, Pittsburgh, Pa, USA, 2000.

[20] S. Mahmood, R. Lai, and Y. S. Kim, "Survey of component-based software development," *IET Software*, vol. 1, no. 2, pp. 57–66, 2007.

[21] X. Cai, M. R. Lyu, K. F. Wong, and R. Ko, "Component-based software engineering: technologies, development frameworks, and quality assurance schemes," in *Proceedings of the 7th Asia-Pacific Software Engineering Conference (APSEC '00)*, pp. 372–379, IEEE, Singapore, 2000.

[22] K. K. Lau and F. M. Taweel, "Data encapsulation in software components," in *Component-Based Software Engineering*, pp. 1–16, Springer, Berlin, Germany, 2007.

[23] T. Wijayasiriwardhane, R. Lai, and K. C. Kang, "Effort estimation of component-based software development—a survey," *IET Software*, vol. 5, no. 2, pp. 216–228, 2011.

[24] H. Koziolek, "Performance evaluation of component-based software systems: a survey," *Performance Evaluation*, vol. 67, no. 8, pp. 634–658, 2010.

[25] E. Roman, R. P. Sriganesh, and G. Brose, *Mastering Enterprise JavaBeans*, John Wiley & Sons, 2005.

[26] S. Vinoski, "CORBA: integrating diverse applications within distributed heterogeneous environments," *IEEE Communications Magazine*, vol. 35, no. 2, pp. 46–55, 1997.

[27] G. L. Saveski, W. Westera, L. Yuan et al., "What serious game studios want from ICT research: identifying developers' needs," in *Proceedings of the Games and Learning Alliance conference (GALA '15)*, Serious Games Society, Rome, Italy, December 2015.

[28] Redmonk programming languages rankings, 2015, http://redmonk.com/sogrady/2015/01/14/language-rankings-1-15/.

[29] E. Gamma, R. Helm, R. Johnson, and J. Vlissides, *Design Patterns: Elements of Reusable Object-Oriented Software*, Pearson Education, 1994.

[30] B. Benatallah, F. Casati, D. Grigori, H. R. M. Nezhad, and F. Toumani, "Developing adapters for web services integration," in *Advanced Information Systems Engineering*, O. Pastor and J. Falcão e Cunha, Eds., vol. 3520 of *Lecture Notes in Computer Science*, pp. 415–429, Springer, Berlin, Germany, 2005.

[31] A. P. Sheth, K. Gomadam, and J. Lathem, "SA-REST: semantically interoperable and easier-to-use services and mashups," *IEEE Internet Computing*, vol. 11, no. 6, pp. 91–94, 2007.

# 11

# Modeling a Virtual World for the Educational Game Calangos

**Angelo C. Loula,**[1] **Leandro N. de Castro,**[2] **Antônio L. Apolinário Jr.,**[3] **Pedro L. B. da Rocha,**[4]
**Maria da Conceição L. Carneiro,**[5] **Vanessa Perpétua G. S. Reis,**[5] **Ricardo F. Machado,**[6]
**Claudia Sepulveda,**[7] **and Charbel N. El-Hani**[8]

[1] *Intelligent and Cognitive Systems Lab, State University of Feira de Santana, 44036-900 Feira de Santana, BA, Brazil*
[2] *Natural Computing Laboratory, Mackenzie Presbyterian University, 01302-090 São Paulo, SP, Brazil*
[3] *Computer Science Department, Federal University of Bahia, 40170-290 Salvador, BA, Brazil*
[4] *Laboratory of Terrestrial Vertebrates, Institute of Biology, Federal University of Bahia, 40170-290 Salvador, BA, Brazil*
[5] *Institute of Education Gastão Guimarães, 44026010 Feira de Santana, BA, Brazil*
[6] *Graduate Studies Program in History, Philosophy and Science Teaching,*
  *Federal University of Bahia and State University of Feira de Santana, 44036-900 Feira de Santana, BA, Brazil*
[7] *Department of Education, State University of Feira de Santana, 44036-900 Feira de Santana, BA, Brazil*
[8] *Institute of Biology, Federal University of Bahia, 40170-290 Salvador, BA, Brazil*

Correspondence should be addressed to Angelo C. Loula; angelocl@uefs.br

Academic Editor: Mark Green

Ecology plays a central role in biology and deserves special attention in scientific education. Nonetheless, the teaching and learning of ecology face a number of difficulties. In order to tackle these difficulties, electronic games have recently been used to mediate ecology learning. This paper presents an electronic game that fulfills these gaps in order to make the students' work with ecological concepts more concrete, active, and systematic. The paper presents the computational model of the ecological system included in the game, based on a real ecological case, a sand dune ecosystem located in the semiarid Caatinga biome, namely, the sand dunes of the middle São Francisco River, in the state of Bahia, Brazil. It includes various ecological relationships between endemic lizards and the physical environment, preys, predators, cospecifics, and plants. The engine of the game simulates the physical conditions of the ecosystem (dune topography and climate conditions with their circadian and circannual cycles), its biota (plant species and animal species), and ecological relationships (predator-prey encounters, cospecific relationships). We also present results from one classroom study of a teaching sequence structured around Calangos, which showed positive outcomes regarding high school students' understanding of thermal regulation in ectothermic animals.

## 1. Introduction

Ecology deserves special attention in biological education because its object of study, namely, the spatial and temporal patterns of distribution and abundance of organisms, as well as their causes and consequences [1, 2] plays a central role in biology. Moreover, ecological knowledge gains additional importance in the current context of environmental crisis.

Despite its relevance, ecology teaching and learning face a number of difficulties. Key ecological concepts, such as ecological succession, food chains, and cycling of matter, are widely recognized as difficult to learn [1, 3, 4]. Accordingly,

there is evidence that the students' knowledge on various aspects of ecology is insufficient [5].

To overcome these difficulties, electronic games have recently been used to support ecology learning, but the available ones usually lack educational goals, are not related to real situations, and do not incorporate tools specifically designed to enhance scientific abilities. The game presented here fulfills these gaps as a resource aimed at promoting learning about ecology by making ecological concepts more concrete to the students and, also, engaging them with conceptual learning in ecology in a more active manner. The game, called Calangos (a popular name for lizards in Northeast Brazil) is based on a real ecological case situated in the dunes of the middle São Francisco River, in the state of Bahia, Brazil, investigated by Brazilian researchers (e.g. [6, 7]). The game (freely available at http://calangos.sourceforge.net/) is intended to provide the students with an environment that allows an adequate understanding of ecological processes. The objective of this paper is to present the model of the simulated ecological system, based on the real ecological case, included in the game and present results from one classroom study of a teaching sequence structured around Calangos. Particularly, the paper addresses the modeled dune environment and the ecological processes involving three lizard species that inhabit this environment.

The computational models developed include graphical models for reproducing the visual aspect of real elements of the sand dunes as game elements, mathematical models to define functions for game variables, and behavior models to describe actions and activities of nonplayable characters based on the behavior of real animals. All of these computational models operate during game play to generate a complex simulation of elements and relationships. Such simulation engine underlying the game corresponds to a flexible set of game rules and provides multiple possible trajectories for an open game play to achieve the proposed goal, a feature that differentiates serious games from mere edutainment games [8]. Serious games combine the analytical and questioning nature of scientific endeavors with the intuitive freedom and rewards of imaginative and artistic acts. In brief, serious games offer a way of exploring serious intellectual and social problems [9, 10].

The paper is organized as follows. The following section presents related work on educational games about ecology. Next, it described the real ecological case in which the game and its ecological model were based. Finally, the Calangos game is described, focusing on the ecological model developed, leading to the final remarks.

## 2. Related Work

The use of games to support educational activities has been studied for a long time [11]. In the case of electronic games, however, it was only recently that teachers started to use them in schools as a tool to help the teaching and learning process. Among the electronic games available to use in educational settings, a number of them are biology/ecology-inspired games that might, at least potentially, help ecology teaching and learning. This section discusses the main features of some of these games.

CellCraft (http://www.carolina.com/category/teacher+ resources/interactive+science+games+and+simulations/cell-craft.do) is a simple online game that takes students inside a cell where they can learn about how a cell works and which challenges it faces to survive in a hostile environment. The game encourages students to balance resources and grow a robust cell to fight off coldness, starvation, and viruses. It follows a linear path: the students are guided to go through fixed steps and perform specific tasks to move to the next step. The strategy is easy to program and control. This

approach guarantees that the students have access to all the information they need to learn a specific topic. Nevertheless, this kind of guided path eliminates the freedom of choice that a real game should provide to the player, forcing the students to follow a standard pattern for acquiring knowledge.

Web Earth Online (http://www.webearthonline.com/) is a multiplayer web-based 2D game where each player can choose to play as a mammal, reptile, or bird. The game simulates a very detailed ecosystem, but it is not clear if it is based on real data. Variables like temperature, weather, rainfall pattern, and direction of air flow are used to control the simulation process. There are many kinds of interaction in the game, such as those between the player and the agents (e.g., predators, preys) and between the player and elements of the ecosystem (e.g., trees, rivers). As a strategy game, the choice of which kind of interaction the player will use is the main challenge of the game. So, for different problems, the player may choose different strategies, and different players may choose different strategies to achieve the same solution. This could be used as a learning tool, but the game did not take advantage of this feature in this way. In fact, there is no explicit educational goal to achieve. The player could play forever or, at least, until it reaches the point where there is no other player to interact with (something common in multiplayer games). Another fact that corroborates the lack of interest about the learning process is the time needed to develop the character. The player must play the game for days to make his/her character grow and evolve. This long period of play does not help the player to perceive the relations between his/her strategy and the ecological concepts involved. It is difficult to evaluate if the model used for the simulations is trustworthy or precise, because there is no indication that the simulation is based on a real ecosystem.

Spore (http://www.spore.com/) is a multigenre single-player God game that allows the player to develop a virtual species. The species starts as a microscopic organism and can evolve into a complex animal. Once the player reaches this stage, he/she can start to guide groups of individuals to develop social relations. In the advanced stages, the user faces the challenge of leading the species to dominate its planet and then finally to its ascension into space, where it interacts with alien species across the galaxy. So, during the evolution of the game, the player experiences different perspectives from different evolutionary stages of a species. Although this game is motivated by many biological concepts like evolution, ecosystems, mutation, and so forth, there is no real model governing these processes. Moreover, there are features that may directly promote the development of misconceptions, such as the fact that the player can obtain new body parts by examining bone piles or skeleton parts found in the landscape, or by defeating some creatures. Thus, from an educational point of view, it is difficult for the player to build any valid correlation between how life evolves during the game and how a real life form could evolve on earth or any other planet. Despite its success as an entertainment game, Spore seems to bring limited educational contributions.

By analyzing the games from a historical point of view, it is possible to see a change between games developed in the 1990's and games developed in the 2000's. Older games, like

SimAnt (http://www.mobygames.com/game/simant-the-ele-ctronic-ant-colony), SimEarth (http://www.mobygames.com/game/simearth-the-living-planet), Lion (http://www.moby-games.com/game/lion), Empire of Ants (http://www.moby-games.com/game/empire-of-the-ants), and SimPark (http://www.mobygames.com/game/simpark), are simulation-based games that try to model, in a precise way, the relations between its elements and players. Some of them (e.g., Lion and SimEarth) have an explicit concern with educational issues. Others (e.g., SimAnt and SimPark) do not have this kind of feature but are based on biological information, which can provide the player with important feedback about what is going on in the environment. However, many newer games are usually based on web technology and poorly developed. They usually borrow strategies from traditional games, like quiz, puzzles, and memory games, changing only the theme, inserting biological or ecological content, or simply using pictures of animals or plants.

In this context, Calangos was developed with a major concern to reproduce a real environment, ruled by a model that is highly precise to give the player a feeling as close as possible to the lizard in its own habitat. At the same time, the game is expected to be able to reinforce the playful atmosphere of a good game, improving the interest of the player to discover which strategy can leave his/her character to achieve the game's goal: grow and reproduce. Finally, the game allows the player to access dispersion graphs that relate variables that describe the past performance of the lizard, allowing him/her to analyze the results of the strategies that he/she adopted in the past, so that he/she can adjust future strategies. Calangos explicitly incorporates tools specifically designed to enhance a key scientific ability, namely, that of interpreting graphs. To the extent of our knowledge, Calangos is the only educational game focused on biology/ecology that has a climate model based on real data and linked to models of the ecological relations between individual organisms and the environment, also based on real data, which, moreover, includes tools for the development of scientific abilities.

## 3. The Real Ecological Case

The ecological case modeled in Calangos is situated in the sand dunes of the middle São Francisco River (Figure 1), in the state of Bahia, Brazil. This ecosystem hosts an endemic and diversified flora and fauna and has been studied by Brazilian researchers for some decades now [6, 7]. Thus, the game not only brings a Brazilian ecosystem to the students' attention, but also the contributions of the Brazilian scientific community to the understanding of this ecosystem.

To succeed in the game, the student must develop an efficient strategy for the day-to-day activity of a lizard (choosing between individuals from three different endemic species, *Tropidurus psammonastes*, *Cnemidophorus* sp. nov., and *Eurolophosaurus divaricatus*). The lizard must be able to choose microhabitats that provide suitable conditions of temperature and humidity and, thus, be capable of behaviorally regulating its temperature. It should also be able to avoid predators and find food to survive and grow, and, after

FIGURE 1: Picture from the sand dunes of the middle São Francisco River.

reaching adulthood, to find a sexual partner and reproduce, after fighting other males, if necessary.

The game simulates the dune environment by taking into account its real features, most of which have been specifically investigated on site. The dunes present a periodic topography, with summits, slopes, and valleys. The topography is associated with changes in the plant communities, as different plant species show different affinities for those positions. The topography, in turn, influences the distribution of resources (thermal environment, food) that are used by the animals (arthropods and vertebrates). Different plant species present different abundances in the dunes and provide different resources to the animals, including food. Animal species exhibit specific patterns of aggregation and use the available resources differently. Some are preys and predators of other animal species, and those eaten by the lizards have species-specific nutritional properties. Other species do not have trophic relationships with the lizards but may influence the resources available to them, as well as other kinds of interactions of the lizards with their environment. This is the case, for instance, of a local rodent (*Trinomys yonenagae*) that digs galleries in the sand that can be used as refuges by the lizards.

Daily changes in the position of the sun lead to changes in the temperature of the air and sand and in the air humidity. Seasonal changes in the climate influences the day temperature and humidity, as well as the primary productivity of plants and, therefore, the availability of food resources to animals.

The relevance of building the game inspired in this real case is twofold: (a) it allows the development of a quite realistic and nature-inspired model, given the availability of field information; and (b) it brings to the focus a relevant Brazilian ecosystem from the Caatinga Biome, which is probably one of the poorest known by most of the students in Brazil. Moreover, if the game is used by international students, this is quite an interesting example of a semiarid, savannah-like ecosystem with several endemic species, which is even more poorly known by foreign students.

# 4. The Computer Game *Calangos*

Calangos is a simulation and action game with 3D visualization in the first and third person. In the currently available game level, the player controls a lizard from one of the three medium-sized endemic species of the sand dunes ecosystem (*Tropidurus psammonastes*, *Cnemidophorus* sp. nov., and *Eurolophosaurus divaricatus*).

It is an electronic educational game that works as a tool to support ecology teaching and learning (and also evolution in Level 4) at the secondary school level. Therefore, it is not a tool for direct exposure of contents to be learned by the student player. Rather, learning is to take place as a consequence of the player's experience in trying to deal with problem situations. While trying to be successful in facing the challenges of the simulated environment, the player has to develop a strategy to control its character and must take into account the game dynamics and rules, and, consequently, the simulated ecological processes. To develop this strategy, the student player has to access dispersion graphs showing relations between variables chosen by him/her from a menu of variables, evaluate what has happened in his/her previous strategy, and modify it aiming at improving the outcomes.

Four game levels are planned for Calangos. At the first level, the student player chooses among the three species of lizards mentioned above and acts as the main character, with the objective of successfully surviving, developing, and reproducing. Level two adds a lizard editor, in which the player can select different morphological, physiological, and behavioral characteristics to build a new lizard to play, with the same objectives of Level 1. The characteristics included in the lizard editor and their variants are also based on biological studies about real lizards. In Level 3, the player goes from a single individual to a population of lizards still in ecological time, with the objective of establishing a dynamical equilibrium for this population. Level 4 is the last level, which changes from the ecological time to the evolutionary time, with the player not only facing population challenges but also having to deal with the evolution of the lizards through many generations. The first level is already developed and Level 2 is currently being implemented; the two last levels are being designed and prototyped. In this paper, the goal is to describe the artificial ecological system modeled on the grounds of the real ecological case described before. This simulated ecology was developed for the first level of the game but also provides a basis for the subsequent levels, being adjusted and expanded for specific requirements. At this first level, the player begins as a lizard early in its life, situated in the dunes terrain, in which there are relevant elements from the ecosystem of the São Francisco River dunes that can be involved in ecological relations with the player-controlled lizard. As a tool to support ecology teaching and learning, the game demands that the student make use of concepts related to different ecological relationships in order to overcome the challenges faced by the lizard to survive, develop, and reproduce successfully. The next sections describe the ecological modeling of the game.

*4.1. Modeling Ecology.* As the player controls a lizard, the relevant ecological relationships modeled for the game were prey-lizard, predator-lizard, vegetation-lizard, lizard-lizard, and lizard-physical environment (Figure 2). Among the elements involved in ecological relationships, there are various species of plants, typical preys of lizards, various species of lizard predators, and also animals not involved in the food chains in which the lizards are engaged. Other cospecific lizards are also present in the environment, engaging in ecological relationships (e.g., competition for territory, preys, and breeding). Besides, there are abiotic elements that are part of the ecosystem, such as the climate and terrain.

Each element and each relationship were initially described by the biologists that are part of the project team by means of texts and pictures based on the published literature and accumulated knowledge [6, 7]. The terrain, animals, and vegetation were visually modeled in three dimensions, so as to reproduce their actual visual aspect. More importantly, computational models were proposed to describe all the relevant elements and relations and establish the game simulation dynamics.

The simulation models underlying the game define an open-ended environment with multiple outcomes and game experiences and, thus, give rise to a game with a complex and flexible set of rules. In the game, simulation represents consequences to causes in an open manner, without using fixed game rules that heavily constrain player actions [3]. The player is free to move the lizard around the environment, establishing ecological relationships with any of the elements modeled. Each player experiences a different game trajectory every time the game is played. The game strategy is the behavior defined by the player when controlling the lizard at every instant of game play, carrying out the challenge of conducting the lizard to survive, develop, and reproduce.

Game simulation dynamics can be evaluated by the player through dispersion graphs made available within the game, which can show relations between variables chosen by the player. The player can make use of such graphs for decision making, by correlating the different simulation variables along time. The better the player understands the constraints and rules underlying simulation, the better he/she understands the relevant ecological relations and the more successful tends to be his/her game strategy.

It is important to note that the developed computational models had particular requirements, as they should be part of a computer game. The proposed models had to be executed in real time in a 3D rendering game engine and, thus, the algorithms involved could not be computationally expensive. Moreover, the goal was not to build predictive, or even fully descriptive, models of the real case. Instead, the proposed models had to describe the real case only partially, in what was necessary for the game requirements, while keeping enough plausibility and adequacy to be used as a learning tool for ecological relationships, providing valid learning experiences for the players. To put it differently, it was not the aim to accurately represent all variables from the real case, but, instead, to meet the requirement that the players' perception of the elements and their relationships should

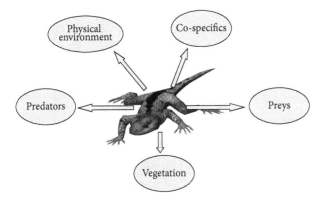

FIGURE 2: Ecological relationships modeled in the game.

be realistic enough for him/her, providing an immersive experience with fidelity to the reality representation. Despite this, it was not arbitrary implementation of the real case, but an approximation of the dynamical ecological model of the real case, considering the demands imposed by the fact that it is a game.

*4.1.1. Physical Environment.* The terrain and the climate were selected as physical elements to be modeled, since they are very important for the game dynamics. The artificial terrain corresponded to dunes with height and length in accordance with the sand dunes of the middle São Francisco River in the Ibiraba village (Municipality of Barra, Bahia, Brazil). Terrain limits were the river itself, a village and fences, also following information from the real region.

To model climate, the relevant variables were temperature, air humidity, and rainfall. More specifically, several variables composed the temperature: air temperature, soil temperature, and temperature in burrows made by the endemic rodent *Trinomys yonenagae*, which are also used by the lizards.

These climate variables affect, directly or indirectly, internal variables of the lizard. They had to model climate dynamics and, therefore, had to vary temporally along the days and months, following seasonal changes. Besides, these variables should also vary spatially, establishing microclimates corresponding to shadows from the vegetation and rodent burrows.

To establish a time flow, a virtual clock was created, parameterized by the computer real clock. Since it is a game and human interaction with the simulation is involved, time flow could not be too slow or too fast, since this could compromise playability. The default time rate is 1 virtual day every 3 minutes and 1 virtual month every 3 days, but the time rate can be configured by the player. This way the student player can experience the day-night cycle and seasons within a single class time. Moreover, a day and night cycle is also visually simulated by varying light conditions in the game and also sun and moon movements in the sky.

The spatial climate variations correspond to microclimates with more amenable or stable climate conditions. These shelters are shadows produced by solar irradiation blockage

by the vegetation and also the gallery systems dug by *T. yonenagae*. These microclimates are crucial for ectothermic animals, such as the lizards.

*Physical Environment: Temperature and Humidity.* The first variable modeled was the air temperature and its temporal variation. Analysis of temperature variations in twenty-four hours cycles from data obtained by the Brazilian National Meteorological Institute (INMET) showed a pattern of daily variations following sunrise and sunset (Figure 3). A similar daily pattern, but in opposing phase, can be observed in the case of air humidity: the higher the temperature, the lower the humidity. In rainy days, air humidity is always high and stable.

This daily pattern of air temperature variation was empirically approximated by a time function with a curve equation for day time and a line equation for night time. This daily temperature function was parameterized by the daily highest and lowest temperatures. To determine the highest and lowest temperatures for each day in the game, historical mean values of highest and lowest temperatures for each month during various years were obtained from INMET (Table 1). The mean and standard deviation values were calculated for each month, estimating normal distribution random variables for the highest and lowest temperatures.

To establish the daily temperature variation for each new day simulated in the game, values are drawn from random variables for the highest and lowest temperatures for a given month, parameterizing the temperature function. The following function was proposed and used to model air temperature:

$$T_{air}(t)$$

$$= \begin{cases} \dfrac{T_{max} - T_{nextmin}}{18} \cdot (t - 6) + T_{nextmin}, \\ \qquad\qquad 0 \leq t \leq 5 \\[2mm] T_{min} + (T_{max} - T_{min}) \cdot \sin\left((t - 6)\dfrac{\pi}{16}\right), \\ \qquad\qquad 5 < t \leq 14 \\[2mm] \dfrac{T_{max} + T_{nextmin}}{2} + \dfrac{T_{max} - T_{nextmin}}{2}\cos\left((t - 14)\dfrac{\pi}{14}\right), \\ \qquad\qquad 14 < t < 22 \\[2mm] \dfrac{T_{max} - T_{nextmin}}{18}(t - 30) + T_{nextmin}, \\ \qquad\qquad 22 \leq t \leq 24, \end{cases}$$

(1)

where $t$ is the time in hours (0–24 hour), $T_{max}$ is the maximum temperature for the current day, $T_{min}$ is the minimum temperature for the current day, and $T_{nextmin}$ is the minimum temperature for the following day.

More important to the game than the air temperature is the soil temperature, since lizards are in close contact with the sand. To estimate the relationship between air temperature

TABLE 1: Monthly mean temperatures measured in a meteorological station at Barra, Bahia, from 1978 to 2008. Data obtained from INMET (http://www.inmet.gov.br/).

| Month | Maximum temperature | Minimum temperature |
|---|---|---|
| January | $32.6 \pm 2.6°C$ | $21.0 \pm 1.7°C$ |
| February | $32.8 \pm 2.5°C$ | $21.4 \pm 1.6°C$ |
| March | $32.3 \pm 2.4°C$ | $21.0 \pm 1.6°C$ |
| April | $32.7 \pm 2.0°C$ | $20.5 \pm 1.7°C$ |
| May | $32.5 \pm 1.9°C$ | $19.1 \pm 2.2°C$ |
| June | $31.9 \pm 1.5°C$ | $17.2 \pm 2.0°C$ |
| July | $32.1 \pm 1.3°C$ | $16.6 \pm 2.0°C$ |
| August | $33.1 \pm 1.6°C$ | $17.5 \pm 2.4°C$ |
| September | $34.5 \pm 1.7°C$ | $19.9 \pm 2.1°C$ |
| October | $35.3 \pm 2.1°C$ | $22.0 \pm 1.8°C$ |
| November | $33.8 \pm 3.0°C$ | $21.7 \pm 1.7°C$ |
| December | $32.9 \pm 2.8°C$ | $21.3 \pm 1.5°C$ |

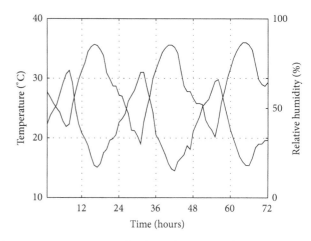

FIGURE 3: Temperature and air humidity measured in a meteorological station at Barra, Bahia, municipality in which the dunes region is located, for a period of 3 days in September 2008. Data obtained from INMET (http://www.inmet.gov.br).

and soil temperature, we relied on measurements made by biologists of the project team. It was verified that soil temperature is higher than air temperature, showing an approximately quadratic relation to the latter and, also, that there is a temporal latency between them, probably due to thermal inertia. Soil temperature was modeled as a quadratic function of the air temperature with a delay of one hour and higher amplitude. The following function was used to model soil temperature:

$$T_{\text{air}}(t) - 0.0425 \cdot \left(T_{\text{air}}(t)\right)^2 + 3.9, \qquad (2)$$

where the constants were empirically determined to approximately fit the data.

Temperature in microclimates (climate spatial variations) was also modeled after air temperature. According to the measurements made by the biologists of the project team, temperature inside burrows also had a delay compared to air temperature, but its amplitude variation was much smaller than the latter. Temperature in the shadow was modeled as being more moderate than the air temperature during sunlight hours, with a reduction of up to 5%. Soil temperature in the shadow was up to 10% lower than soil temperature in sand in open sun.

In addition to temperature, air relative humidity is also an important variable. The air humidity function was modeled as a time function similar to temperature, but in opposing phase. The mean value and amplitude variation of humidity in days without rain were determined from daily temperature values, in a relation estimated by real data. For rainy days, humidity is kept saturated at 100%. The following function was used to model air humidity:

$$H(t) = \begin{cases} -3.9 \cdot T_{\text{air}}(t) + 158, & \text{if not raining} \\ 100, & \text{if raining,} \end{cases} \qquad (3)$$

where the constants were empirically determined to approximately fit the data.

To determine when rain would occur, it was first assumed that if rain occurred, it would last for the whole day. To determine in which days in a month it would rain, historical rain data from INMET were analyzed, establishing mean values and standard deviations for each month and, thus, a random variable with normal distribution for the monthly amount of precipitated rain. Finally, to determine if it would rain in a certain day in the game, it was assumed that the month with the highest rain level was a month in which it rained every day. During simulation, after drawing a value for rain level in a given month from the respective random variable, this value is divided by the highest rain level to determine an estimated number of rainy days. The estimated number of rainy days divided by the number of days in a month gives a probability of rain in each day in that month.

Figure 4 illustrates the simulated air temperature and humidity in the game. It shows a roughly similar pattern to the real data exhibited in Figure 3. Figure 5 shows the different temperature variables modeled in the game.

*4.1.2. Fauna.* The ecological relationships of lizards, predators, and preys and also the relationships between the lizard controlled by the player and its cospecifics are elements of the fauna that need to be modeled. Preys and predators present in the game were defined by the biologists in the team, in accordance with the actual animals found in the real ecological case and in studies on the diet of the lizards. These animals were graphically modeled, reproducing their visual aspect and enforcing immersion, and behaviorally modeled, representing actions and activities that are relevant to the ecological relationships.

Predators include the terrestrial, diurnal bird seriema (*Cariama cristata*), a nocturnal owl, the diurnal hawk southern Caracara (*Caracara plancus*), the nocturnal snake jararaca (*Bothrops neuwiedi*), a diurnal Colubridae snake, the

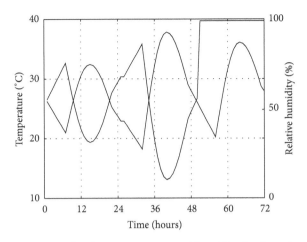

FIGURE 4: Simulated air temperature and humidity for three days, with rain in the third day, for the month of September.

hoary fox (*Lycalopex vetulus*), the wildcat, and the large-sized lizard tegu (*Tupinambis merianae*). All of them have a visual three-dimensional model and exhibit a simple behavior of wandering around the terrain. If a predator approaches a lizard (either the player's or others), it starts chasing the lizard until it gets close enough to attack it (Figure 6). The lizard can only hide from predators if it enters into burrows or if it is close to plants. Every time the player's lizard is attacked, it loses energy. A full predation is not possible upon a single predator attack to preserve game playability.

Ants, termites, maggots, grasshoppers, beetles, and spiders are the preys present in the game, all with a three-dimensional visual representation. We defined three types of behavior for the preys in order to approximate general differences found in the actual behavior of these animals and to add complexity to the building of survival strategies by the students. Beetles, grasshoppers, and maggots keep wandering in the environment, at different velocities. Spiders stay around a plant, moving occasionally. Ants and termites wander in groups around plants. Each prey type appears in different numbers in the environment, depending on whether it is night time or day time.

To eat the preys, the lizard has to get close to them (Figure 7). Each prey type corresponds to a different nutrition level (energy and hydration provided to the lizard) in order to allow the player to experience the dietary diversity observed in the real lizards. These nutrition levels were set based on current biological information in a way that adds plausibility to the model.

There are also interactions between the player's lizard and other cospecific lizards. Male and female cospecific lizards exhibit different behaviors that were inspired by current scientific knowledge on lizard patterns of action during social encounters.

The player always controls a male lizard and every time it gets closer to another male there can be a dispute for territory or for female choice (Figure 8). The dispute starts with head-bobbing, when a lizard nods to indicate that it is ready to fight, trying to make the other individual flee. In the game,

a lizard may flee from the player's lizard with a probability proportional to their size difference but only if the player's lizard executes bobbing. Without bobbing, the other male will always start a fight with the player's character. The fight involves getting close to the other lizard and biting it, taking energy away, proportionally to the difference in size. If the other male reaches a low energy level, it flees and gives up the dispute.

The female lizard interacts with the male lizards only for mating and reproducing. The final objective of the lizard is to live and reproduce as much as possible. The female will only reproduce with a male lizard if it is the only one around her. If two males are near a female, one of them has to flee before the female agrees to mate. As explained above, this may involve fights between the lizards. Once reproduction occurs, the female cannot reproduce again for a whole day. Every time the player's lizard reproduces, its score (which is an egg count) is increased by one. Since the player's lizard begins as an infant, only after twelve months it reaches sexual maturity and is able to reproduce. Before that, the player has to develop and survive.

*4.1.3. Flora.* The flora present in the game is composed of fifteen different species of plants, all graphically modeled, also to enforce immersion. These plants have a characteristic distribution in the real sand dunes: some of them are found in the summit of the dunes, some in the slope, and others only in the valley. The same distribution is also present in the game simulated environment.

In the real dunes, plants are also part of the food chain of the lizards: some of them produce flowers and some produce both flowers and fruits which can be eaten by the lizards, therefore contributing to the lizard's energy and hydration (Figure 9). Moreover, the production of flowers and fruits by the plants follows seasonal variations. All these aspects were simulated by the game and, therefore, the player can notice the influence of seasonal changes in the lizard's diet.

Besides being a food source, plants are also sources of amenable microclimates. Shadows are placed only around plants (Figure 9), which are also hiding spots for the lizards to avoid predators.

*4.1.4. Player's Lizard.* The player's lizard is the main character and source for the experience of ecological relationships. Therefore, it is the most complex element in the game, since every ecological interaction comprises features to be developed in this character.

There are many variables and processes related to the player's lizard that were planned to incorporate relevant biological concepts to the game (Figure 10; see Table 2 for variables). The most relevant variables are energy, hydration, and internal temperature.

Energy is a value between 0% and 100% that represents the energy stored by the lizard. Energy lowers every second due to energy expenditure, which involves basal energy expenditure necessary to keep the lizard alive and energy for movement. Basal energy expenditure can vary depending on the internal temperature: temperatures above the ideal range

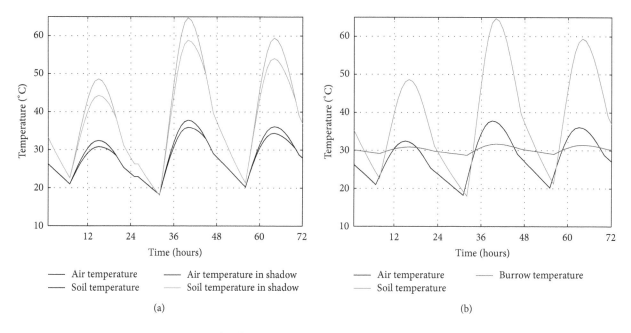

(a)                                                                    (b)

FIGURE 5: Simulated temperatures for three days in different conditions.

FIGURE 6: A predator (seriema) attacking the lizard.

FIGURE 8: Male and female lizards close to the player's lizard.

FIGURE 7: Lizard approaching a prey (spider).

FIGURE 9: Lizard and plants in the dunes. Note the shadows under the plants and the white flower on the floor in front of the lizard.

TABLE 2: Player's lizard main variables.

| Variable | Range/unit |
|---|---|
| Energy | 0% to 100% |
| Hydration | 0% to 100% |
| Internal temperature | 0°C to 50°C |
| Age | 0 to 36 months |
| Energy expenditure | 0% to 100% per time unit |
| Size | 0% to 100% |

raise the basal energy expenditure, whilst temperatures below that lower the expenditure but make the lizard lethargic. Energy for movement depends on the lizard speed: running speed has higher energy expenditure, walking speed has a lower expenditure, and standing still has no expenditure besides the basal one. Energy rises when the lizard eats preys, flowers, or fruits, with each of them contributing to a different amount of energy and hydration.

The current energy for the player's lizard is defined according to the following equations:

$$\text{Energy}(t) = \text{Energy}(t-1)$$
$$-\text{TotalEnergyCost}(t) + \text{FoodEnergy}(t),$$

$$\text{TotalEnergyCost}(t)$$
$$= \text{BasalEnergyCost}(t) \cdot \text{TemperatureCost}(t)$$
$$\cdot \text{MovementCost}(t),$$

$$\text{BasalEnergyCost}(t) = \text{INITENCONS} \cdot \text{SIZEFACTOR},$$

$$\text{TemperatureCost}(t)$$
$$= \begin{cases} \dfrac{1}{\left(1 + \text{TCOST}_{\text{low}} \cdot \left(\text{IT}_{\text{low}} - \text{InternalTemp}(t)\right)\right)}, \\ \quad \text{InternalTemp}(t) < \text{IT}_{\text{low}}, \\[6pt] 1, \\ \quad \text{IT}_{\text{low}} \leq \text{InternalTemp}(t) \leq \text{IT}_{\text{high}}, \\[6pt] 1 + \text{TCOST}_{\text{high}} \cdot \left(\text{InternalTemp}(t) - \text{IT}_{\text{high}}\right), \\ \quad \text{InternalTemp}(t) > \text{IT}_{\text{high}}, \end{cases}$$

$$\text{MovementCost}(t) = \begin{cases} \text{COSTRUN}, & \text{runnning} \\ \text{COSTWALK}, & \text{walking} \\ 1, & \text{stopped}, \end{cases}$$

$$(4)$$

where FoodEnergy is how much energy was gained by eating; INITENCONS is a constant that represents how much time it takes for all initial energy (50%) to be consumed; SIZEFACTOR is a constant proportional to the relative size of the lizard; the bigger the lizard the higher the basal energy expenditure; TCOST is a constant that represents how much total energy expenditure is reduced ($\text{TCOST}_{\text{low}}$) or increased ($\text{TCOST}_{\text{high}}$) when internal temperature is

below the minimum ideal temperature ($\text{IT}_{\text{low}}$) or above the maximum ideal temperature ($\text{IT}_{\text{high}}$); COSTRUN and COSTWALK are constants that represent how much the total energy expenditure is increased when the lizard is running or walking.

Hydration is also a value between 0% and 100%. It rises when the lizard feeds and lowers gradually along time when air humidity is lower than a threshold of 40%.

The internal temperature is a crucial variable for the lizard, since it is an ectothermic animal that cannot rely on internal metabolism to regulate temperature and, thus, must regulate temperature behaviorally, moving to cooler or warmer places when it needs to diminish or increase its temperature, respectively. The player should try to maintain the lizard's temperature at an ideal range, close to 38°C, a value also inspired by the real species. If the lizards' temperature is out of the ideal range, the basal energy expenditure is altered as explained before. When the internal temperature rises above a maximum temperature value, the lizard dies. If the internal temperature is lower than the ideal range, the lizard does not die but suffers a speed reduction and starts having a growing chance of failing to execute actions such as eating (biting food) or fighting other male lizards.

Internal temperature varies according to the soil temperature, but not instantly, as the lizard has a certain thermal inertia to thermal equilibrium

$$\text{InternalTemp}(t) = \text{InternalTemp}(t-1) + \text{TEMPEQ}$$
$$\cdot \left(\text{SoilTemp}(t) - \text{InternalTemp}(t-1)\right), \tag{5}$$

where $t$ is time in hours, InterTemp is the lizard's internal temperature, SoilTemp is the soil temperature, and TEMPEQ is a constant defining how fast internal temperature converges to soil temperature. At the beginning of the game, the thermal inertia is low, with a high value to TEMPEQ, but TEMPEQ lowers as the lizard's size increases.

The lizard's size increases according to its age. At the end of every month, the mean energy value determines how much the lizard's size increases. If the monthly mean energy was 100%, then the lizard grows at a maximum rate at the end of that month. If the mean energy value is lower than 100%, then the lizard's size increases at a proportionally lower rate. As a lizard grows, its walking and running speed increases, but so does the movement and basal energy expenditures. Therefore, a larger lizard can chase preys faster and also flee faster from predators, but it has to eat more to keep its energy level.

## 5. Simulating the Ecological Relationships

The computational models described above amount to a representation of the ecological case upon which the game is based. During game play, all these models are effectively operated, providing a simulated environment where the lizard controlled by the player is situated. To increase awareness and understanding of the different ecological processes and relationships, information about the environment and the lizard, besides being simulated, needs to be observed by the player.

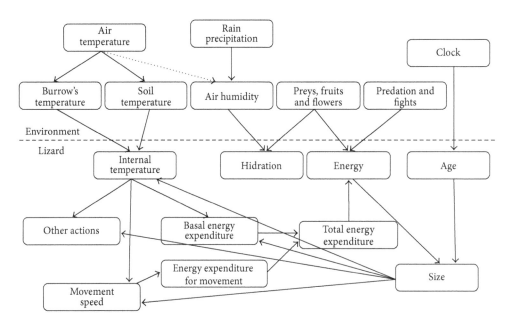

FIGURE 10: Diagram of the most relevant variables for the player's lizard and for the environment, showing also the relations among them.

Therefore, the user interface has to visually present relevant aspects of the various elements. The visualization of elements such as the terrain, fauna, and flora is straightforward, since such elements were graphically modeled and positioned, so the user sees them from a first-person or third-person perspective. Variables, such as soil temperature, internal temperature, and energy, however, have to be exhibited by means of other graphical user interface components.

While playing the game, the student player has instant information regarding the lizard and the environment, such as time, energy level, hydration, internal temperature, air temperature, air humidity, age, sexual maturity, and number of successful reproductions. Moreover, the player can also have access to time graphs for the past 24 hours of many variables, including internal temperature, hydration, air temperature, soil temperature, humidity, energy, and energy expenditure, by means of an interface that allows him/her to select which variables he/she want to plot in two-dimensional dispersion graphs (Figure 11).

To illustrate results obtained by the simulation models during game play, Figure 12 shows a sample of 24-hour graphs of some variables. This sample simulation was done playing the game for one simulated day that lasted 3 minutes in real time. The 24-hour period started at sunrise. The lizard went out in the sun, looking for preys and eating them. As night started, the lizard was attacked by a predator.

As can be noted by the graphs, climate variables are not continuously updated during simulation, but only hourly. This was done because climate variables do not change rapidly and also because it was a way of reducing computational cost.

At sunrise, air and soil temperatures were low and thus the player's lizard had its internal temperature decreased (Figure 12(a)). As the environmental temperature raised and the lizard was under the sun, the lizard's internal temperature

stopped dropping and began to increase. The time where the highest internal temperature was observed did not match the time showing the highest air temperature, as the lizard is more affected by the soil temperature, which has a delay in relation to the air temperature. Besides, the lizards' internal temperature also had a short delay compared to the soil temperature, due to thermal inertia.

While the air temperature increased, the air humidity decreased but never reached a level below 40% (Figure 12(b)). Therefore, the lizard's hydration never decreased in this 24-hour period. But it increased every time the lizard ate a prey and so did its energy value. Every increase in energy and hydration was due to the lizard's feeding.

Energy expenditure varies a lot during this simulation (Figure 12(c)). Every sudden increase with subsequent decrease in energy expenditure was due to the lizard's movements, as running increases energy consumption. Energy expenditure also varied due to changes in basal energy expenditure as the lizard's internal temperature varied. The higher the internal temperature, the higher the basal energy expenditure. At hour 18, energy level dropped considerably. This happened because the player's lizard was attacked repeatedly by a predator while standing still. Every attack promoted an energy level decrease. Afterward, the lizard fled running from predator and got near a tree to hide from it. The lizard stayed in this position as the 24-hour period ended.

Energy, temperatures, humidity, and hydration are variables that can have their instant value and time variation observed by the player inside the game. The sample play described here illustrates how the ecological dynamics inside the game can be evaluated by the player to better understand game play and therefore determine a better game strategy.

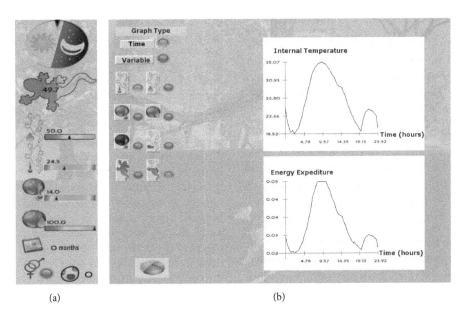

FIGURE 11: During game execution, the player has access to instant values of various simulated variables (a) and also to changes along time of these variables by means of a graph generator interface (b).

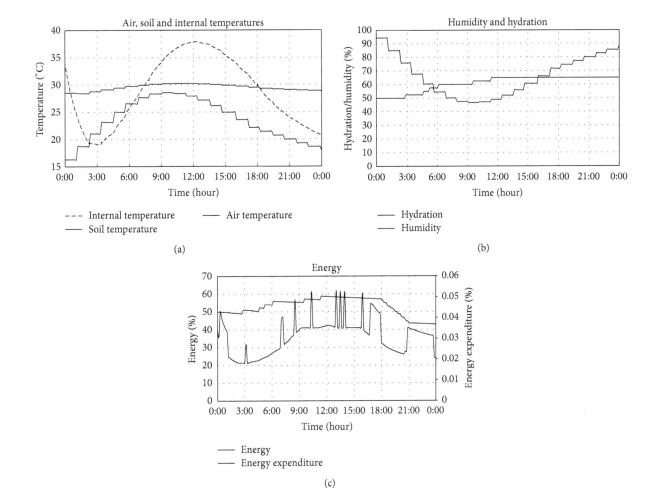

FIGURE 12: Graphs for a 24 h period of game simulation showing temporal variation in (a) temperatures, (b) hydration/humidity, and (c) energy.

## 6. Using Calangos in the Science Classroom

In order to investigate the educational potential of the game Calangos, we used it in the science classroom as part of a teaching sequence for ecology teaching at the high school level, in a public school in Feira de Santana, Bahia, Brazil. Given the educational goals of the teaching, we focused on its contribution to teaching and learning about ecological niche, one of the key subject matters in ecology, which can be addressed through the game.

In many textbooks, the ecological niche is treated as an organism's "profession" in the ecological systems, in connection with Whittaker and colleagues' proposal of distinguishing between niche and habitat [12]. Nevertheless, as discussed by Sepulveda and El-Hani, this conception of niche is inadequate to build an understanding that can help teaching and learning about evolution and, for that matter, also ecology, since it does not stress the role of limiting factors and competition in either the structuring of ecological systems or the evolutionary process [13]. Other conceptions about niche are more appropriate for these educational goals, such as Hutchinson's conception of the niche as a $n$-dimensional hypervolume delimited by the environmental conditions and resources defining the requirements of a species to survive and exhibit its mode of living [14].

We developed the teaching sequence structured around Calangos. In this study, we were guided by the hypothesis that Calangos could help in promoting the construction of an understanding of this conception of ecological niche, more specifically, based on the analysis of thermal regulation as one of the challenges for lizard survival implemented in the game. The teaching sequence include six steps: (1) presentation of the game and its playing dynamics, (2) use of the game by students pairs, (3) proposal of hypotheses for the survival difficulties faced by the lizards (in the game) by means of discursive interactions between students and teacher, (4) discussion of the challenge of thermal regulation in the game, (5) orientation for the students to consider the behavior of the variables found at the side bar and the graphs made available by the game (since they typically pay scant attention to them while playing), and (6) an explicit approach of the Hutchinsonian niche by the teacher, applied to the context of thermal regulation and using students' experience with the game.

The teaching sequence was implemented in three high school first year classes in two 100-minutes sessions, involving 45 students ranging from 15 to 16 years. Both sessions were fully videotaped, comprising 10 recording hours. In the videotaped classes, we selected episodes in which discursive interactions between students and between them and the teacher allowed us to evaluate the students' behavioral engagement in the activities [15] and the meaning making process about the ecological niche in the context of thermal regulation [16]. Moreover, we applied a questionnaire in a pretest-posttest design in order to evaluate the game role in promoting conceptual learning. The questionnaire comprises three task situations evaluating students' understanding about (1) the relation between environmental temperature variation and body temperature variation in ectothermic animals, (2) the

behavioral strategies used by these animals for regulating body temperature, and (3) the concept of ecological niche. For evaluating (1), a graph was presented, showing the increase of environmental temperature and the increase of the lizard internal body temperature along time, followed by one question concerning what information the students were able to extract from the graph, and another question requiring that they explain why frequent temperature variations in a semiarid environment challenged lizard survival. For (2), a picture showing lizard behavioral changes in different periods of the day was provided, and then the students were asked to explain why the lizard remained below a rock at noon, how the shown behavioral changes were related to the relation between environmental and body temperature previously analyzed, and what those behavioral changes revealed with regard to the lizard survival strategies. For (3), the questionnaire provided a scenario describing the sand dunes of the middle São Francisco River, which provided the real case for developing Calangos, and the students were prompted to write a text describing the challenges faced by the lizards to survive and reproduce in that environment. To write the text, they were asked to use the following terms: ecological niche, environmental temperature, soil temperature, lizard internal temperature, hypothermia, hyperthermia, survival, predator, and reproduction. We obtained questionnaires for 18 students in both pretest and posttest. We discuss below some results for providing a glimpse of the results obtained with Calangos use in the science classroom. Finally, to evaluate students' experience while playing Calangos, we asked them to answer the following simple question: "what did you think of the game Calangos?"

In the classroom, discursive interactions during which the biological phenomena simulated in Calangos were discussed, we could observe that the students were capable of articulating their experiences while playing the game with the challenges for the survival of an ectothermic animal. The following excerpt provides an example:

Teacher. What else happened in the game?

Students. We died.

Teacher. Why?

Student 1. Due to high temperature.

Student 2. Due to malnutrition and low temperature.

Teacher. How do you solve this problem, death by high temperature?

Student 3. Isn't just stay in the shadow?

Student 4. But then the lizard dies from the cold.

Student 3. That's true.

Student 5. Then, he should go to the shadow and to the sun to even the body temperature. Not to even... to adjust.

Student 6. To balance the temperature.

Teacher. Kind of adjusting. Why does this happen with lizards? Why do lizards have "cold blood"? What would "cold blood" mean?

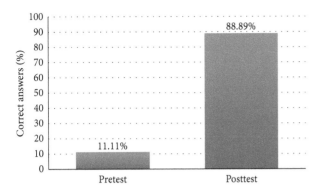

FIGURE 13: Percentage of correct answers to the question about the behavioral strategies used by lizards for regulating body temperature.

Student 5. It depends on the sun to keep...

Teacher. It depends on the environment to regulate internal temperature. They are ectothermic animals.

This finding agrees with the questionnaire data, in which most students (12 out of 18) showed in their answers that they understood how the body temperature of ectothermic animals varies with the environmental temperature. One student, for instance, wrote in the pretest that temperature variation common in semiarid environments are a challenge for the life of a lizard that needs to maintain a stable body temperature. In the posttest, the same student showed a deeper understanding of the phenomenon at stake, writing that the animal needs to control its internal temperature and, thus, should use behavioral strategies to regulate body temperature, exposing itself to the sun or moving to shadowed microenvironments depending on how the body temperature varies with the environmental temperature. With the experience of playing and discussing about Calangos in the classroom, this student's understanding shifted from a superficial view on lizard body temperature control to a deeper view including important aspects related to behavioral strategies for temperature regulation.

When the students were asked in the questionnaire to explain why a lizard remained below a rock at noon, their answers in the pretest did not relate the fact that lizard stayed below the rock to body temperature regulation (Figure 13). As an example, we can mention the following answer: "he is resting, because the sun is too hot and he goes below the rock to rest". In the posttest, in turn, most of them explained that behavior as a strategy used by the animal to keep its body temperature within an adequate range (Figure 13). This student's answer provides an example: "environmental temperature is too high at this time and then it protects itself in the shadow, so that its body temperature is not raised, and, thus, it avoids death."

Concerning the concept of ecological niche, the learning outcomes were much more limited. In the pretest no student used the term "ecological niche" in their texts. In the posttest, only four students used the term "ecological niche" in their texts, suggesting that most of them did not master its meaning after the intervention. This interpretation is reinforced by

answers like the following: "the lizard living in this environment (sand dunes) depends on the soil temperature and the ecological niche to survive." These limited outcomes are likely to be related to the rather abstract nature of the Hutchinsonian niche, showing that it will be necessary in future applications of the teaching sequence using Calangos to expand on the its discussion in the classroom, paying also more attention to the shifting from the more concrete situations experienced by the students in the game and the more abstract reasoning involving in treating the niche as a *n*-dimensional hypervolume.

Other students' answers showed promising outcomes for this shift to a more abstract understanding of the niche, since they identified environmental factors affecting the lizard chances of survival and reproduction, which amount to an important step towards formulating the Hutchinsonian interpretation of the niche. In the pretest, 11 students mentioned some biotic and/or abiotic variable influencing the survival and reproduction chances. In the posttest, this was observed in 17 out of the 18 students. Here is an example: "there are several challenges that the lizard should face, such as escaping predators, feeding, and finding water. But the worst problem is how to keep the temperature and this demands survival strategies, such as staying in the shadow" (posttest).

Besides supporting conceptual learning, the game Calangos motivated the behavioral engagement of the students in interpreting and discussing the biological phenomena simulated in the game, as we could observe in the classroom discursive interactions. This was also shown independently in the questionnaire answers. All 18 students regarded the game as interesting, fun, and educationally important. A student, for instance, described her experience with the game as follows: "very nice and interesting, because we end up getting involved in the game. I felt as I was myself there".

## 7. Conclusion

Electronic games can be a relevant resource for ecology teaching and learning. Calangos is a game that can aid in this task by providing a simulated scenario based on a real ecological case. The simulated ecosystem developed for the game includes a variety of ecological relationships related to a lizard controlled by the student player. The computational models developed, which were discussed in this paper, define a complex network of interrelated elements. To achieve survival and reproductive success, the player must define his/her strategy, facing challenges such as that of deciding when and what to hunt and eat, while paying close attention to the behavioral regulation of the lizard's temperature. To better define a game strategy, the player must understand, however, the game mechanics and this entails that he/she must comprehend the ecological dynamics. In this way, ecological contents can be learned in an active and consistent manner.

An important asset for the development of the simulated ecosystem for the game was the presence of a multidisciplinary team of biological, science education, and computer science researchers. During the whole development process, software requirements were defined and reviewed to better cope with both biological plausibility and educational objectives. We already investigated the game potential for promoting ecology learning and supporting ecology teaching in the classroom, as discussed above, producing evidence for its contributions for teaching and learning about key ecological matters, such as thermal regulation through behavior in ectothermic animals. We found some limits, however, in promoting learning of more abstract concepts, such as the Hutchinsonian niche, through a teaching sequence structure around the game. The next step in the project is to assess and validate the game as a learning tool in a broader set of high school classrooms, using a new version of the teaching sequence addressing the limits observed in this previous study.

## Acknowledgments

The authors would like to acknowledge Marta Vargens, Yupanqui Julho Muñoz, Emerson Silva de Oliveira, Thiago do Carmo Lima, Jairo Henrique dos Santos Calmon, Carlos Bezerra, Paulo César de Alencar Gonçalves Filho, Fladmy Alves de Souza, Jônatas dos Santos Correia, Leonardo Lima and Eduardo de Oliveira, who have participated in the research project, and also the support of FINEP, CNPq, Fapesp, Fapesb, and UEFS. CNPq granted PLBR and CNEL a research fellowship during the development of this work. They are also thankful to the students involved in the high school classroom study reported here.

## References

[1] E. Sander, P. Jelemenská, and U. Kattmann, "Towards a better understanding of ecology," *Journal of Biological Education*, vol. 40, no. 3, pp. 119–123, 2006.

[2] S. M. Scheiner and M. R. Willig, "A general theory of ecology," *Theoretical Ecology*, vol. 1, no. 1, pp. 21–28, 2008.

[3] T. R. Cottrell, "Capturing difficult botanical concepts with a net of previous knowledge," *The American Biology Teacher*, vol. 66, no. 6, pp. 441–445, 2004.

[4] J. D. Proctor and B. M. H. Larson, "Ecology, complexity, and metaphor," *BioScience*, vol. 55, no. 12, pp. 1065–1068, 2005.

[5] B. H. Munson, "Ecological misconceptions," *Journal of Environmental Education*, vol. 25, no. 4, pp. 30–34, 1994.

[6] P. L. B. Rocha, L. P. Queiroz, and J. R. Pirani, "Plant species and habitat structure in a sand dune field in the brazilian Caatinga: a homogeneous habitat harbouring an endemic biota," *Revista Brasileira de Botânica*, vol. 27, no. 4, pp. 739–755, 2004.

[7] P. L. B. Rocha and M. T. Rodrigues, "Electivities and resource use by an assemblage of lizards endemic to the dunes of the São Francisco River, northeastern Brazil," *Papéis Avulsos de Zoologia*, vol. 45, pp. 261–284, 2005.

[8] D. Charsky, "From edutainment to serious games: a change in the use of game characteristics," *Games and Culture*, vol. 5, no. 2, pp. 177–198, 2010.

[9] C. C. Abt, *Serious Games*, University Press of America, Lanham, Md, USA, 1987.

[10] D. R. Michael and S. L. Chen, *Serious Games: Games that Educate, Train, and Inform*, Thomson Course Technology, Boston, Mass, USA, 2005.

[11] D. Fundenberg and D. K. Levine, *The Theory of Learning in Games*, MIT Press, Cambridge, Mass, USA, 1998.

[12] J. H. Whittaker, S. A. Levin, and R. B. Root, "Niche, habitat and ecotope," *American Naturalist*, vol. 107, no. 955, pp. 321–338, 1973.

[13] C. A. S. Sepulveda and C. N. El-Hani, "Adaptacionismo versus exaptacionismo: o que este debate tem a dizer ao ensino de evolução?" *Ciência & Ambiente*, vol. 36, pp. 93–124, 2008.

[14] G. E. Hutchinson, "Concluding remarks," *Cold Spring Harbor Symposium on Quantitative Biology*, vol. 22, pp. 415–427, 1957.

[15] J. A. Fredricks, P. C. Blumenfeld, and A. H. Paris, "School engagement: potential of the concept, state of the evidence," *Review of Educational Research*, vol. 74, no. 1, pp. 59–109, 2004.

[16] E. F. Mortimer and P. H. Scott, *Meaning Making in Secondary Science Classrooms*, Open University Press, Maidenhead, UK, 2003.

# 12

# Nowcasting Mobile Games Ranking using Web Search Query Data

**Yoones A. Sekhavat**

*Faculty of Multimedia, Tabriz Islamic Art University, Hakim Nezami Square, Azadi Blvd., East Azerbaijan, Tabriz, Iran*

Correspondence should be addressed to Yoones A. Sekhavat; sekhavat@tabriziau.ac.ir

Academic Editor: Michael J. Katchabaw

In recent years, the Internet has become embedded into the purchasing decision of consumers. The purpose of this paper is to study whether the Internet behavior of users correlates with their actual behavior in computer games market. Rather than proposing the most accurate model for computer game sales, we aim to investigate to what extent web search query data can be exploited to nowcast (contraction of "now" and "forecasting" referring to techniques used to make short-term forecasts) (predict the present status of) the ranking of mobile games in the world. Google search query data is used for this purpose, since this data can provide a real-time view on the topics of interest. Various statistical techniques are used to show the effectiveness of using web search query data to nowcast mobile games ranking.

## 1. Introduction

Not only does the web contain valuable data that can be integrated and exploited in different applications [1, 2], but also the activities of users when they search on the web can be useful to estimate the real-world activities in a variety of contexts. This web search data has potential to nowcast the current status of activities, since this data is available when search activity happens [3]. The big question is "whether the population's Internet tendencies can represent their subsequent behavior."

Research has shown that no matter whether a customer seeks knowledge on specific attributes of a product or knowledge on how a particular product compares relative to others, the Internet is the primary source of information. Each search for a product on the Internet is a valuable piece of information about an individual's intentions to make a purchase [4]. Since online search is a measure of interest for a topic [5], terms searched by consumers on the web can provide valuable indicators of consumers' interests. Exploiting this knowledge to make business predictions can result in a big change in business decision-making [6]. As discussed in [5], search statistics for a product can represent the interest level for that product and consequently help in predicting the sales of that product.

In [7], it is shown that changes in query volumes for terms related to influenza are indicators of changes in current numbers of influenza cases. Based on this idea, Google Flu Trends, which is used to diagnose outbreaks of influenza in the United States, was developed [7]. The results showed that this tool can predict outbreaks of influenza in the United States 7 to 10 days before releasing CDC's (Centers for Disease Control and Prevention) surveillance report [7]. Although not all of the people searching for influenza related topics, symptoms, and treatments are ill, an increase in the search for terms related to this topic is added together and shows a trend.

In this paper, we show how web search data about mobile games can be an indicator of the world ranking of mobile games. More specifically, we aim to study whether the web search data about mobile games extracted from Google Trends can contribute to the forecasting of the ranking of mobile games reported by App Annie (a business intelligence company and analyst firm that produces market reports for the apps and digital goods industry). Generally, time series regarding the ranking of mobile applications are not reported frequently (e.g., on a monthly or quarterly basis) due to the cost or convention reasons. Because of fast changes in the mobile games market, it would be desirable for developers and investors to make it possible to maintain a current estimate of the value of these time series before it is officially reported or revised. This technique which is called "nowcasting" aims to forecast a current value instead of a future value. In the nowcasting model we propose, the past behavior of the series being modeled (mobile games ranking time series) as well as the values of more easily observed signals (web search query data) occurring in the same period of time is used to predict the current ranking of mobile games.

In a preliminary study in [9], we showed that web search data of mobile games correlates with the market demands of mobile games. We showed that this correlation can be used to nowcast the current status of mobile games where no public report is available regarding the ranking of computer games. More specifically, to find potential areas of interest for game developers in Iran, we studied the trends of web search data for Iranian mobile games. However, in this paper, we show how web search data of mobile games can be used to rank the top mobile games in the world.

The results of this study can reveal market trends for mobile games and make it possible to identify the potential areas of mobile games. Certainly, it is possible to build more sophisticated forecasting models than what we use for this purpose. However, instead of any methodological advances, we argue that the models we propose can serve as baselines to help analysts get started with a basic prediction of trends in this industry.

## 2. Related Work

Web search query data was used in [10] to forecast the present unemployment rate in the United States. Examining the correlation between web search data about oil price and the sales of electricity was studied in [11]. The correlation between search data about terms related to finding jobs and unemployment rate in the United States was considered in [12]. In [13], web search data was exploited to nowcast the private consumption in the United States. In [11], the authors showed that web search data can be more potential to predict indicators for subsequent consumer purchases in cases when consumers start planning purchases, a considerable time before their actual purchase.

In [14], Internet browsing data was used to inform practitioners about real-time consumer behavior in automobile purchases in Chile. In [15], using regression on Google Trends data showed that the volume of searches for cinema related terms has the potential to forecast cinema admissions models. In [16], using Google Trends data about environment-related phrases, it is shown that the public interest in environmental issues, conservation, and biodiversity has decreased since 2004.

## 3. Web Search Query Data on Google Trends

In comparison to surveillance reports that are generally published with delays, web search data can be available timely. Moreover, while traditional surveillance methods use sampling techniques that might affect the accuracy of the results, Internet users do not represent a random sample

(according to the Internet World Stats, the penetration rate of Internet usage in 2015 in the world is 46.1%). Releasing users search queries on Google through a publicly accessible interface (Google Trends) was a big step toward using this valuable source of information for different types of prediction in various areas. This valuable information shows its importance if we take into account the fact that, according to NetMarketShare, Google owns 70.69% of search engine market share.

We employ Google Trends as a source of web search data for mobile games. Google Trends allows gaining access to information about the volume of web searches that were performed by users for different search terms (or a combination of terms), relative to the total number of searches completed by Google over time. The input into Google Trends is a search query (e.g., "Star Wars"), and the output is a time series of the relative popularity of that query over the selected period. Google logs every single query into the Google database, which is accessible through Google Trends interface (https://www.google.com/trends/). Taking into account the fact that people generally enter terms into this search engine because they are interested in something about them makes this database a valuable business intelligence source.

Web search data from Google Trends is publicly available at a weekly frequency. Techniques that aggregate related keywords are used in this tool. Increasing the volume of web queries results in increasing the average of queries related to other queries, which consequently leads to sensitivity in detection of changes in future search volume trends. Google Trends addresses this problem by normalizing the results. Instead of releasing the actual search number, the normalized data is available for users, which is based on the total number of search queries in a particular location during the time period being examined. This normalization takes into account any trends from growth in the total number of Internet users. The normalized data is rescaled to an index with a range of 0 to 100.

## 4. Mobile Games Market

According to Gartner research group [8], global video game sales will reach $111.1 billion by 2015, where mobile games with $22 billion are surpassing PC games. This report states that mobile games are the fastest-growing segment of the market, in comparison to PC games, handheld video games, and video game console, where the game market revenue for mobile game is doubled between 2013 and 2015. The pervasiveness of smartphones as well as the growth in mobile device technologies is driving these trends faster than before. According to this report, the majority of mobile application buyers are from the United States and Europe, where smartphone penetration is considerable and users in these areas have the means to purchase games on multiple platforms.

According to Big Fish Games [17], revenue from games and game content is now surpassing revenue from movie Box Office sales ($10 billion per year), trying to pass television viewing as well. In this report, mobile games are highlighted

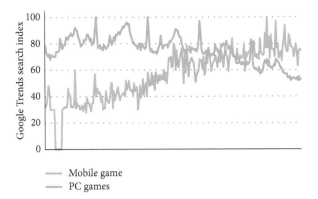

FIGURE 1: Google Trends search index for "mobile games" and "PC games."

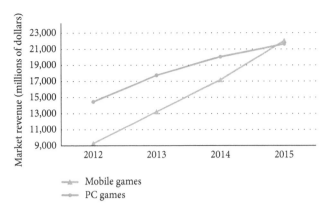

FIGURE 2: Worldwide video game market revenue for mobile games and PC games between 2012 and 2015 based on Gartner group [8].

FIGURE 3: Google Trends search data index and App Annie ranking for Candy Crush Saga.

as a potential type of game that is growing faster than other types (just in the United States, around 48 million people play games on smartphones and tablets). According to this report, 91% of people on the Earth have a mobile phone, where 80% of time on mobile is spent inside apps or games.

According to Newzoo (http://2015.gmgc.info/), 485 million users have spent an average of $4.30 per month in 2015. 64 million mobile game spenders in North America, which is around half of all mobile gamers, spend $7.68 per month on mobile games. Global Mobile Game Confederation (GMGC) expects continuation in mobile games in the coming years ($40Bn by 2017). According to this report, tablet games are growing faster than smartphone games which shows the position of tablets as a potential gaming tool. Due to the importance of mobile games in the game industry, we limit our research to the relation between web search data about mobile games and the actual ranking of mobile games.

*4.1. Mobile Games versus PC Games.* We argue that web search data is correlated with market trends in the mobile game industry. As a first study, to show the effectiveness of using web search data as an indicator of trends in the game market, the results of the search for "mobile game apps" and "PC games" are shown in Figure 1. As you can see in this figure, searches for PC games show a decreasing trend, while there is an increasing trend for "mobile game apps." This is compatible with Gartner's report [8] regarding the market revenue for computer games shown in Figure 2, in which although both PC games and mobile games revenues are increasing, the speed of increase for mobile games is considerably more than for PC games. This is evidence of the fact that the changes in the volume of searches for a topic can be an indicator of changes in the interest and tendency of people for that topic.

*4.2. Correlation between Web Search Data and the Ranking of Mobile Games.* We aim to investigate whether the volume of web search data about mobile games is correlated with the popularity and, consequently, the ranking of these games. More specifically, we study whether the volume of web search data for the name of a mobile game extracted from Google

Trends can be an indicator of the ranking of these games. The results of this finding can help to nowcast the current status and the popularity of games in regions, where there is a lack of official reports.

We selected four mobile games among the top ten mobile games (in terms of the number of downloads) from App Annie (https://www.appannie.com/), which is a company that provides market reports for mobile applications. As an indicator of the popularity of the games, we used the ranking of mobile games produced by App Annie. In particular, we studied *Candy Crush Saga, Clash of Clans, My Talking Angela,* and *8 Ball Pool,* for which Google Trends data is also available. To show the correlation between web search data and the ranking of these mobile games, we mapped web search dates and ranking dates. As shown in Figures 3, 4, 5, and 6, there is a close relationship between the web search data for each game and the corresponding ranking history for the time periods investigated. The differences between starting dates in different diagrams are because the games have been released at different dates.

As shown in Figure 3, Google Trends search index for *Candy Crush Saga* and the ranking of this game in App Annie have a similar decreasing trend since the release of this game in 2013. This correlation is more explicit in the case of *Clash of Clans* (see Figure 4), where an increasing trend from the

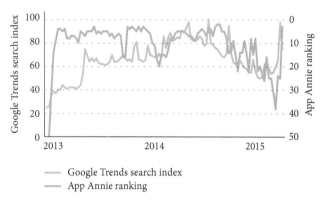

FIGURE 4: Google Trends search data index and App Annie ranking for Clash of Clans.

FIGURE 6: Google Trends search data index and App Annie ranking for 8 Ball Pool.

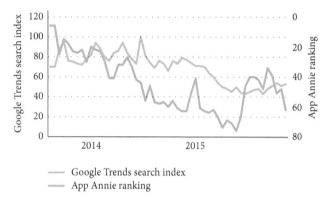

FIGURE 5: Google Trends search data index and App Annie ranking for My Talking Angela.

beginning of 2013 to 2014 is followed with a slight decrease to the beginning of 2015 and then a sharp increase from 2015 to the end of 2015. Accordingly, Google Trends search index for *My Talking Angela* and the ranking of this game in App Annie have a similar decreasing trend (see Figure 5). In the case of 8 Ball Pool (shown in Figure 6), an increasing trend in both Google Trends data and ranking history is followed with a decrease from the beginning of 2015.

*4.2.1. Identifying Correlations.* Although correlation between Google Trends search index and ranking history from App Annie can be seen in Figures 3, 4, 5, and 6, we need a formal method to prove this claim. To this end, we use Granger causality test, which is a statistical hypothesis test to determine whether one time series can contribute to forecasting another [18]. Formally, a variable $X$ Granger-causes $Y$ if $X$ values provide statistically significant information about future values of $Y$. More specifically, $Y$ can be predicted in a better way using the histories of both $X$ and $Y$ in comparison to the use of only the history of $Y$. This technique regresses each variable on lagged values of itself and the other explanatory variable. According to regression model,

$$Y_t = \sum_{j=1}^{m} \left( \alpha_j Y_{t-j} \right) + \sum_{i=1}^{n} \left( \beta_j X_{t-i} \right) + D_t + \varepsilon_t. \quad (1)$$

TABLE 1: Granger causality test result for the top 20 games in App Annie ($P = 0.05$). Games in which the Google Trends search index does not provide statistically significant information about the future values of the ranking are marked with *.

| # | Game name | # of examined points | $F$ | $P$ value |
|---|-----------|---------------------|-----|-----------|
| 1 | Candy Crush Saga | 111 | 4.62951 | 0.03355 |
| 2 | Clash of Clans | 110 | 9.91220 | 0.00211 |
| 3 | My Talking Angela | 50 | 3.57057 | 0.04476 |
| 4 | 8 Ball Pool | 77 | 13.20322 | 0.00050 |
| 5 | Piano Tiles* | 85 | 1.05844 | 0.85428 |
| 6 | Subway Surfers | 121 | 10.02277 | 0.01328 |
| 7 | Color Switch* | 65 | 1.61014 | 0.24453 |
| 8 | Temple Run | 96 | 19.90538 | 0.00213 |
| 9 | Traffic Rider | 94 | 17.69072 | 0.00297 |
| 10 | Pou | 83 | 12.90426 | 0.00166 |
| 11 | Basketball Stars* | 49 | 1.22456 | 0.30063 |
| 12 | Clash Royale | 113 | 10.23644 | 0.00285 |
| 13 | Stack* | 97 | 3.94716 | 0.08219 |
| 14 | slither.io | 64 | 6.65071 | 0.00670 |
| 15 | Disney Crossy Road | 89 | 4.80256 | 0.02357 |
| 16 | My Talking Tom | 74 | 2.79033 | 0.04819 |
| 17 | Hungry Shark World | 102 | 61.19054 | 0.00025 |
| 18 | Dream League Soccer 2016 | 89 | 4.64344 | 0.014555 |
| 19 | Candy Crush Jelly Saga | 75 | 147.517 | 0.000085 |
| 20 | Geometry Dash Meltdown | 95 | 13.16245 | 0.000299 |

When the coefficients of the $X_t$ values are zero, then the series $X_t$ fails to Granger-cause $Y_t$. In this regression model, $D_t$ is a deterministic term, $\varepsilon_t$ is the random error term, $\alpha_j$ is the coefficient on the lagged $Y$ values, and $\beta_i$ is the coefficient on the lagged $X$.

Ideally, all mobile games for which App Annie rankings are available must be examined in order to find whether there are correlations between the Google Trends search index and the ranking history from App Annie. However, this is not practical due to the large number of mobile games available in app stores. Because of this limitation, 20 games among the top mobile games of 2016 were selected. Using Wessa [19], we computed Granger causality for Google Trends search index ($X_t$) and App Annie ranking ($Y_t$). The results of these tests are shown in Table 1. According to the $P$ values in this table, Google Trends search index values provide statistically significant information about the future values of the ranking of the mobile games in 80% of the cases (16 out of 20). As shown in Table 1, in the case of four games (including Piano Tiles, Color Switch, Basketball Stars, and Stack), Google Trends search index does not provide statistically significant information about the future values of the ranking. We attribute this to the general names of the games, as they are not specific names. Consequently, people looking for these names in Google may have something other than games in mind. For example, a user looking for "color switch" may have been looking for techniques to switch color in Photoshop rather than the Color Switch game. Such data impairs the amount of pure searches for the Color Switch game.

### 4.2.2. Identifying Lags.

In the relationship between Google Trends search index time series and App Annie mobile games ranking time series, the App Annie ranking time series may be related to the past lags of Google Trends. To find whether there are time lags between these two time series, we run sample cross-correlation function (CCF). The cross-correlation function of two time series is the product-moment correlation as a function of lag (time-offset) between the series. The cross-correlation function is computed based on Cross-Covariance Function (CCVF). Formally, given two time series $x_t$ and $y_t$, where we can delay $x_t$ by $T$ samples, CCVF is defined as

$$\sigma_{xy}(T) = \frac{1}{N-1} \sum_{t=1}^{n} (x_{t-T} - \mu_x)(y_t - \mu_y). \quad (2)$$

Based on this function and given $\mu_x$ and $\mu_y$ as the means of two time series $x_t$ and $y_t$ with $N$ samples in each, the cross-correlation function is computed as

$$r_{xy}(T) = \frac{\sigma_{xy}(T)}{\sqrt{\sigma_{xx}(T)\sigma_{yy}(T)}}. \quad (3)$$

Using Wessa [19], we computed the cross-correlation function for Google Trends search index ($x_t$) and App Annie ranking ($y_t$). Through this test, we were interested to find whether there are time lags between Google Trends search index and App Annie ranking. Among 20 games shown in Table 1, we selected the top four games based on their rankings in 2016 from App Annie. These games include Candy Crush Saga, 8 Ball Pool, My Talking Angela, and Clash of Clans. For Candy Crush Saga (Figure 7), there are nearly

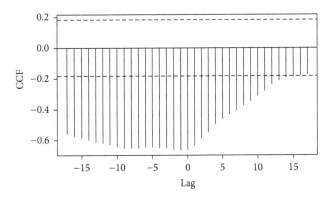

FIGURE 7: Cross functional correlation computed for Candy Crush Saga.

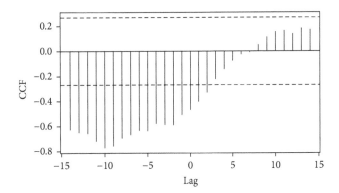

FIGURE 8: Cross functional correlation computed for My Talking Angela.

equal maximum values between 0 and −10. The correlations in this region are negative, indicating that an above-average value of Google search index is likely to lead to a below-average value of App Annie ranking about 5 weeks later. In the case of My Talking Angela (Figure 8), the average of time lag is around 10 weeks. For Clash of Clans (Figure 9) and 8 Ball Pool (Figure 10), the lag is around one week. Although the time lags are different, the correlations for all of them are negative, representing the notion that Google search index is likely to lead to a below-average value of App Annie ranking around 5 weeks later.

### 4.2.3. Forecasting Mobile Games Ranking.

We showed the correlation between Google Trends search index and App Annie ranking for mobile games. We also showed that the above-average value of Google Trends search index is likely to lead to a below-average value of App Annie ranking about 5 weeks later. Now, we aim to investigate to what extent Google Trends search index can be used to forecast the future rankings. To this end, we employed multiple regression technique. Generally, multiple regression, which is an extension of simple linear regression, allows predicting the value of a variable based on the values of two or more other variables. In our case, game ranking is our dependent variable, where we aim to predict its values. Google Trends

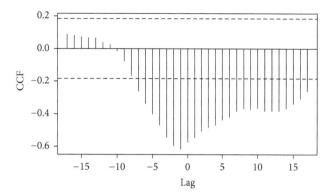

FIGURE 9: Cross functional correlation computed for Clash of Clans.

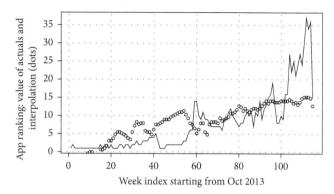

FIGURE 11: Actual values and interpolated values for Candy Crush Saga.

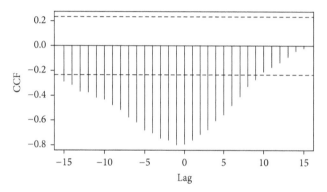

FIGURE 10: Cross functional correlation computed for 8 Ball Pool.

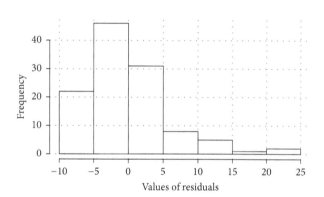

FIGURE 12: Deviations of the observed values from mean (histogram of residuals) for Candy Crush Saga.

search index is our independent variable (a.k.a. the predictor or explanatory variable).

In multiple linear regression, the relationship between independent variables and a dependent variable is modeled by fitting a linear equation to observed data. In this model, values of independent variable $x$ are associated with values of the dependent variable $y$. Given $p$ explanatory variables $x_1, x_2, \ldots, x_n$, the regression line is defined as $\mu_y = \beta_0 + \beta_1 x_1 + \beta_2 x_2 + \cdots + \beta_p x_p$, where this line describes how $\mu_y$ changes with independent variables. The model is expressed as data = fit + residual, where the "fit" term represents the expression $\beta_0 + \beta_1 x_{i1} + \beta_2 x_{i2} + \cdots \beta_p x_{ip}$ and the "residual" shows the deviations of the observed values $y$ from their means $\mu_y$ (shown by $\varepsilon$). Consequently, multiple linear regression, given $n$ observations, is

$$y_i = \beta_0 + \beta_1 x_{i1} + \beta_2 x_{i2} + \cdots \beta_p x_{ip} + \varepsilon_i, \tag{4}$$
$$i = 1, 2, \ldots, n.$$

The results of running regression on Google Trends search index and application ranking for the top four games based on their ranking in 2016 from App Annie are shown in Figures 11, 13, 15, and 17 for Candy Crush Saga, Clash of Clans, My Talking Angela, and 8 Ball Pool, respectively. In addition to representing the actual values and interpolated values based on these data, residuals, which are deviations of the observed values from their mean, are shown in a histogram of residuals (Figures 12, 14, 16, and 18).

4.3. *Nowcasting Virtual Reality Games.* Another important trend in computer games market is games based on virtual reality and augmented reality. Using technologies related to virtual and augmented reality is one of the fast growing areas in computer games that must be considered by practitioners in the game industry. Acquiring Metaio (https://techcrunch.com/2015/05/28/apple-metaio/) (specialized in augmented reality technologies) by Apple and Oculus (https://www.oculus.com/) (specialized in virtual reality solutions) by Facebook shows how big IT firms are moving in this direction. Social media games are another fast growing segment in this industry that takes into account broadband connectivity and networking features to enhance social experiences. As expected, Google Trends also verifies this claim, where tendency to search for virtual reality games has increased in recent years (see Figure 19).

Introducing virtual reality devices such as Oculus Gear VR for Samsung phones as well as many other Gear VR devices makes it possible to experience the virtual reality using mobile phones without the need for a complicated device. Google Cardboard is a simple paper version of this tool that simply allows having the same experience. Introducing these tools has resulted in a significant change in mobile games, where many new mobile games are currently developed based on this technology. Various mobile games such as KioskAR [20] are designed based on augmented

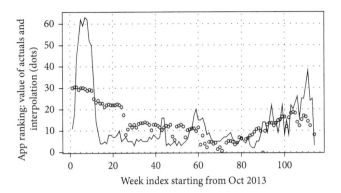

FIGURE 13: Actual values and interpolated values for Clash of Clans.

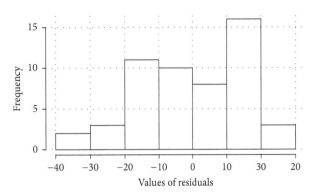

FIGURE 16: Deviations of the observed values from mean (histogram of residuals) for My Talking Angela.

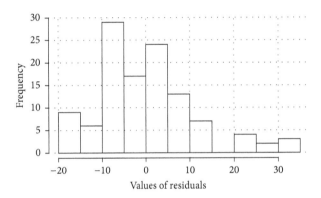

FIGURE 14: Deviations of the observed values from mean (histogram of residuals) for Clash of Clans.

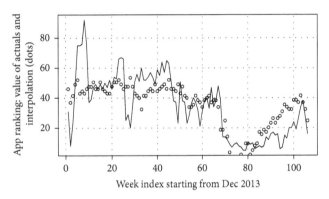

FIGURE 17: Actual values and interpolated values for 8 Ball Pool.

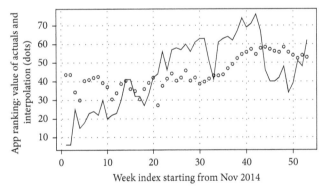

FIGURE 15: Actual values and interpolated values for My Talking Angela.

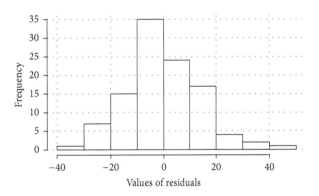

FIGURE 18: Deviations of the observed values from mean (histogram of residuals) for 8 Ball Pool.

reality. Although mobile games based on virtual reality and augmented reality are not currently among the top mobile games, the growth in this area is significant.

Using Google Trends, we extracted the data for the four top virtual reality tools including Samsung Gear VR, HTC Vive, Oculus Rift VR, and Microsoft HoloLens. Samsung Gear VR, which is powered by Oculus, allows using the Samsung Galaxy smartphone as its processor and displaying VR scenes. The Galaxy handset is put in front of the lenses (using a micro USB dock). HTC Vive is a VR headset made in collaboration with Valve at MWC. Oculus Rift

is the virtual reality headset which is currently owned by Facebook. This device is plugged into PCs DVI and USB ports and tracks head movements in order to provide 3D imagery using its stereo screens. Microsoft HoloLens is a virtual/augmented reality tool that combines real world elements with virtual "holographic" images (this device is not released yet). Although some of these tools are not released yet, as shown in Figure 20, searches for them on the Internet, which represent demands and tendencies to use them, are increasing based on Google Trends.

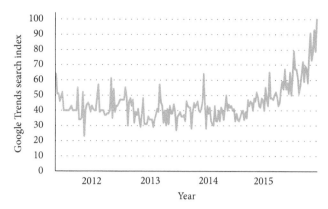

FIGURE 19: Google Trends search index for virtual reality games.

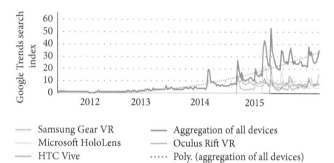

— Samsung Gear VR            — Aggregation of all devices
— Microsoft HoloLens         — Oculus Rift VR
— HTC Vive                   ····· Poly. (aggregation of all devices)

FIGURE 20: Google Trends search index for virtual reality tools including Samsung Gear VR, HTC Vive, Oculus Rift VR, and Microsoft HoloLens.

## 5. Limitations of the Research

One main issue that may affect our assumption about the relation between search volume and the tendency and interest in a specific topic is that online search behavior is not always an indicator of an outbreak. For example, announcing that Rihanna had flu in October of 2011 resulted in an increase in flu-related web queries. This shows the vulnerability of Google Trends to "noisy" queries. As another false positive noisy query, recall of a drug rather than search for treatment may result in an increase in the search volume for flu drugs. One possible solution for this problem in our case is to augment the query with the "game" word. For example, instead of finding the statistics of searches for "color switch," looking for "color switch game" or "color switch mobile game" eliminates the statistics of the queries for color switch that are not related to Color Switch game.

Google Trends provides relative data (search volume index) instead of actual total number of searches. Because of using data sampling techniques and approximation methods, Google Trends data may contain inaccuracies. This problem prevents direct comparison between search volumes [21]. For future work, we aim to address this problem using rank aggregation techniques to combine the ranking of results for similar queries rather than combining actual data.

## 6. Conclusion

In this paper, we showed how web search query data about mobile games (extracted from Google Trends) has correlation with market demands for mobile games and, consequently, the ranking of these games (extracted from App Annie) in the world. We used statistical techniques including cross-correlation function and Granger causality test to show this correlation for the 4 top mobile games extracted from App Annie based on the number of downloads. Finally, regression techniques were used to nowcast the current ranking of mobile games based on web search data extracted from Google Trends for these mobile games. Based on these findings, we argue that this correlation can be used to nowcast the current status of mobile games in regions where no report is published publicly about the ranking and the popularity of mobile games.

Although our model is simple, it shows the potential of using this technique to nowcast the overall status of mobile games market for developers and investors in real time. For future work, we aim to enhance our experiments and use regression techniques to quantitatively predict the present status and the ranking of mobile games, where no ranking history is available in advance.

## Competing Interests

The author declares that there are no competing interests regarding the publication of this paper.

## References

[1] Y. A. Sekhavat, F. Di Paolo, D. Barbosa, and P. Merialdo, "Knowledge base augmentation using tabular data," in *Proceedings of the CEUR Workshop Proceedings*, vol. 1184, Seoul, South Korea, April 2014.

[2] Y. A. Sekhavat and J. Parsons, "SEDEX: scalable entity preserving data exchange," *IEEE Transactions on Knowledge and Data Engineering*, vol. 28, no. 7, pp. 1878–1890, 2016.

[3] M. Mohebbi, D. Vanderkam, J. Kodysh, R. Schonberger, H. Choi, and S. Kumar, Google correlate whitepaper, 2011, http://www.google.com/trends/correlate/whitepaper.pdf.

[4] W. W. Moe and P. S. Fader, "Dynamic conversion behavior at e-commerce sites," *Management Science*, vol. 50, no. 3, pp. 326–335, 2004.

[5] G. Kulkarni, P. K. Kannan, and W. Moe, "Using online search data to forecast new product sales," *Decision Support Systems*, vol. 52, no. 3, pp. 604–611, 2012.

[6] L. Wu and E. Brynjolfsson, "The future of prediction: how Google searches foreshadow housing prices and sales," in *Economic Analysis of the Digital Economy*, University of Chicago Press, 2014.

[7] J. Ginsberg, M. H. Mohebbi, R. S. Patel, L. Brammer, M. S. Smolinski, and L. Brilliant, "Detecting influenza epidemics using search engine query data," *Nature*, vol. 457, no. 7232, pp. 1012–1014, 2009.

[8] R. Van Der Meulen and J. Rivera, *Gartner Says Worldwide Video Game Market to Total $93 Billion in 2013*, Gartner. Haettu, 2014.

[9] Y. A. Sekhavat and P. Abdollahi, "Can Google nowcast the market trend of Iranian mobile games?" in *Proceedings of the*

2nd International Conference on Web Research (ICWR '16), pp. 8–12, Tehran, Iran, April 2016.

[10] H. Choi and H. Varian, *Predicting Initial Claims for Unemployment Benefits*, Google Inc, Mountain View, Calif, USA, 2009.

[11] H. Choi and H. Varian, "Predicting the present with Google trends," *Economic Record*, vol. 88, supplement 1, pp. 2–9, 2012.

[12] F. D'Amuri and J. Marcucci, "'Google it!' forecasting the US unemployment rate with a google job search index," FEEM Working Paper 31, 2010.

[13] N. Della Penna and H. Huang, Constructing consumer sentiment index for US using Google searches (No. 2009–26), 2010.

[14] Y. Carrière-Swallow and F. Labbé, "Nowcasting with Google Trends in an emerging market," *Journal of Forecasting*, vol. 32, no. 4, pp. 289–298, 2013.

[15] C. Hand and G. Judge, "Searching for the picture: forecasting UK cinema admissions using Google Trends data," *Applied Economics Letters*, vol. 19, no. 11, pp. 1051–1055, 2012.

[16] M. L. Mccallum and G. W. Bury, "Google search patterns suggest declining interest in the environment," *Biodiversity and Conservation*, vol. 22, no. 6-7, pp. 1355–1367, 2013.

[17] L. Galarneau, *2014 Global Gaming Stats: Who's Playing What, and Why?* Game News, 2014.

[18] C. W. Granger, "Testing for causality: a personal viewpoint," *Journal of Economic Dynamics & Control*, vol. 2, no. 4, pp. 329–352, 1980.

[19] P. Wessa, *Bivariate Granger Causality (v1.0.3) in Free Statistics Software (v1.1.23-r7)*, Office for Research Development and Education, 2013, http://www.wessa.net/rwasp_grangercausality.wasp/.

[20] Y. A. Sekhavat, "KioskAR: an augmented reality game as a new business model to present artworks," *International Journal of Computer Games Technology*, vol. 2016, Article ID 7690754, 12 pages, 2016.

[21] T. Dimpfl and S. Jank, *Can Internet Search Queries Help to Predict Stock Market Volatility?* European Financial Management, 2015.

# 13

# Heuristics and Recommendations for the Design of Mobile Serious Games for Older Adults

**Mônica da Consolação Machado,**[1,2]
**Ronan Loschi Rodrigues Ferreira** ⓘ**,**[2,3] **and Lucila Ishitani** ⓘ[2]

[1]*Institute of Exact Sciences, University Center Newton Paiva, Belo Horizonte, Brazil*
[2]*Department of Computer Science, Pontifical Catholic University of Minas Gerais, Belo Horizonte, Brazil*
[3]*Department of Engineering, College Santa Rita-FASAR, Conselheiro Lafaiete, Brazil*

Correspondence should be addressed to Lucila Ishitani; lucila@pucminas.br

Academic Editor: Michael J. Katchabaw

As people get older, their physical and cognitive functions decline. Meeting these needs is an important goal to be reached, to propose activities that may contribute to a better quality of life, including leisure and learning. As such, this paper aims to present a set of heuristics and recommendations for the design of mobile serious games for older adults. To elaborate these heuristics and recommendations, we conducted two studies with older people. In the first study, we invited people aged 60 or more to evaluate mobile games, intending to collect data that could help us to adapt the heuristics that were already published to the public of this research. In the period between the two studies, we developed a serious mobile game (*Labuta Batuta*) that met the set of adapted heuristics. In the second study, we invited another group of older people, aged 45 or over, to qualitatively evaluate *Labuta Batuta*, in order to develop a Grounded Theory about the desirable characteristics for the design of serious mobile games for older adults. Besides a Grounded Theory, the second study allowed the identification of nine requirements to be considered when designing the mechanics of mobile games for older adults.

## 1. Introduction

In the last decades, the demand for the so-called "adult games" has grown, due to the ageing of the population [1].

During the ageing process, human being undergoes physical, psychic, and cognitive restrictions, facing new needs and expectations [1–3]. As life expectancy increases, it becomes necessary to offer more options for older adults, including learning and leisure.

Keeping healthy is an indicator of functional independence and longevity. The use of digital games helps to reduce disability and depression and to improve reaction times, balance, and mobility of older adults [4, 5]. Ijsselsteijn et al. [2] state that digital games enhance the self-esteem and mental stimulation of the elderly. Many authors, as [6–8], emphasise that digital games can help older adults in terms of entertainment, relaxation, socialization, mental challenges, and physical fitness, improving the quality of the ageing process.

In order to enjoy all the benefits mentioned, digital games must be suitable for older adults, thus providing them a better life, with more health, fun, and social interaction.

With the technologies available today, especially mobile devices such as smartphones, we need to rethink ways to meet the needs and expectations of older adults. A game designer must know how to create enjoyable virtual experiences [9]. Observing the difficulties and restrictions imposed by age, it is necessary to pay special attention to the development of digital games aimed at older adults, especially regarding gameplay.

Gameplay covers possible actions and reactions generated by the game and the player, the controls, the interaction between players, the role of the characters in the game, and the mechanics of the game.

There are, in the literature, heuristics and recommendations for the evaluation and design of gameplay. However, to date, there are few publications regarding older adults. In addition, many publications address health and cognitive impairments. So, following a different line of research, this work aimed to propose a set of heuristics and recommendations for the evaluation and design of educational games for older adults, focusing gameplay.

It was carried on with two main studies. In the first study, we investigated the validity of the existing heuristics for the evaluation of gameplay, concerning older adults. In the second study, we investigated the validity of Schell's lenses for the scope of this work. Schell [9] states that a good project comes from many possible perspectives and refers to these as lenses, by understanding that each lens is a different way of seeing the project. Each lens is specified by a set of questions about the project, which must be answered by the designer. While studying the lenses of game mechanics proposed by [9], we identified a gap, because they do not guarantee the designers will consider the educational needs of the older player.

Among the results achieved are the identification of new heuristics, nine new requirements or design lenses, and the proposal of a Grounded Theory that contributes to the design of mobile serious games for older adults.

This paper is organized as follows. Section 2 presents the background of this work and some related work. Section 3 presents the method we adopted. Sections 4 and 6 present the method, participants, materials, and results of the first and second studies, respectively. Section 5 describes the main characteristics of "Labuta Batuta", the game developed for the second study. Section 7 briefly discusses the results and Section 8 presents our main conclusions and also suggestions for future work.

## 2. Background

In the following subsections, we present previous work that supported this study, concerning human development in adulthood, digital games, and gameplay.

### 2.1. Human Development in Adulthood.
The human ageing process causes physical, psychological, and cognitive decline.

The best known impairments of older people are those related to vision, which includes presbyopia, macular degeneration, glaucoma, cataract, reduced field of vision, reduced color, depth and contrast perception, decreased adjustment to the dark, and limited perception of small details [1–3, 10].

During the ageing process, cognitive limitations also occur. So, loss of memory, attention, association, perception, and reasoning must be considered in the development of digital games for older adults [11].

Other frequent impairments are related to reduction in hearing, increase of response time, motor difficulties [1, 3], and also cognitive constraints such as [1, 3, 12]: reduced attention to details, reduced short-term memory, difficulty to perform new activities or old activities in a new way; reduced spatial cognition, or the ability to mentally manipulate images and patterns; and inability to remember the goals of a task to

be performed. These impairments can be caused by diseases such as Alzheimer's disease but also by the natural ageing process.

According to Papalia et al. [13], people approaching retirement often wish to expand their minds and their skills to make a more productive and interesting use of leisure. Some adults simply enjoy learning and want to continue learning throughout life. Then, learning activities, work, and leisure should be available for people of all ages. This possibility can help the elderly to slow the impact of ageing on their physical and cognitive abilities, which often determines their emotional state.

In this context, digital games can contribute to the improvement of the ageing process, since they can be used as a means to soften the restrictions due to the age, such as cognitive, motor, perceptive, and psychosocial aspects of people [14–16]. Nguyen et al. [17] stated that, in addition to entertainment, serious games may have beneficial therapeutic effects for older people as they may improve their health and well-being. The authors carried out a Systematic Literature Review (SLR) focusing on the physical, cognitive, and social effects that serious games can provide for the elderly. The SLR results showed that 75% of the articles found confirm positive impacts of serious games for the elderly. In this line of research, Nouchi et al. [18] investigated the impact of the *Brain Age* game on cognitive functions of the elderly. The results showed that the elderly may improve their executive functions and their processing speed when playing Brain Age for 4 weeks.

### 2.2. Digital Games.
Digital games can offer older users new and exciting forms of entertainment as well as stimulate various mental abilities. Koster [19] stated that games are "concentrated chunks ready for our brains to chew on. Since they are abstracted and iconic, they are readily absorbed. Since they are formal systems, they exclude distracting extra details". Because of these characteristics, "games serve as very fundamental and powerful learning tools" [19].

According to Savi and Ulbricht [20], digital games can provide benefits to the teaching and learning process; among them are motivating effect; development of cognitive abilities; learning by discovery; socialization; and motor coordination exercises.

Games whose main objective goes beyond pure entertainment are called serious games. Their main purpose is to convey a message, to teach a lesson, or to offer an experience [21]. These games should provide the challenge and allow players to develop their skills and learn new things that can be applied to the real world, while still being fun and attractive [22].

Older adults have interests and expectations regarding the use of digital games, which include not only fun and distraction but also learning and the expectation of keeping up to date [23]. That is why serious or educational games can attract their interest.

When designing games that meet the interests and expectations of older adults, it is important to consider the cultural characteristics of this audience, given that these characteristics vary for different groups of people and that people identify with the context in which they feel well [24, 25]. In order to develop digital educational games for older adults, it is necessary to take into account a low cost so that they can have access to the game, since many are retired and do not have much money to spend [6, 26].

One of the most important requirements for the development of games projects for older adults is the possibility of offering them the type of content they will enjoy and get involved, even if this requirement is not so obvious and easy to be specified [2]. Digital games design must also consider the knowledge and wisdom that improve with time, the diversity of experiences, and changes in the social and societal roles that come with age.

Older adults are more resistant and afraid to learn new things than young people. For example, they fear making mistakes, they need to know the usefulness of learning, they fear new methods, and they let mistakes decrease their self-esteem. However, because they have more experience and like to help each other, they can also be self-confident and motivated in relation to learning, although they need more time and practice, especially when new learning conflicts with prior knowledge. Thus, they "need guidance, not grades" [27] as a form of evaluation.

*GameFlow* is a scale that can be used to measure the player's skill and it is composed of 8 elements: concentration, challenge, skills, control, clear goals, feedback, immersion, and social interaction [28]. However, the scale *GameFlow* does not adequately describe the increase in knowledge. Based on the scale *GameFlow*, another scale was created to evaluate the improvement of knowledge: *EGameFlow*. This scale can be used as a reference for an educational game project [29].

Currently, mobile games have a large market share among mobile applications as there is a steady increase in the number of users using smartphones and other mobile devices. Statistics show that mobile games represent about 70 to 80% of downloads [4]. According to Chu Yew Yee et al. [7], the growing use of mobile phones by older adults makes mobile games for the elderly a promising niche for game developers, despite the small size of the device screens.

*2.3. Gameplay.* According to Mello and Perani [30], gameplay is the result of the union of three characteristics that are usually associated with games: rules as an internal element; the pursuit of goals by the players, performed through a sequence of tasks given to them; and the skill and experience of the players.

Gameplay includes "the problems and challenges a player must face to try to win the game" [31]; that is, it is the process by which a player reaches the goal of the game.

Gameplay incorporates the game mechanics which consist of rules that define the functioning of the game universe, the core of the game, and the interaction of the player with the game and with other players. Gameplay occurs when the player interacts with the mechanics of the game and possibly with other players [32].

Garris et al. [33] state that gameplay "can lead to certain user judgments or reactions such as increased interest,

TABLE 1: Items and lenses of game mechanics.

| Items of game mechanics | Lenses concerning the items |
|---|---|
| 1- Space | 21 - Functional Space |
| 2- Objects, attributes and states | 22 - Dynamic State |
| 3- Actions | 23 - Emergence and 24 – Action |
| 4- Rules | 25 - Goals e 26 – Rules |
| 5- Skill | 27 – Skill |
| 6- Chance | 28 - Expected Value and 29 – Chance |

enjoyment, involvement, or confidence". These reactions encourage players to persist more and keep playing.

*2.3.1. Game Mechanics.* For the game design, Schell [9] proposed a hundred of lenses, which are small sets of questions to be answered by the designer. The seventh lens focuses on the elemental tetrad, composed of the following elements: aesthetics, mechanics, story, and technology. This lens allows the designer to consider each element separately and then all together.

For this research, we considered separately the element of game mechanics. According to Schell [9], "game mechanics are the core of what a game truly is. They are the interactions and relationships that remain when all of the aesthetics, technology, and story are stripped away". Game mechanics are composed of six main items which are related to nine lenses, as can be seen in Table 1.

Besides the nine lenses directly linked to the six items of the game mechanics, there are 23 other lenses that help to achieve game balance [9]. According to Schell [9], "balancing a game is nothing more than adjusting the elements of the game until they deliver the experience you want", examining the game carefully.

*2.4. Heuristics for Gameplay Evaluation.* Nielsen [34] called "heuristics" his 10 general principles for interaction design "because they are broad rules of thumb and not specific usability guidelines". Desurvire et al. [35] provided a definition of heuristics as "design guidelines which serve as a useful evaluation tool for both product designers and usability professionals".

There are many sets of heuristics to evaluate gameplay. In this study, we used a set of heuristics that we have compiled from a literature review.

Federoff [31] identified heuristics for gameplay evaluation through literature review. In order to evaluate the heuristics found, a field research was carried out with designers of a game developer company. Data collection was performed through observations and interviews with employees of the company. After analysing the results obtained from the comparison of the field research data with the heuristics found in the literature review, new heuristics were proposed.

Desurvire et al. [35] proposed the Heuristic Evaluation for Playability (HEP). It was based on literature and reviews from gameplay experts and game designers. HEP is subdivided into gameplay, game story, mechanics, and usability.

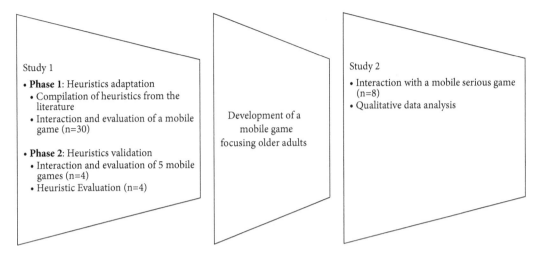

FIGURE 1: Research activities.

It consists of 43 heuristics, of which 16 are heuristics for gameplay evaluation. The heuristics were validated by means of a comparative study between the results of a heuristic evaluation and a user test. The results indicated that using the heuristics allowed to find gameplay problems in the game prototype. The total number of problems identified from the use of HEP was greater than the number of problems pointed out by the user test. According to the authors, HEP is useful in the initial project of the game, because it makes possible to think about the project from the point of view of the user, "avoiding expensive design problems".

Korhonen and Koivisto [32] stated that it is very important for the player to be in control, as it is the player's responsibility to decide what to do or how to do it. They also point out that games are more enjoyable and pleasant when they provide players with satisfying challenges. The authors proposed and validated Playability Heuristics for Mobile Games (PHMG), organized in three main modules: gameplay, mobility, and usability. PHMG consists of 29 heuristics for mobile game evaluation, of which 14 are gameplay-related. "A modular structure suggests that it is possible to use each of these modules separately and evaluate the game against one module at a time" [32]. They also reported that these heuristics are very general and can be applied to any game, regardless of the platform on which the game is played. The proposed heuristics were validated in evaluations of five games of different styles. 64 gameplay problems were found in these games. The results of this work confirm the importance of using gameplay heuristics to identify game design errors.

Desurvire and Wiberg [36] reported in their study that there "are many methodologies for analysing productivity software including Usability Testing and Heuristic Evaluation". The main focus of productivity software is the creation of an easy-to-use interface, helping users to execute tasks, which is the purpose of applications. Concerning games, however, the goals include providing an immersive, fun, and challenging environment. Several times a good pace of challenge makes it worth playing a game. Due to these differences and peculiarities of the games it is important to have a set of design principles. In this way, the authors carried

out a research aiming to adapting the usability principles that exist to the design of games. Among the principles gathered and identified, 22 were related to gameplay. It is important to note that these principles were not related to the elderly, reinforcing the need for specific guidelines for games aimed at older adults, so that the pace and challenge are appropriate for the target audience, and the elderly can have a positive experience.

Korhonen et al. [37] report that in their work they used an expert evaluation method, although this method is not widely adopted for game evaluation. For the effectiveness of the method, heuristics should take into account the characteristics of games. Besides being applicable to games, the expert evaluation method is not too time-consuming or labor-intensive to be carried out. In their work, they used Heuristic Evaluation for Playability (HEP) [35], in addition to the set of Playability Heuristics for Mobile Games (PHMG) [32]. They found that 32% of the problems identified by HEP and 52% of the problems identified by PHMG were related to gameplay. Those problems included, for example, loss of rewards earned by players and repetitive and boring tasks.

From the literature review, one can see the importance of understanding better and of being able to evaluate gameplay so that games become more and more pleasant to be played. There are, in the literature, heuristics for gameplay evaluation. However, to date, no research results have been found that validate the use of these heuristics with games aimed at the elderly.

## 3. The Current Investigation

The results of this work were obtained from two studies. The first one focused on the evaluation, adaptation, and validation of a set of heuristics compiled from the literature. The second one aimed to develop a Grounded Theory about the desirable characteristics for the design of serious mobile games for older adults. Between the two studies, a game was developed, based on the set of heuristics proposed in the first study.

The activities that were conducted to reach the objectives of this work are presented in Figure 1. The details of these activities as well as the results obtained are presented in the next sections.

# 4. Study 1

The first study was organized in two phases. In the first one, gameplay evaluation heuristics were selected after a literature review [38]. Subsequently, thirty older participants interacted with a mobile casual game developed specifically for this audience and evaluated it, through a questionnaire. After the interaction, data analysis was performed and the results enabled the adaptation of gameplay heuristics to the older people [38].

In the second phase of study 1, the adapted heuristics were validated. For this, an evaluation was performed with four older participants interacted with five selected mobile games and evaluated each of them. In addition, an evaluation by four experts was carried out, in order to verify if the results found by them were able to predict the problems and/or difficulties observed by the older adults during the evaluation process. The heuristic evaluation was performed in order to compare the results found with the evaluation with older people. All of the users had already participated in the first phase and agreed to participate in the second phase too. All the experts are participants of the Game Research Group from PUC Minas.

These evaluators applied the heuristics adapted for game-play evaluation when they interacted with the selected mobile games. After comparing the data collected through the evaluation with older adults and the results of the evaluation by specialists, it was possible to draw up a set of heuristics which are essential for evaluation of gameplay directed to the target public of this work.

*4.1. Participants.* The recruitment process followed the snow-ball method [39], beginning with older adults known to the authors of this research.

In order to be selected, the participant should meet the following criteria: aged at least 60 years, having a basic experience in the use of cell phones, having no vision deficit that could not be corrected by corrective lenses or other disability that prevent him/her from using games on smartphones. We chose to invite only old people, and not people ageing 40 or 50, in order to identify the impact of age in the use of mobile games. All the selected people signed the informed consent form.

Among the 30 participants of the first phase, 18 persons were women, which corresponds to 60% of participants and 12 people were men. The average age was 67 years. The youngest participant was 60 and the oldest 92 years old.

Among the four participants of the second phase, three participants were female. The mean age of the group was 64 years. The youngest was 61 years old and the oldest was 67 years old. Two adults were retired; one person was an educator and the other was a housewife. The choice of the participants took into account two variables: the experience with technology and the level of education. Two participants had a basic level of education; one of them was not familiar

with the technology and the other had experience with the use of computers.

Regarding the experts, Cuperschmid and Hildebrand [40] state that an heuristic evaluation (HE) is conducted by experts based on their experience and skills. These experts examine the digital game and make a diagnosis of the problems or difficulties that users are likely to encounter during the interaction. Rocha and Baranauskas [41] state that HE is subjective and advise that the evaluation should be done by a group of three to five evaluators. This recommendation is due to the fact that it is difficult for a single evaluator to find all problems related to the interface. Experience shows that different people encounter different problems. Thus, we invited four specialists to participate in the HE of the games.

*4.2. Materials.* In the first phase of the study, we used questionnaires and a mobile game for older users "Viajando pelo Mundo". In the second phase of the study, we used questionnaires and five casual mobile games.

*4.2.1. Questionnaires.* Three questionnaires were developed to collect data and also the opinion and characteristics of the participants.

The first questionnaire aimed to identify the profile of the participants.

The second questionnaire was applied on the first phase after the participant interaction with the specific mobile game for older adults. It addressed characteristics of the gameplay heuristics compiled from a literature review.

The second questionnaire was developed with 18 objective questions assessed on a 5-point Likert scale and two subjective questions for the evaluation of "Viajando pelo Mundo". This questionnaire contains characteristics included in the proposed set of adapted heuristics, so that older people could reflect and comment on their perception about each heuristic: rules, clarity of objectives, tutorials, the existence of repeated and/or boring activities, fatigue and/or boredom, game progress and rewards, and positive and negative characteristics that participants identified in the game. The 18 items were statements like "The games has clear rules", "The game has boring or repetitive activities", and "The game allows the visualization of the results and players progress in the game".

The third questionnaire was applied in the second phase after the participant played each of the five selected mobile games. This questionnaire addressed the gameplay heuristics compiled from the literature review, after suiting them to the characteristics of older people.

The third questionnaire was composed of 16 items assessed on a 5-point Likert scale and two open questions. The 16 items were statements like "I understood the rules of the game", "I thought it was fun", "I liked the rewards of the game", and "I felt tired or bored". The two open questions were "What did you like the most in the game?" and "What would you change in the game?".

*4.2.2. Viajando pelo Mundo.* For the accomplishment of the first phase of the study, we chose a mobile game that was developed for older people. The game selected was "Viajando

TABLE 2: Games evaluation (average scores).

|  | Question | G1 | G2 | G3 | G4 | G5 |
|---|---|---|---|---|---|---|
| Q1 | I understood the rules of the game. | 4.5 | 5.0 | 4.5 | 4.8 | 4.8 |
| Q2 | I understood the goals of the game. | 4.8 | 4.5 | 4.5 | 5.0 | 4.8 |
| Q3 | I learned from the game. | 4.5 | 5.0 | 4.3 | 5.0 | 4.5 |
| Q4 | I felt a lack of help during the game. | 2.3 | 1.8 | 2.0 | 2.0 | 1.8 |
| Q5 | I liked the images and the sounds of the game. | 5.0 | 4.8 | 3.8 | 4.0 | 4.8 |
| Q6 | I thought it was fun. | 4.8 | 4.8 | 4.3 | 5.0 | 4.8 |
| Q7 | I liked the rewards of the game. | 3.8 | 4.8 | 5.0 | 4.8 | 4.8 |
| Q8 | I liked the challenges of the game. | 4.5 | 5.0 | 4.0 | 4.8 | 5.0 |
| Q9 | I felt that the challenges had increased very quickly. | 2.5 | 2.8 | 3.0 | 3.0 | 2.5 |
| Q10 | I felt tired or bored. | 1.3 | 1.3 | 2.3 | 2.0 | 1.3 |
| Q11 | I found it easy to learn. | 4.0 | 5.0 | 4.5 | 4.5 | 4.8 |
| Q12 | I followed my score in the game. | 4.5 | 4.8 | 4.5 | 5.0 | 4.8 |
| Q13 | I found it interesting. | 4.8 | 5.0 | 4.0 | 4.8 | 5.0 |
| Q14 | I liked the scoring system. | 3.8 | 4.8 | 4.0 | 4.5 | 5.0 |
| Q15 | I found the game boring. | 1.3 | 1.0 | 2.0 | 1.0 | 1.3 |
| Q16 | I feel like playing again. | 4.3 | 5.0 | 4.0 | 4.8 | 4.8 |

G1 = *aTilt 3D Labyrinth Free*, G2 = *Fruit Ninja Free*, G3 = *Find the Difference 2014 HD free*, G4 = *Show do Milhão 2014*, and G5 = *Cut the Rope: Full Free*.

pelo Mundo" [42], which means "a trip around the world", and the version used in the evaluation consisted of a trip to Brazil, France, and Japan. The game was composed of four mini-games and aimed to improve mental abilities like attention, concentration, and reasoning.

*4.2.3. Mobile Games Selected.* The selection of the games considered previous works that reported the factors that motivate and influence the older adults' interest in games [43, 44]. Two of the factors are as follows: the game should be a tool to aid age restrictions and older people enjoy casual games. Thus, for the accomplishment of this study, we chose the following five mobile games:

(i) aTilt 3D Labyrinth Free: this game is based on three-dimensional mazes. The player moves the cell phone to move a ball that must be placed on the target, diverting from black holes. This game exercises control and motor coordination.

(ii) Fruit Ninja Free: the goal of this game is to cut all the fruits that appear on the screen of the mobile phone by dragging the finger, simulating movements of a ninja sword. Besides motor coordination, it requires fast reasoning, lot of attention, and speed.

(iii) Find the Difference 2014 HD free: in this game the player must identify the differences between two images. To do this, one must simply click on the divergences so that they are highlighted with red circles. This game enables the improvement of abilities like attention, concentration, and reasoning.

(iv) Show do Milhão 2014: it is an interactive game of questions and answers, which provides a "prize" of up to one million reais. The questions concern several subjects that can be selected by the player. As the

player evolves in the game, questions become more difficult.

(v) Cut the Rope: Full Free: the goal of this game is to cut ropes at the right time to catch stars and let a candy fall into the mouth of the monster. The game features innovative/mechanics based on physics. This game has won several awards: Apple Design Award, BAFTA Award, Pocket Gamer Award, and GDC Award e Best App Ever Award.

*4.3. Results and Discussion.* In the first phase, the evaluations with older adults occurred during two months.

The results of the evaluation with the game developed specifically for the older people allowed the adequacy of the heuristics compiled in the literature. This adequacy took into account all constraints, difficulties, suggestions, opinions, compliments, and observations evidenced during the evaluation process with the participants.

In the second phase, the evaluations with older adults occurred during three months.

Table 2 shows the average score of each game assigned by the participants for each of the items of gameplay evaluation. In relation to the rules and goals in the game, it can be observed that the lowest score received 4.5 points and the highest score was 5.0 points. This shows that the participants understood the purpose of each game and also the way they should interact with the games. The rewards offered in the game G3: Find the Difference 2014 HD free, pleased all participants (score of 5.0 for Q7), but did not please in the same way in the game G1: aTilt 3D Labyrinth Free, which received a score of 3.8 for the same item. Another important factor for the elderly is learning. Two games received the score of 5.0 for Q3: G2: Fruit Ninja Free and G4: Show do Milhão 2014.

TABLE 3: Number of problems identified by experts.

| Heuristics | G1 Severity | | | G2 Severity | | | G3 Severity | | | G4 Severity | | | G5 Severity | | | Total |
|---|---|---|---|---|---|---|---|---|---|---|---|---|---|---|---|---|
| | L | M | H | L | M | H | L | M | H | L | M | H | L | M | H | |
| H1 | | | 1 | | 1 | | | | 1 | | 1 | | | | | 4 |
| H2 | | | | | | 1 | 1 | | | 1 | | | 1 | | | 4 |
| H3 | | 1 | | | | 1 | | 1 | | | 1 | | | 1 | | 5 |
| H4 | | | 1 | | | 1 | | | 1 | | 1 | | | 1 | | 5 |
| H5 | 1 | | | 1 | | | 1 | | | 1 | | | | | | 4 |
| H6 | | 1 | | | | | | | | | | | | | | 1 |
| H7 | | | | | | | | | | | | | | | | - |
| H8 | | | 1 | | | 1 | | 1 | | | | | 1 | | | 4 |
| H9 | | | 1 | | | 1 | | | 2 | | 1 | | | 1 | | 6 |
| H10 | 1 | | | 1 | | | | 1 | | 1 | | | | | | 4 |
| H11 | | | 1 | | | 1 | | | 2 | | 1 | | | 1 | | 6 |
| H12 | 1 | | | 1 | | | 1 | | | 1 | | | 1 | | | 5 |
| H13 | | | 1 | | | 1 | | | 1 | | 1 | | | | | 4 |
| H14 | | | | | 1 | | 1 | | | | | | | | | 2 |
| H15 | | | | | | 1 | | 1 | | | 1 | | 1 | | | 4 |
| H16 | | | 1 | | | 1 | | | | | | | | | | 2 |
| H17 | | | | | | 2 | | | | | 1 | | | | | 3 |
| H18 | | 1 | | | | | | | | | | | | | | 1 |
| H19 | | | 1 | 1 | | | | | | | | | | | | 2 |
| H20 | | | | 1 | | | 1 | | | | | | | | | 2 |
| H21 | | | 1 | 1 | | | 1 | | | | | | 1 | | | 4 |
| H22 | | | | 1 | | | | | | | | | | | | 1 |
| Totais | 3 | 3 | 9 | 7 | 2 | 11 | 6 | 4 | 7 | 4 | 8 | 0 | 5 | 4 | 0 | 73 |
| | | 15 | | | 20 | | | 17 | | | 12 | | | 9 | | |

G1 = *aTilt 3D Labyrinth Free*, G2 = *Fruit Ninja Free*, G3 = *Find the Difference 2014 HD free*, G4 = *Show do Milhão 2014*, G5 = *Cut the Rope: Full Free*, L = Low, M = Medium, and H = High

As can be seen in Table 3, 73 problems were identified in the Expert Heuristic Assessment. The games G2: Fruit Ninja Free and G3: Find the Difference 2014 HD free were the ones that showed more problems of gameplay, being a total of 20 and 17 problems, respectively.

The results of the second evaluation with older adults and the evaluation by specialists were confronted and analysed, and then, it was possible to verify the concordant and discordant points between the two evaluations.

Table 4 shows that the second evaluation with the older adults identified 27 problems related to gameplay, representing 35.5% of the total encountered. The experts evaluation was able to find 73 gameplay problems, that is, 96% of the total. The results also show that 24 gameplay problems were detected by both older adults and experts during the evaluations.

A certain overlap of heuristics has been reported by two evaluators. In this way, one of the heuristics was discarded from the set of heuristics for gameplay evaluation.

Besidest that, after analysing the results of the evaluation of games by older adults and by experts, it was observed that some heuristics are not essential for evaluation of gameplay aimed at older adults. This is because depending on the game, the heuristics may not apply, since they are not related to all gaming genres. Thus, the validity of 21 gameplay evaluation heuristics for older adults was confirmed, with sixteen heuristics considered essential to evaluate gameplay, and five, optional.

The critical heuristics are presented in Table 5 and the optional heuristics, in Table 6.

## 5. Labuta Batuta: A Game for Older Adults

*Labuta Batuta* [45] is a mobile serious game for older adults, developed considering the set of heuristics proposed as a result of the first study [45]. Its name combines the word *labuta*, which means labor, with the old slang *batuta*, with similar sound, which means great, nice. The main objective of the game was to teach how to make better use of the features of a smartphone. This subject was chosen because it was a suggestion given by older people [46]. The development process lasted for about six months, with many discussion meetings.

The game allows the configuration of an avatar with the appearance of an older adult and is composed of simple mini-games that seek to teach the use of basic navigation

TABLE 4: Number of problems identified.

| Game | In common | Only by experts | Only by older adults | Total |
|---|---|---|---|---|
| aTilt 3D Labyrinth Free | 6 | 9 | 1 | 16 |
| Fruit Ninja Free | 6 | 14 | - | 20 |
| Find the Difference 2014 HD free | 7 | 10 | - | 17 |
| Show do Milhão 2014 | 2 | 10 | 2 | 14 |
| Cut the Rope: Full Free | 3 | 6 | - | 9 |
| **Total** | 24 | 49 | 3 | 76 |

TABLE 5: Critical heuristics.

CH1: The game should provide clear rules, present the main objectives at the beginning, as well as short-term goals throughout the game.

CH2: The game must teach the basic skills needed at the beginning, to be used later by the players.

CH3: The game should provide an interesting, engaging, and absorbing tutorial, that also simulate gameplay, allowing easy understanding.

CH4: The game should use visual and audio effects to arouse interest and interaction, considering the restrictions due to ageing.

CH5: The player should find the game fun and enjoyable, without boring tasks. Repetitive tasks are acceptable as the advanced age can cause memory deficit.

CH6: The game should provide rewards which should be meaningful, enabling immersion in the game as a result of encouraging older people to play more.

CH7: The older player should not be penalized for the same error, since he/she may have attention and memory deficits. Besides that, the player should not lose any earned rewards.

CH8: Challenges should be consistent with the age restrictions of older people, providing positive experiences of the game rather than negative ones, making the player want to play more, rather than giving up.

CH9: The level of difficulty should vary so that the player experiences more challenges as the experience with the game is developed, but at a pace that does not generate frustration.

CH10: Tiredness or boredom should be minimized by varying activities and rhythm during play.

CH11: The game should be fair, engaging, easy to learn and should not be difficult to master, because the older player may have physical or cognitive limitations.

CH12: The player must feel in control.

CH13: The gameplay should be long and enduring to keep the players' interest.

CH14: The first ten minutes of the game and the actions of the players should be obvious and should result in immediate and positive feedback for all types of players, encouraging them from the beginning of the game.

CH15: The player must be able to visualize their progress in the game and also to compare the results.

CH16: The game should be fun first for the player, then for the designer.

commands on smartphones (Figure 2). The game presents the daily life of an older adult into his home using a smartphone. First, the player builds his avatar. Then, the player can navigate the rooms of the virtual house, using the smartphone to carry out various activities, such as taking pictures, sending messages, making calls, and installing and playing mini-games.

*Labuta Batuta* offers the opportunity to learn and practice the following:

(i) Tap on the screen: at the beginning of the game, when the player needs to assemble his/her avatar choosing sex, body shape, skin tone, hair color, eye color, and clothing. It is also used in the mini-game to kill the ants. This activity is important because many old people are used to pressing buttons with force as if it was a physical button, instead of tapping lightly.

(ii) Dragging objects: after creating the avatar the player can walk through the virtual house by dragging his/her finger on the screen in the chosen direction.

(iii) Taking photos, sending and receiving messages, answering and making calls, accessing the Internet, and installing games and other resources are all possibilities of learning that become available as the player progresses in the game.

The user can play six mini-games (Figure 3). In the Formiga mini-game, which means ant, the player practices tapping on the screen while "killing the ants". In the Pontos mini-game, which means points, the player learns to drag the finger on the screen while connecting the dots and forming predetermined images. In the Janela mini-game, which means window, the player will learn to use two fingers to magnify or decrease images, "opening and closing a window".

TABLE 6: Optional heuristics.

| |
|---|
| OH1: The game must be balanced, with several ways to win. |
| OH2: The game should provide consistency between its elements and the story. |
| OH3: The story of the game should be part of the gameplay and should be significant, as the narrative can encourage the participation and interaction of the older player with the game. |
| OH4: The game must have different artificial intelligence sets to provide challenges for all levels of players, whether new or experienced. |
| OH5: The game must support a variety of paths and styles of playing. |

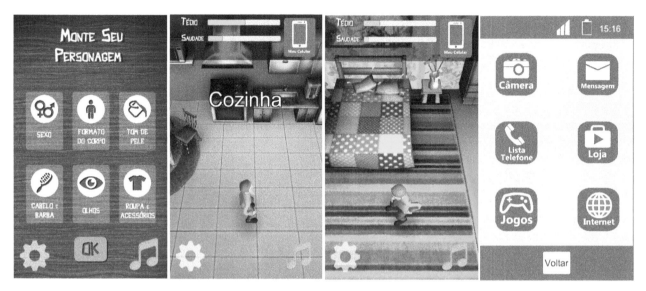

FIGURE 2: Screenshots of Labuta Batuta.

FIGURE 3: Mini-games available in *Labuta Batuta*.

The Memória mini-game, besides allowing the player to exercise cognitive functions such as memory and attention, also allows him/her to exercise the action of tapping the screen. The Eu te pergunto mini-game, which means "I Ask You", allows the player to learn about technical terms relating to social networking and technologies by answering a quiz. The Forca mini-game, which means gallows, uses words related to mobile phones to allow players to practice more and memorize these words.

Ferreira et al. [47] tested out the game with a group of older adults, checking if older adults would learn to use a smartphone after playing the game. The authors applied tests before and after participants played. The authors used a diary and semistructured interviews as data collection instruments and Grounded Theory for analysis. The results indicate that older adults learned to use the features of smartphone, while playing Labuta Batuta, and that they appreciate this learning option.

## 6. Study 2

The data collection took place in an environment known and chosen by the participants. In the trail test, all the participants presented a sufficient level of performance to carry out the proposed activities and to use the cell phone. The trail test was chosen because it verifies the cognitive decline and because it is of easy understanding and application for the older adults.

Next, the mobile serious game Labuta Batuta [45] was installed in the mobile phone used by the participant. Soon after, the researchers explained how to use the game and briefly demonstrated its functions. They also explained to participants how to fill in the diary and that they could stop participating at any time. The participants were asked to play the game every day and to fill the diary for 15 days without any intervention of the authors of this work. The time and duration of each game session were left to the participants.

After this period, the players were interviewed about the experience with the game. These interviews were recorded. Subsequently the diaries and interviews were transcribed for data analysis. The objective of using diary and interview for the data collection was to allow the methodological triangulation.

The data were analyzed using Grounded Theory and followed the guidelines proposed by [48]. The Grounded Theory seeks to meet the following criteria: have an adequate adjustment to data, utility, conceptual density, durability over time, be subject to change, and present explanatory power. In practice, development goes through four phases of data coding. Each phase must be performed judiciously since the quality of the next phase depends on the previous one and impacts on the final construction of the Theory.

In phase 1, line-by-line coding, the sentences that indicated actions and, as far as possible, the participants' words are used to create the codes. In phase 2, focused coding, codes that direct, synthesize, and explain larger data segments, is created. In phase 3, axial coding, categories, and subcategories are developed showing the connections between them. And lastly, in phase 4, theoretical coding, we use codes created during focused coding that help us understand "how codes relate to each other as hypotheses to be integrated into a theory". Theoretical codes should be used to help clarify and stimulate the analysis, but one should avoid imposing a forced structure on the analysis [48].

*6.1. Participants.* For this study, new participants were selected. The criteria for the participants selection were to be at least 45 years old, to consent to voluntarily participate, to be literate, and to have no cognitive, motor, or physical impairment that would prevent the use of the cell phone. The participant did not have to own a cell phone, as the device could be lent by the research group, during the period of data collection.

As in the Study 1, the recruitment process followed the snowball method [39], beginning with older adults known to the authors of this research.

Ten older adults accepted to participate in the study. But two of the participants initially selected interrupted their participation without explanation, leaving only eight participants (six men and two women). According to Singh and Malhotra [49], this number is in agreement with the recommendation to have a minimum of eight participants using diary.

Their average age was 63. The results from the demographic questionnaire showed that the participants had a varied level of education; most of them used cell phones daily, although they found them difficult to use; most of them did not use their cell phones to play; they would like to learn using mobile serious games. All the selected people signed the informed consent form.

A period of 15 days was established so that each participant could play and fill in the diary. This period was ideal because the chosen game does not have many features and would be repetitive if the periods were extended. In the end, the participants answered the interview questions.

It is important to highlight that the saturation of the data was perceived from the sixth participant. Besides that, Charmaz [48] states that small samples do not present a problem when using the Grounded Theory.

*6.2. Materials.* The instruments used in this research were a demographic questionnaire to know the profile of the participants, a trail test [50] to assess the participant's cognitive ability, and a diary for the participant's record of his/her experience while playing the game and a semistructured interview. In this study, because the game *"Labuta Batuta"* aimed to teach how to use the features of a mobile phone, we had to apply a trail test to find out if the participant was able to use the game and to learn.

According to Lazar et al. [51], a diary allows collecting the data over time, and the participants are responsible for choosing the places and times for the records. This makes it easier for them to record details of events as it would be harder to remember everything by the end of the data collection period. The diary needs to be well prepared to ensure a valid outcome.

The use of a diary aims to "understand the thinking processes that the gamer experiences as a human during the course of game play" [52]. This is because the players can record their impressions on the interface with more freedom.

According to [53], a diary study "minimizes the effects of observers on participants". They allow greater autonomy of the participants when registering their answers, due to the fact that the researchers are absent at the time of the events. In addition, since there is no interaction with the participant during the annotations in the diary, the participant tends to act more naturally which may allow the researcher a better perception of the events that were really important for the participants, differently from what happens when the researcher is present during the recording of the data, when the participant may feel inhibited. Besides, the use of the diary as another method of data collection allowed the comparison of the data with those collected by the interview method, configuring the methodological triangulation.

*6.2.1. Development of Questions for the Diary and for the Interview.* To develop the fields for the diary and the question for the final interview, we considered the six items related to game mechanics with their respective lenses [9], the 23 lenses for balancing game mechanics, and also the factors of the scale *EGameFlow* [29], except the *social interaction* factor, since the questions were directed to a single player game. To establish these correlations we observed a set of questions that are made in each of the lenses [9] and, judiciously, searched for a correlation with each of the factors of the EGameFlow scale [29]. The criterion for correlations was the use of keywords: for instance, lenses that had a question about concentration in the game were correlated to the concentration factor of the EGameFlow scale. After

TABLE 7: An example of correlation and definition of the questions for the diary and interview.

| EGameFlow Factor | Questions for the diary | Lens number | Questions for the interview |
|---|---|---|---|
| Concentration | | 21 | 1- What elements of the game have kept your concentration on learning and which hindered it. Explain. |
| | | 22 | |
| | | 23 | |
| | | 24 | 2- Were the game activities interesting for your learning or would you like to have other activities in the game? Explain. |
| | Number of relationships | **4** | |
| Feedback | 1- Explain what you think of the feedback about your performance during the game. | 28 | |
| | | 40 | |
| | | 41 | |
| | Number of relationships | **3** | |

this correlation, a new question was elaborated. For example, the first question of the interview has a direct link with lenses 21 and 22 which in turn has a direct correlation with the concentration factor of the EGameFlow scale. Therefore, the interview and the diary allowed approaching different factors of the scale without making the process tiring for the participants [54]. Part of this result can be seen in Table 7.

Thus, four questions were proposed for the diary and seven questions for the interview. In addition, the following criteria were used to formulate the questions: short, easy-to-understand questions that do not allow only yes or no responses and a small number of questions to avoid tiring the participants.

The note fields of the diary were as follows:

(1) Explain what you think of the feedback about your performance during the game.

(2) Explain if the game's challenges were suited to your skills.

(3) Explain if you forgot the time or worries of life while playing.

(4) What did you learn?

The questions of the interview were as follows:

(1) What elements of the game have kept your concentration on learning and which hinderer it. Explain.

(2) What you did was interesting for your learning or would you like to have other actions in the game? Explain.

(3) Have the goals of the game been clearly stated? Explain.

(4) How did the game help you to overcome the challenges and how did you feel? Explain.

(5) What should a game have so that you feel in control and excited to play and learn? Explain.

(6) Were you motivated to apply what you learned in the game? Explain.

(7) What in the game called more of your attention and was it good for your learning? Explain.

*6.3. Results.* This section presents the main results related to study 2. The theoretical coding allowed us to specify the possible relationships among the categories developed. The relationships were generated from the answers given by the participants, in the interviews.

*6.3.1. Coding of the Data Collected.* 316 codes were generated in line-by-line coding, with 78 codes generated from data extracted from the diaries and 238 from the interviews.

After analysing the 316 codes generated in line-by-line coding, 81 codes were generated during focused coding. To generate the focused codes, we considered the line-by-line codes that allowed us to synthesize and explain larger data segments. In the axial coding, 15 categories were generated and for this, the most significant and/or frequent codes of the focused coding were considered. 81 subcategories were related to these 15 categories. For example, the category *improvement of knowledge* gather the following codes or subcategories: *learning to use the touch screen, putting into practice what he/she learned through the game, considering that what he/she did in the game was interesting for his/her learning, relating game elements to day-to-day practices, relating technological terms to those presented in the game,* and *learning through the game.*

It was observed that, of the 15 categories, six were already covered in the literature: *challenges, feedback, improvement of knowledge, clear objective, immersion,* and *autonomy* [9, 29]. The nine new categories were *mini-games, performance assessment, progressing in the game, entertainment and learning, levels, use of mobile devices, concentration in learning, enjoying playing,* and *external links.* The discovery of these nine categories reinforces the gap in the literature and causes new requirements to emerge for designing the mechanics of mobile serious games focusing on older adults.

Theoretical coding allowed us to specify the possible relationships among the categories developed. The relationships were deduced from the interviews with the participants

TABLE 8: Theoretical codes and their relationships.

| Num. | Theoretical code |
| --- | --- |
| 1 | Enjoying playing affects: Improvement of knowledge, Entertainment and learning, Progressing in the game, Use of mobile devices, Immersion, Performance assessment. |
| 2 | Entertainment and learning affect: Improvement of knowledge, Levels, Use of mobile devices, Enjoying playing, External links. |
| 3 | Improvement of knowledge affects: Entertainment and learning, Use of mobile devices, Challenges, Levels, Enjoying playing. |
| 4 | Use of mobile devices affects: Entertainment and learning. |
| 5 | Clear objectives affect: Entertainment and learning, Use of mobile devices, Enjoying playing, Performance assessment, Progressing in the game, External links. |
| 6 | Progressing in the game affects: Enjoying playing, Improvement of knowledge, Challenges. |
| 7 | Mini-games affect: Improvement of knowledge, Use of mobile devices, Enjoying playing, Entertainment and learning. |
| 8 | Feedback affects: Enjoying playing e a Performance assessment. |
| 9 | Levels affect: Enjoying playing, Entertainment and learning. |
| 10 | Challenges affect: Improvement of knowledge, Levels, Enjoying playing |
| 11 | Immersion affects: Progressing in the game, Entertainment and learning. |
| 12 | Autonomy affects: Concentration in learning, Improvement of knowledge, Enjoying playing. |
| 13 | Performance assessment affects: Progressing in the game. |
| 14 | Concentration in learning affects: Enjoying playing. |

[54]. The sets of theoretical codes generated are presented in Table 8.

For example, in the following statements (all names are fictitious), one can observe some of these relationships:

(i) Relationship between the categories *concentration in learning* and *enjoying playing* (code #14):

*"Ah, yes. What attracted me to games is scores, which encouraged me more and more to continue ... And the time, we do not worry about the time, in closing that game, and get more coins and more games, very good. This help us a lot to be concentrated."* [Alda, P1, interview]

(ii) Relationship between improvement of knowledge and entertainment and learning (code #3):

*(...) if I need to use the Face, now I already know how to do it; and before I had difficulties, I called someone to help me, ... not now, after I learned in the game, ... I started to associate and learn, I learned better.* [Arcia, P6, interview]

(iii) Relationship between *clear objective* and *Enjoying playing* (code #5):

*(...) it was all very well explained, I had no difficulty, I did not find it difficult, I thought it was cool. (...).* [Equel, P3, interview]

*6.3.2. Building a Grounded Theory.* The relationships established and the theoretical model served as the basis for the construction of a Grounded Theory with requirements for the design of mobile serious game for older adults.

The categories *enjoying playing, entertainment, and learning* and *improvement of knowledge* are the central categories of the theoretical model because they establish the largest number of relationships and were the most affected and the ones that most affect the opinion of the players. This indicates that when older people like to play a mobile serious game they value the union of entertainment with learning and understand that this union leads to improvement of knowledge which favors immersion and continuous learning. Therefore, it is recommended that a design of the mechanics of mobile serious games for older adults considers these relationships as main requirements.

The relationships of the category *use of mobile devices* show that, by using a mobile device to play and learn, the older adults arouse their interest in the use of mobile technologies, which contributes to digital inclusion, entertainment, and learning of this audience.

The category *clear objective* and its relationships show that, by clearly understanding the goals of a mobile serious game, older adults understand better how to play. As so, they achieve the goals of the game and value the opportunity to have fun and learn at the same time, besides overcoming the barriers of using mobile technologies.

The category *progressing in the game* and its relationships show that as the older adult progresses in the game, he/she will becomes more interested, curious, and willing to win the game's challenges. It is worth remembering that these challenges must be appropriate to the player's abilities [28] and preferably organized in levels, because the lack of this balance can frustrate the player and stop him/her from playing.

For older adults, mini-games helped in concentration, motivated player learning, and enabled better use of the mobile device used to play. Therefore, the relationships of the category *mini-game* show another recommendation for the design of the mechanics of mobile serious games for older adults. This recommendation is to include mini-games that arouse attention and that also allow the players to evaluate their performance in the game.

The relationships of the category *feedback* show that feedback encourages players and influences them to enjoy the game and to continue playing, so feedback should be well-designed and well-balanced.

Another requirement for the player to feel in control of the game is to consider his/her physical and/or cognitive limitations. An alternative is to insert *external links* to stimulate the older adult to exercise other movements and to learn other information.

## 7. Discussion

We identified the categories *enjoying playing, entertainment, and learning* and *improvement of knowledge* as the central categories to be considered in the design of serious game mechanics, focusing on older adults.

This indicates that when older people like to play a mobile serious game, they value the union of entertainment with learning and understand that this union leads to improvement of knowledge which favors immersion and continuous learning. Therefore, it is recommended that a design of the mechanics of mobile serious games for older adults considers these relationships as main requirements. This means that this type of game should meet requirements that allow the older adult to enjoy playing, to have fun, and mainly to improve their knowledge through play.

To meet these requirements, the game designer must consider the impairments due to ageing (Section 2.1), the set of heuristics proposed as a result of Study 1 (Section 4.3), Schell's recommendations [9], and the nine new elements that emerged from the Grounded Theory process. These nine new elements could be understood as follows:

(i) Include mini-games with educational content.

(ii) Offer frequent feedback during the game, which may also be related to the learning process.

(iii) Offer the older gamer the possibility of progressing in the game, because this progress favors the learning process.

(iv) Design an amusing game, because entertainment can lead to learning and a monotonous game can hinder learning.

(v) Include levels that allow a gradual perception of learning.

(vi) Develop games for mobile devices as they are getting increasingly used.

(vii) Avoid elements in the game that may distract the player.

(viii) Design a game that makes the older player feel good and relaxed.

(ix) Present suggestions of external links with educational content.

In order to evaluate the performance and learning of the older adult through mobile educational games, we also suggest the recommendations from Fu, Su, and Yu [29].

## 8. Conclusions

This article presents some heuristics and recommendations for the design of mobile serious games for older adults. In the first study, a bibliographic survey was carried out to identify a set of gameplay heuristics. These heuristics were validated by a user evaluation process performed by thirty older people who interacted with a game developed exclusively for the elderly. The results of this evaluation allowed the adaptation of heuristics for evaluation of gameplay to the elderly, considering the age-related constraints.

The adapted heuristics were validated through an evaluation with four older people with a mean age of 64 years who interacted with five mobile games and an evaluation conducted by four experts. After analysing the results, the validity of 21 heuristics adapted for evaluation of gameplay for older adults was confirmed.

These heuristics can help game evaluators and game developers to identify specific gameplay problems for older adults, as they present a set of rules that aim to support the development of games for these people with quality and perspective of acceptance. The set of heuristics will also be useful for evaluating games that are not specific for the older people, and it is possible to find out if older adults will be able to interact with games developed for another age group. From these guidelines, it was possible to develop the Labuta Batuta game for the older people.

Based on Grounded Theory approach, the data analysis of the second study allowed the identification of nine important topics to be considered in game design: *mini-games, performance assessment, progressing in the game, entertainment and learning, levels, use of mobile devices, concentration in learning, enjoying playing,* and *external links.* These topics complement the ones proposed by Fu et al. [29] and Schell [9].

From the participants' point of view, the following text reinforces the importance of a mobile serious game for the older adult:

> *I think it ..., for me it was a great pleasure to participate ... because I have never used the Internet, to tell the truth, I have never used it, so it was a learning process for me, and I thank you for it, ... I still want a cell phone like that with more ..., more modern to use.*

As future work, we suggest a study covering the heuristics that were not evaluated in this research. This includes the use of artificial intelligence to define levels of difficulties for games focusing on older people.

Future work should also include the development of a mobile serious game following the recommendations for game mechanics presented in the Grounded Theory proposed in this article. And then, test the game developed with older adults to validate this theory. One can also evaluate the potential of this type of game to promote the digital inclusion of the older adult.

In addition, the following research questions are suggested for future studies on mobile serious games for older adults:

(i) What topics do older adults prefer to entertain and learn while playing a mobile serious game?

(ii) How should the level design of mobile serious games for older adults be?

(iii) Which genres of games would be preferred by older adults for entertainment and learning?

## Acknowledgments

This research received financial support from PUC Minas and from CNPq [475311/2012-4].

## References

[1] A. Vasconcelos, P. A. Silva, J. Caseiro, F. Nunes, and L. F. Teixeira, "Designing tablet-based games for seniors: the example of CogniPlay, a cognitive gaming platform," in *Proceedings of the 4th International Conference on Fun and Games (FnG '12)*, pp. 1–10, ACM, New York, NY, USA, September 2012.

[2] W. Ijsselsteijn, H. H. Nap, Y. De Kort, and K. Poels, "Digital game design for elderly users," in *Proceedings of the 2007 Conference on Future Play, Future Play '07*, pp. 17–22, ACM, New York, NY, USA, November 2007.

[3] A. Lopez-Martínez, S. Santiago-Ramajo, and A. Caracuel, "Game of gifts purchase: Computer-based training of executive functions for the elderly," in *Proceedings of the IEEE 1st International Conference on Serious Games and Applications for Health (SeGAH '11)*, pp. 1–8, Braga, Portugal, November 2011.

[4] A. Ponnada and A. Kannan, "Evaluation of mobile games using playability heuristics," in *Proceedings of the International Conference on Advances in Computing, Communications and Informatics (ICACCI '12)*, S. M. Thampi, E. El-Afry, and J. Aguiar, Eds., pp. 244–247, ACM, New York, NY, USA, 2012.

[5] M. Rice, M. Wan, M. Foo et al., "Evaluating gesture-based games with older adults on a large screen display," in *Proceedings of the ACM SIGGRAPH 2011 Game Papers (SIGGRAPH '11)*, 8 pages, ACM, New York, NY, USA, 2011.

[6] S.-T. Chen, Y.-G. L. Huang, and I.-T. Chiang, "Using somatosensory video games to promote quality of life for the elderly with disabilities," in *Proceedings of the 2012 4th IEEE International Conference on Digital Game and Intelligent Toy Enhanced Learning, DIGITEL 2012*, pp. 258–262, Japan, March 2012.

[7] S. L. Chu Yew Yee, H. B. Duh, and F. Quek, "Investigating narrative in mobile games for seniors," in *Proceedings of the SIGCHI Conference on Human Factors in Computing Systems (CHI '10)*, pp. 669–672, Atlanta, Georgia, USA, April 2010.

[8] D. Kaufman, L. Sauvé, L. Renaud, A. Sixsmith, and B. Mortenson, "Older adults' digital gameplay: patterns, benefits, and challenges," *Simulation and Gaming*, vol. 47, no. 4, pp. 465–489, 2016.

[9] J. Schell, *The Art of Game Design: A Book of Lenses*, Taylor and Francis Group, New York, NY, USA, 1st edition, 2008.

[10] A. L. Pelletier, L. Rojas-Roldan, and J. Coffin, "Vision loss in older adults," *American Family Physician*, vol. 94, no. 3, pp. 219–226, 2016.

[11] M. Foukarakis, A. Leonidis, I. Adami, M. Antona, and C. Stephanidis, "An adaptable card game for older users," in *Proceedings of the 4th International Conference on PErvasive Technologies Related to Assistive Environments (PETRA '11)*, 7 pages, ACM, New York, NY, USA, May 2011.

[12] J. Borg, A. Lantz, and J. Gulliksen, "Accessibility to electronic communication for people with cognitive disabilities: a systematic search and review of empirical evidence," *Universal Access in the Information Society*, vol. 14, no. 4, pp. 547–562, 2015.

[13] D. E. Papalia, S. W. Olds, and R. D. Feldman, *Human Development*, McGraw-Hill, 11th edition, 2009.

[14] S.-T. Chen, I.-T. Chiang, E. Z.-F. Liu, and M. Chang, "Effects of improvement on selective attention: Developing appropriate somatosensory video game interventions for institutional-dwelling elderly with disabilities," *The Turkish Online Journal of Educational Technology*, vol. 11, pp. 409–417, 2012.

[15] M. J. Rodríguez-Fórtiz, C. Rodríguez-Domínguez, and P. Cano, "Serious games for the cognitive stimulation of elderly people," in *Proceedings of the 2016 IEEE International Conference on Serious Games and Applications for Health (SeGAH)*, pp. 1–7, Orlando, FL, USA, May 2016.

[16] H. Chi, E. Agama, and Z. G. Prodanoff, "Developing serious games to promote cognitive abilities for the elderly," in *Proceedings of the 5th IEEE International Conference on Serious Games and Applications for Health, SeGAH 2017*, pp. 1–8, Perth, WA, Australia, April 2017.

[17] T. T. Nguyen, D. Ishmatova, T. Tapanainen et al., "Impact of Serious Games on Health and Well-being of Elderly: A Systematic Review," in *Proceedings of the 50th Hawaii International Conference on System Sciences*, pp. 3695–3704, 2017.

[18] R. Nouchi, Y. Taki, H. Takeuchi et al., "Brain training game improves executive functions and processing speed in the elderly: a randomized controlled trial," *PLoS ONE*, vol. 7, no. 1, Article ID e29676, 2012.

[19] R. Koster, *Theory of Fun for Game Design*, O'Reilly, Sebastopol, CA, USA, 2nd edition, 2013.

[20] R. Savi and V. R. Ulbricht, "Jogos digitais educacionais: Benefícios e desafios," *Renote*, vol. 6, no. 1, 10 pages, 2008, http://seer.ufrgs.br/index.php/renote/article/view/14405/8310, Accessed on 2018-29-05.

[21] D. Michael and S. Chen, *Serious games: Games That Educate, Train and Inform*, Thomson, Boston, Mass, USA, 1st edition, 2006.

[22] B. Bergeron, *Developing serious games (game development series)*, Charles Riber Media, Hingham, Mass, USA, 1st edition, 2006.

[23] R. N. S. D. Carvalho and L. Ishitani, "Motivational factors for mobile serious games for elderly users," in *Proceedings of XI SBGames*, pp. 19–28, 2012.

[24] B. D. Schutter and V. V. Abeele, "Designing meaningful play within the psycho-social context of older adults," in *Proceedings of the 3rd International Conference on Fun and Games, Fun and Games 2010*, pp. 84–93, Belgium, September 2010.

[25] S. Pedell, J. Beh, K. Mozuna, and S. Duong, "Engaging older adults in activity group settings playing games on touch tablets," in *Proceedings of the 25th Australian Computer-Human*

*Interaction Conference: Augmentation, Application, Innovation, Collaboration (OzCHI '13)*, H. Shen, R. Smith, J. Paay, P. Calder, and T. Wyeld, Eds., pp. 477–480, ACM, New York, NY, USA, 2013.

[26] K. M. Gerling, F. P. Schulte, and M. Masuch, "Designing and evaluating digital games for frail elderly persons," in *Proceedings of the 8th International Conference on Advances in Computer Entertainment Technology (ACE '11)*, 8 pages, ACM, New York, NY, USA, November 2011.

[27] G. J. Pine and P. J. Horne, *The Adult Learner*, Routledge, 2005, http://www.umt.edu/sell/fire/FireWeb/m410prework/The%20Adult%20Learner.pdf. Accessed on 2018-05-29.

[28] P. Sweetser and P. Wyeth, "Gameflow: A model for evaluating player enjoyment in games," in *Computing and Entertainment*, vol. 3, p. 24, 2005.

[29] F.-L. Fu, R.-C. Su, and S.-C. Yu, "Egameflow: A scale to measure learners enjoyment of e-learning games," *Computers and Education*, vol. 52, no. 1, pp. 101–112, 2009.

[30] V. Mello and L. Perani, "Gameplay x playability: defining concepts," in *Proceedings of the SBGames*, pp. 157–164, 2012, http://sbgames.org/sbgames2012/proceedings/papers/artedesign/AD_Full20.pdf, Accessed on 2017-08-10.

[31] M. A. Federoff, "Heuristics and usability guidelines for the creation and evaluation of fun in video games," Tech. Rep., Indiana University, Bloomington, 2002.

[32] H. Korhonen and E. M. I. Koivisto, "Playability heuristics for mobile games," in *Proceedings of the 8th International Conference on Human-Computer Interaction with Mobile Devices and Services (MobileHCI '06)*, pp. 9–16, ACM, New York, NY, USA, September 2006.

[33] R. Garris, R. Ahlers, and J. E. Driskell, "Games, motivation, and learning: a research and practice model," *Simulation & Gaming*, vol. 33, no. 4, pp. 441–467, 2002.

[34] J. Nielsen, "10 usability heuristics for user interface design," https://www.nngroup.com/articles/#popular, Accessed on 2017-06-10, 2014, 1995.

[35] H. Desurvire, M. Caplan, and J. A. Toth, "Using Heuristics to Evaluate the Playability of games," in *Proceedings of the CHI '04 Extended Abstracts on Human Factors in Computing Systems (CHI EA '04)*, pp. 1509–1512, New York, NY, USA, April 2004.

[36] H. Desurvire and C. Wiberg, "Game usability heuristics (play) for evaluating and designing better games: The next iteration," in *Proceedings of the 3d International Conference on Online Communities and Social Computing: Held as Part of HCI International 2009 (OCSC '09)*, pp. 557–566, Springer-Verlag, Heidelberg, Berlin, 2009.

[37] H. Korhonen, J. Paavilainen, and H. Saarenpää, "Expert review method in game evaluations: comparison of two playability heuristic sets," in *Proceedings of the 13th International MindTrek Conference: Everyday Life in the Ubiquitous Era (MindTrek '09)*, A. Lugmayr, H. Franssila, O. Sotamaa, P. Näränen, and J. Vanhala, Eds., pp. 74–81, ACM, New York, NY, USA, 2009.

[38] M. C. Machado and L. Ishitani, "Heurísticas para avaliação de gameplay direcionadas a adultos mais velhos," *Revista de Sistemas e Computaππo-RSC*, vol. 5, no. 1, pp. 3–14, 2015.

[39] P. Biernacki and D. Waldorf, "Snowball sampling: problems and techniques of chain referral sampling," *Sociological Methods and Research*, vol. 10, no. 2, pp. 141–163, 1981.

[40] A. R. M. Cuperschmid and H. R. Hildebrand, "Avaliação Heurística de Jogabilidade Counter-Strike: Global Offensive," in *Proceedings of XII SBGames*, pp. 371–378, 2013.

[41] H. V. Rocha and M. C. C. Baranauskas, *Design e Avaliação de Interfaces Humano-Computador*, NIED/UNICAMP, Campinas, Brazil, 2003.

[42] R. S. Silva, A. Rocha, M. S. Nery, and Á. A. Rocha, "Viajando pelo mundo: um projeto de jogo para smartphone com foco em idosos," in *Proceedings of XIII SBGames*, pp. 148–157, 2014.

[43] L. G. N. D. O. Santos, L. Ishitani, and C. N. Nobre, "Uso de jogos casuais em celulares por idosos: um estudo de usabilidade. uso de jogos casuais em celulares por idosos: um estudo de usabilidade," *Revista de Informática Aplicada (RIA)*, vol. 9, no. 1, pp. 24–44, 2014.

[44] T. T. Cota, N. Vieira, and L. Ishitani, "Impacto do gênero de jogo digital na motivação dos idosos para jogar," in *Proceedings of XIII SBGames*, pp. 361–368, 2014.

[45] R. S. Silva, A. Rocha, M. S. Nery, and Á. A. Rocha, "Labuta batuta: um jogo educacional móvel para adultos mais velhos," in *Proceedings of XIV SBGames*, pp. 463–472, 2015.

[46] A. M. Mol and L. Ishitani, "Avaliação de interface de um aplicativo para uso em telefone celular e voltado para a terceira idade," in *Proceedings of the IX Symposium on Human Factors in Computing Systems (IHC '10)*, pp. 1–10, Brazilian Computer Society, Porto Alegre, Brazil, 2010.

[47] R. L. R. Ferreira, R. B. Silva, and S. R. I. Yoshioka, "Aprendizagem do uso de smartphones por adultos mais velhos mediada por jogo educacional," in *Proceedings of XIV SBGames*, pp. 945–954, 2015.

[48] K. Charmaz, *A Construção da Teoria Fundamentada: Guia prático para análise qualitativa*, Artmed, Porto Alegre, Brazil, 2009.

[49] A. Singh and S. Malhotra, "A researcher's guide to running diary studies," in *Proceedings of the 11th Asia Pacific Conference on Computer Human Interaction (APCHI '13)*, pp. 296–300, ACM, New York, NY, USA, 2013.

[50] T. N. Tombaugh, "Trail Making test A and B: normative data stratified by age and education," *Archives of Clinical Neuropsychology*, vol. 19, no. 2, pp. 203–214, 2004, http://goo.gl/Qt2Twv, Accessed on 2016-03-01.

[51] J. Lazar, J. H. Feng, and H. Hochheiser, *Research Methods in Human-Computer Interaction*, John Wiley, Chichester, England, 2010.

[52] L. Q. En and S. S. Lan, "Social Gaming — Analysing Human Computer Interaction Using a Video-Diary Method," in *Proceedings of the 2nd International Conference on Computer Engineering and Technology (ICCET)*, pp. 509–512, 2010.

[53] S. Carter and J. Mankoff, "When participants do the capturing: the role of media in diary studies," in *Proceedings of the SIGCHI Conference on Human Factors in Computing Systems (CHI '05)*, pp. 899–908, USA, April 2005.

[54] L. R. R Ferreira, "Um modelo de mecânica para construção de jogos educacionais móveis para adultos mais velhos," *Dissertação de mestrado Pontifícia Universidade Católica de Minas Gerais. Programa de Pós-Graduação em Informática*, pp. 794-681, 2016.

# 14

# Integrated Solution of a Back Office System for Serious Games Targeted at Physiotherapy

**Tiago Martins,**[1] **Vítor Carvalho,**[1,2] **and Filomena Soares**[1]

[1]*Algoritmi Research Centre, University of Minho, 4804-533 Guimarães, Portugal*
[2]*IPCA, 4750-810 Barcelos, Portugal*

Correspondence should be addressed to Vítor Carvalho; vcarvalho@ipca.pt

Academic Editor: Michela Mortara

Serious games targeted at physiotherapy can be a solution to help the physical therapy professionals. However, the entire game management, in its various aspects, is under the professional's responsibility. One way to reduce the professional management work will be to integrate a Back Office system in the game. Following this trend, the purpose of this paper is to present a modular Back Office system for centralized management of one or more games targeted at physical therapy.

## 1. Introduction

Several studies have shown that serious games have enormous potential in health interventions, including rehabilitation and physiotherapy. The pleasant atmosphere they create and the feedback forms they usually include promote the interest of patients, who are increasingly motivated and involved in their rehabilitation [1].

If the game itself is enough for patients to perform the proposed activity, it may not be for the health professionals. In fact, these professionals have to make the management of the game with regard to the players' profiles, their responsible peers, and their physical therapy programs and the state of the disease and its evolution, among other topics. Back Office development becomes an important tool in the management of this clinical information.

The original concept of Back Office suffered fast evolution with regard to either operational efficiency, process automation, application responsibility, or even the application areas [2]. Two areas closed to the Back Office concept are information systems and informatics. Therefore, Back Office is defined as the set of features and characteristics of an information system with different restricted areas. The Front Office is visible for all users. Authenticated users are allowed to change the system functions by using the Back Office [3].

Demographic trends, whether in developed countries or in third-world countries, point to a sharp increase in the number of elderly people with motor problems. Otherwise, the number of people that work is decreasing. These facts will contribute to a decrease in the number of professionals dedicated to physical therapy. It will be required to equip the clinics with technologies that may support the health professionals in their task of assisting older people [4].

With this in mind, the purpose of this paper is to provide a modular solution of a Back Office that supports one or more games targeted at physical therapy, allowing the management of patients (players), of the staff, of Health Units, and of the games' performance.

This paper is structured as follows. Section 2 presents the state of the art in this topic, Section 3 states the idea and model proposal, Section 4 details the Back Office Design, Section 5 presents the database, Section 6 defines the users hierarchy and privileges, Section 7 shows the main functions and features of Back Office, Section 8 refers to system's messages and alerts, and finally Section 9 addresses the conclusions of the work.

## 2. State of the Art

Despite an extensive bibliographic search, only few serious games targeted at physical therapy and with integrated Back Office systems have been found. Therefore, we opted to present some serious games that have Back Office systems regardless of the purpose of healthcare. StrokeBack is a telemedicine project using a virtual reality (VR) scenario targeted at rehabilitation in home environment of patients who suffered a stroke. This project is complemented by a system in line with Health Personal Storage of each patient. A Back Office integrated solution allows healthcare professionals to access the data of each patient, enabling them to constantly monitor their health status and their rehabilitation progress [5].

The Nu!RehaVR system is another rehabilitation teletechnology, based on VR, used in patients who have traumatic brain injury or have suffered from a stroke and, therefore, need long periods of rehabilitation. With this system, they feel encouraged to perform exercises increasingly difficult and complex, confident in the recovery of their autonomy and optimizing their quality of life. Nu!RehaVR integrates three distinct environments, one of them being the Back Office that the therapist can access to choose among the available exercises proposed by the doctor those which are most appropriate to each patient [6].

Within the scope of his doctoral thesis, Artemisa Dores [7] presents the development, the implementation, and the evaluation of the Computer-Assisted Rehabilitation Program-Virtual Reality (CARP-VR). It is a program with different environments that are simulations of real-life contexts, in which patients will perform diverse activities based on daily situations. To face the patient mobility problems, several training stations are located in different medical institutions. The architecture of this system includes a centralized Back Office, enabling performing synchronized remote updates and configuration of training stations. Furthermore, it also keeps the results obtained by each participant in each training session updated. With this data, the therapist can evaluate the patient's condition and his/her evolution, which allows him/her to define the appropriate training program.

For rehabilitation, Sarathkumar and Sawal [8] recommend a wireless sensor network, which is a low-cost and easy-to-use system. The data is collected and stored in a database (acceleration and angular velocity at which the patient moves his/her limbs). One of the system components is the Back Office, which allows health professionals to access the information and check the physical performance of the patients optimizing the appropriate therapies.

Sheep Herding, Labyrinth, Letter Tracing, and Writing are four games embedded in an interactive application used to support, in a motivating and fun way, the rehabilitation of writing skills in people suffering from paralysis after stroke. The Back Office of the application allows therapists to adjust various parameters of the games, for example, the difficulty level of the game, adapting the exercises to the needs and interests of the patient [9].

Lanfermann and Willmann [10] registered a patent of a system and method for rehabilitation or physical therapy of patients with neuromotor disorders such as stroke. This invention consists of a camera system that records the patient exercises and an interaction system that gives the user instructions to start or stop a given exercise. The Back Office offers an easy solution for the therapist to watch the video recording of the full exercise and to evaluate the patient's performance.

Mercury is a platform that allows a wide range of clinical applications to be inserted in a wireless sensor network, for the acquisition and processing of high-resolution signals. One of the referred applications enables the monitoring of patients with Parkinson's disease and another allows detecting epileptic convulsions. The sensor data are released in the Back Office, to be processed later [11].

## 3. Model Proposal

The authors felt the need to design and develop a generic and integrated system that allows the management of the information gathered from different serious games, in a single remote platform, supported by a centralized database (Figure 1).

The games to be used by this system try to promote the patients motivation to carry out the conventional physical therapy exercises when they are performed in a clinical rehabilitation centre. Back Office system aims to make the management of serious games for the therapy to be used exclusively within the clinic, not with the objective of monitoring patients in remote environment since the supervision by a professional of physical rehabilitation is always imperative. In extreme cases, it may be used in home physical therapy, when accompanied by a professional, thus avoiding negative effects on the use of these games.

The main objective of this type of game targeted at physical therapy is to motivate the patients to continue with their rehabilitation programs as long as possible, since the traditional physical therapy exercises are repetitive and boring, which leads them to give up early on their treatments.

Although the games usually have score systems, more importantly than achieving any score, the main aspect is that the patient performs correctly each exercise. Therefore, the supervision by a health professional is extremely important in order to avoid excessive strain on the patient to get better scores, damaging his health.

As the authors' goal was to develop a modular solution to allow adding the management of new games, new features, and updates, among other functionalities, a web-based platform was developed.

The fact that the database and the Back Office system are located on a remote server allows users to access the application, anywhere and anytime, requiring only an Internet connection. Moreover, everything is centralized, both in research purposes and in the clinical information management. Remotely, the system administrator can install new games, fix bugs, update the application, and add new modules, among others.

The Back Office was designed taking into account some basic principles of safety, integrity, stability, and reliability. It is divided into five main areas: Health Unit's management, personnel management, patient management (players), games management, and statistics. All these areas are managed by

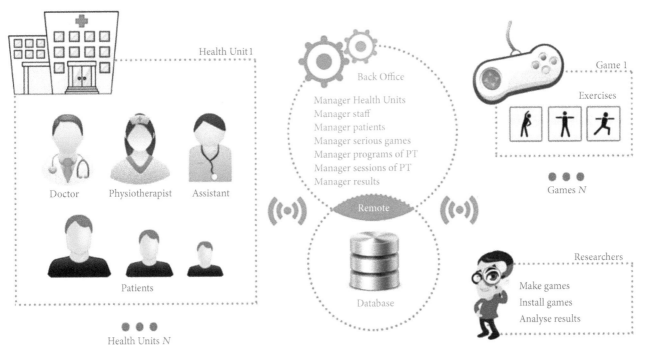

FIGURE 1: System generic architecture.

a hierarchy of users privileges (administrators, doctors, physiotherapists, assistants, and others), with specific limitations for each of them.

In addition to the management functions, the Back Office is multilingual and its users can opt for English or Portuguese languages.

Although the final model of the application is more complex than that which is shown in Figure 2, this represents, generally, the application behavior in a three-dimensional situation (doctor, physical therapist, and patient), whose goal is to create a physical therapy program based on the use of a serious game. In this case, the doctor logs in to the Back Office and creates a patient (player) profile as well as his/her physical therapy program, citing the professionals responsible for it (physiotherapists and respective assistants). In the clinic, the physical therapist logs in to the game and chooses the player and his/her physical therapy program is loaded so that the patient (player) starts playing. The nucleus of this architecture is the database that stores all the generated information, and the Back Office is the manager of this information. The game makes use of this information to load the programs of the players and send all results to the database, which can be consulted in the Back Office by the doctor or by those responsible for the patient.

## 4. The Back Office Design

When developing a web page, it should be taken in mind the warnings of the World Wide Web Consortium (W3C), which is the board responsible for recommending development standards for the Internet (web standards). Nowadays, with the diversity of devices (computers, smart television, smart phones, and tablets) that allow access to the Internet, it becomes imperative to use these patterns in order to ensure that the solution is fully functional in most browsers. These W3C recommendations were followed by the research team to avoid in the future compatibility formatting problems.

In the programming area, various languages were used for different purposes. At the level of aesthetic and structural construction, HTML5 program was used together with CSS3 for creating styles. For interpreted programming, executed by the browser, JavaScript was used with different frameworks based on jQuery. In what concerns the language server side, it was decided to use the PHP5 along with SQL to access the databases. The languages used are currently the most commonly used in the market for reasons of reliability, security, and integrity, when programmed in accordance with the recommended guidelines and standards.

The system takes all necessary and legally required precautions to ensure the protection of information collected from its users through the Back Office. These precautions ensure safety online and offline of that information. Whenever sensitive information is collected or used, the data are encrypted using SSL certificates. Thanks to the 128-bit SSL (Security Sockets Layer), which protects the transmission of all sensitive data over the Internet, all information is treated with the greatest security. The user's privacy is ensured and the risk of interception of data during the communication is safeguarded. All passwords and sensitive data stored in the databases are also encrypted.

With regard to data protection, all those which are collected by the Back Office are treated according to Directive 95/46/CE that provides the notion that the collection and then the processing of data can only be made for legitimate purposes, with specific and defined goals, with data

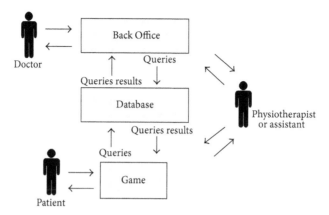

FIGURE 2: System behavior in a three-dimensional model.

accuracy and only allowing the identification of the holder at specified times. The law provides also the principle of prior authorization, so data processing can only be carried out with the consent of the owner. The system also follows Directive 2002/58/CE that establishes rules to ensure safety with regard to the processing of personal data, the notification of the violation of personal data, and the confidentiality of communications. In addition, it prohibits unsolicited communications whenever the user has not given his/her consent.

Another advantage in the use of the presented technological solutions is that they can run on free software such as Linux operating system and LAMP, which is a solution that incorporates the Apache (web server), PHP (programming language), and MySQL (database software) that allows running web applications of high availability and high performance.

In the graphic design field, we opted for a minimalist style with simple and clear elements (menus, tables, icons, and images, among others), most of them created through Cascading Style Sheets (CSS). One of the application's goals was to make it neutral, without using the design of a specific game, in order to support multiple types of games with different designs. The colors chosen for the graphics and the typography are between gray and blue, opting for a sans serif font type, which is the most used in this kind of application.

Considering that the Back Office is responsible for managing all the information at the level of Health Units and serious games, one of the difficulties is the way to overcome entropy, that is, the state of natural disorder of any system. For that issue, the research team had to take into account the architecture of the information, that is, the way how it is treated and is presented to the end user.

Usability, which can be defined in five dimensions (learning, efficiency, memory, strength, and satisfaction), may be the "key success" of an application. If the user does not feel comfortable in using a particular application, he/she tends to give up easily. Following this trend, we considered some guidelines for the organization of contents in the Back Office. First, the importance of creating a responsive layout, adaptable to different target devices (computers, smartphones, and tablets) was considered, with the aim of promoting adequate usability to its size and shape. Secondly, it was necessary to

idealize the organization structure of information. The main functions are accessible through a side menu on the left, always available from any part of the application. Along the main menus, submenus can be opened containing the main functions of the first. Navigation is rather intuitive and fluid, based on the logical structure of various applications that are on the market and have already been tested, such as Facebook (user research, user profiles, messaging between users, and boxes alerts, among others) (Figure 3).

## 5. The Database

The database plays a central role in the overall system as it is responsible for storing all the information generated in the Back Office and in the games.

To ensure safety, reliability, availability, and integrity of the database, we opted for the currently most widely used model, the relational model, which is based on the concept of relationships where a relationship is a table of values.

The database structure was normalized to allow for efficient storage, low data redundancy, and efficient access to stored data.

The Entity Relationship (ER) diagram of the database is shown in Figure 4.

## 6. Users and Privileges Hierarchy

As mentioned, the Back Office contains several areas that are conditioned to a hierarchy of users. Figure 5 shows a flow chart with the structure of each section of the Back Office and the respective restricted areas.

The users' hierarchy is divided into five distinct classes: managers, doctors, physiotherapists, physiotherapy assistants, and others.

Administrators are usually research team users that can access all sections of the Back Office. Only administrators can install new games' modules, add Health Units, and access global and specific statistics of the use of games and of the Back Office itself.

In Back Office, doctors are responsible for creating the profiles of their patients, as well as their physical therapy

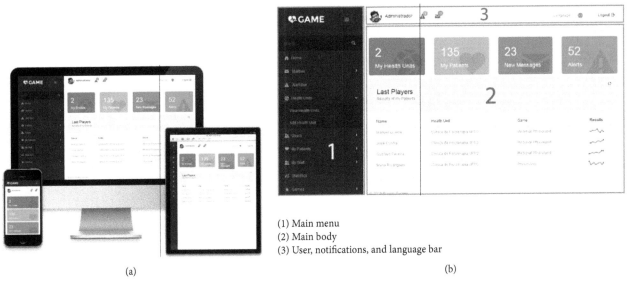

(1) Main menu
(2) Main body
(3) User, notifications, and language bar

(a)                                                                                                (b)

FIGURE 3: (a) Web application with responsive layout. (b) Main application areas.

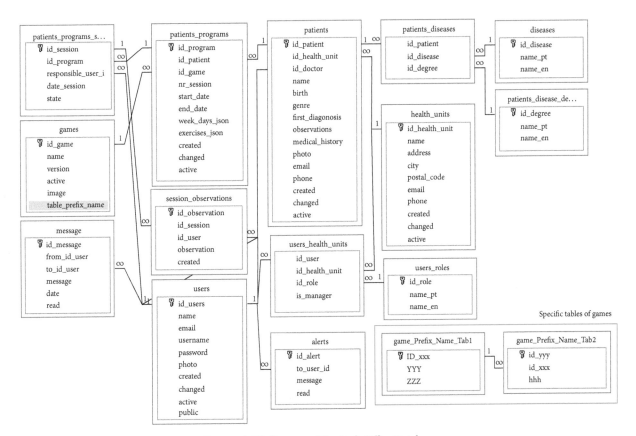

FIGURE 4: ER diagram of the Back Office Database.

programs based on serious games, delegating responsible people (physiotherapists and assistants).

Physical therapists are responsible for going along with their patients while they are performing their physical therapy programs, prescribed by the doctor. While performing a physical therapy program, they can enter the Back Office,

choose the physical therapy session for a particular patient, and write additional information that can be consulted in the future.

Physical therapy assistants can only navigate through the areas common to all users.

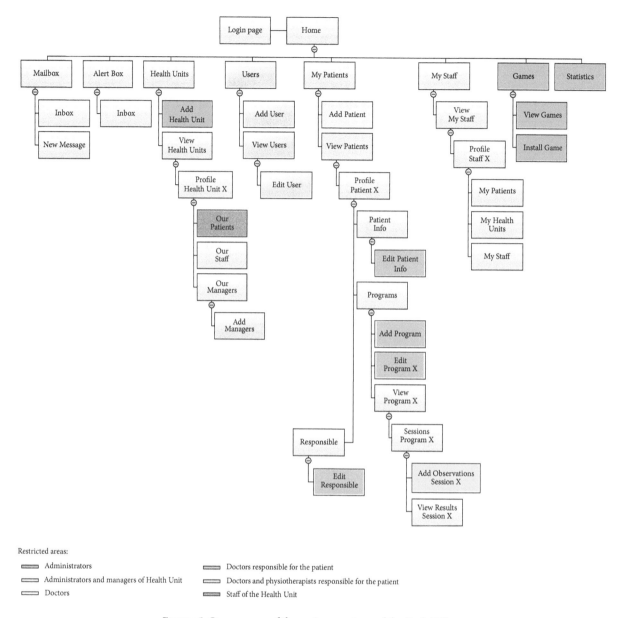

FIGURE 5: Organogram of the various sections of the Back Office.

The class "others" may be associated, for example, with a Health Unit director.

The manager is a secondary class that is a complement to the primary (doctor, physiotherapist, or others), which allows the user to manage the staff (team) of his/her Health Unit, with the possibility of adding, for example, doctors, physical therapists, assistants, or even new managers.

## 7. Main Functions and Features of the Back Office

Currently, the system is autonomous, aiming especially at doing the management of the staff of Health Units and their users with the use of serious games.

When accessing the Back Office, a login page appears. Each user must enter his/her username and password and choose the language he/she wants. After this authentication, the user is redirected to the main page of the Back Office, a dashboard that presents some notifications such as new alerts, new messages, and score of the latest players. On the side (always present), the menu is displayed with the main sections (it varies according to the hierarchy level of the user). At the top, a notification bar of alerts and messages, a language selector, a user menu, and the "Log Off" option are also presented.

Before any other task, the administrator must install the serious games on the computers of the Health Units. The administrator may install the game modules, which are contained within a ZIP file. He/she accesses the submenu "Install

FIGURE 6: Process of installing a new game module.

Game" on the "Games" menu, selects the file containing the modules of a game specifically created for use with the Back Office, and clicks "Install." These games will be the basis for physical therapy programs (Figure 6).

The games are available to be downloaded online and installed locally. Whenever there is a new update, the game will ask for the same update. Local administrators should only have the necessary permissions to do so.

The games modules contain the information specific to each game, like exercise and difficulty levels, among other parameters. They also contain scripts that create tables in the database to keep the results and game parameters, but they also provide the pages that serve as a basis for consultation and management of the results obtained from the sessions. Thus, the Back Office can manage several games, regardless of the Back Office structure, with the only necessary requirement being to install the respective modules.

Administrators are the only users that can make the management of games modules from their installation to their removal.

When there are yet no Health Units, the administrator is responsible for adding them. He/she must enter the submenu "Add Health Unit," on the "Health Units" menu. Then, a form is presented to fill in with all the Health Unit information like name, address, telephone, and email, among other relevant information. After the creation of the Health Unit, it is required to add a user "manager" of that Health Unit (Figure 7).

From here, the administrator or the new manager of the created Health Unit can edit its information and add staff as well as new managers, but only administrators can eliminate a Health Unit.

As previously stated, only administrators and managers of a Health Unit can add new users (staff of a Health Unit). It should be noted that a user may be associated with various Health Units, with the same position or different positions. Only administrators can add new users with the position of administrator. To add a user, it is needed to access the submenu "Add User," on the "Users" menu, and fill in the user's profile (name, Health Unit, and position, among others).

In the management of users, administrators can see all the users of all Health Units, being able to edit them or delete them. However, managers can only see the users of the units they manage.

User profiles are only available to the elements of the Health Units, unless the user profile is defined as "public." If it is a public profile, the users of other Health Units may contact him/her and see the Health Units where he/she is associated (Figure 8).

The task of creating (or eliminating) patient profiles is exclusive of doctors; only they can create a patient profile. For this, the doctor must access the submenu "Add Patient" on the menu "My Patients" and fill in the form with patient information like Health Unit (he/she can only choose a Health Unit he/she belongs to), name, date of birth, email, phone, diseases and respective degrees, and medical history, among other relevant information. The doctor should also choose the persons (physiotherapist and assistants) who will be responsible for him/her during physical therapy sessions (Figure 9).

Patient profiles are only accessible to staff of his/her Health Unit.

After creating a patient profile, the doctor responsible for him/her can create physical therapy programs based on the serious games. The doctor has to access the patient's profile, enter the tab "Programs," and click "Add New Program." The page presents a form where the doctor chooses the game and the respective physical therapy exercises he/she wants his/her patient to perform, sets the number of sessions

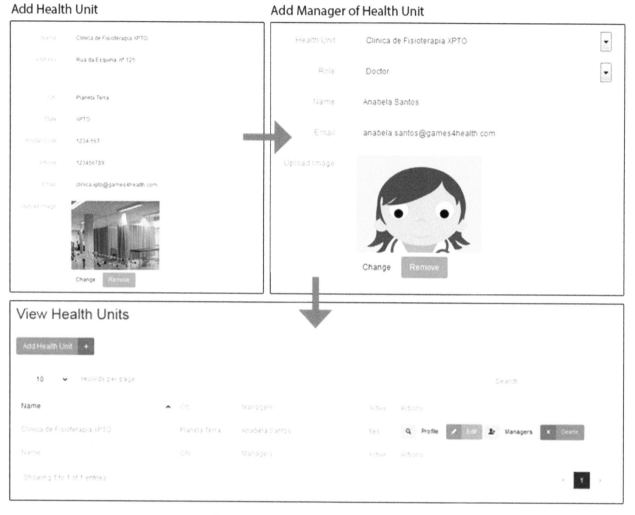

FIGURE 7: Creating process of a Health Unit.

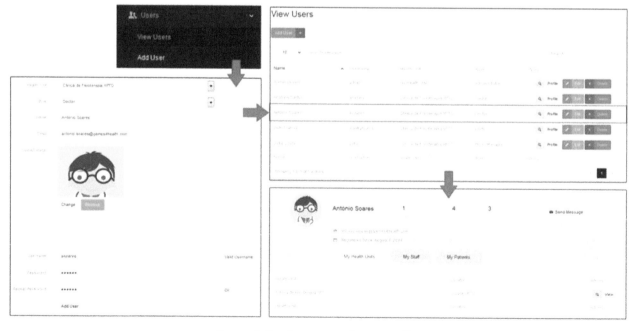

FIGURE 8: Creating process of a user profile.

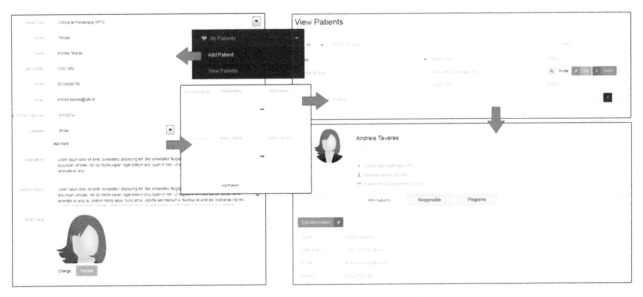

FIGURE 9: Creating process of a patient's profile.

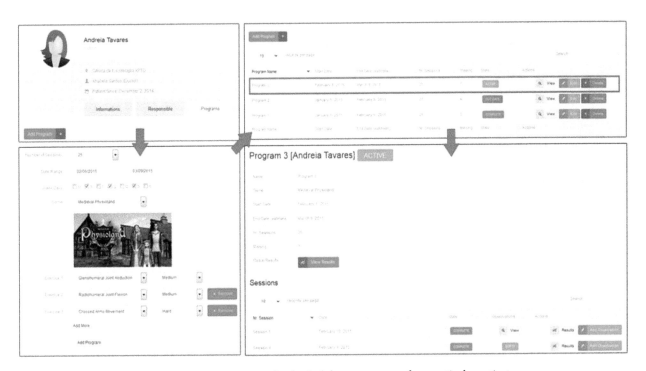

FIGURE 10: Creating process of a physical therapy program for a particular patient.

and the start and end date (forecast) of the program, and chooses the days of the week on which the patient must play (Figure 10).

Only physicians responsible for the patient can edit or delete a physical therapy program; however, physical therapists and assistants can consult it.

All physiotherapy sessions for a particular patient are recorded in his/her current physical therapy program and the results may be consulted by all those responsible for the patient. The physical therapists and the doctors of the patient can also insert comments on a particular session.

The pages that display the results are specific for each game, since each of them has specific objectives. Doctors, physiotherapists, and assistants can consult the individual results of each session or of all sessions already performed (Figure 11).

General statistics of the application are only available for administrators and serve to have an overview on using the

Patient Sessions

Session Results

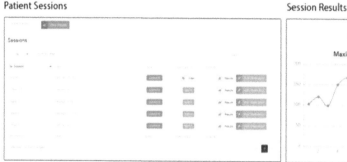
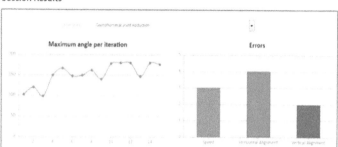

FIGURE 11: Specific results of a physical therapy session.

FIGURE 12: General statistics for administrators.

Back Office and installed games (access the menu "Statistics"; and a variety of graphics are presented with results on the use of the application, such as number of daily, monthly, and annual access instances and number of new registrations of users, patients, and Health Units, among others). With regard to the games, there is also an analysis of the number of players per month, by gender, and by fulfillment of a physical therapy program, among others (Figure 12).

## 8. Messages and Alerts

The exchange of messages between the staff members of a Health Unit and among elements of another unit may become interesting in the sense of sharing knowledge, solutions, and results.

Alerts are messages that the system sends to the users and the patients. Several alerts are scheduled to be sent automatically to doctors and physical therapists, like absence of the sessions, performance report, weekly evolution of the patients, and end of physical therapy program, among other relevant alerts.

If patients choose, they can receive in their mailbox or on their mobile phone alerts for scheduled physical therapy sessions, as well as their absences and weekly results.

The notification bar, always present on the top of the page, indicates to the users the number and the content of new alerts and messages (Figure 13).

## 9. Final Remarks

The Back Office is an indispensable tool for the management and processing of information. The Back Office developed and presented management in a centralized way, with all the information gathered from several serious games spread over different Health Units, improving the efficiency of time management and results, in terms of clinical approach as well as in terms of research. The ability to install management modules of new games makes it versatile and powerful. Thereby, it will benefit physiotherapy professionals, researchers, and, above all, those who are the target of the investigation, the patients.

The serious games management platform oriented for physiotherapy becomes unique because, instead of having

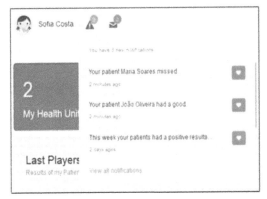

FIGURE 13: Boxes of alert notifications and messages.

multiple Back Office systems for different games, it includes the management of several games, also including the staff management of Health Units, thus avoiding the information redundancy generated by different systems. This allows the management and the treatment and filtration of all information generated by the system.

As future work, we intend to use the information collected by this Back Office system to perform the analysis of the patients' rehabilitation progress. Moreover, future work data will also include the acceptance level of the system by all the actors involved, including the patients and the health technicians.

## Competing Interests

The authors declare that they have no competing interests.

## Acknowledgments

This work has been supported by Fundação para a Ciência e Tecnologia (FCT) in the scope of the project: UID/CEC/00319/2013. The authors are also grateful to the Portuguese Foundation (FCT) for funding through SFRH/BD/74852/2010 Ph.D. scholarship.

## References

[1] T. Martins, V. Carvalho, and F. Soares, "Monitoring of patients with neurological diseases: development of a motion tracking application using image processing techniques," *International Journal of Biomedical and Clinical Engineering*, vol. 2, no. 2, pp. 37–55, 2013.

[2] M. J. King, *Office and Beyond—A Guide to Procedures, Settlements and Risk in Financial Markets*, Harriman House, Petersfield, UK, 2nd edition, 2003.

[3] P. M. O. Martins, *Back Office para Plataformas Web de Gestão de Conferências Científicas: Desenvolvimento e Avaliação*, Universidade do Porto, Porto, Portugal, 2013.

[4] S. Valenti, S. Fioretti, M. Maurizi, M. Panti, and T. Leo, "Teaching motor disability assessment over the web: MODASPECTRA," *Educational Technology and Society*, vol. 5, no. 1, pp. 184–198, 2002.

[5] E. Vogiatzaki and A. Krukowski, "Serious games for stroke rehabilitation employing immersive user interfaces in 3D virtual environment," *Journal of Health Informatics*, vol. 6, pp. 105–113, 2014.

[6] O. Gervasi, R. Magni, and M. Zampolini, "Nu!RehaVR: virtual reality in neuro tele-rehabilitation of patients with traumatic brain injury and stroke," *Virtual Reality*, vol. 14, no. 2, pp. 131–141, 2010.

[7] A. Dores, *Reabilitação Cognitiva Através de Ambientes Virtuais: Inovações Metodológicas e Tecnológicas*, Instituto de Ciências Biomédicas Abel Salazar, Porto, Portugal, 2012.

[8] B. Sarathkumar and R. Sawal, "Towards a hi-fi wireless sensor network for rehabilitation supervision," *International Journal of Engineering Sciences & Research Technology*, vol. 3, no. 4, pp. 7063–7068, 2014.

[9] J. S. Curtis, L. S. Ruijs, M. H. De Vries, R. Winters, and J.-B. Martens, "Rehabilitation of handwriting skills in stroke patients using interactive games: a pilot study," in *Proceedings of the 27th International Conference Extended Abstracts on Human Factors in Computing Systems (CHI '09)*, pp. 3931–3936, Boston, Mass, USA, April 2009.

[10] G. Lanfermann and R. D. Willmann, U.S. Patent no. 0299232, U.S. Patent and Trademark Office, Washington, DC, USA, 2009.

[11] K. Lorincz, B. Chen, G. Challen et al., "Mercury: a wearable sensor network platform for high-fidelity motion analysis," in *Proceedings of the 7th ACM Conference on Embedded Networked Sensor Systems*, pp. 183–196, ACM Press, Berkeley, Calif, USA, November 2009.

# 15

# KioskAR: An Augmented Reality Game as a new Business Model to Present Artworks

**Yoones A. Sekhavat**

*Faculty of Multimedia, Tabriz Islamic Art University, Hakim Nezami Square, Azadi Boulevard, Tabriz, East Azerbaijan 51647-36931, Iran*

Correspondence should be addressed to Yoones A. Sekhavat; sekhavat@tabriziau.ac.ir

Academic Editor: Ali Arya

This paper presents the architecture of KioskAR, which is a pervasive game implemented using augmented reality (AR). This game introduces a new business model that makes it possible for players to present their artworks in virtual kiosks using augmented reality, while they are having fun playing the game. In addition to competition between the players in the game, this game requires social interaction between players to earn more points. A user study is conducted to evaluate the sense of presence and the usability of the application. The results of experiments show that KioskAR can achieve a high level of usability as well as sense of presence.

## 1. Introduction

Recent years have witnessed a widespread success of computer games as cultural and commercial phenomena. The computer games market is a fast growing market that is reported to reach $128 billion by 2017 [1]. In physical real-world games, players can navigate and communicate with each other in natural ways. This is an advantage of these games, in which the interface with the real-world is intuitive. On the other hand, providing sophisticated and animated contents that can be fantastic or even impossible in the real-world is an advantage of computer games [2].

Traditionally, computer games are locked within the confines of a computer or a smartphone display [3]. In these games, small windows provide a view into the virtual game world, where the player is disconnected from the surrounding physical environment. Pervasive games are a new type of digital games that have recently emerged and attracted academic attention. In pervasive games, players occupy a game world that is present within the ordinary world [4]. These games by extending the gaming experience out into the real-world make it possible for players to move with their smartphones in a room, street, or wilderness. Pervasive games incorporate the real-world in the game so that common objects from everyday life can become a part of the game. In this setting, players may have to walk to the place where an object resides in order to play the game. This is an important advantage of pervasive games that is not possible in traditional computer games [5].

Different techniques can be used to implement pervasive games. In Alternate Reality Games (ARG) [6], the real-world is used as a platform, in which multiple media and game elements are employed to create a storyline that infiltrates real life. In these games, story elements are spread throughout the players' information space, which are used by players to participate in building the story. In ARGs, the information space of players is Web sites, email messages, and physical locations. In situated games that are deeper rooted within a context, players must physically attend in a location designed for the game to participate in the game. Urban games such as Songs of North [7] are examples of situated games that depend on contextualized play. Pervasive games can also be implemented using augmented reality (AR) to bridge the gap between real-world games and computer games. Augmented reality has introduced new ways of interacting with digital contents, where real-world interaction and computer-controlled contents are mixed seamlessly. This introduces a new class of games, in which the physical environment becomes an integral part of the game. AR games make it possible to create a new game environment, where virtual objects are overlaid on the real-world.

The focus of this paper is on a pervasive game based on augmented reality. Unlike virtual reality, which is an artificial and computer-generated view of a real life environment, augmented reality is the blending of virtual reality and real life that layers computer-generated multimedia on existing reality. In the recent years, various industries such as entertainment, e-commerce education, psychology, navigation, and tourism increasingly use augmented reality. According to Gartner research group, AR will be one of the top ten disruptive technology trends for the coming years that will result in considerable changes in relations between consumers and producers [8]. Acquisition of Metaio (an Augmented Reality Company) by Apple, Google's investment in Google Glass (an optical AR head-mounted display), and Microsoft efforts to produce Microsoft HoloLens show the significance of augmented reality in future applications. Augmented reality (AR) redefines the retail experience by boosting e-commerce in multiple ways and makes it possible for brands to differentiate themselves from competitors.

Digital games based on augmented reality have the potential to change the business models. AR by bringing 360-degree product views and enabling consumers to virtually visualize products in their homes can increase the likelihood of a purchase. Either at a retail store or in a website, AR makes it possible for consumers to experience the products before making purchase decisions. Using AR, customers can virtually try on a product and experience how garments look on them. A recent research in advertising shows that representing 3D models of products to customers in online shopping results in more product knowledge, better brand attitude, and, consequently, an increase in the purchase intention [9]. Augmented reality, by blurring the line between real and computer-generated worlds, provides additional information for buyers that is realized by visualizing virtual objects in the real-world on the screen.

This paper outlines a game with an augmented reality (AR) interface that allows art students to compete and collaborate with each other in a pervasive game, while presenting their artworks to other players. Artworks can be any handcraft made from wood, metal, clay, bone, horn, glass, paper, leather, stone, or other materials. Paintings, typographies, and other forms of 2D arts can also be presented in this game. In the AR game we propose, which is called KioskAR, virtual kiosks are established using augmented reality in physical places. KioskAR is a mobile application that employs the built-in cameras in devices to capture a user's physical world in real time, augments camera view with layers of multimedia contents (including 3D models, videos, and photos of artworks), and makes it possible for users to interact with these multimedia contents (viewing the artworks from different viewing angles, leaving comments on the artworks, and playing the slide shows).

During the game, players (i.e., art students) are encouraged to establish virtual kiosks. Kiosk owners can present their artworks through these virtual kiosks in forms of 3D models, videos, or slide shows of photos. Players by attending near the physical spot of a kiosk can visit this kiosk. They can physically turn around a virtual kiosk to see the kiosk as well as artworks in the kiosk from different viewing angles.

This is provided by augmented reality technology, where the synthesized images of artworks and virtual kiosks are shown on the image captured by the built-in cameras of a handheld device. Several sensors of the devices including GPS, accelerometer, and compass are used to decide how this multimedia content must be shown to a player. Kiosk owners can physically stand near the physical spot of their kiosk to meet visitors and explain their artworks. However, the artworks are visible to visitors even if the owners are not there. This game values social behaviors by encouraging team work. Players earn more score when playing in a team. An integral part of this game is mobility, where players need to physically explore the environment looking for virtual kiosks. In this application, a user or a group of users must be positioned at predefined spots to view and interact with virtual and computer-generated multimedia content. The results of interaction are shared and spread out on all AR devices.

This paper discusses technical challenges, usability issues, and the sense of presence in AR game design and proposes the KioskAR game that

(i) makes it possible for players to present their artworks in virtual kiosks that are visible in real geolocation spots through augmented reality;

(ii) promotes real social interactions between players through prioritizing group activities to individual activities;

(iii) employs various encouraging factors to get players more involved in the game.

## 2. Augmented Reality Games

The design of a pervasive game based on augmented reality requires considering many issues including the architecture of pervasive games, social interactions between players, and AR tracking techniques that are discussed in the following.

### 2.1. Pervasive AR Games

*2.1.1. Overview.* In [4], the pervasive mobile game is defined as "a context-aware game that necessarily uses mobile devices." Context-awareness involves sensing the environment such that the gameplay is adapted based on the current sensed conditions. This sensed data provides a source for game content and customized behaviors. In pervasive games, players are mapped onto real-world settings such that they must literally move from place to place to control their avatars (e.g., Human Pacman [10] and ARQuake [11]). In pervasive mobile games, the world boundary is not well-defined and, sometimes, it can be unconstrained. Players are called colocated, when they can interact inside an area defined by a local network. A pervasive game may last for several weeks or months, affecting the daily lives of players. This requires creating a persistent world that progresses without the player's intervention, while notifying the player to take an action if some event happens [12]. Players can access remote resources, while they are located anywhere.

*2.1.2. Related Work.* A survey of existing pervasive games and their technologies is provided in [13]. The chase game Can You See Me Now? [14] allows the interaction between real players on a city street with online players in a parallel virtual city. In Gbanga, virtual world is connected to the real-world locations visited by the player. This game involves walking around the city, moving between different areas, exploring new places, finding items, and meeting with other players. In Uncle Roy All Around You [15] and PAC-LAN [16], players are required to literally go to specific physical locations to complete the game activities.

IPerg [17] (Integrated Project in Pervasive Gaming) is a European research project with the focus on extending gaming experiences in spatial, social, and temporal dimensions. In GPS Mission, players are guided to checkpoints, where they can find virtual gold used to claim special virtual trophies. In this game, players leave marks to show they have already visited that place. In REXplore [18], which is a game designed for tourists, location information is used to encounter players with historical figures associated with historical buildings. In Insectopia [19], players run about to collect virtual insects, which are traded between players. In this game, players compete and collaborate in pairs in order to collect more insects. In UbiFit Garden [20], gamification is employed to sense physical activities of players and make the virtual garden blossom. In Fish'n'Steps [21], players feed a virtual fish to grow.

In AR-Bowling [22], players throw virtual bowling balls using hand gestures detected by pinch gloves. In AR ping-pong [23], players receive force feedback through optically tracked ping-pong racket handles. In [24], which is an AR game performed in a tracked area, a player moves around this area to collect treasures. ARQuake [25] is a multiuser game, in which the player is positioned in the real-world (tracked by an AR marker, a GPS sensor, and a digital compass). In this game, the player moves around shooting monsters to collect items. TimeWarp uses certain historical or cultural locations related to the environment in which the game is played. NetAttack [26] is an indoor/outdoor AR game that employs GPS and other tracking techniques to localize game objects. The Rooms [27] is a collaborative horror game in which the projected augmented reality is used to support collaborative immersive gaming.

Some pervasive games have been proposed with educational purposes. In [28], students play the role game of hunting as lions in groups on a school playing field. The purpose of this game is to encourage learning through highly physical role play. Gigaputt helps players to learn a three-hole golf course, in which the player's location is tracked. In this game, after teeing off, players physically move to where their virtual balls have landed while retracing their paths. Playful Toothbrush [29] is an educational game designed to encourage children for proper brushing habits.

*2.2. AR Design for Social Interaction.* Participation in a social activity, which the players can enjoy with their friends, is one of the important parameters of creating fun in digital games [30]. Pervasive games by focusing on the social aspects of computer games preserve the rich social interactions

found in traditional games (Pirates [31] and STARS [32]). These games are played across different media channels (e.g., smartphones) that make it possible to explore mixed reality environments. Through these games, the social quality of traditional games is integrated with computer games.

The design of an AR game that involves the collaboration of participants must deal with some changes. In these games, participants share a physical space surrounding them as well as the virtual space bounded to the physical space. Although social interaction in game design is not unique to AR game design, employing this technology provides new opportunities to design novel forms of social interaction in digital games [33]. More specifically, AR can provide a new environment in which virtual and real social interaction between the players can simultaneously occur in the game environment. To engage in a colocated activity or a virtual social interaction, players can perform physical movements, which may require implementing effective interface metaphors. Tracking and communication is another important requirement in AR game design. In BragFish [34], AR technology is used to create a shared virtual space in a fishing game, which results in social interaction among the players. In this game, physical actions are employed to allow players to gain situation awareness. In Art of Defense [35], by moving of tangible objects, players collaborate to defend their bases. In this game, players in the same place perceive the physical presence of others. A team-based competitive AR game is proposed in [2], in which players physically explore the game environment, while communicating with other players.

*2.3. Location-Based versus Marker-Based AR.* Mobile AR applications are classified into marker-based and location-based AR that differ in the techniques used to track and sense the environment [36]. In location-based AR, which is generally used outdoor, sensors such as GPS, compass, and gyroscope are used to indicate the location of a user. This geolocation data indicates what multimedia content must be rendered over the camera view. Arusma (https://www.aurasma.com/) and Layar (https://www.layar.com/) are examples of location-based AR applications. On the other hand, in marker-based AR, easily detectable and predefined target images are used to register the position of data that is augmented. In marker-based AR, the rotation and translation of the image detected in relation to the camera of the smartphone indicate where to augment data.

In pervasive games based on location-based AR, sensors such as GPS and compass and accelerometer provide information about the current context of players employed to deliver a gaming experience. This information is changed based on location, action, and feelings of the players [28]. However, some difficulties may decrease the usability of this technique. Location-based AR applications not only are resource-intensive but also are limited due to sensor accuracy [37] (GPS accuracy is anywhere between 10 and 50 meters and compass data is only accurate to around 20 degrees) [38]. Techniques have also been proposed to interact with virtual contents in the real-world. The interaction with the environment can be achieved through automatically detecting the environment by location sensors, gesture identification, or speech recognition.

AR games can be marker-based such that the game environment is activated when scanning a marker (already registered to the AR game) by the built-in camera of the device. This way, the game environment and the game objects appear on the marker when the player looks through the camera of the device. On the other hand, in location-based games (a.k.a., markerless AR games), GPS, compass, and gyroscope sensors indicate when and how to augment virtual objects on the screen. The KioskAR we propose in this paper is a markerless AR game that employs GPS, accelerometer, and compass data to indicate where and from what direction to show virtual kiosks.

## 3. Game Design

KioskAR is a social game, which bridges the gap between real and virtual social behavior. The students of art universities are target players of this game. Through the game, players compete with each other to receive more points to enhance their kiosk, while at the same time, they collaborate with other players to receive more points. This game makes it possible for players to present their artwork through a virtual kiosk presented in a physical place using augmented reality. This game implements a dimension of social interaction through cooperation with players to create an amusing gaming experience. Players can employ KioskAR to facilitate existing social interaction in groups to which they belonged. The more involvement in the game, the more credit for players that can be used to enhance virtual kiosks.

*3.1. KioskAR Scenario.* A player receives a predefined initial credit once he/she registers to the game. Using this credit, the player is able to establish a new virtual kiosk. Kiosks can be established in open areas on the campus. To establish a kiosk, a player must stand physically in the spot he/she wants to establish a kiosk and indicate the direction from which the kiosk is visible through the camera view. A kiosk can be established in spots where there is no overlap with the boundaries of other kiosks. A kiosk is visible to a player when this user stands nearby the geographical location of that kiosk, and through the built-in camera of the device, the player looks at the direction where the kiosks are located. This way, the virtual kiosk is augmented on the image captured by the camera of the device.

Kiosk owners can present their artworks in terms of 3D models, videos, or slide shows of photos. Players can physically turn around a kiosk and see the kiosk as well as artworks in the kiosk from different viewing angles. These features of augmented reality presentations are achieved by employing compass, accelerometer, and GPS sensors of a smartphone. Kiosk owners can physically stand near the physical spot of their kiosk to meet visitors and explain their artworks. However, the artworks are visible to visitors even if the owners are not there.

A player receives credits when (1) he/she regularly updates his/her kiosk through adding new 3D models, videos,

and photo collections of artworks, (2) he/she hangs around the physical spots of other kiosks and regularly visits them, (3) either the player views other players' works or others view the player's work, and (4) either the player leaves comments on artworks of other kiosks or others leave comments on the player's work. To promote the real social interaction between players, simultaneously visiting the kiosks in a group results in receiving more credits. The more credit a player gains, the more new kiosks this player can open in the campus. Although there is no limit on the number of kiosks a player can establish, the cost of opening new kiosks is increased exponentially to prevent dominating the physical area by some specific players.

Since the visibility of a kiosk depends strongly on the traffic of people in the physical spot of that kiosk, kiosks can be traded between players. In other words, some players might like to spend their credit to establish new kiosks in neighborhoods where people tend to hang out. There are also virtual bulletins that are visible using augmented reality located in some predetermined areas on the campus. Players can use their credit to advertise their kiosks on the bulletin.

*3.2. KioskAR Overview.* The overall architecture of the KioskAR including user interface (UI), communication (CM), game engine (GE), and data access (DA) components is presented in Figure 1. As shown in this figure, five main parts of the interface of KioskAR that appear in client side are map view, AR view, kiosk view, spot view, and configuration view. The overall process model of KioskAR including activities that are performed while playing the game as well as activities to configure the virtual kiosks is shown in Figure 2.

*3.2.1. Map View.* Map view provides a 2D map of the playing environment and the locations of kiosks. This view presents a big picture of the campus and kiosks that are already established on the campus. A snapshot of the map view for IAU (http://www.tabriziau.ac.ir/) campus (which is also used in our user study) is shown in Figure 3. To reduce visual search time, a good color coding is crucial. In map view, colors are selected based on "opponent" process theory of colors [39], which is widely used in information visualization [40]. According to this theory, red versus green, blue versus yellow, and black versus white are three opponent color pairs. Each color in a pair can be easily distinguished from the other color. Using this theory, the background of the map view is pale yellow, while Kiosks that are already established in the campus are shown by blue kiosk logos. Grey areas on this map are indoor places that cannot be used to establish a kiosk. Similar to standard map views, players can zoom and pan the map view to explore the gaming environment. A user's position and orientation are shown on the map view. Kiosks are selectable in this map. Once a user clicks a kiosk icon on the map, a pop up window is displayed representing the certificate of this kiosk including the name of kiosk, the name of the owner, the picture of the owner, a brief description of what is represented in the kiosk, the popularity score of the kiosk, and the credit of the owner. The size of display font is compatible with the zooming scale.

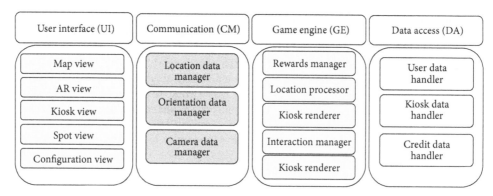

FIGURE 1: The architecture of KioskAR including client and server side components.

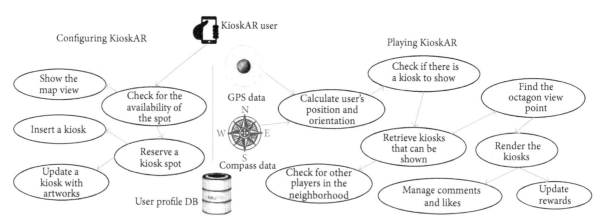

FIGURE 2: The overall process model of KioskAR including activities that are performed while playing the game as well as activities to configure the virtual kiosks.

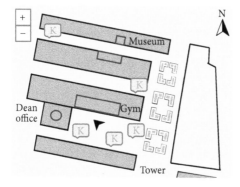

FIGURE 3: The map view of KioskAR including the available spots as well as spots that are already occupied by the kiosks.

FIGURE 4: The 3D model of the kiosk is augmented on the image captured by the built-in camera of the device.

*3.2.2. AR View.* AR view is the main view of KioskAR. If a player stands near the physical spot of a kiosk and looks through the AR view of the application, the 3D model of the kiosk is augmented on the image captured by the camera of the device (Figure 4). The goal of AR view is mixing real and virtual multimedia content to enhance the perception of a user from the current location and kiosks. There are six predetermined kiosk templates that can be selected by players. They all provide spots on the kiosks that can be used to put 3D models, videos, or photos of artworks. By clicking

on an item on the AR view, a player can leave a comment for an item in that kiosk. Players can physically turn around a kiosk to see the kiosks from different viewing angles.

In marker-based AR, an image (already registered to an AR component) is used as a target image that activates an AR application. In this method, a user can turn around the target image to see the 3D model augmented on the image captured by the camera from different viewing angles (Figures 5 and 6). However, in location-based AR, we need to find a way to indicate from what viewing angle a player is looking at

FIGURE 5: The AR view, watching at a kiosk from the north-east side of the kiosk.

FIGURE 6: The AR view, watching at a kiosk from the north-west side of the kiosk.

a kiosk. To this end, we assume there exists a hypothetical octagon boundary around a kiosk (see Figure 8). Each side of this octagon indicates from what viewing angle a user is looking at the kiosk.

Let $p = (p_x, p_y)$ be the user's position on the 2D map of the game field. Given an octagon with the side size of $L$, where $s_i$ represents the side between $a_i$ and $a_{i+1}$ corners, we compute the distance from the user's position to all sides of octagon around the the kiosk.

We need to compute the distance from the user's position $p = (p_x, p_y)$ from the line between $a_i = (x_i, y_i)$ and $a_j = (x_j, y_j)$. The vector perpendicular to the line between $a_i$ and $a_j$, denoted by $v$, and the vector from the point $p$ to the first point on the line between $a_i$ and $a_j$ are calculated as

$$v = \begin{bmatrix} y_j - y_i \\ -(x_j - x_i) \end{bmatrix},$$

$$r = \begin{bmatrix} x_i - p_x \\ y_i - p_y \end{bmatrix}. \tag{1}$$

The distance from $p = (p_x, p_y)$ to the side $s_i$ (i.e., the line between $a_i$ and $a_j$) is given by projecting $r$ onto $v$ such that

$$\text{distance}(p, s_i) = |\hat{v} \cdot r|$$
$$= \frac{(x_j - x_i)(y_i - p_y) - (x_i - p_x)(y_j - y_i)}{\sqrt{(x_j - x_i)^2 + (y_j - y_i)^2}}. \tag{2}$$

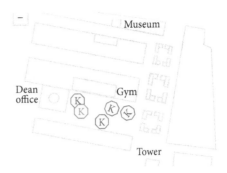

FIGURE 7: The spot view allows specifying the physical location of a new kiosk. Overlapping boundaries are shown in red.

By computing the distances from a user's position $(p_x, p_y)$ to different sides of the octagon ($s_i \in S$), the side with the minimum distance to player's position is selected as a view that is shown to user. The selected side is changed when the players move around the kiosk and the distances to different sides are changed:

$$\text{selected edge} = \underset{s_i \in S}{\text{argmin}} \, \text{distance}(p, s_i). \tag{3}$$

*3.2.3. Spot View.* A kiosk can be established in a spot where there is no overlap between the boundary of this kiosk and other existing kiosks. This view shows the boundary of existing kiosks in terms of octagons on the map and the boundary of the new kiosk to be established. The boundary of the new kiosk is shown in green, which turns into red in case there is an overlap with the boundaries of existing kiosks (see Figure 7).

*3.2.4. Kiosks View.* To establish a new kiosk, the kiosk view makes it possible to browse different kiosk templates already available for the players. In the first version of KioskAR, users can select among six default kiosks (four of them are shown in Figure 9). The 3D models of kiosks are obtained from sketch up warehouse (https://3dwarehouse.sketchup.com/) with slight changes to show scores, rankings, and comments on the kiosks. All kiosks provide facilities to present artworks in forms of 3D models, photos, videos, and audios. However, kiosks have different capacities to upload such multimedia. Depending on the features of these kiosks, players require different ranges of credits to establish the kiosks.

*3.2.5. Configuration View.* The configuration view of KioskAR provides a wide variety of features including registration and editing profile information. In this section, users can also exchange real money for credits or trade their kiosks with other players. Some hot spots (not all of them) are already reserved by the game engine which require more credit to be purchased by the players. This encourages those who are new to the game to exchange credits with real money to accelerate their progress in the game. This view also shows the statics of top players including players who own hot kiosks, players with top credits, and players with more views

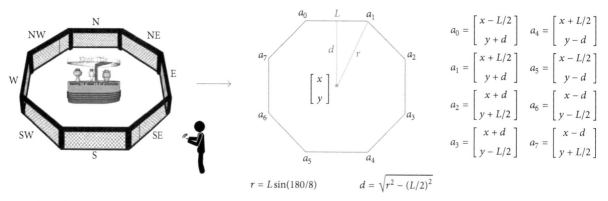

$$r = L\sin(180/8) \qquad\qquad d = \sqrt{r^2 - (L/2)^2}$$

FIGURE 8: A hypothetical octagon around the kiosk. A side having minimum distance from the user's position is selected as a view from which the kiosk is shown to the user.

FIGURE 9: A snapshot of four different default kiosks used in KioskAR. The user selects one of these kiosks once establishing a virtual kiosk.

and comments. The configuration view allows users to post information of their kiosks in the news bulletin of the game to encourage players to be involved in the game.

*3.2.6. Credit Collection Module.* A player receives the initial credit of 1000 points once he/she registers to the game. Although a basic kiosk can be established by this credit, a player needs more credit to enhance the kiosk or to establish other kiosks. Each view from other visitors (that requires visiting the physical location of the kiosk and seeing the kiosk through augmented realty) is one point for the kiosk owner and visitor. There is a limit of one view per kiosk per day, unless the kiosk is updated between the views. When a visitor leaves a comment during the visit to a kiosk, both the visitor and the kiosk owner receive extra two points.

To promote real social collaboration, visitors who visit in groups receive more points. More specifically, $n$ players simultaneously visiting a kiosk each receive $n$ points. This way, we promote real social collaboration between players, which is one of the goals of this game. An update in the kiosk is five points, which is limited to one update per day. The progress in the game is achieved through finding the right spots to establish your kiosk, opening kiosks near well-known kiosks, using and representing good artworks in kiosks, and regularly updating the kiosks.

*3.2.7. Technical Requirements.* KioskAR is an Android location-based mobile game which can be installed on

smartphones and tablets. This game requires awareness of the location (using GPS sensor) and the orientation (using compass and accelerometer) of the devices. Obviously, an AR application requires a built-in camera of the device to present the real-world onto the device's screen. On the server side of the application, MySQL is used to store a player's profile, the multimedia presented in virtual kiosks, and the status of the game and players. In KioskAR, players can view and interact with multimedia provided by other users. This requires the server side processing of interactions in the game and updating all users with the latest state of the game. The blackboard communication model is used in KioskAR where players receive the updated information directly from the server, without P2P correspondences between the players.

## 4. Evaluation Methodology

As discussed in [41], user experience in augmented reality has not been studied appropriately. Although various design choices are made into design and development of KioskAR, the true value of this application is verified using a user study. KioskAR was designed to virtually present artworks in real physical locations through an augmented reality game, where players compete and socially collaborate to receive more scores. In this study, we aim to empirically measure qualitative data related to *usability* and *sense of presence* in order to make well-supported statements about the usefulness of KioskAR.

*4.1. Study Design.* We asked participants to join the game and play for a period of two months. During this time, players were asked to play with KioskAR at least 3 times a week. The data of participants not engaging actively in the game during this period were eliminated from the results. Although all participants were compensated for their time to participate in this study, to encourage more activity, players with high activities and high scores were compensated with extra gift cards. Although these extrinsic rewards may impair the results of measuring the desirability of the KioskAR, we noticed this technique is effective to keep participants engaged in our long-term study. Another study without any extrinsic rewards can be useful to measure the desirability of KioskAR. However, this will need another form of motivation to keep participants engaged in the game.

We conducted a prestudy questionnaire to measure educational level, prior experience, and knowledge of participants with AR technology as well as social network games. We manually installed the game on participants' smartphones. We had a quick presentation session to teach participants how to use the application. Participants were told that their general information including location and usage information will be stored, when they are connected to Internet and the application is active. Before starting the study, we gained informed consent for participating in the study and gathering usage information. Participants were asked to complete questionnaires regarding usability and sense of presence two months after they played the game. They also completed a poststudy questionnaire which was designed to measure subjective reactions to the use of KioskAR.

*4.1.1. Participants.* A total of 56 participants including 24 males and 32 females were purposely recruited from the students of IAU University. Participants were asked to have experience of using smartphones. The prestudy questionnaire verified all participants have a similar level of knowledge of AR applications. The results of 8 participants were removed from the study for not actively playing the game. During the first week of study, few bugs were reported by participants that were fixed immediately, and we contacted participants to update the application.

*4.2. Sense of Presence.* As discussed in [42], the *sense of presence* is an important issue with regard to augmented reality games. Unlike virtual reality games, in which we aim to disconnect the player from the real-world, AR games require players to be present in the real-world as a game environment. In [43], *presence* is defined as "the subjective expression of being in one place or environment, even one is physically situated in another." As discussed in [42], presence can be stated in terms of physical (or spatial) presence and social presence. In [44], physical presence is defined as "the sense of being here." On the other hand, social presence is defined as "the sense of being together with another." Both physical and social presence are important factors in KioskAR. Physical presence is important because players must feel they are exploring a real kiosk. Social presence is important because a player must collaborate and interact with other players and kiosk owners to receive more points.

In spite of existing definitions of spatial and social presence, measuring presence is a challenging issue in AR games. As discussed in [42], *level of interactivity* and *realism* are two important factors affecting the sense of presence in AR games. Playing a game results in a higher sense of presence in comparison to observing a game. As discussed in [45], this interaction also results in a higher degree of entertainment. On the other hand, realism can be realized in several ways such as using first-person view instead of 3rd-person view, using real sounds and virtual representation of bodies. Presence has another side in collaborative games, where a player interacts with other players in addition to interaction with virtual world and objects. As discussed in [46], playing with a friend results in a better sense of presence in comparison to playing with a stranger. In KioskAR, players playing together share a mutual goal, which is trying to receive more points when the players visit kiosks in groups. To this end, players physically move as a team through the real-world. In this study, we aim to find how people feel towards the real and virtual elements.

There are several factors affecting the sense of presence from which the actual space where KioskAR is used has a significant effect on the sense of presence. Since the main goal of KioskAR is to help artists to present their artworks, the establishment of virtual kiosks in an artistic space can be crucial to ensure the visibility of the kiosks by target customers. What we measure in terms of *sense of presence* for KioskAR is the overall sense of presence by considering factors related to the application as well as the environmental parameters in which the application is used. Studying the effect of actual space on the sense of presence is a separate study that will be taken into account in future work.

*4.2.1. Measures.* MEC Spatial Presence Questionnaire (MEC-SPQ) [47] is a questionnaire to measure the sense of presence that covers several aspects of presence. This questionnaire is derived from a solid theory of spatial presence [48], which is designed to be filled by participants immediately after media exposure. Originally, variables including attention, involvement, suspension of disbelief, spatial situation model, and spatial presence are considered in this questionnaire. This questionnaire is widely adapted and used in the literature to measure the sense of presence for different media. In [42], to measure the presence experienced by players in an AR game, a questionnaire is proposed which is inspired by MEC-SPQ. The questionnaire we used in our experiments is adapted from the questionnaire in [42] which makes it possible to measure the sense of presence in terms of involvement, perceived interactivity, spatial presence, and social presence. The questions used to measure each of the four factors are shown in Table 1. Participants were asked to answer the questions that were rated on a 5-point Likert scale. Some of the statements in the original questionnaire were vague. Since the user study was conducted in Persian language, we made a clear and easy to understand translation of the statements.

*4.2.2. Results.* The results of experiments evaluating the sense of presence in terms of four different parameters including involvement, interactivity, spatial presence, and social

TABLE 1: The statements used in the questionnaire to evaluate the sense of presence.

| | Questions |
|---|---|
| Involvement | Q1: I thought most about things having to do with the game. |
| | Q2: I imagined precisely what the artworks were. |
| | Q3: I thought the game could have personal meaning for me. |
| | Q4: I considered things that were presented in the AR view. |
| | Q5: The experience activated my thinking. |
| Interactivity | Q1: I felt as if I could interact with virtual kiosks. |
| | Q2: I felt as if I could interact with virtual objects. |
| Spatial presence | Q1: At the end of the game, I felt as if I came back to reality. |
| | Q2: At the start of the game, I felt as if I were entering a new world. |
| | Q3: I felt as if I were part of a game that was not part of the reality. |
| | Q4: All my senses were stimulated by the (game) experience. |
| | Q5: The virtual objects felt real to me. |
| Social presence | Q1: I felt the presence of another person. |
| | Q2: I feel that the person is watching me and is aware of my presence. |
| | Q3: The person seemed alive to me. |
| | Q4: I perceived the kiosks as computer-generated images, not as a real. |
| | Q5: The thought that the kiosk was not real came often to my mind. |

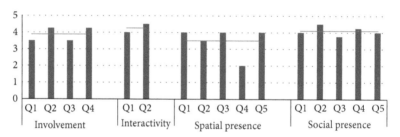

FIGURE 10: The average score of questions for the sense of presence questionnaire [42] answered by participants to measure the sense of presence in KioskAR.

presence are shown in Figure 10. As shown in this figure, KioskAR shows a high level of sense of presence according to the responses of participants (the average score greater than 4 for all parameters).

We were interested to find if players perceive game actions taking place within the real environment. We were also interested to know if the players feel the existence of virtual objects in the real-world. By analyzing the log data, we noticed that the strongest sense of presence was among the participants playing in a team, indicating the positive effect of social collaboration in the sense of presence. In particular, participants felt more sense of interactivity and social presence in the case of collaboration. One of the main challenges with an AR game is to provide continuous sense of presence to players. Participants reported that they felt they were in the game space, while navigating on the campus and visiting different kiosks.

*4.3. Usability.* Usability is an important factor in the evaluation of AR systems indicating how well users can exploit the functionalities of a system [49]. To study the usability of applications for handheld devices, Mobile Phone Usability Questionnaire (MPUQ) has been used in literature [50]. However, some specific issues related to augmented reality

are not considered in MPUQ. In this paper, we employ Handheld Augmented Reality Usability Scale (HARUS) that includes *comprehensibility* and *manipulability* scales [49]. Comprehensibility refers to the "ease of understanding the information presented" by an AR application. On the other hand, the manipulability refers to "ease of handling AR application as user performs a task." As shown in Table 2, the HARUS questionnaire includes 16 statements (8 statements for comprehensibility scale and 8 statements for manipulability scale). Users were asked to answer to what extent they agree to the statements. We use a 5-point Likert scale ranging from strongly disagree to strongly agree.

Mixing positive and negative questions makes the respondents think more and avoid the tendency to tick the same response for every question [51]. More specifically, using a balance of negative and positive questions results in cautiously responding to the questionnaire. Obviously, to calculate the sum of scores for the questions, negatively worded questions were scored in a reverse manner.

*4.3.1. Results.* The result of applying HARUS questionnaire [49] on participants is shown in Figure 11. As expected, KioskAR shows a high level of comprehensibility according to the responses of participants. In terms of manipulability,

TABLE 2: The statements used in HARUS questionnaire to evaluate usability.

| | Questions |
|---|---|
| Comprehensibility | Q1: Interacting with this application requires a lot of mental effort. |
| | Q2: The amount of information displayed on screen was appropriate. |
| | Q3: The information displayed on screen was difficult to read. |
| | Q4: The information display was responding fast enough. |
| | Q5: The information displayed on screen was confusing. |
| | Q6: The words and symbols on screen were easy to read. |
| | Q7: I felt that the display was flickering too much. |
| | Q8: The information displayed on screen was consistent. |
| Manipulability | Q1: Interacting with KioskAR requires a lot of body muscle effort. |
| | Q2: Using the application was comfortable for my arms and hands. |
| | Q3: The device difficult to hold while operating the application. |
| | Q4: It is easy to input information through the application. |
| | Q5: My arm or hand became tired after using the application. |
| | Q6: The application is easy to control. |
| | Q7: I was losing grip and dropping the device at some point. |
| | Q8: The operation of this application is simple and uncomplicated. |

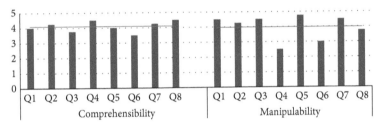

FIGURE 11: The average score of questions in HARUS questionnaire [49] answered by participants to measure the usability of KioskAR.

although the overall score is acceptable, the average of scores for Q4 (it is easy to input information through the application) and Q6 (the application is easy to control) are somehow low in comparison to other questions. We argue that this is a common problem to all AR applications designed for handheld devices. In these applications, a user needs to hold his/her device with one hand, while he/she may not have full control on the device, specifically when it is required to tap on the screen or to use the keyboard. Using head-mounted augmented reality glasses can be a solution for this problem. However, this requires carrying this device while playing KioskAR, which may not be convenient for all users. An alternative solution for handheld devices can be fixing the kiosk in AR view such that it does not require the user to tap on the window or use the keyboard in the AR view.

## 5. Conclusion

In this paper, we proposed KioskAR, which is an AR game that allows students to present their artworks in terms of 3D models, videos, and photos in virtual kiosks. Virtual kiosks, which are augmented on the camera view of a handheld device, are visible to all players when they stand in predetermined locations. KioskAR is a location-based augmented reality application that employs GPS, accelerometer, and compass sensors to find geolocation information and the direction of players. KioskAR not only provides a novel business model through gaming but also encourages physical social interactions. To gain more points, players need to physically move as a team and visit virtual kiosks located in different spots on the campus.

A user study was conducted to evaluate the sense of presence as well as the usability of KioskAR. The results of experiments show that participants reported a high level of social presence in addition to spatial presence, involvement, and interactivity. During the study, we noticed that KioskAR does not sufficiently support social interaction between players who do not know each other in advance, representing the need for something more to enhance the experience of a meaningful social interaction. There are also some problems regarding the usability of the kiosks (e.g., the difficulty of typing while looking at a kiosk and fixing the AR view while there are slight changes in the location or the direction of a user), which we aim to fix in future work. In addition, we plan to perform additional user studies to measure the scalability of the approach as the number of kiosks and players grows.

## Competing Interests

The author declares that he has no competing interests.

## Acknowledgments

The author would like to thank Saeedeh Sadighjamali (a Ph.D. candidate of folklore studies in Memorial University in Canada) for rigorous proofreading of the paper.

# References

[1] Gartner, *Gartner Says Worldwide Video Game Market to Total $93 Billion in 2013*, 2013, http://www.gartner.com/newsroom/id/2614915.

[2] A. Mulloni, D. Wagner, and D. Schmalstieg, "Mobility and social interaction as core gameplay elements in multi-player augmented reality," in *Proceedings of the 3rd International Conference on Digital Interactive Media in Entertainment and Arts (DIMEA '08)*, pp. 472–478, ACM, September 2008.

[3] O. Oda, L. J. Lister, S. White, and S. Feiner, "Developing an augmented reality racing game," in *Proceedings of the 2nd International Conference on Intelligent Technologies for Interactive Entertainment (INTETAIN '08)*, article 2, ICST (Institute for Computer Sciences, Social-Informatics and Telecommunications Engineering), 2008.

[4] M. Montola, J. Stenros, and A. Waern, *Pervasive Games: Theory and Design*, Morgan Kaufmann Publishers, Burlington, Mass, USA, 2009.

[5] L. Valente and B. Feij, *A Survey on Pervasive Mobile Games*, MCC07/13, Departamento de Informática, PUC-Rio, Rio de Janeiro, Brazil, 2013.

[6] J. Y. Kim, J. P. Allen, and E. Lee, "Alternate reality gaming," *Communications of the ACM*, vol. 51, no. 2, pp. 36–42, 2008.

[7] P. Lankoski, S. Heliö, J. Nummela, J. Lahti, F. Mäyrä, and L. Ermi, "A case study in pervasive game design: the songs of north," in *Proceedings of the 3rd Nordic Conference on Human-Computer Interaction (NordiCHI '04)*, pp. 413–416, ACM, October 2004.

[8] Gartner Emerging Trends and Technologies Roadshow, *Gartner Identifies Top Ten Disruptive Technologies for 2008 to 2012*, 2008.

[9] H. Li, T. Daugherty, and F. Biocca, "Impact of 3-D advertising on product knowledge, brand attitude, and purchase intention: the mediating role of presence," *Journal of Advertising*, vol. 31, no. 3, pp. 43–57, 2002.

[10] A. D. Cheok, K. H. Goh, W. Liu et al., "Human Pacman: a mobile, wide-area entertainment system based on physical, social, and ubiquitous computing," *Personal and Ubiquitous Computing*, vol. 8, no. 2, pp. 71–81, 2004.

[11] W. Piekarski and B. Thomas, "ARQuake: the outdoor augmented reality gaming system," *Communications of the ACM*, vol. 45, no. 1, pp. 36–38, 2002.

[12] L. Valente, B. Feijo, and J. C. S. do Prado Leite, "Mapping quality requirements for pervasive mobile games," *Requirements Engineering*, pp. 1–29, 2015.

[13] K. J. L. Nevelsteen, *A Survey of Characteristic Engine Features for Technology-Sustained Pervasive Games*, Springer, Berlin, Germany, 2015.

[14] M. Flintham, S. Benford, R. Anastasi et al., "Where on-line meets on the streets: experiences with mobile mixed reality games," in *Proceedings of the SIGCHI Conference on Human Factors in Computing Systems*, pp. 569–576, ACM, Fort Lauderdale, Fla, USA, April 2003.

[15] S. Benford, M. Flintham, A. Drozd et al., "Uncle roy all around you: implicating the city in a location-based performance," in *Proceedings of the International Conference on Advances in Computer Entertainment Technology (ACE '04)*, pp. 21–47, Singapore, June 2004.

[16] O. Rashid, W. Bamford, P. Coulton, R. Edwards, and J. Scheible, "PAC-LAN: mixed-reality gaming with RFID-enabled mobile phones," *Computers in Entertainment*, vol. 4, no. 4, article 4, 2006.

[17] A. Waern and K. P. Kesson, "IPerG position paper," in *Proceedings of the 2nd International Conference on Pervasive Computing*, Vienna, Austria, April 2004.

[18] R. A. Ballagas, S. G. Kratz, J. Borchers et al., "REXplorer: a mobile, pervasive spell-casting game for tourists," in *Proceedings of the Extended Abstracts on Human Factors in Computing Systems (CHI '07)*, pp. 1929–1934, ACM, San Jose, Calif, USA, May 2007.

[19] J. Peitz, H. Saarenpää, and S. Björk, "Insectopia: exploring pervasive games through technology already pervasively available," in *Proceedings of the 4th International Conference on Advances in Computer Entertainment Technology (ACE '07)*, pp. 107–114, ACM, June 2007.

[20] S. Consolvo, D. W. McDonald, T. Toscos et al., "Activity sensing in the wild: a field trial of UbiFit Garden," in *Proceedings of the 26th Annual CHI Conference on Human Factors in Computing Systems (CHI '08)*, pp. 1797–1806, Florence, Italy, April 2008.

[21] S. Kang, J. Lee, H. Jang et al., "SeeMon: scalable and energy-efficient context monitoring framework for sensor-rich mobile environments," in *Proceedings of the 6th International Conference on Mobile Systems, Applications, and Services*, pp. 267–280, ACM, June 2008.

[22] C. Matysczok, R. Radkowski, and J. Berssenbruegge, "AR-bowling: Immersive and realistic game play in real environments using augmented reality," in *Proceedings of the ACM SIGCHI International Conference on Advances in Computer Entertainment Technology (ACE '04)*, pp. 269–274, ACM, September 2004.

[23] B. Knoerlein, G. Székely, and M. Harders, "Visuo-haptic collaborative augmented reality ping-pong," in *Proceedings of the 4th International Conference on Advances in Computer Entertainment Technology*, pp. 91–94, ACM, June 2007.

[24] A. D. Cheok, X. Yang, Z. Z. Ying, M. Billinghurst, and H. Kato, "Touch-space: mixed reality game space based on ubiquitous, tangible, and social computing," *Personal and Ubiquitous Computing*, vol. 6, no. 5-6, pp. 430–442, 2002.

[25] A. D. Cheok, W. Wang, X. Yang et al., "Interactive theatre experience in embodied + wearable mixed reality space," in *Proceedings of the International Symposium on Mixed and Augmented Reality (ISMAR '02)*, pp. 59–68, October 2002.

[26] I. Lindt and W. Broll, "NetAttack—first steps towards pervasive gaming," *ERCIM News*, vol. 57, pp. 49–50, 2004.

[27] J. Michelsen and S. Bjrk, *The Rooms-Creating Immersive Experiences Through Projected Augmented Reality*, Foundations of Digital Games, 2014.

[28] S. Benford, D. Rowland, M. Flintham et al., "Life on the edge: supporting collaboration in location-based experiences," in *Proceedings of the SIGCHI Conference on Human Factors in Computing Systems (CHI '05)*, pp. 721–730, ACM, Portland, Ore, USA, April 2005.

[29] Y.-C. Chang, J.-L. Lo, C.-J. Huang et al., "Playful toothbrush: ubicomp technology for teaching tooth brushing to kindergarten children," in *Proceedings of the SIGCHI Conference on Human Factors in Computing Systems (CHI '08)*, pp. 363–372, ACM, Florence, Italy, April 2008.

[30] M. Montola, J. Stenros, and A. Waern, *Pervasive Games. Theory and Design: Experiences on the Boundary between Life and Play*, Morgan Kaufmann, 2009.

[31] S. Bjrk, J. Falk, R. Hansson, and P. Ljungstrand, "Pirates! using the physical world as a game board," in *Proceedings of the Interact*, pp. 423–430, Tokyo, Japan, July 2001.

[32] C. Magerkurth, T. Engelke, and M. Memisoglu, "Augmenting the virtual domain with physical and social elements: towards a paradigm shift in computer entertainment technology," *Computers in Entertainment*, vol. 2, no. 4, p. 12, 2004.

[33] Y. N. Chang, R. K. C. Koh, and H. B. L. Duh, "Handheld AR gamesA triarchic conceptual design framework," in *Proceedings of the IEEE International Symposium on Mixed and Augmented Reality-Arts, Media, and Humanities (ISMAR-AMH '11)*, pp. 29–36, Basel, Switzerland, October 2011.

[34] Y. Xu, M. Gandy, S. Deen et al., "BragFish: exploring physical and social interaction in co-located handheld augmented reality games," in *Proceedings of the International Conference on Advances in Computer Entertainment Technology (ACE '08)*, pp. 276–283, ACM, Yokohama, Japan, December 2008.

[35] D.-N. T. Huynh, K. Raveendran, Y. Xu, K. Spreen, and B. MacIntyre, "Art of defense: a collaborative handheld augmented reality board game," in *Proceedings of the ACM SIGGRAPH Symposium on Video Games*, pp. 135–142, ACM, August 2009.

[36] T. Jung, N. Chung, and M. C. Leue, "The determinants of recommendations to use augmented reality technologies: the case of a Korean theme park," *Tourism Management*, vol. 49, pp. 75–86, 2015.

[37] S. Jung, S. Kim, and S. Kim, "Augmented reality-based exhibit information personalized service architecture through spectator's context analysis," *International Journal of Multimedia and Ubiquitous Engineering*, vol. 8, no. 4, pp. 313–320, 2013.

[38] D. Marimon, C. Sarasua, P. Carrasco et al., *MobiAR: Tourist Experiences through Mobile Augmented Reality*, Telefonica Research and Development, Barcelona, Spain, 2010.

[39] E. Hering, *Outlines of a Theory of the Light Sense*, University of Chicago Press, Chicago, Ill, USA, 1964.

[40] Y. A. Sekhavat and O. Hoeber, "Visualizing association rules using linked matrix,graph, and detail views," *International Journal of Intelligence Science*, vol. 03, no. 1, pp. 34–49, 2013.

[41] T. Olsson, T. Kärkkäinen, E. Lagerstam, and L. Ventä-Olkkonen, "User evaluation of mobile augmented reality scenarios," *Journal of Ambient Intelligence and Smart Environments*, vol. 4, no. 1, pp. 29–47, 2012.

[42] A. M. Von Der Pütten, J. Klatt, S. Ten Broeke et al., "Subjective and behavioral presence measurement and interactivity in the collaborative augmented reality game TimeWarp," *Interacting with Computers*, vol. 24, no. 4, pp. 317–325, 2012.

[43] B. G. Witmer and M. J. Singer, "Measuring presence in virtual environments: a presence questionnaire," *Presence: Teleoperators and Virtual Environments*, vol. 7, no. 3, pp. 225–240, 1998.

[44] F. Biocca, C. Harms, and J. Gregg, "The networked minds measure of social presence: pilot test of the factor structure and concurrent validity," in *Proceedings of the 4th Annual International Workshop on Presence*, pp. 1–9, Philadelphia, Pa, USA, May 2001.

[45] P. Vorderer, S. Knobloch, and H. Schramm, "Does entertainment suffer from interactivity? the impact of watching an interactive tv movie on viewers' experience of entertainment," *Media Psychology*, vol. 3, no. 4, pp. 343–363, 2001.

[46] N. Ravaja, T. Saari, M. Turpeinen, J. Laarni, M. Salminen, and M. Kivikangas, "Spatial presence and emotions during video game playing: does it matter with whom you play?" *Presence: Teleoperators and Virtual Environments*, vol. 15, no. 4, pp. 381–392, 2006.

[47] P. Vorderer, W. Wirth, F. R. Gouveia et al., "MEC spatial presence questionnaire (MEC-SPQ): short documentation and instructions for application," Report to the European Community, Project Presence: MEC (IST-2001-37661), 3, 2004.

[48] D. Weibel and B. Wissmath, "Immersion in computer games: the role of spatial presence and flow," *International Journal of Computer Games Technology*, vol. 2011, Article ID 282345, 14 pages, 2011.

[49] M. E. C. Santos, J. Polvi, T. Taketomi, G. Yamamoto, C. Sandor, and H. Kato, "Toward standard usability questionnaires for handheld augmented reality," *IEEE Computer Graphics and Applications*, vol. 35, no. 5, pp. 66–75, 2015.

[50] Y. S. Ryu and T. L. Smith-Jackson, "Reliability and validity of the mobile phone usability questionnaire (MPUQ)," *Journal of Usability Studies*, vol. 2, no. 1, pp. 39–53, 2006.

[51] W. C. Leung, "How to design a questionnaire," *Student BMJ*, vol. 9, no. 11, pp. 187–189, 2001.

# Permissions

The contributors of this book come from diverse backgrounds, making this book a truly international effort. This book will bring forth new frontiers with its revolutionizing research information and detailed analysis of the nascent developments around the world.

We would like to thank all the contributing authors for lending their expertise to make the book truly unique. They have played a crucial role in the development of this book. Without their invaluable contributions this book wouldn't have been possible. They have made vital efforts to compile up to date information on the varied aspects of this subject to make this book a valuable addition to the collection of many professionals and students.

This book was conceptualized with the vision of imparting up-to-date information and advanced data in this field. To ensure the same, a matchless editorial board was set up. Every individual on the board went through rigorous rounds of assessment to prove their worth. After which they invested a large part of their time researching and compiling the most relevant data for our readers.

The editorial board has been involved in producing this book since its inception. They have spent rigorous hours researching and exploring the diverse topics which have resulted in the successful publishing of this book. They have passed on their knowledge of decades through this book. To expedite this challenging task, the publisher supported the team at every step. A small team of assistant editors was also appointed to further simplify the editing procedure and attain best results for the readers.

Apart from the editorial board, the designing team has also invested a significant amount of their time in understanding the subject and creating the most relevant covers. They scrutinized every image to scout for the most suitable representation of the subject and create an appropriate cover for the book.

The publishing team has been an ardent support to the editorial, designing and production team. Their endless efforts to recruit the best for this project, has resulted in the accomplishment of this book. They are a veteran in the field of academics and their pool of knowledge is as vast as their experience in printing. Their expertise and guidance has proved useful at every step. Their uncompromising quality standards have made this book an exceptional effort. Their encouragement from time to time has been an inspiration for everyone.

The publisher and the editorial board hope that this book will prove to be a valuable piece of knowledge for researchers, students, practitioners and scholars across the globe.

# List of Contributors

**Wei Shi**
Faculty of Business and I.T., University of Ontario Institute of Technology, Oshawa, ON, Canada L1H 7K4

**Jean-Pierre Corriveau and Jacob Agar**
School of Computer Science, Carleton University, Ottawa, ON, Canada K1S 5B6

**Imma Boada, Antonio Rodriguez-Benitez and Juan Manuel Garcia-Gonzalez**
Graphics and Imaging Laboratory, University of Girona, 17071 Girona, Spain

**Santiago Thió-Henestrosa**
Departament Informatica, Matemàtica Aplicada i Estadística, University of Girona, 17071 Girona, Spain

**Mateu Sbert**
Graphics and Imaging Laboratory, University of Girona, 17071 Girona, Spain
School of Computer Science and Technology, Tianjin University, Tianjin 300072, China

**Alexandre Greluk Szykman, André Luiz Brandão and João Paulo Gois**
Federal University of ABC–UFABC, Avenida dos Estados 5001, Santo André, Brazil

**Azrulhizam Shapi'i and Sychol Ghulam**
Faculty of Information Science & Technology, Universiti Kebangsaan Malaysia (UKM), 43600 Bangi, Selangor, Malaysia

**Amir Zaib Abbasi and Ding Hooi Ting**
Department of Management and Humanities, Universiti Teknologi PETRONAS, Tronoh, Malaysia

**Helmut Hlavacs**
Research Group Entertainment Computing, University of Vienna, Vienna, Austria

**Liang Wang and Yu Wang**
School of Computer Science and Technology, Hebei University, Baoding 071000, China

**Yan Li**
School of Mathematics and Information Science, Hebei University, Baoding 071002, China

**Anis Zarrad**
Department of Computer Science and Information Sciences, Prince Sultan University, Riyadh 11586, Saudi Arabia

**Shahenda Sarhan, Mohamed Abu ElSoud and Hebatullah Rashed**
Computer Science Department, Faculty of Computers and Information, Mansoura University, Mansoura 35516, Egypt

**Filipe M. B. Boaventura and Victor T. Sarinho**
State University of Feira de Santana, Feira de Santana, BA, Brazil

**Wim van der Vegt, Wim Westera and Enkhbold Nyamsuren**
Open University of the Netherlands, Valkenburgerweg 177, 6419 AT Heerlen, Netherlands

**Atanas Georgiev**
Sofia University "St. Kliment Ohridski", Boulevard Tzar Osvoboditel 15, 1504 Sofia, Bulgaria

**Iván Martínez Ortiz**
Complutense University of Madrid, Avenida de S´eneca 2, 28040 Madrid, Spain

**Angelo C. Loula**
Intelligent and Cognitive Systems Lab, State University of Feira de Santana, 44036-900 Feira de Santana, BA, Brazil

**Leandro N. de Castro**
Natural Computing Laboratory, Mackenzie Presbyterian University, 01302-090 São Paulo, SP, Brazil

**Antônio L. Apolinário Jr.**
Computer Science Department, Federal University of Bahia, 40170-290 Salvador, BA, Brazil

**Pedro L. B. da Rocha**
Laboratory of Terrestrial Vertebrates, Institute of Biology, Federal University of Bahia, 40170-290 Salvador, BA, Brazil

**Maria da Conceição L. Carneiro and Vanessa Perpétua G. S. Reis**
Institute of Education Gastão Guimarães, 44026010 Feira de Santana, BA, Brazil

**Ricardo F. Machado**
Graduate Studies Program in History, Philosophy and Science Teaching, Federal University of Bahia and State University of Feira de Santana, 44036-900 Feira de Santana, BA, Brazil

**Claudia Sepulveda**
Department of Education, State University of Feira de Santana, 44036-900 Feira de Santana, BA, Brazil

**Charbel N. El-Hani**
Institute of Biology, Federal University of Bahia, 40170-290 Salvador, BA, Brazil

**Mônica da Consolação Machado**
Institute of Exact Sciences, University Center Newton Paiva, Belo Horizonte, Brazil
Department of Computer Science, Pontifical Catholic University of Minas Gerais, Belo Horizonte, Brazil

**Ronan Loschi Rodrigues Ferreira**
Department of Computer Science, Pontifical Catholic University of Minas Gerais, Belo Horizonte, Brazil
Department of Engineering, College Santa Rita-FASAR, Conselheiro Lafaiete, Brazil

**Lucila Ishitani**
Department of Computer Science, Pontifical Catholic University of Minas Gerais, Belo Horizonte, Brazil

**Tiago Martins and Filomena Soares**
Algoritmi Research Centre, University of Minho, 4804-533 Guimarães, Portugal

**Vítor Carvalho**
Algoritmi Research Centre, University of Minho, 4804-533 Guimarães, Portugal
IPCA, 4750-810 Barcelos, Portugal

**Yoones A. Sekhavat**
Faculty of Multimedia, Tabriz Islamic Art University, Hakim Nezami Square, Azadi Blvd., East Azerbaijan, Tabriz, Iran

# Index